AIDS in the Industrialized Democracies

AIDS in the Industrialized Democracies

Passions, Politics, and Policies

David L. Kirp and
Ronald Bayer, editors

Rutgers University Press
New Brunswick, New Jersey

Library of Congress Cataloging-in-Publication Data

AIDS in the industrialized democracies : passions, politics, and policies
  / co-editors, David L. Kirp and Ronald Bayer.
      p.   cm.
   Includes bibliographical references.
   ISBN 0-8135-1821-0 (cloth)—ISBN 0-8135-1822-9 (pbk.)
    1. AIDS (Disease)—Government policy—North America. 2. AIDS
(Disease)—Government policy—Europe. 3. AIDS (Disease)—Government
policy—Japan.   4. AIDS (Disease)—Government policy—Australia.
I. Kirp, David L.   II. Bayer, Ronald.
RA644.A25A363545   1992
362.1'969792—dc20   91-40630
                                                                CIP

British Cataloging-in-Publication information available

Contents

List of Tables and Figures

Foreword

Jonathan M. Mann

This foreword begins with the book's final point: that since the HIV/AIDS pandemic will not be the last, it is vitally important that we explore and analyze how the new global problem of AIDS was discovered, not only at a medical and then a scientific level but also in public health and, finally, in societal and political terms. In all countries, this process of discovery and response was discontinuous, involving periods of rapid progress and frustrating delays. Yet in general, there was a delay of two to four years between the first report of a person with AIDS in a country and the start of a serious national AIDS awareness campaign.

The careful analysis of each stage of the societal reaction to AIDS provides powerful insights into particular countries. Yet AIDS also offers a nearly unique opportunity for productive international comparisons, due both to the global nature of the epidemic and to the relatively brief period (a few years) between the first report of AIDS in 1981 and case reports in many countries. Thus, the stage is set to describe and analyze the public policy responses to the initial, as well as the emerging and evolving, challenges of AIDS. How the industrialized countries reacted to the epidemic, how it was conceptualized, and how different societal elements—governmental and nongovernmental—responded, are of central importance both for understanding the future directions of AIDS policy and for learning lessons of enormous practical value for the next pandemic.

The similarities among industrialized countries are impressive. From the first reports in mid-1981, information about AIDS was widely and rapidly accessible to scientific, medical, and public health experts in all the industrialized countries. The health care infrastructure of all industrialized countries is in theory competent to absorb health care challenges posed by a new disease, and the general public was also informed about AIDS, reflecting the substantial news value of this epidemic of fatal sexually transmitted disease.

This fine book, edited by David Kirp and Ronald Bayer, examines what happened next, beyond the fundamental similarities, where the mysteries and complexities of each national response to AIDS begin. The editors have assembled a fascinating collection of national stories—what do they tell us?

These chapters show that in the industrialized countries, financial resources were not the critical factor in determining AIDS policies; nor were individuals, as prominent as they appeared at the time in the daily press. Rather, the response to AIDS illuminates each nation's political culture. The strength of this book is its attention to national details of person, place, and time. Each chapter, although developed according to a similar format, is flavorful, distinctive, and pungent. German penchant for system and classification, Dutch tolerance, and Swedish rigor inform their respective chapters' tone and style, as well as their content. For those countries the reader already knows rather well, the description of AIDS policy will resonate with inevitability; for unfamiliar countries, the chapter will provide a privileged glimpse into the heart and soul of the nation. For as HIV dissects the immune system, so HIV/AIDS lays bare the social, cultural, and political character of entire societies.

Yet there is another dimension, less visible in a collection of national accounts, that may yet be critical for the future. Networks of concerned people and organizations that are either international (composed of member nations) or transnational (international council of AIDS service organizations, Global AIDS Policy Coalition, international council of people living with HIV and AIDS) create a growing capacity for sharing, communication, and solidarity that crosses national boundaries. Global interdependence is a reality that we in health have been rather slow (unlike our colleagues in business or communications) to recognize, and it is bringing about a growing capacity to transcend national borders, to join community activism with a global consciousness and conscience.

Yet there is a tension between the continued relevance of community and national specificity and global thinking. We need not choose among the extremes of tribalism, nationalism, or globalism—yet the future of more than AIDS may depend upon how these tendencies are negotiated. Thus, a global epidemic of infectious disease helps us not only to explore health and science, but also to appreciate further the forces that are shaping the modern world. The community, national, and international response to the AIDS pandemic mirrors and helps to shape the global future.

Acknowledgments

A project of this scope acquires many debts along the way. A generous grant from the University of California's AIDS Task Force made the enterprise possible, and timely support from the American Foundation for AIDS Research enabled us to expand the scope of the project. The Conanima Foundation provided support to Ronald Bayer's work on this undertaking.

Research assistance was provided by University of California M.P.P.-M.P.H. student James Soos and Harkness Fellow Jill Rutter. At Columbia University, Amy Fairchild assisted in the preparation of the tables appearing in each chapter. Daniel Shostak, a graduate of the Berkeley M.P.P-M.P.H. program, served as recording secretary (and occasional interlocutor) at an August 1990 conference in Talloires, France, that brought together the contributors to exchange drafts and frame common concerns.

At Columbia University, Lela Cooper, Amy Fairchild, and Margot Lovett; at Berkeley, Robi Carmack, Rosemarie Scholz, and E. J. Koch deciphered the authors' scribbles and produced a presentable whole, under conditions of stress sometimes bordering on duress.

Kenneth Arnold, director of Rutgers University Press, made an early and enthusiastic commitment to the venture. Karen Reeds at the Press ably shepherded the book through the review and publication process.

AIDS in the
Industrialized
Democracies

Introduction An Epidemic in Political and Policy Perspective

Ronald Bayer and David L. Kirp

The first cases of AIDS were reported by the Centers for Disease Control (CDC) in the United States in mid-1981. Not until three years later was the viral agent responsible for the new lethal and infectious disease identified. It then became possible to understand that the sudden outcropping of disease represented the end stage of the introduction of a deadly virus, HIV, years earlier. By then, AIDS had affected gay men, intravenous drug users, their sexual partners and children, as well as recipients of blood transfusions and anticoagulant therapy. Within a year or two after the CDC's initial report, AIDS had appeared in countries throughout the world. Thus had begun a pandemic that many saw as representing the greatest threat to public health in the last years of the twentieth century.[1]

A single viral threat had imposed itself on nations at very different levels of economic development; with very different political systems, cultural backgrounds, and attitudes toward sexuality, drug use, and privacy; and with very different conceptions of the role of the state in protecting the public health. The impact of AIDS also varied, and the dimensions of the epidemiological challenge posed by AIDS in particular countries determined the extent to which it would have an impact on fundamental institutions, practices, and values. At the same time, pre-existing patterns of public policy concerning infectious and sexually transmitted diseases, the content of social norms regarding sexuality—and in particular homosexuality—and drug use, popular attitudes toward those populations most at risk, and the existence of government mechanisms for the provision of care to the sick and frail: all would have a profound effect on how AIDS and those with HIV infection would be treated.

AIDS is a medical condition, the clinical course of which is dictated by the pathogenesis of a viral agent. In that sense it exists at a supranational, supracultural level. But like all diseases, AIDS is also embedded in distinctive societies at distinct moments in their history, and so it is also socially constructed.[2] This volume examines how particular nations confronted with a single viral threat faced the challenge of AIDS.

The focus is entirely on AIDS policy and politics in economically

1

advanced democratic nations, not in the Third World. This does not reflect a lack of awareness of the terrible burden of AIDS in the world's
poorer nations. A decade after the official onset of the epidemic, it is plain
that the overwhelming toll of AIDS will be taken not in those countries
where the disease was first officially recognized, but rather in nations
where high poverty levels and inadequate medical infrastructures make it
all but impossible to take advantage of therapeutic advances in treating
AIDS: in many of these poor nations, the cost of an HIV test exceeds the
per capita health budget. That gulf means that, for AIDS as for so many
things, the rich nations and the poor have too little to say to one another;
and redistribution on a scale necessary to narrow that gulf is nowhere on
the political agenda. By restricting our focus to economically advanced
democracies, we can see how differing national cultures have affected the
response to AIDS and have shaped the experience of the epidemic, even
when embedded in economic systems able to provide decent (if not always equitable) health care and in political systems that share a commitment to liberal democratic values. We can also examine the prospects for
countries to learn from one another.

Just as the spread of HIV infection was radically affected by technologi-
cal innovations that made world-wide travel so easy and by the level of
economic development that made such travel a cultural norm for the
citizens of well-to-do nations, knowledge about the new epidemic could
also move quickly. The World Health Organization played a key role in
gathering data and developing international policy recommendations.
Swift transnational communication meant that public health officials, politicians, physicians, scientists, and advocates could track not only the world-
wide epidemiological patterns of the epidemic, but also governments'
policy responses and the actions of nongovernmental organizations.

The United States assumed center stage in the AIDS epidemic. AIDS
was first identified in America, and among the industrialized democracies
it would bear the greatest burden of AIDS cases: indeed, there have been
more AIDS cases in the United States than in the rest of the economically
advanced democratic world combined. What the United States government did—and did not—do, what gay community-based organizations in
America sought by way of public policies and accomplished in terms of
delivering services and education, have served as international points of
reference. America has been both an instructively positive model and a
negative example of how to face the challenge of AIDS. Thus, what the
Centers for Disease Control recommended to protect the blood supply,
what San Francisco did when faced with deciding whether to shut gay
bathhouses, how the Gay Men's Health Crisis in New York City and the
AIDS Foundation and the Shanti Project in San Francisco provided ser-

vices to people with AIDS: these initiatives frequently became part of the policy discourse elsewhere.

Coincidentally—but consequentially—AIDS came to America at the very moment that a conservative administration presided over by Ronald Reagan assumed office. In that regard the United States was not very different from several of the other economically advanced democracies— Canada, Japan, Germany, and Britain among them—which at the time had conservative leaders. But the political coloration of the ruling governments has proved less significant than long-established traditions for dealing with matters of sexuality, drug use, privacy, the rights of vulnerable minorities, and perceived threats to the public health.

There are striking differences that need explanation:

- Why did the Swedish government bring AIDS within the ambit of the preexisting law on venereal diseases, with its harsh commands, while virtually every other country rejected that course?
- Why did public health officials in New York City and San Francisco choose to close or regulate the bathhouses while authorities in Australia, the Netherlands, and Denmark rejected such control?
- Why have needle exchange schemes been uncontroversial in the Netherlands but a source of bitter debate in Germany and the United States?
- Why did the British, Swedes, and Australians choose AIDS campaigns designed to raise fears about the threat of AIDS to the general community, while the Dutch, French, Spanish, and Danes fostered a more benign effort?
- Why did the subject of schoolchildren with AIDS produce significant public outcries in Spain and the United States but not elsewhere?
- Why were studies to track the epidemiology of HIV infection uncontroversial in the United States and Canada but a source of deep division in Great Britain and Holland?
- Why have countries as diverse in their approach to AIDS as Denmark, Great Britain, and Japan chosen to make special financial awards to hemophiliacs infected with HIV because of contaminated blood clotting agents while other nations have not done so?

To date, much of what has passed for comparative analysis of AIDS policy has entailed extracting a single strand of policy from its context: needle exchange, for example, or the treatment of HIV-positive prisoners. We seek, quite differently, to locate the development of AIDS policy within the broader framework of social policy formation. (To facilitate comparisons among the countries studied, we have converted all national

expenditures on AIDS into 1990 U.S. dollars.) No single set of institutions
or cookbook-like formulas could have served as a guide to those who
prepared the accounts, experts in their own countries' experiences. As
shapers of the inquiry, we developed orienting questions meant to guide
the research of individuals with very different intellectual and professional
backgrounds. The contributors were asked to consider:

- *Public Health.* What is the public health tradition with regard to
mandatory measures such as testing, screening, and reporting by
name of carriers and those with infectious diseases, including venereal diseases? What is the tradition of reliance on contact tracing
and the imposition of restraints on those deemed a threat to themselves or others? Since much of public health law is a product of an
earlier era of infectious disease, what restraints have been imposed
on the plenary exercise of public health powers in the past two
decades?
- *Drug Abuse.* What is the main thrust of programs controlling
drug use? What is the role of the criminal law? of treatment? of
opiate maintenance?
- *Homosexuality.* What is the current legal status of homosexuality? To what extent has the law sought to protect homosexuals from
discrimination? How well organized is the gay community? What
form has opposition to homosexuality taken?
- *Sex Education.* What is the tradition of sex education in public
schools and in other institutions? To what extent have moralistic
concerns shaped the content of this education?
- *Confidentiality and Discrimination.* What is the tradition and
current state of confidentiality protections for medical reports? Is
confidentiality a matter of custom or enforced by law? Are there
national policies on discrimination, and if so, what groups do they
protect? Are those with "handicapping conditions" protected?
- *Health and Social Security.* Who bears the cost of illness in the
society? Does the system of health insurance protection extend to
long-term in-home care? Is there a continuum of care that covers
those with chronic diseases?
- *The Policy-making Process.* Is there a tradition of consultation
with, or formal incorporation of, interest group constituencies in
formulating and implementing health and social policy?

The mix of policy decisions on AIDS adopted by any country is not
reducible to single, simple formulations. Nevertheless, it seemed crucial
that each case study consider the extent to which the policy components
fit together to form a more or less coherent whole. We hypothesized two
polar ideal types: a *contain-and-control strategy,* which would seek by

compulsory means to identify those with HIV infection and then to isolate them as a way of preventing the further spread of disease; and a *cooperation-and-inclusion strategy*, which would attempt to engage those most vulnerable to AIDS through education, voluntary testing, and counseling, and by protecting their privacy and social interests as members of the commonwealth.

These competing approaches to AIDS represent two very distinct approaches to public health generally. The contain-and-control strategy derives from the historical tradition of public health, which developed in the context of sometimes virulent epidemic diseases and was codified nearly a century ago. Because of medical advances in therapeutics and transformed patterns of morbidity and mortality in industrialized nations during the latter part of the twentieth century, this approach has rarely been applied to public health threats in recent decades. But the contain-and-control philosophy continues to inform elements of the public health response to sexually transmitted diseases, particularly the emphasis upon compulsory identification through screening. By contrast, the strategy of cooperation-and-inclusion reflects a newer tradition in public health. It is based on the effort to confront chronic noninfectious diseases such as alcoholism, lung cancer, and heart disease—all of which are linked to patterns of behavior. This tradition emphasizes the role of mass persuasion in modifying life-styles linked to disease.

AIDS represents a public health threat at once viral and behavioral. Each of the industrialized democracies thus had to decide a fundamental question: Which elements of each tradition would be drawn upon to contain its spread? The answers reflect the balance of political forces in each nation, the importance placed upon matters of privacy, the relative commitment to personal liberty, the value placed upon voluntarism, and the changing face of the disease. In short, the politics of AIDS is the politics of democracy in the face of a critical challenge to communal well-being.

For this comparative venture, we sought contributors whose professional interest would permit them to prepare careful and candid descriptions of the experiences of their own countries. The interdisciplinary nature of the inquiry led us to recruit a Noah's Ark of social scientists: some are political scientists by training, others sociologists, yet others lawyers and policy analysts. Some came to the task as outsiders critical of their nation's response to AIDS; others had been insiders, directly involved in the formulation of AIDS policy; and of course there were those who were more disinterested. Whatever their perspective, we asked our collaborators to write in a way that would interest—and be useful to—the broad international community of scholars, public health officials, policymakers, and AIDS activists that has been forged by the common confrontation with AIDS.

Each chapter, with its engrossing particularities, says a great deal about how a single virus produced public policy unique to each nation, its politics, and its culture. Taken as a whole, though, the volume captures the sweep and drama of how different nations with a shared commitment to democratic institutions faced the kind of challenge many had believed would never again confront economically advanced countries.[3] In so doing, these renderings tell us a great deal not only about our recent past but also about how the next out-of-the-ordinary challenge to communal health might be faced. If AIDS has taught us anything, it is that we can no longer believe that we are secure against such a threat.

Notes

1. See generally Mirko Grmek, *History of AIDS: Emergence and Origin of a Modern Pandemic* (Princeton, N.J.: Princeton University Press, 1990).

2. See generally Susan Sontag, *AIDS and Its Metaphors* (New York: Farrar Straus, 1989).

3. Compare William McNeill, *Plagues and Peoples* (Garden City, N.Y.: Doubleday, 1976).

Chapter 1 # The United States: At the Center of the Storm

Ronald Bayer and David L. Kirp

Among the industrialized nations of the world, the United States has been most influential in shaping social attitudes and policy responses to AIDS. As the Introduction notes, the disease was first detected in the United States, and the course of the disease first became apparent in the American experience. Not surprisingly, policymakers in other countries looked to the United States for models of what to do—and what *not* to do.

AIDS is a virulent and deadly disease. It is also a contagion of metaphors, which has evoked images of taint, deviance, and defilement. Those moralist associations helped mold both private and public responses to the disease. Initially they prompted panic, particularly at the thought that AIDS might "break out"—might have significant impact on what was euphemistically called the general population. Those associations also discouraged activist government reaction, particularly during the crucial early years of the epidemic.

Yet the voice of AIDS hysteria, an aspect of a broader American right-wing politics, never carried the day. In ideological terms, the story of AIDS is ultimately not a tale of conspiracy-building and witch-hunting of the kind urged by the vocal extremists, but more a tale of consensus-building across professions, political ideologies, and sexual preferences. The most remarkable examples of that consensus are the strikingly liberal reports of national AIDS committees, most or all of whose members were appointed by two conservative Republican presidents, and the leadership exercised during the 1980s by a surgeon general previously best known for his anti-abortion activism.

Except at wartime, activist government is seldom characteristic of the United States. The fragmented structure of the American government militates against quick action, an intentional aspect of the handiwork of the framers of the Constitution. The executive, legislative, and judicial branches compete with one another for dominion within each level of government, and there is also competition among federal, state, and local levels of government.

AIDS placed special strains on this system of governance. To address it effectively required scarce resources, both of dollars and leadership.[1]

7

Often enough in the AIDS arena the competition took the form of a dance of avoidance. Until the mid-1980s, Washington remained largely on the sidelines. Responses varied widely, even among the states like New York and California and cities like New York City and San Francisco that were most affected. Part of the American AIDS policy story, then, is the development of generalized institutional capabilities inside and outside the sphere of government to cope with the spread of the disease, and the eventual willingness, epitomized in 1990 federal legislation, to finance those institutions. Another part of this story is the fragility of those commitments as the character of AIDS continues to change. In the United States as elsewhere, what was initially most remarkable about AIDS was its evident uniqueness. Part fearsome medical contagion, part social crisis, it demanded ways of responding appropriate to its newness. In a host of areas, from candor in discussions of matters sexual to the development of public–private ventures in public health, from rules about privacy to the structures of funding, AIDS changed the policy landscape. Everything about it seemed exceptional. Whether AIDS exceptionalism will carry on into the 1990s, even as the character of the disease itself continues to change, is the central current puzzle of the American experience with AIDS.

When AIDS first made its appearance in the early 1980s, it shattered the illusion that advanced industrial societies had placed behind them the threat of infectious disease. Once again, it became necessary for America to consider the role of public health practices as a defense against the threat of epidemic disease. Had AIDS struck at a different moment in American political history, the balances struck—indeed, the very questions asked—would have been far different.

AIDS posed its challenge to the American polity at a unique juncture. For almost twenty years the judiciary had been deepening and extending the scope of the constitutionally protected realm of privacy.[2] Paralleling these developments and drawing upon the same reformist spirit, the courts had redefined the standards against which all measures limiting fundamental rights would be judged. Although there were only limited indications of how those changes would affect the tradition of deference to decisions made by officials acting to protect the public health—for such questions had rarely arisen in recent decades—it was almost certain that their exercise of authority would not remain unchallenged.

AIDS, a lethal disease transmitted in the most private settings, would test the vitality of the jurisprudence of privacy, the durability of the commitment to individual rights and due process, and the capacity of those responsible for the defense of the public health to adjust their professional

traditions—the authoritarian measures that defined the historical repertoire of responses to epidemic threats—to a social and legal milieu far
different from what had given rise to and endowed them with legitimacy.
Would the standard practices of public health for dealing with sexually
transmitted and communicable diseases be applied to AIDS, or would
HIV infection be treated as exceptional, requiring a unique set of measures? What efforts would be made to modify the behaviors of tens of
millions of men and women? How would the initial impact of AIDS on gay
men, a group at once popularly despised and politically resourceful, shape
these initiatives? How would the illicit status of drug use inform attempts
to interrupt the spread of a lethal disease among IV drug users? How
would the historical antagonism to homosexuality and the illicit nature of
drug use shape these efforts? How would the linkage of intimacy and
lethality serve to inform debates about the protected realm of privacy?
Would coercion be used to identify those who were infected with HIV?
How would the claim of confidentiality be balanced by public health officials and the courts against public health concerns that might be thought to
require disclosure? Would the power to quarantine ever be used to restrict
individuals whose behaviors posed a threat of HIV transmission?

During the two preceding decades, first the courts and later Congress
extended the protection of antidiscrimination measures, initially applied
to race, to other potentially stigmatizing characteristics such as gender
and handicap. Those with AIDS—unlike those touched by other mysterious new diseases, such as Legionnaires' disease—were likely candidates
for stimgatization. When confronted with claims of discrimination against
those with AIDS, would courts intervene—and would lawmakers adopt
antidiscrimination rules for this new and potentially aggrieved class, at
once medically and politically defined? How would the jurisprudence of
rights configure the response to AIDS?

Even as this epidemic struck, Ronald Reagan, newly elected to the
presidency, was initiating a wholesale assault on an already fragile welfare
state. The Reagan administration was also encouraging political and social
forces committed to a traditional and restrictive vision of moral norms in
public life. Consequently, at a time when vigorous federal action was
demanded to deal effectively with the new epidemic—when a massive
infusion of resources for research and prevention efforts would be called
for, when great sums for social and medical services would be needed, and
when a capacity to break with the anti-gay trends in American culture
would be required—the administration consistently minimized the issue
and denigrated those who urged a more activist national role. For their
part, right-wing political groups such as the Moral Majority helped define
a national policy agenda in which perceived deservingness, innocence, or

guilt were critical in determining whom government would and would not help.

Although the failures and missteps that characterized Washington's response to AIDS had a profound impact on the political course of the epidemic, no understanding of AIDS in the United States could emerge from a focus on national decisions alone. In the federal system, much of public health policy is made and implemented at the state and local level. The political character of the fifty states has provided much of the context of AIDS policy-making. Responses in New York City and California were especially critical. The fact that HIV infection so disproportionately afflicted gay men in San Francisco and New York City, two cosmopolitan and liberal cities, did much to affect the course of response to the epidemic. Despite important differences between the two urban centers, they established a pattern of response to the epidemic, most critically a rejection of compulsory measures, which served as a standard that others would either emulate or explicitly seek to reject. In Washington, representatives of these two states became leading players, molding the efforts of Congress to prod the Reagan administration into doing more. .

In the period between 1981 and 1990, roughly the first decade of the AIDS epidemic, four major transformations occurred, each of which modified perceptions, politics, and policy. Epidemiologically, the focus shifted from gay white males to inner-city black and Hispanic drug users and their sexual partners, as the incidence of infection dropped dramatically among homosexuals. Clinically, remarkable advances in therapeutics held out the prospect for a radical modification of the early conception of HIV infection as a progressive and invariably fatal disease. The impotence of medicine in the epidemic's first years had, by 1990, been replaced by a sober optimism on the part of treating physicians. Increasingly, AIDS was being thought of as a chronic disease. From the perspective of public health policy, the early framing of AIDS as exceptional—requiring a unique set of measures unlike those typically brought to bear in the response to other sexually transmitted and communicable diseases—began to yield to the "mainstreaming" of AIDS. Finally, with increasing attention to the care of those with HIV-related diseases came a marked shift in the ideological focus of policy debates. The tension between privacy and the needs of the public health, at the center of debate in the epidemic's first years, remained at issue, most pointedly as it related to health professionals with HIV. But increasingly it has been overshadowed by concerns about the implications of the inequitable nature of the American health care system for assuring access to medical services for those with HIV disease.

These transformations are the focus of this chapter on AIDS in America.

Epidemiology

In June 1981, the Centers for Disease Control (CDC) began to note the appearance in previously healthy gay men of diseases that in the past had occurred only in individuals whose immune systems had been severely compromised.[3] In that month, *Morbidity and Mortality Weekly Report,* the CDC's official publication, reported that between October 1980 and May 1981, five young men in Los Angeles had been diagnosed with pneumocystis carinii pneumonia. In an editorial comment, the outbreak was termed "unusual." The *Report* suggested, by way of explanation, "an association between some aspect of homosexual lifestyle or disease acquired through sexual contact and pneumocystis pneumonia in this population. Based on clinical examination of each of these cases, the possibility of a cellular immune dysfunction related to a common exposure might also be involved."

One month later, the CDC announced that in the prior thirty months, Kaposi's sarcoma, a malignancy unusual in the United States, had been diagnosed in twenty-six gay men in New York City and California.[4] Each of the patients had died within two years of diagnosis. In all of the cases two factors were striking: the youth of the victims (in the past, Kaposi's had been reported only in elderly Americans) and its "fulminant course."

By the end of 1990, as America prepared to enter the second decade of the epidemic, more than 160,000 cases of CDC-defined AIDS had been diagnosed and more than 100,000 people were dead. Although the epidemiological picture has changed since the epidemic's first years, one feature has remained constant. AIDS is primarily a disease of the socially marginal: gay and bisexual men, intravenous drug users, their sexual partners and their children (see Table 1.1). Blacks and Hispanics are significantly overrepresented. Among men the proportion of new cases linked exclusively to homosexual behavior has declined from 77 percent in the period before 1983 to 55 percent in 1990. Among women, the cases attributed to intravenous drug use have remained at 50 percent. The proportion of cases linked to heterosexual transmission remained low: 6 percent. Seventy percent of all cases among women are black or Hispanic. Although all fifty states have now reported at least two cases of AIDS, the burden of the epidemic has fallen most heavily on California, Florida, New Jersey, New York, and Texas. Washington D.C., the nation's capital, with its small but overwhelmingly minority population, has also experienced a heavy impact from the epidemic (see Table 1.2). This epidemiological pattern has had a profound effect on the shape of the policy response to AIDS.

That it was white middle-class gay men who bore so heavy a burden of

Table 1.1. AIDS Cases by Year of Report and Category of Risk Exposure for the United States, 1981–1990

Risk category	1981	1982	1983	1984	1985	1986	1987	1988	1989	1990	Total
Homosexual/bisexual activity	145	381	1,293	2,892	5,494	8,590	13,610	18,069	19,917	23,911	94,302
Homosexual/bisexual activity and IVDU	13	59	199	420	605	994	1,569	2,194	2,233	2,381	10,667
IVDU	21	120	376	798	1,428	2,294	3,642	7,632	8,125	10,114	34,550
Blood products	0	11	44	95	268	462	914	1,253	1,131	1,264	5,445
Heterosexual activity	6	49	108	171	287	560	919	1,617	2,011	2,765	8,493
Mother to child	0	8	24	42	106	159	263	480	564	689	2,335
Other/unknown	4	19	59	97	135	221	417	815	1,216	2,195	5,178
Total cases	189	650	2,103	4,515	8,323	13,280	21,334	32,060	35,197	43,319	160,970

SOURCE: National Research Council, *AIDS: The Second Decade* (National Academy Press, 1990), 44.

Table 1.2. AIDS Cases and Annual Rates per 100,000 Population by State, 1990

Locale	Per 100,000 1990	Cumulative adults	%	Cumulative children	%	Total	%
District of Columbia	121.1	2,672	2	40	1	2,712	2
New York	46.7	33,694	21	802	29	34,496	21
New Jersey	31.5	10,091	6	280	10	10,371	6
Florida	31.2	13,607	9	386	14	13,993	9
California	24.0	30,462	19	212	8	30,674	19
Texas	19.2	11,320	7	111	4	11,431	7
U.S. total	17.0	158,186		2,784		160,970	

SOURCE: Adapted from data provided by the U.S. Centers for Disease Control.

AIDS in the epidemic's first years has had an indelible impact on the nature of the public policy debates. Only since the 1970s had gays begun to emerge from the closet, organizing politically to defend their interests.[5] The advent of AIDS accelerated this process. Thus, they had the capacity to mount a powerful defense of their rights, most critically the right of privacy. Indeed, despite the challenges from the political right, the organized elements of the gay community set the terms of public debate on AIDS prevention in the first phase of the epidemic. When the question of access to drug trials emerged in 1988, gay groups combined technical expertise with political artfulness. They were able to force a reconsideration of the reigning paradigm of research, of the control over new therapeutic agents. Poor black and Hispanic drug users and their sexual partners lacked the power to force attention to their own interests. But in this very helplessness, they compelled attention to the question of how America—with a health care system uniquely inequitable among the industrialized democracies—would meet the challenge of providing medical attention to those, one American in three, without adequate medical insurance.

Combating Discrimination in the Name of Public Health

Central to the public health strategy for confronting AIDS in the epidemic's first years was the recognition that threats of discrimination could undermine efforts to effect behavioral changes. The concerns of those committed to protecting the rights of the infected and vulnerable merged with public health concerns in shaping an alliance against discrimination.

In the political struggle to fashion policy on AIDS discrimination, it was inevitable that the important American tradition of using legislative instruments at both state and federal levels to codify the rights of vulnerable minorities would be called upon. The protection of public law, rooted in the century-old movement to protect racial minorities, had slowly been extended to other minorities, including those with medically-based handicapping conditions. That extension would prepare the groundwork for demands that explicit laws be enacted to protect those with AIDS and HIV infection.

Unsurprisingly, the public schools became an early focal point of controversy over discrimination. Parents, terrified by the new disease, acted to protect their children from what they believed was the unacceptable, if remote, threat of a lethal disease.[6] Although no more than a handful of schoolchildren were publicly involved, the ensuing, widely publicized conflicts dramatized the chasm separating those who argued that great care was necessary when exclusionary policies were being considered from others who believed that, in the face of a threat like that posed by

AIDS, no precaution was too great. That it was children who would either suffer the consequences of exclusion—shame, stigma, isolation—or bear the risk of infection only sharpened the conflict.[7]

Anticipating such challenges to what it considered rational public health policy and social order, the CDC convened a group of consultants in June 1985, to assist in preparing recommendations on issues raised by the presence in classrooms of children infected with the AIDS virus as well as those clinically diagnosed as having the disease itself. At the end of August, just before the beginning of the school year, the CDC issued its recommendations.[8] Reassuring in tone, the statement reviewed the epidemiological evidence and concluded that "casual person to person contact as would occur among schoolchildren appears to pose no risk." Only in the case of very young children and those who were neurologically impaired, where control over bodily secretions was limited, was there even a "theoretical" risk of transmission. Though this formulation left open questions concerning day care for and the foster placement of infants born to infected mothers—issues that would haunt later discussions—it was adequate to the immediate task. There were no grounds for excluding from the classroom most infected children, many of whom had acquired HIV infection from blood transfusions or the clotting factor used by hemophiliacs. "Mandatory screening as a condition for school entry [is] not warranted," the CDC concluded.

But the CDC's guidelines came too late to avert public alarm. That July, Rock Hudson had died from AIDS, an event that made the disease headline news across the country. Although Hudson was a gay man, many took his death as signaling the possibility that AIDS might actually affect them; the response was often panicky. And panic was a particularly understandable reaction when children—"innocent children," as they were described—seemed threatened by the disease.

In the fall of 1985, several school boards yielded to parental anxiety and barred children who had AIDS or were suspected of being HIV-infected from the classroom. Where local boards, acting on the advice of health officials, refused to take such action, parents sometimes organized classroom boycotts. In New York City, a bitter controversy pitted two local community school boards against the city's central Board of Education and Department of Health.[9] Parents angered by the insistence of public health officials that pupils with AIDS be permitted to attend class marched with placards that declared: "Our children want grades, not AIDS"; "Better safe than sorry"; and "Stop the lies: We want facts." Ten thousand children boycotted the city's public schools for a week. Parents responded to the efforts at reassurance with the disbelief of those who expected manipulation by medical experts and public officials.

Even as exclusion of a thirteen-year-old boy named Ryan White from a

Kokomo, Indiana, public school, another headline-making story, seemed to many to show the heartlessness of this heartland town, stories revealing a different side of America went unnoticed. In Swansea, Massachusetts, parents and classmates, prodded by a very different school administration, warmly welcomed another thirteen-year-old with AIDS back to school. Ultimately, the New York City and Kokomo cases—as well as several others across the country—led to court rulings allowing children with AIDS to attend school, on the grounds that they posed no significant risk of transmitting the disease.[10] Through these decisions, judges began extending the protections of antidiscrimination law to people with AIDS.

Concern by employers and workers also provoked a rash of efforts to bar from the workplace those considered to pose some risk of transmitting AIDS.[11] By mid-1985, the epidemiological evidence and scientific understanding of the transmission of HIV had made such acts groundless from a public health perspective. Nonetheless, some private as well as public sector employers responded with alarm, and some trade unions sought exclusions. Unions representing prison guards pressed for the screening of inmates so that the infected could be subject to special handling and even segregation.[12]

The CDC, committed to an anti-alarmist course, tried to stanch the tide of AIDS-related anxiety in the workplace. In so doing, it infuriated right-wing politicians who believed the public health was being sacrificed to protect the interests of gay men. The CDC drafted a special set of recommendations to those who performed invasive procedures where blood contact was possible because of the theoretically greater risk they posed.[13] Here, too, the CDC concluded that there were no grounds for the exclusion of workers otherwise capable of performing their jobs because of AIDS or for routinely screening asymptomatic workers to detect the presence of HIV infection.

But if infected workers posed no risk to clients, customers, and patients, what of the risk posed by infected patients to those who came into contact with them—and especially with their blood and other body fluids? Here, too, the CDC provided a voice of reassurance: the adoption of standard infection control precautions for all patients would be sufficient to protect health care workers from those infected with the AIDS virus.[14]

The debate surrounding infected clinicians and patients was not, however, to be put to rest. Despite the CDC recommendations, many physicians continued to argue for their right to know the HIV status of their patients. In 1990, the CDC confirmed the transmission of HIV from a dentist to five patients. That event led the CDC, as well as the American Medical Association and the American Dental Association, to reopen the question of whether infected clinicians should be permitted to undertake invasive procedures, as well as whether hospitals should be permitted to undertake mandatory screening of all clinicians to identify those who were infected. In mid-1991, after an extraordinarily protracted process involving public conflict, debate within the Public Health Service itself, and political pressure, the CDC finally declared that HIV-infected clinicians who performed invasive procedures should be barred from such procedures. Although it did not endorse mandatory screening to identify those who would be excluded, the decision provided those who had long opposed the limitations on testing for HIV infection with an opportunity to press their case with renewed vigor. Just after the CDC recommendations were made public, the U.S. Senate voted overwhelmingly for legislation that would make it a crime punishable by ten years' imprisonment for a physician to fail to disclose his or her HIV status to a patient.

In 1985 it was still possible to resist the move toward discrimination. Despite objections on the part of some political conservatives the antiexclusionary posture of the CDC was endorsed by the broad spectrum of public health officials in the United States, who made clear their opposition on public health grounds to discriminatory measures. *Report on AIDS*, the statement of the nation's chief health officer, Surgeon General C. Everett Koop, to the American people in the fall of 1986, epitomized the opposition of public health officials to exclusionary policies. Throughout this report, Koop stressed that casual, nonsexual contact posed no risk; that the presence of those with AIDS or HIV infection in public represented no danger. Reassuringly, he asserted:

> Shaking hands, hugging, social kissing, crying, coughing or sneezing will not transmit the AIDS virus. Nor has AIDS been contracted from swimming pools or bathing in hot tubs or from eating in restaurants (even if a restaurant worker has AIDS and carries the AIDS virus). AIDS is not contracted from sharing bed linens, towels, cups, straws, dishes or any other eating utensils. You cannot get AIDS from toilets, doorknobs, telephones, office machinery or household furniture.[15]

Thus, over the full range of social encounters, from the most remote to the most "intimate" of nonsexual contacts, those infected with the AIDS virus represented no hazard. Having thus dismissed as unfounded the fears that fueled proposals to exclude HIV-infected individuals from work, school, housing, and public accommodations, the surgeon general could reject discrimination based on HIV status as without medical warrant.

Nevertheless, the federal government itself had embarked on a policy of barring those with HIV infection from a number of employment settings. In October 1985, the secretary of defense initiated a policy of mandatory screening in the armed forces which required exclusion of all HIV-infected recruits.[16] A year later, the Foreign Service undertook the exclusion of all infected job applicants.[17] The Department of Labor determined that it would screen all applicants to the Job Corps, an employment program for impoverished youth; those who were infected would be barred from the program.[18] In 1987, the Congress endorsed, with virtually no dissent, a policy of screening all immigrants for HIV. Those who were infected were to be barred from seeking residence in the United States.[19] Despite enormous efforts to reverse the policy, it was reaffirmed by the secretary of health and human services in 1991.

The persistent problem of discrimination was highlighted by the Presidential Commission on the HIV Epidemic appointed by President Reagan. "HIV-related discrimination is impairing the nation's ability to limit the spread of the epidemic. . . . As long as discrimination occurs and no strong national policy with rapid and effective remedies against discrimination is established, individuals who are infected with HIV will be reluctant to come forward for testing, counseling and care."[20] This declaration came against a background of resistance on the part of the Reagan administration to act on behalf of those exposed to medically unwarranted exclusions. Indeed, the Justice Department had stated in 1986 that the federal law that protected handicapped indviduals from discrimination in.programs receiving funds from Washington did not shield individuals from acts based on "fear of contagion, whether reasonable or not."

Despite such resistance, the states moved to extend their legislative protection to individuals with AIDS and HIV infection. All fifty states have laws that protect individuals with medical handicaps against unjustified discrimination; more than half have extended the scope of such statutes to include those with HIV infection. In addition, the attorneys general of many states, as well as state human rights commissioners and some municipalities, have declared HIV-related discrimination to be illegal.

In 1987, the Supreme Court ruled that the statute protecting individuals with handicaps against discrimination extended to those with contagious diseases.[21] Irrational fear was no grounds for discrimination, said the justices; indeed, protection against irrationality lay at the heart of federal law. While the facts of the case concerned tuberculosis, not AIDS, that statement of law was a direct rebuff to the Reagan administration's announced policy on AIDS. Finally, and perhaps most importantly, the 1990 Americans with Disabilities Act, which extended civil rights protections to handicapped individuals who face discrimination in both the public and private sectors, includes individuals with HIV infection. Reflecting the breadth of support for such legislation, President George Bush supported a law many viewed as the most important civil rights legislation in almost two decades.

It is difficult to determine the extent of HIV-related discrimination, to know the extent to which state laws and policies as well as the persistent advice of health officials have been effective in stemming the spread of fear against individuals because of AIDS. A survey undertaken by the American Civil Liberties Union found more than thirteen thousand complaints of HIV-related discrimination between 1983 and 1988—and in 1988 the ACLU found that the number of such reports had increased by 50 percent over the prior year.[22] But some knowledgeable observers have noted a marked improvement in the social climate. Thus Larry Gostin, writing in the *Journal of the American Medical Association*, observes:

> The early cases, still winding their way through the courts, often involve discriminatory practices by employers based on prejudice or fears of transmission in the work force. . . . [Now] employers appear much less likely to exclude employees from ordinary workplaces. The new wave of cases involves workplace settings where there is likely to be some exposure to blood such as health care settings, laboratories, and forensic examiners.[23]

Privacy and the Public Health: First Wars

Even before the discovery of HIV, public health officials had been compelled to recognize that the fight against AIDS would require adopting a strategy designed to reassure those most at risk about the benign intentions of state agencies perceived as antagonistic. This suspicion was hardly baseless: gay men still suffered the legacy of official repression and social exclusion; homosexual acts were still illegal in twenty-four states; only in 1973 did the American Psychiatric Association delete homosexuality from its classification of mental disorders.[24] An effective public health response would require public health officials to negotiate differences rather than impose solutions. To reassure intravenous drug users and to reach them with messages of prevention, policies would have to depart radically from repressive drug control programs that had become the hallmark of the government's response. For Haitians, who were in the early days of the epidemic perceived as being at special risk, reassurances were necessary that public health efforts would be untainted by efforts of the immigration authorities to locate and expel undocumented aliens. In all, the emerging campaign against AIDS would have to display a respect for confidentiality and privacy unprecedented for professionals whose traditional ideology had emphasized responding aggressively to perceived risks and not worrying overmuch about privacy.

In the epidemic's first phase, tensions emerged between public health officials, gay activists, and civil liberties organizations. Nowhere was this more obvious than in the bitter debates over whether to close or regulate gay bathhouses, quasi-public commercial establishments where gay and bisexual men engaged in sexual activity linked to the spread of AIDS. On October 9, 1984, San Francisco's director of public health, Mervyn Silverman, announced:

> The [gay bathhouses] that I have ordered closed today have continued in the face of this epidemic to provide an environment that encourages and facilitates multiple unsafe sexual contacts, which are an important contributory factor in the spread of this deadly disease. When activities are proven to be dangerous to the public and continue to take place in commercial settings, the Health Department has the duty to intercede and halt the operation of such establishments.[25]

Thus did the liberal chief health official of the city known as the country's gay Mecca reject the claims of those who sought to protect the gay bathhouses by the invocation of the principles governing the state's attitude to private sexual behavior between consenting adults. For Silverman, the commercial nature of the establishments removed the protective mantle and provided the warrant for intervention. Responding to those who would view his actions as reversing the social and legal advances attained by San Francisco's gay community, the commissioner ended his statement by declaring: "Make no mistake about it. These fourteen establishments are not fostering gay liberation. They are fostering disease and death."

Because of the public health challenge of AIDS and the anxiety it produced, the bathhouses—those bold expressions of an unfettered gay sexuality—had become the subject of an acrimonious controversy that divided the gay community and forced a confrontation over privacy, sexual behavior, and the limits of state intervention. Despite occasional suggestions that the gay community might have to collaborate with public health officials to regulate the bathhouses or to limit the activity permitted to occur within them, the dominant voice, projected by the gay press, was hostile to state intrusion and to claims that the defense of public health by government officials might entail restrictions on commercial establishments serving the sexual desires of their gay clientele. It resisted as well the suggestion that the gay community should act to force changes in the institutions providing the setting for anonymous sexual encounters. Having so recently emerged from long, bitter struggles against statutory prohibitions on homosexuality in many states and the socially sanctioned pattern of discrimination that made privacy so central to the struggle for survival, it is not surprising that gay political thought was so libertarian in its orientation.

Public health officials in a number of cities, including New York, ultimately moved to close or tightly regulate the bathhouses, the way having been led by San Francisco.[26] That they as well as others had not responded earlier, despite the insistent calls for closure from conservative public officials, was partly a consequence of the political constraints imposed by charting a course compatible with a policy of cooperation with gay men. Public health officials were also restrained by the impact of liberal political values. The centers of the AIDS epidemic were cosmopolitan cities with political cultures of relative tolerance in which sexual privacy was a preeminent concern. Indeed, public health director Silverman had said that if heterosexual behavior had been involved, he would have closed San Francisco's bathhouses immediately. Officials also recognized that bathhouse behavior was but a very small part of the vast problem of potentially deadly sexual behavior occurring in settings beyond the reach of the state.

Viewed from the perspective of public health measures designed historically to control the spread of infectious diseases, the decision to close the baths was not remarkable. After all, periodic raids had closed houses of prostitution during panics about venereal disease.[27] What *was* remarkable was the prudence and restraint that characterized such moves. The closing of the baths could thus be seen as reflecting both the traditional orientation of public health and the exceptionalism that characterized AIDS policies in the epidemic's first decade.

Blood, Privacy, and Stigma: The Politics of Safety

For the first year of the epidemic, AIDS remained almost exclusively a disease of the marginal—gay and bisexual men, intravenous drug users, recent immigrants from Haiti. Such an epidemiological pattern was regarded as delivering to the broader community a reassuring message: virtually all heterosexuals who did not engage in socially aberrant behavior had little to fear. But on July 16, 1982, a report in the CDC's *Morbidity and Mortality Weekly Report* shattered the illusion of security.[28]

Three cases of pneumocystis carinii pneumonia had been reported among patients with hemophilia A, the most severe form of the disorder. Two had died; one remained critically ill. All three were heterosexual. None had a history of intravenous drug use. In commenting on these cases, the CDC stated: "Although the cause of the severe immune dysfunction is unknown, the occurrence among the three hemophiliac cases suggests the possible transmission of an agent through blood products." If this was true, the implications both for hemophiliacs treated with Factor VIII, a clotting agent that in concentrated form is derived from the pooled plasma of large numbers of donors, and for transfusion recipients, could be disastrous.

It was the threat of transfusion-associated AIDS that, for the first time, galvanized media attention and provoked concern about how "innocents" could fall victim to the epidemic. *Time* magazine typified the response. "A majority of experts believe that what was once known as the 'gay plague' will enter the general population" and that the most likely route of entry would be through blood.[29]

If the bathhouse debate had focused on the clash between the demands of sexual privacy and the protection of the public health, the controversy over how to protect the blood supply from those who might infect it centered on questions of social stigma, the consequences of identifying whole classes as the potential sources of contamination. Just as the threat to blood, symbolic of life itself, evoked communal anxiety, the threat of exclusion from the blood donor pool represented a profound threat to the social standing of those who would be classed as a danger to the public health. In addition to concerns over privacy so central to the bathhouse controversy, the debate over the blood supply called into question the gay struggle for social integration.

While some gay physicians felt that the situation required the withdrawal of homosexual men who led "fast lane" sexual lives from the donor pool, for the gay political leadership the potential for a socially catastrophic turn in policy was all too easy to discern. But the effort of gay leaders to prevent the government from urging the exclusion of high-risk individuals from the blood donor pool was ultimately untenable, given the increasing frequency with which gay men themselves had sought to educate those at increased risk about the dangers of donation. On March 4, 1983, the Public Health Service issued its recommendations on the "Prevention of Acquired Immune Deficiency Syndrome (AIDS)."[30] Given the available evidence, the Centers for Disease Control, the Food and Drug Administration, and the National Institutes of Health, which had collaborated in preparing the new recommendations, declared that "physical examinations alone [would] not identify all persons capable of transmitting AIDS." There was, therefore, no alternative but to treat all members of groups at increased risk for AIDS as posing a threat of transmission. Included were homosexual and bisexual men with multiple sex partners, as well as those who had sex with such individuals.

In measured language, and with full recognition that the blood banking community had expressly rejected the explicit screening of potential donors for sexual orientation, the Public Health Service put forth its "prudent" proposals calling on members of groups at increased risk to refrain from donating plasma and blood. Although specifying that laboratory tests, personal histories, and physical examinations be included among the potentially useful approaches to identifying those at risk, the recommendations carefully avoided any reference to the explicit use of questions about sexual orientation, the method proposed by the National Hemophilia Foundation but so opposed by gay leaders.

Gay political leaders came tacitly, if reluctantly, to accept the Public Health Service recommendations on exclusion as a temporary expedient. Ultimately, they believed, the development of a specific blood test would obviate the need for screening procedures, no matter how carefully designed, based upon sexual orientation.

A little more than a year after the Public Health Service delivered its donor exclusion recommendations, Secretary of Health and Human Services Margaret Heckler announced at a national press conference that a retrovirus, HTLV-III (also called LAV at the time, but ultimately named HIV), had been identified as the agent responsible for AIDS.[31] The discovery—which would fundamentally affect all future efforts to understand AIDS—also had immediate implications for protection of the blood supply. Government officials were quick to announce that a blood test for the antibody to the virus, which could potentially protect the blood supply, would be commercially available within six months. But no sooner had the prospect of the availability of such a long-awaited test been made public than concern about how it would be applied began to surface. Such anxieties were compounded by uncertainty about the clinical significance of the presence of the antibody.

In the face of the impending licensing of a test designed to protect the blood supply, a broad consensus developed around the need to create alternative test sites for individuals seeking knowledge of their antibody status. These sites, where testing was most often done under conditions of anonymity, were designed to divert people from using blood banks to determine their HIV status, and would ultimately emerge as the nucleus for all publicly funded testing for infection with the AIDS virus.

The Battles Over Testing

From the outset, the test developed to detect the antibody to the AIDS virus—and first used on a broad scale in blood banking—was mired in controversy. Uncertainty about the significance of the test's findings and about its quality and accuracy provided the technical substrate of disputes that inevitably took on a political character.

Months before the AIDS virus antibody test was licensed by the Food and Drug Administration for use in blood banks, anxiety had already surfaced in the discussions of gay leaders, fueled by the fears engendered by the repressive calls of the political right. "Don't take the test" became the rallying cry. In an editorial, the *New York Native*, a gay newspaper, declared:

> No gay or bisexual man should allow his blood to be tested. . . . The meaning of the test remains completely unknown, beyond indicating exposure to the virus. [What was far from uncertain, however, was the] personal anxiety and socioeconomic oppression that [would] result from the existence of a record of a blood test result. . . . Will test results be used to identify the sexual orientation of millions of Americans? Will a list of names be made? How can such information be kept confidential? Who will

be able to keep this list out of the hands of insurance companies, employers, landlords, and the government itself?[32]

Gay and bisexual men needed to modify their behaviors in order to protect their own health and that of their sexual partners. For those purposes, what role could such an ambiguous and potentially dangerous test play?

Opposition to the use of the antibody test, outside the context of blood banking and research protocols, was not restricted to gay groups. A number of local health departments also expressed alarm. In New York City, the health commissioner, responding to the fears of those who foresaw a future in which those identified as infected would be exposed to discrimination, not only refused to establish testing sites but sought to impede the use of the test outside of blood banking. New York, the epicenter of the American AIDS epidemic, thus became the only major American city where voluntary, confidential, or anonymous testing would not be readily available.

At the same time, some began to perceive the test as a potentially invaluable adjunct in the struggle against AIDS—especially when the ELISA test (which by design tended to overdiagnose the presence of infection) was done in conjunction with the technically more difficult and more expensive Western Blot confirmatory test. The proponents of testing did not deny that there were lingering technical problems, but they asserted that similar problems were associated with virtually every test done in medicine. They did not view the test as a substitute for individual counseling and mass education but as a potent tool for fostering the behavioral modifications that everyone understood to be essential to any AIDS control program. They did not discount the risks posed by threats to confidentiality, but sought to protect the privacy of those who needed testing, frequently by arguing that the option of anonymity be available. Finally, and most critically, those who supported the use of the test believed that the emerging understanding of the significance of positive findings was of great personal and public health relevance. Unlike those who persisted in asserting that the test demonstrated little about current infectivity, the test's proponents relied on studies revealing that the presence of the antibody indicated current infection with the AIDS virus—and of a presumed capacity to transmit infection to others. In sum, at each juncture where uncertainty and ambiguity led opponents of the test to stress the threats to privacy and civil liberties and the absence of compensating public health benefits, public proponents of testing underscored the potential for a contribution to the campaign against AIDS.

It was not only those officially involved with public health who had begun to argue that testing for the antibody to the AIDS virus was important. In November 1985, nine months after the test was licensed, the

American Association of Physicians for Human Rights, a gay medical organization, urged gay and bisexual men to take the test if they needed it "to practice low risk sexual behavior all the time."[33] The chair of its AIDS Task Force acknowledged that his deepening realization that AIDS posed the "most serious threat of our lifetime" had impelled him to a change of mind.[34] "In 1984 . . . I saw the test as the greatest threat to the gay community and advised loudly 'don't take the test.' I was wrong . . . the greatest threat to gay and bisexual men is not the test (at least where it is anonymous), it is infection with HTLV-III."[35]

While increasing numbers of gay leaders were beginning to accept the need for testing under carefully defined circumstances, many within the public health community were beginning to place even greater stress on the potential benefits that would result from the large-scale voluntary testing of those at increased risk for HIV infection. In August 1985, the Association of State and Territorial Health Officials (ASTHO), an organization of state health commissioners concluded that, when properly used, "test information may enhance the education efforts which remain for now the principal intervention to prevent HTLV-III transmission."[36]

But an increased reliance on voluntary testing was predicated on the capacity to protect the confidentiality of test results. Acknowledging the skepticism of the gay community, the ASTHO report stressed the importance of convincing those at risk that all measures would be taken to preclude the unwarranted disclosure of test findings. The defense of confidentiality was not antithetical to the protection of public health; it provided the condition for the required interventions.

In March 1986, after months of deliberation, the CDC published recommendations placing federal health authorities behind proposals that would involve the voluntary testing of all Americans at risk.[37] Among those included were homosexual and bisexual men, present or past intravenous drug users, persons with clinical laboratory evidence of HIV infection, persons born in countries where heterosexual transmission was believed to play a major role in the spread of AIDS, male and female prostitutes, sex partners of infected persons or persons at increased risk, all persons with hemophilia who had received anticoagulants, and newborn infants of high-risk or infected mothers. In short, millions of Americans were brought within the scope of the CDC's proposals. Such testing was necessary to "facilitate the identification of seropositive asymptomatic individuals," so that they might be counseled about risk reduction and the importance of ongoing clinical evaluation. Large-scale testing and counseling would, in turn, require a vast expansion of the settings within which efforts would be made to reach those at increased risk. Counseling and voluntary testing had to be routinely offered to those at increased risk wherever they received medical care; clinics for the treatment of those with sexually transmitted diseases and drug abusers were singled out. The CDC used the occasion to underscore the importance of confidentiality protections to the new strategy of public health intervention. Only if those at risk believed their privacy was protected would efforts succeed to increase the numbers seeking testing. So important was such confidence-building that the CDC supported testing under conditions of anonymity if confidentiality could not be assured.

Entailed in the CDC's defense of the aggressive promotion of voluntary testing was a rejection of any recourse to coercive screening. Indeed, the strategy was voluntarist at its core. Both Surgeon General Koop and a special committee established by the Institute of Medicine of the National Academy of Sciences underscored these themes in reports issued in the fall of 1986. In his *Report on AIDS*, Koop rejected proposals for mass mandatory screening as "unnecessary, unmanageable, and cost prohibitive."[38] The Committee on a National Strategy for AIDS, created by the Institute of Medicine and the National Academy of Sciences, similarly rejected compulsory testing as a way to identify the infected. Proposals for more targeted mandatory screening of at-risk individuals were rejected as impractical and infeasible in an "open society." Instead of such compulsory measures, the committee endorsed large-scale "voluntary, confidential testing (but with provision for anonymous testing if desired)."[39]

While the political, public health, and medical mainstream opposed mandatory testing, those on the right wing of the political spectrum continued to press for it. The most striking example of such a move came in California in late 1985 and 1986, when forces aligned with Lyndon LaRouche, an avatar of what has been called the paranoid style in American politics, solicited more than six hundred thousand signatures from Californians.[40] This placed on the ballot a measure requiring state public health officials to enforce a range of coercive AIDS policies, including mass testing, the reporting of seropositives to public health registries, and the exclusion of the infected from a range of jobs. Opposed by a bipartisan coalition of the medical, cultural, religious, and political elite of California, the referendum nevertheless won the support of almost 30 percent of the seven million voters who cast ballots on the issue in November 1986.[41]

There was only one domain within which testing without consent, or even the knowledge, of individuals whose blood was being examined for the presence of HIV infection, did not arouse opposition in the United States. That involved the epidemiological study of samples drawn for non-HIV-related purposes that were stripped of all personal identifiers. Such blinded seroprevalence studies were first proposed by the CDC in late 1985 as a way of determining the level of infection in the general population, as well as in specific population groups such as patients attending clinics for sexually transmitted diseases or child-bearing women. Because such studies could not be used to identify particular individuals, it was widely believed by gay groups and civil liberties organizations as well as public health officials that they were ethical. But such epidemiologically driven testing, which in other industrialized democracies such as England and the Netherlands provoked strong opposition, had little to do with the commitment to testing individuals for purposes of encouraging behavioral change, a central element of the CDC's prevention strategy.

By 1990, more than two million persons had been tested throughout the United States at federally-funded counseling and testing sites. Of those tested, almost 150,000 were infected. Since public health officials believed that as many as one million Americans were infected with HIV, these data suggested that the vast proportion of infected persons had chosen not to be tested.[42] To those who saw testing of the infected as critical to the process of behavioral change, it was clear that still more vigorous encouragement and support of screening programs were necessary.

To assure that testing would in fact be voluntary, some states enacted statutes requiring that written specific consent be obtained before testing occurred. The insistence on such rigor stood in marked contrast to the standard American practice in medicine, where consent to diagnostic blood tests is assumed once an individual has come for treatment. To many clinicians, the demand for specific consent represented a burdensome intrusion into the practice of medicine. Despite the voluntarist consensus and the statutory requirements, many physicians and hospitals undertook surreptitious testing of patients, justifying their practices by claims that the protection of health care workers and sound diagnostic work required such screening.[43] In New York State, four medical societies, including the New York Medical Society, unsuccessfully brought the Commissioner of Health to court because of his failure to designate AIDS a sexually transmitted disease, a determination that would have permitted testing without consent.[44] This effort represented but one of many signs that, in the last years of the 1980s, the voluntarist orientation of the epidemic's first phase and the perspective of HIV exceptionalism were increasingly subject to erosion.

With the announcement, in mid-1989, that clinical trials had revealed the efficacy of early therapeutic intervention in slowing the course of illness in asymptomatic but infected persons and preventing the occurrence of pneumocystis carinii pneumonia, the political debate about testing underwent a fundamental change. Gay groups such as Project Inform in San Francisco and the Gay Men's Health Crisis in New York began to encourage those they had formerly warned against testing to determine whether they were infected.[45] Physicians pressed more vigorously for the "return of AIDS to the medical mainstream," so that testing might be routinely done under conditions of presumed consent.[46] State and federal public health officials launched aggressive campaigns for voluntary testing.

Although physicians and public health officials have typically avoided the language of compulsion, stressing instead "routine" testing, the threat of coercion—as well as the risk of increased discrimination within the context of medical institutions—loomed before gay activists, their liberal political allies, and proponents of civil liberties.

With the promise of early therapeutic intervention came the unraveling of alliances that had been forged in the first phase of the epidemic. Nowhere was this clearer than in the emergence of a powerful movement, supported by obstetricians and pediatricians, for the routine screening of pregnant women who could transmit HIV to their offspring and the mandatory screening of infants at high risk for infection. In both cases, traditions of public health practice served as models for what might be done in the case of the AIDS epidemic.

Public Health Reporting and Contact Tracing

The erosion of the alliance that had resisted the application of traditional public health epidemic control practices could be seen also in the shifting trends on the issue of reporting the names of those infected with HIV to confidential public health department registries. AIDS itself had been reportable in every state since 1983, as local public health officials, encouraged by the CDC, sought to adopt long-standing public health practice to the new epidemic. Little controversy surrounded the imposition of such reporting requirements.

That was not the case, however, with the reporting of individuals with HIV infection who had not been diagnosed with AIDS. Soon after the initiation of antibody testing in 1985, some health officials argued that reporting be extended to HIV test results, and the LaRouche campaign in California made such reporting a centerpiece of its efforts. Calls for reporting were fiercely resisted by gay groups because of concerns about privacy and confidentiality; they were also opposed by public health officials in states and cities with large numbers of AIDS cases because of the potential impact on people's willingness to seek voluntary HIV testing. As a consequence, named reporting of HIV had become the practice in only a handful of states, typically those with few cases. It was thus a great setback for those who opposed reporting that the Presidential Commission on the HIV Epidemic, reluctantly appointed by President Reagan under pressure from public health officials and political liberals dismayed by the failure of the White House to apprehend the gravity of AIDS, urged in its 1988 final report that HIV be made reportable.[47]

Ultimately more significant were the fissures that had begun to appear in the alliance opposing named reporting in states where the prevalence of HIV infection was high and where gay communities were well organized. In New York, for example, major elements of the medical community sought to compel the state commissioner of health to declare HIV infection a reportable condition.[48] In June 1989, the commissioner of health in New York City declared that HIV reporting was crucial to the public health, asserting at the same time that it was time to bring AIDS within the ambit of classical disease control programs.[49] These moves were part of a national trend at the outset of the 1990s. Although by the end of 1989 only nine states required named reporting without any provision for anonymity, states increasingly were adopting policies that required reporting in some circumstances. At the end of 1990, the CDC itself urged the states to undertake named reporting.

This move toward reporting was only partly linked to the argument that state health departments needed the names of individuals to assure adequate clinical follow-up. As important was the assertion by public health officials that effective contact tracing had become more critical than ever because of the need for early clinical intervention. The identification of infected individuals could only be assured if those with HIV infection but not yet diagnosed as having AIDS could be interviewed by public health investigators, in order to elicit the names of their sexual and needle-sharing partners.

Despite its well-established role in venereal disease control in the United States, such contact tracing in the context of AIDS had been a source of ongoing conflict between gay groups and civil liberties organizations, on the one hand, and those public health officials who had proposed such a strategy in the early years of the epidemic, on the other. Though the laws were sometimes coercive in language, in fact contact tracing was predicated on the willingness of those with sexually transmitted diseases to provide public health workers with the names of their partners, who could then be contacted and urged to undergo serological testing and treatment. It also entailed a commitment to protect the anonymity of the index case. Nevertheless, this disease control measure was viewed by AIDS activists as a threat to confidentiality and as a potentially coercive intervention. Opponents typically denounced contact tracing as "mandatory," and their fears were amplified by conservative demands that tracing be made compulsory. In the state of Minnesota, one opponent warned that the lists created by contact tracing would pose a grave threat to gay men: "The road to the gas chambers began with lists in Weimar Germany."

The Centers for Disease Control have been most important in pressing for the adoption of contact tracing programs at the state level, where all such programs are organized and funded. In 1988, the CDC stipulated that all states that received funds from its AIDS prevention program had to have in place procedures for partner notification. Support for voluntary contact tracing was ultimately to come from the public health establishment: the Institute of Medicine and the National Academy of Sciences, the Presidential Commission on the HIV Epidemic, the American Bar Association, and the American Medical Association.[50] By the beginning of the 1990s, as a better understanding emerged of how contact tracing functioned in the context of sexually transmitted diseases, some of the most vocal opponents yielded their principled opposition and instead centered their concerns on the cost of so labor-intensive an intervention.

In addition to essentially voluntary partner notification, health officials have debated whether there were circumstances under which it was permissible for physicians to breach confidentiality in order to warn individuals who might be placed at risk by HIV-infected patients who refused to modify their behavior.[51] A long tradition in the United States permitted such breaches, and the law in some states made them obligatory. Early concerns about confidentiality in the context of the AIDS epidemic had resulted in many state enactments that precluded physicians from warning individuals endangered by their patients. Ultimately, the American Medical Association took the position that breaches of confidentiality to prevent the possible transmission of HIV infection were a professional responsibility.[52] Although no state has enforced such a legal duty to warn, by 1990 about a dozen had granted physicians the "privilege to disclose" for purposes of warning unsuspecting partners, protecting them from lawsuits by patients angered by the violation of confidentiality.[53]

Quarantine and the Criminal Law

The question of how best to respond to individuals who might infect others inevitably forced the issue of quarantine to the fore. The most plenary of public health powers, the capacity to isolate individuals whose infectious conditions posed a threat to communal welfare, had rarely been exercised in recent years. Yet a strategy that would seek to contain and control those with HIV infection did find some support from those at the far right of the political spectrum.

Perhaps the most forthright call for quarantine appeared in the *American Spectator*, a conservative journal of opinion:

> There are only three ways that the spread of lethal infectious diseases stops: it may be too rapidly fatal, killing off all its victims before the disease can spread; the population affected may develop natural or medically applied immunity; it may not be able to spread because uninfected individuals are separated sufficiently well from those infected. [At this point the only way] to prevent the spread of the disease is by making it physi-

cally impossible. This implies strict quarantine, as has always been used in the past when serious—not necessarily lethal—infections have been spreading. Quarantine in turn implies accurate testing.[54]

Lamenting the failure of nerve on the part of Americans, the article noted that neither quarantine nor universal testing was palatable to the American public where AIDS was concerned, despite the fact that they had been used "without hesitation in the past."

On grounds of science, pragmatics, and constitutional values, proposals for the mass isolation of all HIV-infected individuals have found no support among public health professionals or even conservative politicians. But the more targeted use of the quarantine power to control those with AIDS or HIV infection who seemed unwilling to stop their unsafe behavior did elicit support from some public health officials. Unlike proposals such as LaRouche's, which carried in their sweep those who posed no threat to others, the prospect of controlling, as a last resort, people who demonstrated their willingness to inflict harm seemed tailored to the requirements of a public health practice cognizant of both practical and constitutional limits.[55]

In a nation attentive to individual liberty, all proposals for the management of "recalcitrants," no matter how carefully framed, provoked questions about the due process protections that would be brought to bear in the determination of infectiousness, the substantiation of charges of irresponsible and dangerous sexual behavior, and the establishment of the appropriate period of confinement and control. Some believed that the risks involved in granting authority to state officials were simply too great, the benefits of quarantine too uncertain, to warrant the extension of public health law to the control of private sexual behavior. The issues were aired on national television when the public broadcasting network described the case of Fabian Bridges, a poor black male prostitute and drug user in Texas who, though infected, had continued to solicit customers despite the fact that he knew he had AIDS.

Unlike those who viewed public health law as a humane application of the state's power without the punitive implications of the criminal law, opponents of quarantine saw primarily the threat of an unbridled exercise of power. Thus, many defenders of civil liberties asserted that they would prefer that the criminal law, with its well-developed protections for the accused, be brought to bear in response to those who knowingly and willfully put others at risk for AIDS. The assault on quarantine and the defense of the criminal sanction in the context of AIDS was part of a much broader liberal test of the fundamental premises of public health law, with its open-ended and discretionary character. While the vision of a forward-looking, scientific, and nonpunitive law, deriving its inspiration from medicine and inspired by a rehabilitative ideal, had once stood as a critical standard against which the archaic and retributive features of the criminal law could be judged, there had been a radical shift of perspective in the 1960s and 1970s.[56] Now it was the procedurally bounded and restricted exercise of the state's power to punish that stood as a model for the reform of public health law.

Despite fierce opposition to all efforts to bring AIDS within the scope of state quarantine statutes, more than a dozen states have done so since 1987.[57] Typically, those states have simultaneously modernized their disease control laws to reflect contemporary constitutional standards. These detail procedural guarantees and require that restrictions on freedom represent the "least restrictive alternative" available to achieve a "compelling state interest."

Since there have been only a few notable cases in which newly revised quarantine statutes have been applied to the AIDS epidemic, this issue has proved more problematic in theory than in practice. More typically, the power these laws vested in public health officials has been used to warn rather than incarcerate those whose behavior has posed a risk of HIV transmission.

The enactment of statutes criminalizing behaviors linked to the spread of AIDS parallels the political receptivity to laws extending the authority of public health officials to control those whose behavior poses a risk of HIV transmission.[58] Such use of the criminal law, broadly endorsed by the Presidential Commission on the HIV Epidemic, called upon a tradition of state enactments that makes the knowing transmission of venereal disease a crime.[59] Although they almost never were enforced, the existence of these older laws served as a rationale for new legislation. Between 1987 and 1989, twenty states enacted such statutes, the vast majority of which defined the proscribed acts as felonies, despite the fact that most earlier statutes had treated knowing transmission of venereal disease as a misdemeanor.[60] In 1990, federal legislation providing for increased support for states and cities with large numbers of AIDS cases stipulated that the receipt of funds depended on the existence of state authority to prosecute those who willfully behaved in a manner that could result in HIV transmission to unsuspecting partners.

Some aggressive prosecutors have relied on laws defining assault and attempted murder to bring indictments, even in the absence of AIDS-specific enactments. One survey estimates that between fifty and one hundred prosecutions were initiated during the epidemic's first decade, involving acts as varied as spitting, biting, blood splattering, blood donation, and sexual intercourse with an unsuspecting partner.[61]

These cases, while few in number, have drawn great attention. Most have not resulted in guilty verdicts. But punishment for those found guilty has sometimes been unusually harsh. In Nevada, where prostitution is both legal and regulated, a woman was sentenced in 1989 to twenty years' imprisonment under a statute that makes solicitation by those who test positive for HIV a felony. In the same year, an Indiana appeals court upheld a conviction for attempted murder against a man who had splattered blood on emergency workers seeking to prevent him from committing suicide.[62]

Prevention Through Education

In the face of continued conservative and right-wing challenges and early libertarian concerns, the central thrust of AIDS prevention campaigns has been on education. At every encounter with the threat of coercive public health measures—calls for mandatory screening and the isolation of those capable of transmitting HIV infection—the broad alliance of physicians and public health officials committed to a voluntarist strategy has insisted that education provide the central element in prevention. More money, more inventiveness, more explicitness: all were necessary if individuals were to be taught how to protect themselves from HIV infection, how to protect their sexual partners or those with whom they shared intravenous drug equipment, how to prevent the birth of babies with AIDS.

There was little dispute that education in its various forms, from mass public health campaigns to private counseling, had a critical role to play in combating AIDS. What was cause for conflict was the extent to which education ought to represent the sole element in the strategy of prevention; the detail with which governmentally-funded programs would address matters of sexual behavior and intravenous drug use; the extent to which it would be possible to use language that many would find offensive, or pictures that many would consider pornographic.

Despite the very early and widespread appreciation of the role that risk reduction education might play in controlling AIDS, the federal government did virtually nothing to fund such efforts in the first years of the epidemic. While part of the more general inadequacy of the government's response, the failure to support educational efforts was nevertheless striking. In its *Review of the Public Health Service's Response to AIDS*, the Office of Technology Assessment of the U.S. Congress wrote in February 1985: "So far, efforts to prevent AIDS through education have received minimal funding, especially efforts targeted at groups at highest risk."[63] When the National Academy of Sciences and the Institute of Medicine issued the report *Confronting AIDS* in the fall of 1986, they stressed the importance of education and were sharply critical of the efforts made during the first five years of the epidemic.[64] Persistent pressure from the alliance of forces brought together by the struggle against AIDS led to rapidly increasing funds for education and counseling. To AIDS activists, though, these expanded resources were still inadequate.

Inadequate federal funding for AIDS education had roots deeper than fiscal constraints from the onset. The prospect of a major government effort to underwrite risk reduction education was deeply controversial. How could it have been otherwise? How could government agencies teach gay men about "safer" sexual practices when homosexual acts were criminal offenses in twenty-four states and the nation's capital, the District of Columbia? How could such agencies teach addicts about sterilizing drug paraphernalia when the possession of heroin and cocaine constituted criminal offenses in every state?

The important influence of religion in American social life has played a crucial role in shaping and limiting the content of AIDS prevention efforts. Although liberal religious denominations have expressed deep concern about those infected with HIV and those subject to stigmatization, Protestant fundamentalists have used their considerable influence to restrict the capacity of public health officials to launch effective campaigns. Thus, in a nationally televised sermon, Jerry Falwell of the Moral Majority declared that AIDS was a "lethal judgment of God on America for endorsing this vulgar, perverted and reprobate life-style."[65] For Falwell and many of his followers, the epidemic taught the importance of a return to sexual and moral convention: "Do it and Die" was the lesson of AIDS.

The Catholic Church, while committed to the care of those with AIDS and rejecting the doctrine of "God's judgment," has nonetheless insisted that its opposition to condom use not be modified in light of the need for safer-sex education. Indeed the U.S. Conference of Bishops rejected a church document, "The Many Faces of AIDS," which exhibited some tolerance for condom education.

Even when public health departments sought to fund AIDS education through intermediaries, they were forced to confront the question of how explicit these groups could be. In 1985, AIDS Project Los Angeles, a community-based group under contract with the state of California, began to distribute "Mother's Handy Sex Guide," a brochure with a cover photograph of a seductively seated man wearing nothing but an athletic supporter. The warnings contained in the pamphlet were direct: "When you share urine, shit, cum, blood and possibly saliva, you are at greatest risk for getting AIDS." Under the heading "Playing Unsafely," the pamphlet listed "Fucking without a condom. Your partner coming in your mouth. Water sports. Pissing in the mouth or on the skin with cuts or sores." The bulk of the material included in "Mother's Handy Sex Guide" was devoted to three erotic gay fantasies, which depicted sexual encounters involving mutual masturbation and anal intercourse with the use of condoms, safe or "relatively safe" sexual acts. A conservative member of the Los Angeles County Board of Supervisors was outraged: "It goes beyond all boundaries of good taste and decency. . . . The material is not educational, it's hard core pornography."[66] California consequently created a Materials Review Committee, which concluded: "It is preferable to use clinical or descriptive terms describing sexual contact or behavior . . . rather than their slang or 'street language' equivalents." Photographs and other "visual messages" were not to be explicitly suggestive.[67]

The CDC's decision to impose similar constraints on educational materials developed under grants it made to local AIDS programs had far-reaching implications. As a result of intervention from the White House, the CDC moved to prohibit the funding of material that might be deemed offensive by broad community standards, and to create local review panels to ensure that those standards would not be violated. One CDC official told a gay physicians' group: "You would be naive to think that we can spend tax dollars to eroticize homosexuality."[68]

Although the CDC guidelines initially had a chilling effect on the content, style, and language of programs seeking federal support, some states created review panels sympathetic to the concerns voiced by gay leaders. But the assault on the public funding of safer-sex educational material went beyond revulsion provoked by the use of "street language" and sexually explicit drawings and photographs. To conservative politicians and some religious groups—those who believed that AIDS was the consequence of the erosion of traditional values, of a sexuality unrestrained by heterosexual monogamy—the very premises of the AIDS education being encouraged by public health officials were profoundly flawed.

Ultimately, the controversy pitted Surgeon General C. Everett Koop, a voice of public health pragmatism, against Secretary of Education William J. Bennett, who was closely associated with the morally most conservative elements within the Reagan administration. Bennett's influence ultimately prevailed when the attorney general issued the following directive:

> Any health information developed by the federal government that will be used for education should encourage responsible sexual behavior . . . based on fidelity, commitment, maturity, placing sexuality within the context of marriage. . . . Any health information provided by the federal government that might be used in schools should teach that children should not engage in sex and should be used with the consent and involvement of parents.[69]

The influence and constraining impact of moralism was vividly revealed in the spring of 1988, when the U.S. Senate overwhelmingly voted to support an antihomosexual amendment put forth by conservative

Republican Senator Jesse Helms. Enraged by a sexually explicit "safer-sex" comic book produced by the New York City–based Gay Men's Health Crisis, a recipient of federal funds, Helms denounced the "promotion of sodomy" by the government. The threat of AIDS would never be met effectively "as long as [the U.S. Senate encourages] groups that advocate homosexuality, which was the original source of the AIDS virus."[70] The conservative Republican senator proposed precluding the use of federal funds "to provide AIDS educational information, or prevention materials and activities that promote or encourage homosexual activities."[71] Less surprising than Helms's proscriptive move was the ease with which he was able to elicit support from almost all of his senatorial colleagues.

Safer Drug Use and the Problem of Drug Abuse

Attempts to address intravenous drug users about the risks they posed to themselves and their sexual partners as a result of their behaviors have also been embroiled in controversy from the outset. If "safer"-sex literature provoked conflict because of its explicit language and implicit toleration of homosexuality, messages to addicts about the importance of avoiding contaminated drug paraphernalia suggested a temporary truce in the seven-decade medicolegal effort to suppress the illicit use of drugs.

The first major encounter over how to address drug users at risk for HIV infection and transmission occurred in Los Angeles. It was provoked by the distribution by public health officials of a pamphlet entitled "Shooting Up and Your Health." The pamphlet warned about the hazards associated with intravenous drug use, but nevertheless rejected the condemnatory stance of those who sought to extirpate such behavior.

> There are always risks associated with any use of drugs by injection. The only way to avoid these risks is not to use needles. If you continue to inject drugs, the following measures will reduce your risk. DON'T SHARE NEEDLES! Sharing drugs can share diseases too. Obtain your own "works" and don't let anyone else use them. CLEAN YOUR OWN WORKS. Wash them with alcohol after each use, then leave them to soak in alcohol until the next use. CLEAN YOUR SKIN with alcohol before injecting.

"Shooting Up" was brought to the attention of the county's board of supervisors at the same time that the pamphlet "Mother's Handy Sex Guide" was stirring outrage. It was assailed as "impl[ying] the official approval of the government of the county and city of Los Angeles toward drug use."[72] One conservative local politician saw in it another example of "radical liberals using taxpayers' dollars to subsidize deviant behavior and another example of bureaucrats gone crazy." Bowing to the fury, officials withdrew the pamphlet, acknowledging that it had been "inappropriate" to inform addicts about how best to use drugs.

For those who saw the prevention of drug abuse as their professional mission, the publicly-funded distribution of such literature was troubling. Representatives of the National Institute on Drug Abuse declared that "NIDA does not feel comfortable sending information which tells drug abusers not to use dirty needles or share needles. NIDA's position is based on [the clear] message, Do Not Use Drugs,"[73] Ultimately, however, public agencies could not avoid the imperatives of an anti-AIDS campaign among drug abusers. Unlike the situation that prevailed among gay men, where voluntary and community-based organizations could assume responsibility when public agencies abdicated it, there was nothing done for addicts unless publicly-funded agencies acted.

The critical dimensions of the AIDS problem among drug users, especially in East Coast cities, were recognized by health experts who acknowledged that HIV could spread to other regions. But until the end of the decade the response of state and federal authorities was feeble. Long waiting lists for entry into drug abuse treatment, both methadone maintenance (available for about two decades) and abstinence-based, continued to exist into the 1990s.

The dimensions of that failure were underscored in the 1988 report of the Presidential Commission on the HIV Epidemic.[74] An additional $1.5 billion a year would be necessary for drug abuse treatment and education, said the commission, since only such an investment would provide immediate treatment to all drug users who might seek it. For the Reagan administration, which had placed its emphasis on a moral appeal to abstinence and had contemplated the return to harsh street-level enforcement of drug use and possession statutes, the call for the massive funding of drug abuse treatment programs seemed the siren song of a discredited liberalism. For those familiar with the inadequacy of available services and the difficulties that would go unresolved even with an infusion of resources, the commission's declaration provided some small reason for hope.

The call for greater attention to the problem of drug abuse in the light of the AIDS epidemic was repeated by the Institute of Medicine and the National Academy of Sciences, which in 1988 had painted a bleak picture linking intravenous drug use, heterosexual transmission, and the birth of infants with HIV infection. "The Committee believes that the gross inadequacy of federal efforts to reduce HIV transmission among IV drug users, when considered in relation to the scope and implications of such transmission, is now the most serious deficiency in current efforts to control HIV infection in the United States."[75] Relying on the report of the Presidential Commission, these institutions also called for an annual expenditure of $1.5 billion.

Despite these appeals, little has been done. Concern about budgetary deficits, ten years of ideological opposition to welfare state–like programs by conservative national administrations, and the absence of a strong political constituency capable of effectively clamoring for the needs of the underclass have resulted in a policy of un-benign neglect.

The failure to provide adequate treatment for drug users and a recognition that, even were such treatment to be made available, many drug users would choose to continue to use drugs, led some local public health officials to urge that sterile drug injection equipment be provided. Clean needles might do for those who shared injection equipment what condoms could do for the interruption of the spread of AIDS through sexual contact. In 1986, the adoption of what became known as the "Amsterdam model" became a rallying cry for reformers. New York City's commissioner of health urged Mayor Edward Koch to adopt a policy of providing sterile injection equipment to addicts.

The proposal provoked fierce opposition, not only from law enforcement officials but also from the black community. For some black leaders, needle exchange disregarded the true needs of impoverished communities; indeed, it was nothing less than "genocidal." Not until the winter of 1988, in the wake of reports that one out of every sixty-one women who had given birth in New York City during a recent survey period was infected with the AIDS virus, was the municipal government granted permission by state health officials to conduct a trial needle exchange program.[76]

But that effect was short-lived. In 1990 New York elected its first black mayor, David Dinkins, who then appointed the City's first black commissioner of health, Woodrow Myers. Among the commissioner's first official acts was to end the experiment with needle exchange. Myers went further, however, and took the unique stance that the city should withdraw all financial support for efforts at bleach education and bleach distribution among drug users. On this issue the politics of AIDS prevention had produced an alliance between the liberal, black, and Hispanic elite and the most conservative political forces in the United States. Despite such broad-based opposition, small needle exchange programs have begun to operate in the United States.

Access to Treatment, Access to Research

From the outset of the AIDS epidemic, the Reagan administration, committed to fiscal restraint and hostile to the interests of gay men, was unwilling to devote significant resources to study the treatment of HIV infection. At a time when funds were critically short, the administration compelled its senior health officials to testify before Congress that there were no shortfalls.[77] A congressional oversight committee, chaired by a representative from New York City, denounced these maneuvers and charged that research into AIDS had been "unnecessarily delayed."[78] But as the enormity of the potential impact of the much-publicized epidemic impressed itself upon the political elite, and as the demands of a broad alliance of AIDS activists, scientists, public health officials, and liberal politicians made itself felt, the picture began to change. Table 1.3 reveals the marked increases that then occurred.

By 1990, the federal government had spent more than $5.5 billion on HIV-related programs, $2.2 billion of which had been for research. But if the funding of AIDS research was the result of political conflict, the fruits of that investment have set the stage for new series of controversies.

In the first years of the epidemic, the tradition of public health practice was challenged by those who claimed that the authoritarian repertoire of interventions was unnecessary, politically unacceptable, and potentially counterproductive in preventing the further spread of HIV. In the late 1980s, very differently, the regulatory regime surrounding the development of new drugs that might slow the progression of HIV disease in those already infected became the subject of intense debate. Most dramatically, People With Aids Coalition and ACT UP sought to speed the process of drug development, insisting on a greater commitment of resources, demanding a radical restructuring of the conduct of clinical research. With the emergence of these new groups came a new style of protest: direct action. Sit-ins, "zaps," and mass demonstrations—including raids on the New York Stock Exchange, a blockade of San Francisco's Golden Gate Bridge, and an occupation of the Washington, D.C., offices of the Food and Drug Administration—largely displaced lobbying and more decorous forms of political negotiation. Like the protesters of the 1960s, the new AIDS activists sought to marshal the power of disruption.

While ACT UP's slogan, "Silence = Death," drew its power from a blunt simplicity, the issues forced onto the political agenda were anything but simple. They brought into focus not only bureaucratic delay and fiscal neglect, but also a set of federal regulations adopted to protect research subjects from the dangers of abuse. It was the specter of such abuse, as exemplified by the notorious Tuskegee syphilis experiment, that informed the contemporary history of human experimentation in the United States.[79] In the mid-1970s, the National Commission for the Protection of Human Subjects of Biomedical and Behavioral Research developed ethical principles to govern researchers' work; those norms were later codified in regulations enacted by the Department of Health and Human Services and the Food and Drug Administration.[80] At the core of those guidelines was the radical distinction between research, designed to produce socially necessary, generalizable knowledge, and therapy, designed to benefit individuals. In the

Table 1.3. Federal Spending on AIDS/HIV Research in the United States, 1982–1991 (in millions of 1990 U.S. dollars)

Year	Amount
1982	4.1
1983	28.9
1984	74.2
1985	104.5
1986	243.3
1987	407.3
1988	641.6
1989	1,033.0
1990	1,163.0

SOURCE: Adapted from U.S. Congress, Office of Technology Assessment, "How Has Federal Research on AIDS/HIV Disease Contributed to Other Fields?" (April 1990), Table 2, p. 3.

conduct of research, individuals, especially those who were socially vulnerable, needed protection against conscription and undue risk. Restrictive—protective—standards of access were developed in the name of ethics. In the name of science, the orthodoxy insisted upon adherence to the "gold standard" of the randomized clinical trial.

AIDS activists forced a reconsideration of these standards. Their struggle ironically has linked very conservative opponents of all government regulatory efforts—including those who, for example, fought for the right to treat cancer with Laetrile—with groups speaking on behalf of the vulnerable. Blurring the distinction between research and treatment—"A Drug Trial is Health Care Too"—those insistent upon radical reform have sought to open wide the points of entry to new "therapeutic" agents, both within and outside clinical trials. They have demanded that the paternalistic ethical warrant for protecting the vulnerable from research be replaced by an ethical regime informed by respect for the autonomous choices of potential subjects, who could weigh for themselves the potential risks and benefits of new treatments for HIV infection. Women (especially pregnant women), drug users, prisoners, children—all those previously excluded from research or severely restricted from access to drug trials—had to be given opportunities to participate in clinical studies.[81] Moreover, the revisionists have demanded a reconceptualization of the relationship between researchers and subjects. In place of protocols imposed from above, they have proposed a more egalitarian and democratic model in which negotiation would replace scientific authority.

Proponents of the new ethos hold out the prospect of a new regime that respects both individual rights and the requirements of good science.[82] Those who are less sanguine warn that the blurring of the distinction between research and treatment can only bring false hope to the desperate.[83] Some researchers have gone farther, arguing that the already initiated reforms represent a threat to the research enterprise itself.

With the first signs that research on the treatment of AIDS was beginning to bear fruit, the failure of the American health care system to cover the cost of illness and of the federal government to assist localities compelled to bear the burden of providing care for large numbers of AIDS patients became stunningly apparent. These patients were just a small fraction of those who would increasingly be defined as in need of care. Writing in the *Journal of the American Medical Association* in 1990, researchers predicted that "rather than a fulminant disease treated primarily inside the hospital, [HIV infection] will become a largely chronic condition requiring years of outpatient monitoring and pharmacologic intervention."[84] To meet the challenge of chronic HIV infection, it would be necessary to create and fund an infrastructure capable of providing ongoing clinical services to upward of a million individuals.

This challenge has demanded attention at a moment when the growing inequalities of the American health care system are widely evident, and the potential cost of fashioning a collective remedy for such inequities paralyzes the political system. Some thirty to forty million Americans, one American in six, has no health insurance at all. Of those who are insured, at least sixty million more are inadequately protected, bearing (for example) the entire cost of prescription drugs. Could such a health care system meet the challenge of providing virtually all HIV-infected individuals, many of whom were impoverished, with the outpatient clinical services they would need and with the expensive drugs they would require? Would it be possible for a health care system that failed to meet the chronic health care needs of poor Americans to meet the needs of those infected with HIV? These questions dwarfed in significance the important and continuing debates about discrimination by private medical insurers.

Some relief came from emergency federal programs to assist the states in paying the cost of the drug AZT for those without insurance, reimbursement policies by Medicaid, the joint federal–state program that provides protection for less than half of America's poor, as well as a host of patchwork programs in the states. But these efforts were clearly inadequate.[85] In its December 1989 Report to the President, the National Commission on Acquired Immune Deficiency Syndrome, appointed by President Bush but chaired by unspoken liberal proponents of increased federal efforts to meet the challenge of AIDS, warned that medical breakthroughs would "mean little unless the health care system can incorporate them and make them accessible to people in need."[86] The existence of a medically disenfranchised class meant that, for many, access to care was almost solely through the "emergency room door of one of the few hospitals in the community that treats people with HIV infection and AIDS."

Throughout the epidemic's early years, the volunteer efforts of gay community-based groups provided an extraordinary array of social support services to those with HIV-related disease. Such efforts had met needs where government had failed. By 1983, an estimated forty-five self-help groups had emerged around the country, and by 1990 these numbered over six hundred. Many were small, but a few had become highly professionalized, with budgets in the millions of dollars (a significant proportion coming from state and federal contracts for services), dozens of paid staff members, and hundreds of volunteers.

But the increasing medicalization of the epidemic meant such efforts would be insufficient: physicians, nurses, laboratories, and medications would be needed to deal with the full range of HIV-related problems. These were the conditions under which a sharp split began to emerge between gay community-based organizations that defined themselves primarily as care providers, on the one side, and activists, on the other side, who dismissed such work as inadequate, sometimes so inadequate as to amount to an act of collaboration with the antagonist state.

The looming crisis in health care for those with HIV disease set the stage for congressional action that could scarcely have been imagined a short time earlier. It represented the fruit of persistent efforts on the part of AIDS activists, their allies, and some political leaders from the cities and states that had borne the disproportionate share of AIDS cases. In the winter of 1990, Massachusetts Senator Edward Kennedy, the exemplar of Democratic party liberalism, and Utah Senator Orrin Hatch, a Republican whose stance on abortion and other social issues often cast him in the role of a conservative, jointly sponsored legislation to provide a major infusion of federal assistance to localities most severely burdened by AIDS. Just as the government had responded to natural disasters, the Kennedy-Hatch Bill—ultimately named the Ryan White Act, after the Kokomo, Indiana, boy with hemophilia who had been barred from his classroom and who had since died—asked government to respond to the medical disaster of AIDS. "The Human Immunodeficiency Virus constitutes a crisis as devastating as an earthquake, flood, or drought," Senator Kennedy declared. "Indeed, the death toll of the unfolding AIDS tragedy is already a hundredfold greater than any natural disaster to strike our nation in this century."[87]

As remarkable as the joint sponsorship of this legislation, which would provide $2.9 billion over five years, was the overwhelming support the legislation received in the Senate; there the vote was 95 to 4.[88] When similar legislation with even greater resource commitments was voted on by the House of Representatives, the vote was 408 to 14.[89]

This legislation represented an important act of national solidarity on both symbolic and practical levels. But the hopes inspired by congressional action were shattered when, under the pressure of a budgetary crisis, less than 20 percent of the promised funds was appropriated for the 1991 fiscal year. And this may represent the high-water mark of Washington's concern. Without the promised federal relief, the states and cities that have borne so disproportionate a share of the burden of the AIDS epidemic enter the second decade of the epidemic with an ever-increasing caseload and little hope for the assistance that only Washington can provide.

Conclusion

Public policy on AIDS has begun to undergo a profound transformation. Professional, epidemiological, and clinical factors have all played a role in this change.

Public health policy is always more than the application of a repertoire of standard professional practices to threats to communal welfare. Officials must also take into account a range of extra-professional considerations, including the prevailing political climate and the unique social forces brought into play by a particular public health challenge. In the first years of the AIDS epidemic, these officials were thrown off balance by the sudden emergence of an unexpected lethal threat. Under those circumstances, they were compelled to negotiate the course of the public health strategy with representatives of a well-organized gay community and their allies in the medical and political establishments. In this process, many of the traditional practices of public health, such as routine screening, reporting of HIV infection by name, and contact tracing were dismissed as inappropriate. But as the first decade of the epidemic has come to an end, public health officials have begun to reassert their professional dominance over the policy process, and in so doing have begun to rediscover the relevance of their own professional traditions to the control of the AIDS epidemic.

This process has been fostered by changing perceptions of the dimensions of the threat posed by AIDS. Early fears that HIV infection might spread broadly in the population have proven unfounded: the epidemic has remained largely confined to those groups first identified as being at increased risk. As the focus of public health concern has shifted from gay men, among whom the incidence of HIV infection has remained low for the past several years, to poor black and Hispanic drug users and their sexual partners, the influence of gay spokespersons has begun to wane. Racial minorities and drug users are less adept at influencing policy, and those who speak on their behalf often lack the commitment to privacy and consent that characterizes gay organizations. Furthermore, policy directed toward the poor is often authoritarian in cast, and it is precisely such authoritarianism that evokes the traditions of public health. Finally, in the United States as in virtually every Western democracy, the estimates of the level of infection first put forth several years ago have proven to be too high. As AIDS has become less threatening—more "normal"—the claims of those who argued that the exceptional danger posed by the epidemic necessitated exceptional policies have begun to lose their force.

But most important in accounting for the changing contours of public health policy have been the important advances in the treatment of HIV infection. The prospects for better management of HIV-related opportunistic infections and the hopes of slowing the course of HIV progression itself through prophylaxis, which mean longer lives for those who are infected, have heightened the importance of early identification. That, in turn, has invited a new willingness to consider traditional public health approaches to screening, reporting, and partner notification.

The broad political context within which decisions will be made about the availability of resources for prevention, research, and the provision of care will be affected by the changing perspective on AIDS. The availability of such resources has always been the outcome of a competitive process, however implicit. The desperate effort to wrest needed resources from an initially unresponsive political system, in the context of a health care system that failed to provide universal protection against the cost of illness, compelled AIDS activists to argue that this disease was different, and so required funding commitments of a special kind. It was inevitable that, in a resource-constrained climate, there would be challenges to the federal AIDS allocations that were so belatedly made.

In 1989, a former official at the federal Health Care Financing Administration could thus write that public resources being allocated to research into and the prevention of AIDS had approached the levels devoted to cancer, a disease responsible for over five hundred thousand deaths a year, and exceeding spending on heart disease, which accounted for over seven hundred thousand annual deaths. More strikingly, such expenditures were more than four times those devoted to diabetes, from which 5.8 million Americans suffered and which accounted for thirty-six thousand annual deaths. If the increases in spending on AIDS were to continue, "their equity could be questioned."[90] Although such comparisons distort and oversimplify complex issues, this perspective has become increasingly common.

As the process of "normalizing AIDS" progresses, the contours of policies for prevention and care will increasingly come to reflect the broad pattern of public health and social welfare practice in the United States. Both the vitality and the singular weaknesses of these policies will determine the shape of the American response to AIDS in the coming years.

Notes

1. See Office of Technology Assessment, *The Public Health Service's Response to AIDS* (Washington, D.C.: Government Printing Office, 1985); The National Academy of Science, *Confronting AIDS: Update 1988* (Washington, D.C.: National Academy of Science Press, 1988).

2. This chapter is largely based on Ronald Bayer, *Private Acts, Social Consequences: AIDS and the Politics of Public Health* (New Brunswick, N.J.: Rutgers University Press, 1991).

3. "Pneumocystis Pneumonia—Los Angeles," *Morbidity and Mortality Weekly Report* (June 5, 1991), 250–252. This journal hereafter is referred to as *MMWR*.

4. "Kaposi's Sarcoma and Pneumocystis Pneumonia Among Homosexual Men—New York City and California," *MMWR* (July 3, 1981), 305–308.

5. See Dennis Altman, *The Homosexualization of America* (Boston: Beacon Press, 1982).

6. David Kirp, *Learning by Heart* (New Brunswick, N.J.: Rutgers University Press, 1989).

7. See Viviana Zelizer, *Pricing the Priceless Child: The Changing Social Value of Children* (New York: Basic Books, 1985).

8. "Education and Foster Care of Children Infected with Human T-Lymphotropic Virus type III/Lymphadenopathy Associated Virus," *MMWR* (August 30, 1985), 517–521.

9. Dorothy Nelkin and Stephen Hilgartner, "Disputed Dimensions of Risk: A Public School Controversy Over AIDS," *Milbank Quarterly*, Supplement 1 (1986), 118–142.

10. Kirp, *Learning by Heart.*

11. Dennis Altman, *AIDS in the Mind of America* (Garden City, N.Y.: Anchor Books, 1986), 60–62. See also Mark Rothstein, "Screening Workers for AIDS," in *AIDS and the Law*, ed. Harlan Dalton, Scott Burris, and the Yale Law Project (New Haven, Conn.: Yale University Press, 1987), 126–141, and Arthur S. Leonard, "AIDS in the Workplace," ibid., 109–125.

12. *Detroit Free Press* (October 18, 1985), 15A.

13. "Recommendations for Preventing Transmission of Infection with Human T-Lymphotropic Virus Type III/Lymphadenopathy-Associated Virus during Invasive Procedures," *MMWR* (April 11, 1986), 221–223.

14. "Recommendations for Preventing Transmission of Infection with Human T-Lymphotropic Virus Type III/Lymphadenopathy-Associated Virus," *MMWR* (November 15, 1985), 681–686, 691–695.

15. *Surgeon General's Report on Acquired Immune Deficiency Syndrome*, 21.

16. *Washington Post* (August 31, 1985), 1.

17. *New York Times* (November 29, 1986), A10.

18. *New York Times* (December 17, 1986), B19.

19. *New York Times* (June 3, 1987), B8.

20. Presidential Commission on the HIV Epidemic, *Final Report* (June 1988), 119.

21. School Board v. Arline, 480 U.S. 273 (1987).

22. American Civil Liberties Union, "Epidemic of Fear" (mimeo) (1990).

23. Lawrence O. Gostin, "The AIDS Litigation Project: A National Review of Court and Human Rights Commission Decisions, Part II: Discrimination," *Journal of the American Medical Association* (April 18, 1990), 2091.

24. Ronald Bayer, *Homosexuality and American Psychiatry: The Politics of Diagnosis* (New York: Basic Books, 1981).

25. Mervyn Silverman, Press Statement (October 9, 1984).

26. Bayer, *Private Acts*, 53–67.

27. Allan Brandt, *No Magic Bullet* (New York: Oxford University Press, 1987).

28. "Pneumocystis Carinii Pneumonia Among Persons with Hemophilia A," *MMWR* (July 16, 1982), 365–367.

29. *Time* (March 28, 1983).

30. "Prevention of Acquired Immune Deficiency Syndrome (AIDS) Report of Interagency Recommendations," *MMWR* (March 4, 1983), 101–103.

31. *New York Times* (April 24, 1984), C1.

32. *New York Native* (October 8–21, 1984), 5.

33. American Association of Physicians for Human Rights (November 12, 1985).

34. Neil Schram, "Open Letter to the Gay and Lesbian Community" (mimeo) (January 14, 1986).

35. *New York Native* (February 3–9, 1986), 4.

36. Association of State and Territorial Health Officials, ASTHO *Guide to Public Health Practice: HTLV-III Antibody Testing and Community Approaches* (Washington, D.C.: Public Health Foundation, 1985), 16.

37. CDC, "Additional Recommendations to Reduce Sexual and Drug Abuse-Related Transmission of Human T-Lymphotropic Virus Type III/Lymphadenopathy-Associated Virus," *MMWR* (March 14, 1986), 152–155.

38. *Surgeon General's Report on Acquired Immune Deficiency Syndrome* (October 1986), 33.

39. Institute of Medicine and National Academy of Sciences, *Confronting AIDS* (Washington, D.C.: National Academy Press, 1986), 125.

40. See generally Richard Hofstader, *The Paranoid Style of American Politics and Other Essays*, Phoenix Edition (Chicago Press, 1979).

41. Bayer, *Private Acts*, 147–153.

42. CDC, "Publicly Funded HIV Counseling and Testing, 1985–1989," *MMWR* (March 9, 1990), 140.

43. *New York Times* (February 17, 1990), 1.

44. *New York State Society of Surgeons, New York State Society of Orthopoedic Surgeons, New York State Society of Obstetricians and Gynecologists, and the Medical Society of New York v. David Axelrod.*

45. *PI Perspective* (April 1988), 7; *New York Times* (August 16, 1989), 1.

46. Frank S. Rhame and Dennis A. Maki, "The Case for Wide Use of Testing for HIV Infection," *New England Journal of Medicine* (1989), 1248–1254.

47. Presidential Commission *Final Report*, 76.

48. *New York State Society of Surgeons, New York State Society of Orthopoe-*

dic Surgeons, New York State Society of Obstetricians and Gynecologists, and the Medical Society of New York v. David Axelrod.

49. Stephen C. Joseph, "Remarks at the Vth International Conference on AIDS" (mimeo) (June 5, 1989).

50. Institute of Medicine and National Academy of Sciences, *Confronting AIDS: Update 1988* (Washington, D.C.: National Academy Press, 1988), 82; Presidential Commission, *Report*, 76; American Bar Association, AIDS Coordinating Committee, *ABA Policy on AIDS* (August 1989); *American Medical News* (July 8–15, 1988), 4.

51. Vanessa Merton, "Confidentiality and the 'Dangerous Patient': Implications of *Tarasoff* for Psychiatrists and Lawyers," *Emory Law Journal* (Spring 1982), 263–343.

52. Board of Trustees, American Medical Association, December 1989.

53. Intergovernmental Health Policy Project, "1989 Legislative Overview," *Intergovernmental AIDS Reports* (January 1990), 3.

54. J. F. Grutsch and A. D. J. Robertson, "The Coming of AIDS: It Didn't Start with Homosexuals and It Won't End with Them," *American Spectator* (March 1986), 12.

55. "Conference of Local Health Officers Report to U.S. Conference of Mayors, Task Force on AIDS" (mimeo) (January 1986).

56. Ronald Bayer, "Crime, Punishment, and the Decline of Liberal Optimism," *Crime and Delinquency* (April 1981), 189–190.

57. Based on data in the files of the Intergovernmental Health Policy Project, George Washington University, Washington, D.C.

58. Larry Gostin, "The Politics of AIDS: Compulsory State Powers, Public Health, Civil Liberties," *Ohio State Law Journal* (1989), 1041.

59. Presidential Commission, *Final Report*, 130–131.

60. Based on data in the files of the Intergovernmental Health Policy Project, George Washington University, Washington, D.C.

61. Lawrence O. Gostin, "The AIDS Litigation Project: A National Review of Court and Human Rights Commission Decisions, Part 1: The Social Impact of AIDS," *Journal of the American Medical Association* (April 11, 1990), 1963.

62. Gostin, "The Politics of AIDS."

63. U.S. Congress, Office of Technology Assessment, "Review of the Public Health Service's Response to AIDS" (Washington, D.C.: Government Printing Office, 1985), 53.

64. National Academy of Science, *Confronting AIDS*, 97.

65. Cited in Earl E. Shelp and Albert R. Jonsen, "The Impact of AIDS on Religious Denominations" (unpublished manuscript (1991).

66. *Advocate* (October 1, 1985), 22.

67. Douglas Conway, "For the Sake of Words: Language Restrictions and AIDS Education" (unpublished manuscript) (1986).

68. Alvin Novick, telephone interview (October 10, 1986).

69. Edwin Meese III, Memorandum for the Domestic Policy Council (February 11, 1987).

70. *Congressional Record* (October 14, 1987).

71. *New York Times* (April 29, 1988), B4.

92. Los Angeles *Times* (August 29, 1988), B4.

73. U.S. Public Health Service, Executive Task Force on AIDS, Minutes (April 8, 1985).

74. *New York Times* (February 25, 1988), 1.

75. National Academy of Sciences, *Confronting AIDS*, 84.

76. *New York Times* (January 13, 1988), 1.

77. Randy Shilts, *And the Band Played On* (New York: St. Martin's Press, 1987).

78. Sandra Panem, *The AIDS Bureaucracy* (Cambridge, Mass.: Harvard University Press, 1988), 91.

79. See James Jones, *Bad Blood: The Tuskegee Experiment* (New York: Free Press, 1981).

80. National Commission for the Protection of Human Subjects of Biomedical and Behavioral Research, *The Belmont Report* (Washington, D.C.: Department of Health, Education and Welfare, 1978).

81. Carol Levine, "Women and HIV/AIDS Research: The Barriers to Equality," *Evaluation Review* (October 1990), 447–463; Theodore M. Hammett and Nancy Neveloff Dubler, "Clinical and Epidemiologic Research on HIV Infection and AIDS Among Correctional Inmates: Regulations, Ethics, and Procedures," *Evaluation Review* (October 1990), 482–501; Kathy Nolan, "AIDS and Pediatric Research," *Evaluation Review* (October 1990), 464–480.

82. Martin Delaney, "The Case for Patient Access to Experimental Therapy," *Journal of Infectious Diseases* vol. 159; no. 3 (March 1989), 416–419.

83. George Annas, "Faith (Healing), Hope and Charity at the FDA: The Politics of AIDS Drug Trials," *Villanova Law Review* volume 34, No. 5 (1989), 771–797.

84. Peter S. Arno et. al, "Economic and Policy Implications of Early Intervention in HIV Disease," *Journal of the American Medical Association* (September 15, 1990), 1494.

85. Intergovernmental Health Policy Project, "AZT: Who Will Pay?" *Intergovernmental AIDS Reports* (May–June 1989), 4; Intergovernmental Health Policy Project, "State Financing for AIDS: Options and Trends," *Intergovernmental AIDS Reports* (March–April 1990), 1–8.

86. National Commission on AIDS, "Report Number One."

87. Senator Edward Kennedy, letter (February 1990).

88. *New York Times* (May 17, 1990), B10.

89. *New York Times* (June 14, 1990), B9.

90. William Winkenwerder, A. R. Kessler, and R. M. Stolec, "Federal Spending for Illness Caused by the Human Immunodeficiency Virus," *New England Journal of Medicine* vol. 320; no. 4 (June 15, 1989), 1598–1603.

Chapter 2   Canada: Community Activism, Federalism, and the New Politics of Disease

David M. Rayside and Evert A. Lindquist

On May 17, 1988, Jake Epp was burned in effigy. In a country not usually given to such public dramas—a country with a tradition of political reserve and accommodation—the attack on the federal minister of health and welfare was a turning point in the AIDS epidemic in Canada.

By 1988, there were more than twenty-four hundred cases of AIDS and almost two thousand deaths; as many as fifty thousand Canadians were estimated to be HIV-positive. Despite the loss of life, the growing proportions of the epidemic in Canada, the extensive media coverage of the U.S. epidemic, and Canada's self-image as being more socially progressive than the United States, a national AIDS strategy had yet to be articulated.

Growing frustration with the lack of government leadership had led to the radicalization of AIDS activists in Vancouver, Montreal, and other major cities determined to pierce through the bureaucratic and political fog of Ottawa. The May seventeenth protest was organized by the Toronto-based AIDS Action Now! and was staged at the National Conference on AIDS, which brought together government officials, public health professionals, and representatives of community-based organizations. The display of activist anger captured national media attention and sent shock waves through the corridors of power in Ottawa.

Two months later, Epp announced a $116 million (all dollars in this chapter are given in 1990 U.S. dollars) funding commitment to AIDS. Then, following the November 1988 election, which returned the Progressive Conservative government to power, Prime Minister Mulroney replaced the morally conservative Epp with Perrin Beatty, a younger minister widely regarded as more at ease dealing with AIDS and gay-related issues. In June 1989, as host of the Fifth International Conference on AIDS in Montreal, Beatty, catching many of his own officials by surprise, promised that a national AIDS strategy would soon be forthcoming. This strategy was announced a year later, and while it provided no additional funding, most AIDS activists believed the strategy was more congruent with their objectives than previous federal policy initiatives.

49

Federal policymakers were not the only targets of activists. Confrontations also occurred in several provincial capitals and municipalities, with AIDS activists and medical professionals raising the alarm about inadequate programs for public education and health care. But even if politicians in Canada's most right-wing governments were scrambling to revise policies and establish new approaches for responding to an epidemic that, by July 1991, had killed three thousand Canadians, the policy response has been uneven and largely uncoordinated. Part of the explanation lies in Canada's highly decentralized federal system, which gives primary responsibility for health care to the provinces; within that system, a substantial portion of the responsibility for public health is devolved to municipal governments or regional health agencies. As a result, the issues posed by AIDS have led policymakers and activists into an inter-jurisdictional thicket, exacerbated by the federal government's reluctance to coordinate.

Much more important in explaining the inadequacy of government response has been the slowness of key policymakers to take AIDS seriously or to treat it as exceptional. Many administrative officials relied on routines established for earlier epidemics, not asking for more than modest budgetary increases until the late 1980s. Early on, elected politicians were typically more than ready to avoid dealing with AIDS themselves and to let ordinary administrative routines take their course. Jake Epp was part of a Conservative government that was intent on limiting the growth of social spending, even though its moral conservatism was not so prominent as that of the Reagan administration. But just that kind of fierce moralism was in evidence in parts of the federal Conservative caucus, in the province of British Columbia, and in some Quebec political circles. Although progressive politicians and administrators could be found in the city governments of Vancouver and Toronto, municipalities are the most financially constrained of the three levels of government.

In the unfolding of AIDS policy in Canada, it is possible to discern a fundamental struggle between two visions of health care. One, drawing on elements of contain-and-control models, was based on a well-entrenched traditional approach insinuated into much of the medical establishment and most public health bureaucracies. For most of the 1980s, the actions of many public officials followed routines developed to deal with other diseases: focusing on protecting those not yet infected, treating the sick as irresponsible and in need of policing, leaving drug testing initiatives to pharmaceutical companies, and retaining hypercautious methods for approving drugs. This perspective did not enlist the participation of community groups and politicians: the critical tasks were to be undertaken by medical doctors, researchers, and epidemiologists.

Clashing with this approach was a more inclusionary policy vision. Community AIDS activists, reformist public health officials, and some of the doctors with large HIV/AIDS practices attached more significance to patients' rights. They called for comprehensive and frank education programs aimed at the entire population, generous funding of community groups to work with those most affected by the disease, extensive distribution of condoms and needles for intravenous drug users, recognition of the significance of discrimination associated with AIDS and HIV infection, greater funding for and coordination of medical facilities specifically for AIDS, a larger and more geographically dispersed network of doctors trained to deal with HIV and AIDS, more funds for research, and greater involvement in the policy process on the part of community groups and people with AIDS. What gave this view special prominence in Canadian AIDS policy was that its proponents, working within community groups or in their own medical practices, had borne much of the burden of providing services to people living with AIDS and had generated safer-sex educational materials for the populations most seriously affected by the epidemic. Governmental avoidance of AIDS in the first few years left public officials without the expertise to address the broad range of educational and social issues posed by the disease, and established the community groups and their allies in critical program delivery and agenda setting roles. The persistently high proportion of gay men among the numbers of Canadians with AIDS has given gay men (and in some places lesbians) a dominant role in AIDS community group organizing, though groups representing Haitians, Natives, women, and prostitutes have started to play more prominent roles.

In the confrontation between government policymakers and AIDS activists, the impact of two factors must be kept in mind. The first is the presence of socialized health insurance throughout Canada. There is uneven access to medical personnel with an interest and expertise in AIDS, particularly outside major cities, and there are also serious financial burdens on people with HIV and AIDS who wish to use drugs that are not "approved" by provincial drug policies, but few of these problems are so severe as in the more privatized American health care system.

The second important factor to keep in mind is the effect of U.S. developments on Canadian public policy and community activism. Unlimited access to the American media meant that Canadians were made aware of the disease at about the same time as Americans, before substantial numbers of Canadians became sick. That lead time may well have encouraged a calmer public reaction; there were fewer cases of panic about casual contact in Canada than there were in the United States, and more readiness on the part of most media outlets to avoid sensationalization. The view that AIDS was justifiable retribution for an immoral life-style has never had as strong a public voice as in the United States, Britain, or Australia.

The proximity of the United States has meant that the work of government epidemiologists and medical researchers has largely been shaped by their American counterparts. Canadian AIDS activists, especially in English Canada, have also been greatly influenced by the agendas and tactics of their American counterparts, for example in developing community-based AIDS prevention programs and acquiring information on experimental drugs. The long-standing reluctance of Canadian branches of multinational drug companies to place much priority on research has also meant that the availability of drugs is greatly dependent on the research priorities and marketing plans of American pharmaceutical firms.

The evolution of public policy on AIDS in Canada has moved through three distinct stages. The first began in the early 1980s, as many politicians and officials ignored the epidemic or responded very cautiously. The second stage began in mid-1985, when Rock Hudson's illness became public knowledge, greatly intensifying public interest and concern in Canada, and when the development of HIV blood tests raised new issues for debate. In this period, Canadian governments began to make significant but usually ad hoc commitments to AIDS programs. As the number of AIDS cases increased, community groups grew in size and proliferated, with new militant voices broadening the range and intensity of criticism directed at governmental inactivity. The third period began in the spring of 1988, when the pressure on all levels of government to develop coherent AIDS strategies was dramatically increased by the protests of community group activists at the National AIDS Conference. Most recently, there are signs of a "normalization" of AIDS policy and the possibility that it may be reintegrated into other areas of health education and care. Although it is too early to tell, this may demarcate the beginning of a fourth stage.

Canada's Health Care System

Although all Canadians are covered by publicly-funded medical insurance, health care is primarily a provincial responsibility, with the provinces organizing the delivery of services, chartering and negotiating with various professional bodies to determine fee schedules, funding hospitals for capital and operating expenditures, and establishing regional and local public health networks. However, the federal government plays an important role through its spending power. On several occasions in the past, the federal government agreed to match provincial contributions to hospital and medical insurance as long as their health delivery systems met a set of minimum criteria.[1] The influence of federal spending is also evident in the fact that most medical research grants in Canada come from federally-funded agencies (the Medical Research Council, the Natural Sciences and

Engineering Research Council of Canada, and the National Health Research and Development Program administered by the federal Department of Health and Welfare). In a more general way, the federal government has influenced the provinces by coordinating the flow of information and organizing federal–provincial meetings of politicians and officials in the health field.

There is considerable variation in how provinces organize health care systems. This diversity is partly a product of the fact that federal funding during the 1960s was geared toward the delivery of health care services by physicians and hospitals, excluding, for example, many of the costs associated with public health. And as medical services provided by paraprofessionals, outpatient and freestanding clinics, hospices, and the like have become more widespread, with the costs generally falling to provincial authorities, variation in the extent and style of service has developed. The health care role given to local authorities and the extent of centralization also vary considerably, with Quebec notable for the extent of decentralization within the health care delivery system itself.

Several areas of jurisdiction shared by provincial and federal governments pertain to AIDS. The first is epidemiology and laboratory testing. Local and provincial officials collect data on various diseases and patient conditions, and provinces offer testing facilities for physicians and hospitals. The Laboratory Center for Disease Control, located in the Health Protection Branch of the Department of Health and Welfare in Ottawa, acts as an expert of last resort if provincial laboratories have difficulty identifying diseases or interpreting test results. It also develops and tests new identification procedures and trains scientists and technicians learning those new procedures. A second area of shared jurisdiction entails blood supply regulation. In 1981, the Canadian Blood Committee was established within the Health Services and Promotion Branch of the federal Ministry of Health and Welfare to coordinate provincial funding of the Canadian Red Cross, which collects virtually all of the country's blood supply from volunteer donors and is responsible for screening that blood. A third area of joint jurisdiction concerns drugs. The federal government's Drug Directorate, located within the Health Protection Branch, is solely responsible for the testing, approval, and regulation of new drugs, and it covers the cost of those drugs while they are in the experimental phase. It has an Emergency Drug Release Program intended for the release of medications that are not in enough demand for pharmaceutical companies to seek approval for regular marketing. Once a drug is approved, it falls to the provinces to determine to what extent the cost of the drug will be covered by public funds.

The complexity of AIDS policy in Canada emerges not only from the

Table 2.1. AIDS Cases by Year of Report and Category of Risk Exposure for Canada, 1979–1990

Risk Category	Before 1983	1983	1984	1985	1986	1987	1988	1989	1990	Through April 2, 1991	Total
Homosexual/bisexual activity	15	29	116	270	461	703	794	845	469	19	3,721
Homosexual/bisexual activity and IVDU	0	4	3	8	20	27	31	43	25	0	161
IVDU	2	0	0	3	1	10	11	20	11	1	59
Blood Products	1	3	1	22	31	43	59	47	24	1	232
Heterosexual activity[a]	14	15	29	29	42	52	73	82	25	1	362
Mother to child	4	5	5	11	3	6	7	6	0	0	47
Other/unknown	1	3	7	8	18	24	14	50	74	0	199
Total cases	37	59	161	351	576	865	989	1,093	628	22	4,781

SOURCE: Federal Centre for AIDS (April 2, 1991).
[a] A substantial number of these cases have been in Montreal's Haitian community. The proportion of heterosexual cases originating in "Pattern II" countries was 70% or more until 1987, after which it has varied from 37% to 56%.

decentralization built into its federal structure but also from the complex structural pattern within each level of government. AIDS policy has been influenced by the politicians in electoral office at various levels of government and by a variety of administrators, some lodged within bureaucratic units with a strong culture that severely restricts policy options.

One of the very first recorded cases of AIDS occurred in Canada, in 1979, although it was not recognized as AIDS for several years. As Table 2.1 shows, Canada's pattern of AIDS cases is comparable to the United States and northern Europe, with over three-quarters of the cases reported among gay men and bisexuals (not including intravenous drug users who are also gay or bisexual). That proportion has declined very slightly in recent years, with corresponding increases in the incidence of AIDS among drug users and heterosexual women.

AIDS Policy in Three Provinces

Because they contain the three largest cities in Canada—Toronto, Vancouver, and Montreal—and because they are themselves the three largest provinces, Ontario, Quebec, and British Columbia have a special importance in the story of AIDS policy (see Table 2.2). Since each province is separated from the others either by enormous geographic distance or by language, policymakers and AIDS activists have often followed strikingly distinct paths, and at times have had remarkably little contact with one another. The primacy of provincial jurisdiction in the health care field and the failure of the federal government to play much of a coordinating role in the battle against AIDS has reinforced the distinctiveness of AIDS policy in each of the major population centers.

Until 1985, there was in all three provinces a widespread view that established administrative routines could respond adequately to this new disease. AIDS was added to the list of medical conditions that had to be reported to the provincial ministries of health, and the matter was generally kept out of "politics."[2] However, community-based groups recognized the special character of the epidemic. In Vancouver, Toronto, and more haltingly in Montreal, they mounted the first counseling and safe-sex educational programs to respond to the newly sick and the worried well. Concerns about discrimination were raised from the outset, although most AIDS groups concentrated on the provision of services unavailable through the established medical and public health systems.

But beginning in 1985, the public profile of the disease became dramatically higher. The range of political issues posed by the epidemic was also expanded by the availability of HIV testing and the development of new drug treatments. AIDS groups grew and diversified in all three cities,

Table 2.2.   Total Accumulated AIDS Cases in Canadian Provinces

Province	No. of cases	Rate/million population
Ontario	1,858	194.2
Quebec	1,505	225.0
British Columbia	866	283.5
Alberta	322	132.6
Nova Scotia	75	84.7
Manitoba	52	48.0
Saskatchewan	47	46.7
New Brunswick	28	39.0
Newfoundland	20	35.1
N.W. Territories	3	56.6
Prince Edward Island	3	23.1
Yukon	2	80.0

Source: Federal Centre for AIDS, "Surveillance Update: AIDS in Canada" (April 2, 1991).

though least effectively in Montreal. It was during this period that more activist and confrontational voices were added to the community group arsenal, criticizing governmental inaction and traditional public health policies on issues such as testing for HIV, drug testing and availability, and the quality of health care.

Responding to the pressure, some local and provincial governments moved to develop new policies and administrative routines, but others did little. The Ontario provincial government and the City of Toronto were the first to develop major public education programs and initiatives in other areas. In Ontario, it was the elected leaders of a new Liberal government concerned to establish its reformist credentials, not health officials, who provided the first impetus to respond with other than traditional public health procedures. In British Columbia, the reverse pattern was evident. A right-wing Social Credit government actively sought to avoid dealing with AIDS or evincing support for gay community initiatives, while health administrators were prepared to apply to AIDS innovative policies already in place for sexually transmitted diseases—policies that in effect broke with traditional public health orthodoxies about reporting, contact tracing, and the like. In Quebec, the development of new initiatives was hampered by a continuing sense of confidence in the capacity of an ostensibly community-based health care system already in place to respond to any challenge, by the determination of the Liberal government to control public spending, and by a health minister uncomfortable about AIDS and gay-related issues. There were health professionals and administrators in Quebec who recognized that AIDS was a serious problem that needed special responses, but they lacked resources; and the decentralized character of health policy-making in the province made for uneven development of programs and facilities.

During the late 1980s, there was some convergence in AIDS policy across the provinces. All governments were under considerable pressure to establish comprehensive policies and to adopt coordinating mechanisms within health departments and ministries. Issues that were once administrative matters could no longer be avoided, even by right-wing politicians; individual politicians who felt personally uncomfortable talking about AIDS, sexuality, or gay-related issues were quietly shunted out of the health portfolio. Quebec was still least inclined to devote substantial budgets to AIDS (see Tables 2.3 and 2.4), but by 1991 provincial and municipal policies stood in less stark contrast with one another.

Ontario is Canada's largest province and its wealthiest. Toronto, the provincial capital, is the country's largest metropolitan area, its 1986 population of 3.3 million understating the size of the urban region in which it is located. The city has Canada's biggest and most organized lesbian and gay communities, and it has more AIDS cases than any other urban area in the country. Some Toronto health officials recognized early that AIDS was a serious epidemic for which they were unprepared. But most municipal and provincial public health administrators initially adopted a business-as-usual approach: the retention of the principle of full named reporting for HIV as well as AIDS is the most obvious example. Since the mid-1980s, though, the province has been governed by political parties determined to appear progressive on health care issues, so that when political leadership was called for, accommodation was made to reformist pressures from community groups and medical professionals.

Before the AIDS epidemic, lesbian and gay political networks were more firmly established in Toronto than anywhere else in the country, and AIDS community organizing built on that base. Such organizing has not been unproblematic, but in providing services, in mounting political pressure on governments, and in cooperating with one another, the major community groups in Toronto have been very effective. They established for themselves a legitimate place in policy networks and have helped shift government policy at the provincial and municipal level.

The first U.S. reports of "gay cancer" had little media impact in Canada, even among Toronto's lesbians and gays. The September 1981 issue of *The Body Politic*, then Canada's major gay magazine, carried its first article on the subject; it was suspicious of the U.S. Centers for Disease Control for "distortions" linking the spread of Kaposi's sarcoma to homosexual activity. In the October 1981 issue, two medically trained contributors to the magazine acknowledged that gay men seemed especially vulnerable to this

Table 2.3. AIDS/HIV Policies in Canada

Policy	Ontario	Quebec	British Columbia	Federal government
AIDS advisory comm. created	June 1983	June 1982	June 1987	August 1983
AIDS center/section created	August 1987	June 1989	none	July 1987
Comprehensive AIDS strategy	none	none	April 1991	June 1990
AIDS made reportable	June 1983	October 1986	February 1983	: : : :
HIV made reportable	September 1986	no	no	: : : :
Blood screened	November 1985	November 1985	November 1985	: : : :
Testing widely available	November 1985	November 1985	October 1985	: : : :
First public education program	February 1986	Fall 1987	Fall 1987	March 1987
AIDS school curriculum	September 1987	September 1989	September 1987	: : :
Community group funding[a]	May 1986	April 1987	none	May 1986
First AIDS clinics established	January 1987	December 1989	May 1987	: : :
AZT available/funded	May 1987	May 1987	May 1987/1991[b]	December 1986
Needle exchange program	August 1989	July 1989	March 1989	: : :
Discrimination barred				
—for HIV/AIDS	c	June 1989	October 1988	May 1988
—for sexual orientation	December 1986	December 1977	no	no

[a]First systematic funding program for community group funding.
[b]British Columbia began paying the costs of AZT for all recipients in 1991.
[c]Ontario's Human Rights Code includes in its definition of "handicap" any degree of physical disability or infirmity. The Code also explicitly includes sexual orientation, but its equality rights provisions are widely believed to cover sexual orientation implicitly. The Canadian Human Rights Act has not yet been amended to include sexual orientation.

disease, but warned that the apparent link to multiple sexual partners might be rooted less in scientific evidence and more in conservative morality. For gay leaders to perceive early speculation about this new disease as morally driven was not surprising. The gay political agenda had sexual liberation at its center, and for several years local police had been raiding gay bathhouses and bars in Toronto. In that light, AIDS looked to be a convenient new excuse to push an old cause.

But a year later, when twenty-five AIDS cases had been reported in Canada, the gay community became more attentive to the threat and by 1983, concern about the spread of the epidemic was great enough that the AIDS Committee of Toronto (ACT) was established, using $58,000 in government job-creation grants to employ half a dozen staff—although there were still some gay political voices resisting the suggestion that AIDS ought to change sexual practices and dismissing calls for increased protection of the blood supply. For the next few years, this was the only major AIDS community group in the city, and until mid-decade it was the major producer of AIDS prevention and counseling programs. [3]

Several Toronto doctors with large gay practices began seeing patients with AIDS in 1983. Only a few doctors were knowledgeable about the disease, and over the next two years they were to see their work load expand considerably. By June 1983, there were twenty-three cases of Aids-Related Complex (ARC) and eight of AIDS in Toronto. City health officials suggested launching education programs aimed both at informing the gay population about ways of avoiding infection and at allaying fears among health care workers and the rest of the public. [4] The readiness of city officials to act was partly a result of the earlier development of a progressive program on sexually transmitted diseases (STDs), which recognized that established public health routines did not necessarily work. But AIDS education still had a budget of only $9,400, and even though substantial staff time was being increasingly devoted to AIDS, the city's medical officer of health was wary of diverting too many resources to AIDS.

Ontario's Conservative government made AIDS a reportable disease in June 1983, requiring the same full nominal reporting mandated for other communicable diseases. In the following month, a Provincial Advisory Committee on AIDS (OPACA) was named; it was dominated by medical professionals preoccupied more with physician-related referral services and health care worker training than with public education. Through these early years, provincial and local officials sought to maintain the low profile of AIDS programs, believing that it was better to keep AIDS away from elected politicians.

In 1985, there were 129 new cases of AIDS reported in Ontario, 38 percent of the Canadian total, and in the middle of that year, Rock Hudson's

Table 2.4. AIDS Budgets for Canada, 1983–1991 (in millions of 1990 U.S. dollars)

	1983–84	1984–85	1985–86	1986–87	1987–88	1988–89	1989–90	1990–91
Federal Government								
Research/surveillance	.03	.33	.59	1.94	4.60	7.90	7.69	11.36
Public education/hot lines					.26	3.16	4.06	5.55
Community group funding			.04	.63	1.36	3.08	4.06	7.52
Red Cross								
HIV tests/testing clinics		.37	.35	.35	.66	.86	1.29	1.54
Drugs								
Care/treatment					.33	.65	1.18	2.38
Hospices/residences								
Coordination/administration					1.53	3.71	4.06	3.97
Total	.03	.70	.98	2.93	8.72	19.36	22.34	32.32
Ontario								
Research/surveillance	.14	.41	.34	.32	.36	.47	.47	.54
Public education/hot lines			.10	.36	8.49	4.50	9.93	9.38
Community group funding		.02	.06	.09	.37	1.25	3.15	3.32
Red Cross			.73	.86	.88	.89	.87	.89
HIV tests/testing clinics			.18	.46	2.32	1.26	1.93	2.05
Drugs					2.38	5.02	7.82	11.41
Care/treatment					1.85	2.33	3.50	6.08
Hospices/residences		.07		.86	2.03	2.15	2.18	2.41
Coordination/administration			.18	.17	.18	.19	.19	.24
Total	.14	.51	1.76	3.13	18.87	18.03	30.04	35.75
Quebec								
Research/surveillance				.05	.04	.05	.28	.40[a]
Public education/hot lines						.09	.99	3.04[a]
Community group funding			.03	.07	.29	.42	.79	.45
Red Cross				.98	1.06	1.16	1.22[a]	1.30[a]
HIV tests/testing clinics			.16	.22	.61	1.06	1.14	.72[b]

Drugs		.88	1.79	3.06	3.21
Care/treatment	.17		.27	1.40	1.35
Hospices/residences				.39	.50
Coordination/administration	.22	.10	.06	.37	.36
Total	1.51	2.97	4.90	9.63	12.25c
British Columbia[d]					
Research/surveillance		...	...	...	...
Public education/hot lines		.88	1.07	1.05	1.07
Community group funding		.02	.03	.04	.09
Red Cross		.44	.45	.44	.45
HIV tests/testing clinics		.22	.22	.22	.22
Drugs		1.57	1.64	1.73	1.80
Care/treatment		3.95	5.36	5.85	7.04
Hospices/residences					
Coordination/administration		...	...	...	...
Total		7.08	8.37	9.33	10.67

SOURCES: All figures provided by AIDS sections or centers in respective governments, though some may not include all AIDS-related expenditures. Because they include expenditures from only three provinces, though representing close to 75 percent of the Canadian population, the total expenditures enumerated in this table do not constitute all federal and provincial expenditures for the country as a whole.

Note: Research expenses are combined with those associated with epidemiological surveillance and clinical trial networks. Public education expenses include IV drug use strategies, governmental staff education programs, and in Ontario, monies directed to regional public health units. Care/treatment expenses for provincial governments include the costs of AIDS hospital units, outpatient clinics, and home care; for the federal government they include such costs as those associated with establishing a treatment information network, professional development for medical personnel, and the testing for AIDS-related medical devices. Coordination and administrative expenses include the costs associated with advisory committees and AIDS conferences, but are not reported for all governments.

[a] Estimates.

[b] Costs for HIV lab testing unavailable.

[c] Budget estimates provided by Quebec's AIDS Coordination Centre left $.92 million unaccounted for.

[d] In British Columbia, the costs of surveillance and administration have been absorbed into other budget categories.

death intensified public interest in AIDS. Even though there was less panic than in parts of the United States, heightened concern about heterosexual spread increased the burdens placed on Ontario's AIDS community groups, particularly in Toronto. New political voices were heard in debates about AIDS, including people living with AIDS and gay activists radically critical of what was seen as governmental inaction. Although the Ontario and Toronto governments were expanding their AIDS programming, community groups began to raise new questions of government policymakers, health researchers, and medical practitioners.

Before 1986, public health authorities in the City of Toronto had done more on AIDS than their counterparts in other provinces; they expanded their commitment that year. In 1985, the city made its first grant to the AIDS Committee of Toronto (ACT), signaling a recognition of the skills acquired by community groups, especially in safer-sex education. Although some of the city's public health administrators were wary of AIDS activists and reluctant to incorporate them fully into advisory networks, the grant to ACT marked a new departure in responding to disease. In 1986, Toronto's Board of Health acquired a new chair who helped multiply the city's AIDS budget. Jack Layton was a progressive city councillor representing a downtown ward with a large gay population, and his concern about AIDS policy provided encouragement to city health officials who recognized that existing programs did not meet the challenges posed by the epidemic. By early the following year, a $5.1 million thirty-month program had been developed and approved.[5]

The provincial government also began to go beyond existing routines in the mid-1980s. Early in 1985, the Conservative government was persuaded by one of its ministers, Susan Fish, to give money to the AIDS Committee of Toronto. The 1985 Ontario election resulted in the Liberal party's forming a minority government with the support of the social democratic New Democratic party. The new government portrayed itself as reformist, and the dramatic increase in heterosexual concern about AIDS helped make the issue unavoidable. The government created the Ontario Public Education Advisory Panel on AIDS (OPEPA). With a modest budget and little administrative support from the provincial health ministry, it put Ontario in the lead among provincial governments in preparing and distributing educational materials, and in recognizing the importance of the more explicit and targeted messages that community groups could provide. OPEPA represented an effective collaboration between medical scientists, media experts, social workers, educators, public health officials, government administrators, Red Cross officials, and AIDS community group representatives. The Ontario government's commitment of $25.7 million to AIDS in 1986 and an additional $10.8 million the following year provided resources for public education to regional health units across the province, and regularized funding for community groups across the province. The provincial government also took over the AIDS hot line, initiated by the AIDS Committee of Toronto and for a time operated by the City of Toronto, and expanded it to cover the whole province with counseling in English and French. In 1987, Ontario became the first of the major provinces to require AIDS education in all schools, starting in the seventh grade.

In 1986, discrimination against people with AIDS or HIV infection was barred by provincial legislation when the provincial human rights code was amended to include "disability" and "sexual orientation." Even though the Ontario Human Rights Commission had a reputation for slowness in responding to complaints, the code it administered could be used to send clear signals to private firms, individuals, school boards, and government agencies themselves.[6] The addition of sexual orientation to the code had been particularly controversial, and the Liberal government was initially reluctant, but once forced by a New Democratic party amendment to address the issue, the government gradually became emboldened. The homophobia in the intensity of right-wing opposition, some of it from fundamentalist and Roman Catholic groups, only increased the resolve of the Liberals and New Democrats.[7]

New treatment measures were also adopted. The provincial government allocated some of its resources for AIDS outpatient clinics in a number of Toronto hospitals; and once AZT had been approved for use by the federal government, the province provided it to AIDS patients free of charge.

A special AIDS section within the Public Health Branch of the health ministery was also set up in 1987—an unusual administrative response to a single disease. This increased the staffing allocated to AIDS and institutionalized a degree of coordination between branches within the ministry. There was still a certain "business-as-usual" approach to AIDS within some units of the ministry, though, with continuing resistance to conceding unusual routines or resources to AIDS. The creation of the AIDS section allowed a degree of autonomy from a relatively traditional ministry culture, an autonomy strengthened by the determination of Ontario's elected politicians to avoid being embarrassed by inaction.

That fear of embarrassment continued to give community groups considerable leverage. Although the AIDS Committee of Toronto remained the largest AIDS group, it was soon joined by several other organizations. The PWA (People With AIDS) Coalition was formed in early 1987 by a small group of gay men, though it was not until 1989 that the group was firmly established. The Safe Sex Corps (later the Safe Sex Project) was founded at about the same time by the Toronto-based Canadian Organization for the Rights of Prostitutes to mount educational and prevention programs among female and male prostitutes. AIDS Action Now! (AAN!), formed in late 1987, drew on an enormous reservoir of activist energy and anger about political inaction, forming a militant political wing analogous to ACTUP in the United States. From the beginning, the relationship between ACT, AAN!, and other AIDS groups in Toronto was cordial. The fact that ACT was generally supportive of new groups helped sustain a more cooperative spirit than what prevailed in Montreal and Vancouver. Activists in AAN! were often impatient with ACT and PWA for their political caution, but most recognized that each organization had a distinct, complementary role to play. For its part, most ACT members recognized that the angry tone and militant tactics employed by AAN! added weight to ACT's lobbying for intensified government attention to the epidemic.

During this period, criticism emphasized the insufficiency of government's attention to AIDS policy and the underfunding of research and public education. AIDS Action Now! focused on the difficulty of obtaining promising new treatments for AIDS, the tradition-bound methodologies used in drug experimentation, and the inadequacy of patient care in Toronto hospitals. As testing for HIV became common, activists were more critical than ever of the requirement that the name of anyone testing HIV-positive be supplied to the Ontario government. In contrast to some of their U.S. counterparts, though, these activists did not encounter officials inclined to establish compulsory screening programs or close bathhouses.

While in earlier years, AIDS policy in Toronto and Ontario was driven by cautious administrators generally inclined to keep AIDS out of politics, by the mid-1980s elected politicians were actively involved in generating extensive and highly publicized initiatives. A few years later, AIDS had become even more attractive to reformist policymakers, and AIDS community groups were thought to be worth courting. In Toronto's civic politics, this political shift was reinforced at the administrative level by the 1988 appointment as medical officer of health of Dr. Perry Kendall, who put aside some traditional canons of public health. In 1989, a needle exchange program was established for IV drug users. Even though city officials insisted on controlling the program, it was not long before they were considering supplementary programs that would be administered by community groups more closely linked to drug users.[8] That same year, following a suggestion by Kendall, the public school board agreed to place condom dispensers in all city high schools. Programs were also expanding at the provincial level. By 1990, the Ontario government's annual spending on AIDS programs had reached $25.7 million, the highest per capita of any province and the highest spending per AIDS case.[9] A number of the educational and curricular materials developed with provincial funding were by then serving as national models.

Despite these new commitments, community groups' criticism of government policy persisted. In what was billed as a consensus conference on AIDS organized by the health ministry late in 1988, bringing together researchers, primary care physicians, community group representatives, public health officials, and other policymakers, division was at least as apparent as agreement, particularly on the subject of anonymous testing. Chief Medical Officer of Health Richard Schabas staked out a position clearly at odds with that of community groups and strongly supported by medical professionals within his ministry and public health officials across the province. The medical officer of health for the Ottawa area, for example, declared:

> Non-[named] reporting may be quite appropriate where public health authorities are satisfied that complete counseling of infected people and thorough follow-up of partners has been completed. When this criterion has not been met, it is incumbent on public health to require [named] reporting so that these fundamental public health activities can be ensured. Furthermore, anonymous linked testing precludes any public health follow-up and should be unanimously opposed within the public health community.[10]

His Toronto counterpart was more willing to countenance the possibility of non-nominal testing but vigorously opposed anonymous testing:

> Hundreds of thousands of tests have been performed via the public health system in Ontario. Not a single breach of confidentiality has occurred or been alleged. . . . What might be the price of anonymous testing? Our data base would suffer. Critical information on the numbers of infected individuals and the extent of spread into various groups in society would become harder to collect and be subject to serious distortions. . . . Our regular follow-up with reporting physicians would cease and with it our emphasis and assistance in contacting and assisting at-risk partners. The assistance that we offer family physicians would be severely curtailed as would our ability to monitor the very rare individual who behaves irresponsibly and exposes others to risk.[11]

On the other hand, the Ontario AIDS Advisory Committee, which replaced OPACA and OPEPA in 1989, recommended anonymous testing at selected sites across the province. The Liberal minister of health, Elinor Caplan, was intent on maintaining cooperative relations with community groups and so accepted that advice. Her New Democratic party successors seemed inclined toward the comprehensive and permanent establishment of anonymous testing throughout the province, and finally began pilot projects early in 1992.

The lines between the province's chief medical officer of health and AIDS activists were drawn even more sharply in 1990, when Schabas, supported by the Ottawa and Toronto medical health officers, called for the reclassification of AIDS as a "virulent" disease, in order to grant powers of "isolation" (in effect, quarantine) to health authorities. For AIDS activists, this was an example of the traditional public health practice of portraying the sick or infected as "dangerous," and gave public health officials too much discretionary authority. To a provincial government intent on avoiding controversy, the proposal was not attractive.[12]

Treatment issues have pitted AIDS activists and physicians with large AIDS practices against policymakers in Ontario. The mounting burden on health care providers, and the problems confronting patients and doctors arising out of cumbersome procedures and weakly coordinated health facilities, were the object of mounting criticism. The toll on Toronto medical practitioners with large AIDS practices was one measure of the epidemic's costs. Philip Berger, who has one of the largest number of AIDS-affected patients in the country, notes:

> There are now another twenty, twenty-five doctors in Toronto who are knowledgeable, and patients who are infected tend to go to these doctors. That's one of the problems in this whole epidemic: there's only a very small number of doctors seeing most of the patients. And we had to educate ourselves, by listening to our patients, reading the medical literature, attending international conferences. There was no one to sit there and tell us about it. [The] pressure is there from all sorts of angles. . . . [One] source of pressure is the amount of work involved in taking care of patients. They have tremendous physical and emotional needs, and they need to be guided through the social system to obtain legal aid, welfare, lower OHIP [health insurance] premiums, or hospital services. Thirdly, keeping up with medical knowledge is very, very difficult. . . . What's more, it seems everybody wants us to do research for them. Clinical investigators testing new drugs or social scientists . . . are soliciting our cooperation because of our knowledge of AIDS and our experience with AIDS patients. . . . Another part of this "volunteer work" involves being consulted by government policy-makers. . . . And there's the political side, the lobbying and the intervention by our group of doctors [Toronto HIV Primary Care Physicians Group], putting pressure on the government policy makers to get moving, which, as you know, they have not done.[13]

By a 1991 estimate, sixteen of the thirty-six Toronto doctors with large AIDS caseloads have closed their practices to new patients, and a number have abandoned the AIDS field altogether.[14] According to one: "I just can't treat everyone who wants to be seen by me, none of us can. Every day I have to turn away one or two patients who call looking for a physician. I feel like I'm working in the middle of a war zone."[15]

The lack of an overall provincial strategy has created inconsistencies from one medical practitioner to another. "Patients go to one specialist to get one type of treatment and to another to get a different kind. Or they go to a GP to get another dose of a drug. Everyone's doing things differently, because the profession has no agreed upon, community-wide standards."[16] In the words of one AIDS Action Now! activist: "There is no management system in place to properly instruct doctors as to what is known and what is unknown about these treatments. . . . Proper treatment of the PLWA [people living with AIDS] demands consultation and cooperation across disciplines that is rare given the present organization of hospitals and medical care."[17] The problems facing people living with AIDS or HIV are more acute outside Toronto because of the paucity of doctors with an interest or skill in AIDS. The province has developed public education programs to be administered by regional public health units, but medical care for AIDS is still concentrated in the province's major cities, further increasing the burdens on doctors with already established reputations for treating AIDS. Another problem identified by AIDS community groups and physicians is the reluctance of provincial authorities to add new experimental drugs to the Ontario Drug Benefit Plan. Without government funding, these drugs are beyond the means of many people with HIV and AIDS.

Still, in comparison to other jurisdictions in Canada, elected political leaders in strategic health portfolios were moving toward an accommodation with community groups, and had developed policies as comprehensive as any in Canada. Within the public health departments of such cities as Toronto and in the AIDS section of the provincial Health Ministry, there were administrators who recognized the urgency of the AIDS crisis and its particular characteristics. Recently, too, the Ontario AIDS Section was shifted into a branch of the health ministry more concerned with community health. In the summer of 1990, when the New Democratic party came to power in Ontario, a number of AIDS activists believed that the new government would be more progressive than its predecessor. It was the New Democrats who had initiated the 1986 amendment adding sexual orientation to the Human Rights Code, and they had been most critical of spending curtailments in social services and health. By mid-1991, though, little had happened, and AIDS activists and medical practitioners were becoming restive.[18]

Vancouver's population of 1.3 million makes it less than half the size of Toronto or Montreal, but it has had the highest per capita incidence of AIDS of any of Canada's largest cities. The first AIDS community group in Canada was formed in Vancouver, as was the first organization for people with AIDS. Although not always as cordial in their relations with one another as their Toronto counterparts or as cooperative with one another,

Vancouver AIDS activists at times have been at the forefront of expanding the national policy agenda. The smaller size of the city, and the concentration of gay men and lesbians in the West End, have also created unusual opportunities for cooperation in the delivery of services by governments and health professionals. But the policy response of both local and provincial governments has often been slower than in Ontario.

In the mid-1980s, when Ontario's provincial government was taken over by a Liberal party portraying itself as progressive, British Columbia remained in the hands of a right-wing Social Credit party led by Bill Vander Zalm, a conservative Roman Catholic determined to distance himself as much as possible from initiatives that could be construed as supporting a gay life-style (a stance shared by his first health minister, Peter Dueck). This hampered the work of AIDS community groups; and the paucity of provincial funding limited the activities of health administrators. Nevertheless, innovative policies did emerge at both city and provincial levels. The Sexually-Transmitted Diseases Division of British Columbia's Centre for Disease Control was able to take advantage of policies developed before the installation of the current government. Provincial AIDS administrators actually were more prepared than their Ontario counterparts to challenge traditional public health orthodoxies.

In the early years of the epidemic, in Vancouver and throughout British Columbia, the contrast between gay community activism and government inactivity was starker than in Ontario. AIDS Vancouver became the first AIDS community group in the country, formed in 1983 by a small group, a number of them gay doctors. The board was very cautious in its approach to political issues and not rooted in gay community organizing. Still, the organization offered a number of crucial services in counseling and public education at a time when no one else was equipped to deal with AIDS.

In January 1983, British Columbia became the first government jurisdiction in North America to make AIDS a reportable disease. By the beginning of 1985, forty-eight cases of AIDS had been reported in the province—over a quarter of the Canadian total—but the provincial government did little to respond to the epidemic. Even in Vancouver, which was not governed by politicians who were as right-wing as the provincial government, health administrators had done little to establish policies or advisory networks for AIDS. But when Dr. John Blatherwick, the city's new medical officer of health, sent a colleague to San Francisco to investigate what was happening in that city, the dramatic and sobering tale that he returned with helped provoke municipal action.

During the mid-1980s, while the province's political leadership continued to avoid AIDS and refused any significant funding to community groups, that very avoidance created maneuvering room for provincial public health officials. Proximity permitted informal contact and considerable cooperation among provincial and local public health administrators in Vancouver, particularly since provincial officials were less encumbered by conservative political masters located in Victoria. There was little of the sharp disagreement, so evident in Ontario, on the question of anonymous testing for HIV. Unlike Ontario, British Columbia has never made HIV infection reportable. Public health officials were much more favorably inclined to unnamed, even anonymous, testing and reporting, and equally skeptical of the usual public health view of contact tracing. As one administrator rhetorically asked of his Ontario colleagues: "What do they do with that information?" In 1985, British Columbia became the first province to offer free testing and counseling throughout the province, and although doctors or clinic nurses were to keep track of the names of patients being tested for HIV, there was no requirement for further registering of names. A special AIDS testing and counseling clinic was established by the health ministry in Vancouver. There patients could easily supply pseudonyms to doctors or clinics, and so could have de facto anonymous tests. This system was installed after AIDS Vancouver representatives convinced public health officials that no one would show up for testing at a clinic where names would be on file.

Vancouver's AIDS community groups grew and divided between 1985 and 1988. While they were sometimes unable to attain the complementary relationships of their Toronto counterparts, they played a leading role in challenging established government policy on the testing and release of drugs. The first group in Canada to organize people living with AIDS was Vancouver's PWA Coalition, formed in early 1986 as a breakaway from AIDS Vancouver. It grew quickly and developed a critical political profile that the parent group generally lacked. It forced the federal Health and Welfare Department to release AZT by threatening to smuggle supplies of the drug from the United States.

In 1987, the provincial government proposed an amendment to the Health Act giving medical health officers powers of sanction, including quarantine, to restrict those likely to expose others to HIV or AIDS. This was the change Ontario public health officials had wanted, but which had become politically impossible because of the opposition of AIDS community groups, and it intensified concern among British Columbia activists about the government's conservative agenda. The legislation was changed after protests from various quarters, including the British Columbia Civil Liberties Association, although fears persist that the newly granted powers of quarantine are excessive and the protections for confidentiality insufficient.[19]

Mailings on AIDS went out to all British Columbia households in the fall of 1987, and a toll-free AIDS information line was established. The

Ministry of Education developed an optional Family Life Program for grades 7 through 11. Generally, the educational materials and curriculum were thought tame by observers outside the provinces. Tempered by the provincial government's moral agenda, they emphasized sexual abstinence and used such themes as "Be Responsible . . . For Life." Meanwhile, the capacity of community groups to develop their own programs was hampered by the reluctance of the provincial government to fund their activities.

However, one program did illustrate the capacity of the province's AIDS administrators to use established programs in innovative ways. The street nurse program had been developed in 1947, and had launched a "nurses in blue jeans" program for drug users in the 1960s. Without the need for legislative approval, the program grew from one nurse to seven, operating out of three storefront offices. The nurses had already been distributing condoms prior to AIDS, and simply continued doing so (along with offering counseling and anonymous testing) to prevent infection from HIV.

Vancouver's Health Department had its own educational programs, and was more willing to fund community groups, although it was only in 1987 that the political climate in the city seemed right for major policy initiatives. In that year, the city institutionalized protections against discrimination for city employees with AIDS or HIV infection. Health officials also encouraged the Vancouver school board to develop AIDS programs more effective than the provincially sponsored curriculum then being put into place.

The record on treatment and palliative care has been mixed. When AZT was released by federal authorities in late 1986, British Columbia was the only province in Canada to refuse to provide it free to AIDS patients: until 1991, AZT was officially provided free of charge only to people eligible for welfare. Some other drugs for treating AIDS are also harder to obtain in British Columbia than in Ontario. There have been proposals for an AIDS hospice in Vancouver—a proposal backed by AIDS community groups, health care professionals, and some health administrators—but the provincial government refused funding, a refusal thought by many to have resulted from a direct intervention by Premier Vander Zalm.

Yet Vancouver seems to have fewer problems of doctor burnout and lack of coordination in the delivery of medical services than Toronto. In 1985, as the number of AIDS cases rose dramatically, St. Paul's Hospital, a large Catholic hospital located close to the city's West End, decided to establish the institution as a center for excellence in the treatment of AIDS, and soon formed an interdisciplinary team of about thirty general practitioners, nurses, specialists, and social workers. The inpatient services of the hospital and a provincially-funded outpatient clinic eventually found itself treating 90 percent of the province's AIDS cases, offering more integrated and coherent hospital care than was available anywhere else in Canada.

Vancouver's AIDS community groups continued to be underfunded through the late 1980s.[20] In 1990, ACTUP was formed by a group that broke off from the PWA Coalition. Like its American counterparts, ACTUP used aggressive, dramatic techniques to criticize not only the provincial government but also the otherwise much-praised St. Paul's Hospital. The relationship between community groups has remained in flux, although in 1990 the British Columbia AIDS Network was formed to bring together representatives of community groups, along with health and social agencies from across the province.

At both the municipal and provincial levels in British Columbia, this period has witnessed moves to establish comprehensive AIDS policies. The head of Vancouver's Health Department prepared an AIDS plan in early 1988, which was approved by the city council. The program specified substantial support for community groups and educational programs directed at all six thousand city employees. In 1989, Vancouver became the first Canadian city to establish a needle exchange program to combat HIV infection among IV drug users, building on the approach of the provincial street nurse program.[21]

At the provincial level, there has been less specific policy development. While protection against discrimination for people with AIDS or HIV was secured by a 1988 decision of the British Columbia Council of Human Rights, which applied provisions of the 1984 Human Rights Act on physical disability, there was no serious talk of extending provincially regulated human rights protections to lesbians and gays. Through the 1980s, Premier Vander Zalm resisted making AIDS a priority issue and was reluctant to approve educational materials that contained explicit messages or verged on "condoning" behavior he regarded as immoral. As late as 1989, one provincial official likened AIDS to a self-inflicted wound, and Health Minister Dueck suggested that some people's life-styles had "invited" the disease.

John Jansen, a new health minister who did not find sexual or gay issues as repugnant as his predecessor, was appointed in 1989. The next year, partially motivated by the imminent unveiling of a national AIDS strategy, provincial authorities began to develop their own strategy. For the first time, the matters that most divided community groups and the government were being openly debated within the government, and two community groups were given funding to undertake needs assessments. In 1991, the health minister unveiled the new provincial AIDS strategy, which included government provision of all approved AIDS drugs free of charge, and creation of a "center of excellence" for medical professionals. Later that year, the New Democratic party defeated the Social Credit party in a provincial election. The new government is more likely to follow through more vigorously on new policy directions suggested by the AIDS strategy.

Quebec has had a relatively high incidence of AIDS, second only to British Columbia. Four-fifths of the province's cases have been in metropolitan Montreal, reflecting the pattern of concentration in Canada's two other largest provinces. The most distinctive features of the epidemic in Quebec have been the relatively high proportion of heterosexual cases (over 20 percent), and the number of Haitian cases (15 percent). Two-thirds of Quebec's cases have resulted from homosexual activity, relatively low by Canadian standards.

Quebec's health system is much more decentralized than other provincial systems.[22] The province is divided into sixteen regions for planning and management, and thirty-two Departments of Community Health (DSC) for the public health work once done by municipalities. Work formerly under the control of the Island of Montreal's municipal health departments is now the responsibility of the eight DSC in the metropolitan region, and to some extent of the community health centers (CLSC) that form the operational base of the system.[23] AIDS has revealed the unevenness in programs and policies that can emerge, even within the Montreal region, because of decentralization. The system encourages entrepreneurial initiative, but since AIDS emerged during a period of fiscal restraint, the entrepreneurial advantages of the system have not been particularly evident.

None of the community groups in Montreal or the province of Quebec has been able to develop a profile and influence comparable to those of their counterparts in British Columbia and Ontario. This may be partly because Quebec is the only province where AIDS has affected more than one clearly identifiable and mobilizable group in large numbers. Montreal's Haitian community contained a substantial number of Canada's earliest AIDS cases, and the regularity of personal contact with a home country in which the spread of AIDS was alarming posed acute problems for a poor constituency at the economic margins of Quebec society. The Groupe Haitien pour la Prévention du SIDA was formed in 1985, and with the help of federal government grants was able to raise community consciousness about modes of transmission.

Gay community mobilization had begun earlier, but not as effectively as in Toronto and Vancouver. In December 1983, several months after the formation of AIDS Vancouver and the AIDS Committee of Toronto, the Montreal Gay Association established a committee on AIDS called the Montreal AIDS Resource Committee (MARC-ARMS). This group, and the organization that supplanted it in 1985 as the largest AIDS community group in Montreal, the Comité SIDA Aide Montréal (C-SAM), attracted a disproportionate number of the city's anglophone minority. The increased coverage given to AIDS in North America's English-language press, both gay and mainstream, did not immediately influence Quebec's francophone gay population, most seeming to believe that AIDS was a risk only to those who traveled to the United States. Beyond the question of AIDS, Quebec's gay Francophone population was politically complacent, partly because of the perception that Quebec was more tolerant toward lesbians and gays than English-speaking North America. While elsewhere in Canada it was gay-dominated community groups that exerted critical pressure on governments, in Quebec such groups suffered from recurrent turf warfare and fragmentation along linguistic and ideological lines.

In Quebec, government spending on AIDS and policy development also lagged behind the other major provinces. Provincial government and regional health administrators have always been reluctant to take community groups seriously. Since the system was designed to deliver services at the community level, politicians and officials resisted calls for providing significant funding to community groups. In the earliest stages of the epidemic, even the social democratic Parti Québécois health and social services minister complacently assured gay representatives that "the health care system will look after you."

Matters did not improve when the Liberal party replaced the Parti Québécois as the governing party early in the AIDS epidemic. Premier Robert Bourassa tightened the financial screws on virtually all departments as part of a general program of government restraint. Bourassa did not share British Columbia Premier Vander Zalm's moral conservatism, but the minister of health and social services did. Thérèse Lavoie-Roux was a conservative Catholic who avoided the AIDS issue and resisted launching major public education programs on AIDS.[24] As late as fiscal year 1986–1987, the provincial government's budgetary commitment to AIDS (apart from $950,000 to the Red Cross for blood testing) was $534,000.

Some positive steps were taken. The Public Health Protection Act was amended in 1986 to add AIDS as a reportable disease, and there was an explicit decision not to require reporting for seropositivity. In fact, the law stipulates that no information be required that might permit the identification of an infected person.[25] The provincial government also has had a good record on combating discrimination. The Quebec Charter of Rights had been amended in 1977 to include sexual orientation, and the Quebec Human Rights Commission did not wait for complaints about AIDS or HIV status discrimination before adopting a policy that treated both as disabilities protected by the human rights charter. In 1985, the Ministry of Education directed school boards to ensure that no child be deprived of education because of HIV or AIDS. The following year, the Ministry of Health and Social Services directed local community health and social service centers, hospitals, and nursing homes to ensure that no one suspected of being HIV-positive was excluded.

After foot-dragging on the issue, the provincial government did initiate a public education program in 1987, dealing with all sexually transmitted diseases but HIV/AIDS in particular, and it was a high-profile campaign using well-known entertainers. A provincewide information line was also established that year. Development of an AIDS–related curriculum for the schools was slower in coming, although the Protestant School Board of Greater Montreal, serving a majority of the province's anglophones, developed an AIDS curriculum in cooperation with C-SAM.

AIDS was forced more than ever into Quebec's political spotlight in 1988, when a provincial AIDS Task Force recommended an increase in research funding, more education programs especially for high risk groups, greater protections against discrimination for HIV-infected people, opposition to mandatory HIV testing except for the blood supply and tissue donations, increased support for community groups, greater availability of condoms, and the provision of an integrated system of care to HIV-infected persons, including home care, day care, and foster care. Several of these recommendations were taken up by the provincial government.

The government also began implicitly to recognize the inability of the existing health system to cope adequately with AIDS. In 1988, AIDS action teams were established, including two in downtown Montreal and one in Quebec City, and they began offering anonymous testing for HIV. A year later, the government centralized all of its AIDS-related responsibilities in the Centre Québécois de Coordination sur le SIDA, and instructed it to coordinate programs, not only with the various agencies in the decentralized health care system, but with community groups as well. The center was located in Montreal and reported directly to the associate deputy minister of health and social services. Creating an administrative unit for a single disease was a departure for the ministry, which had treated AIDS as a sexually transmitted disease in the "Service de prévention" branch. The government committed itself to spending $6.3 million a year for the following three years on AIDS; and in the 1989–90 budget, about $890,000 was given to community groups. Although this was less than one-third the level of Ontario's support for community groups in the same year (and even at that it included funds for a new AIDS shelter in Montreal), it still constituted a significant improvement.

After the September 1988 election, Marc-Yvon Côté replaced Thérèse Lavoie-Roux as health and social services minister; he was more comfortable with the full range of issues associated with the epidemic and listened to a wider range of voices. Since Côté's appointment, AIDS education has been mandated for all the province's schools, even in the face of continuing reluctance on the part of the Montreal Catholic School Board. Progress has also been made in providing residential assistance for people with AIDS. The Quebec government, in cooperation with the City of Montreal and Centraide (Quebec's equivalent to the United Way), established a residence for twelve people with AIDS, the first of three residences eventually established in Montreal, and access to the province's home care service was also fully extended to those with AIDS. One of the most important policy innovations occurred without provincial government involvement. In mid-1989, a highly successful needle exchange program was inaugurated, and was so successful that by 1990 it was receiving more than one thousand visits per week.

Quebec's record on treatment is less praiseworthy. Both people with AIDS and community group activists are critical of hospital care. Underfunding has led to such overcrowding that the quality of care has been jeopardized in the hospitals with expertise in AIDS. The burdens on doctors and clinics with large AIDS caseloads have started to show, evoking images of the burnout in Toronto.

There has been less confrontation in Quebec between AIDS community groups and government policymakers over matters that elsewhere caused considerable conflict. Traditional public health orthodoxies on such issues as reporting and testing had little impact in Quebec, human rights protections have been clearly laid out, and payment for AIDS-related drugs has been assured. However, the extreme slowness of the provincial government response to AIDS has made AIDS community groups skeptical about the seriousness of government initiatives, a skepticism reinforced by the continuing reluctance of provincial authorities to consult community groups and to fund them at a level comparable to Ontario.

Despite the fact that the Medicare systems in place in Ontario, British Columbia, and Quebec ensured more uniform access to health care than in the United States, there has been considerable diversity in the character of the institutions designated to respond to AIDS, in the political coloration of the major protagonists, and in the governmental budgetary commitment to combating the epidemic (see Table 2.4). Ontario has had the best-organized community group network, one that was resilient during the onslaught of the epidemic and skillful in the application of political pressure, and that network was faced with a relatively supportive political leadership in the provincial government. In contrast, British Columbia's Social Credit government resisted taking a proactive stance on AIDS, though in ducking the issue it left room for creative provincial and local health officials. While fewer of British Columbia's community groups

were as effective as those in Ontario, strong voices were heard on a
number of issues, notably drug treatment. The central role of St. Paul's
Hospital in delivering institutional care was problematic for people living
with AIDS outside Vancouver, but this centralization avoided the problem
of fragmentation evident in Toronto and Montreal. Quebec is characterized not only by a complex and decentralized health care system, but also
by a strong belief among policymakers in that system's ability to cope with
AIDS without significant adaptation and by a government long reluctant
to concentrate resources on AIDS. In 1989–90, for example, per capita
spending on AIDS was $1.29 for Quebec, contrasted to $3.03 for Ontario
and $2.68 for British Columbia (equivalent to $6,190, $16,503, and
$10,126 per AIDS case respectively). Quebec's community group net-
work has been weak, not only because the numbers of Haitian and other
heterosexual cases has meant a more diversified set of communities affected by the disease, but also because the gay and lesbian community
itself is less united in its concern about AIDS.

However, even with the institutional and political diversity across provinces and the ad hoc character of much policy-making on AIDS, there are
signs of growing consistency across jurisdictions in the early 1990s. All
three provinces now have needle exchange programs, all provide funding
for at least some AIDS drugs, all have offered de facto anonymous testing
for HIV (if only experimentally in Ontario), all have mounted extensive
public education campaigns, all have instituted AIDS curricula in the
school systems, and all have involved community groups in planning and
implementing policy.

AIDS Policy at the National Level

Federal AIDS policy in Canada has evolved in isolation from developments in the provinces. Ottawa's policymakers did not have large numbers of AIDS cases close at hand, and were removed from day-to-day
issues that AIDS poses. In addition, most areas of federal jurisdiction are
more distant from the front lines of health care than provincial or municipal jurisdiction: medical research funding, blood supply coordination,
drug testing and approval, and coordination of intergovernmental relations within Canada and with other countries and international organizations. Yet because the federal government has enormous potential
leverage through its spending power, it could have played a more aggressive role than it chose to. Apart from undertaking early epidemiological
tracking and testing, and providing a certain amount of community group
funding, federal authorities were reluctant to assume their usual role in
federal–provincial coordination, this reluctance a product of the general
timidity and conservatism of officials in key AIDS positions in the federal

Health and Welfare Department. As federal inactivity persisted in the face of an increasingly serious epidemic, local AIDS community groups were more and more critical of the national political and administrative leadership. These groups eventually established a national presence and their high-profile work eventually helped shift the national AIDS political agenda away from traditional approaches to medical care and public health.

Scientists at the Laboratory Centre for Disease Control (LCDC) first learned of what would eventually be known as AIDS through reports from the United States Centers for Disease Control in 1981. Early the next year, they established a system of national surveillance for the disease, and it was in epidemiology that federal authorities took a rare lead. When the viral agent responsible for AIDS was identified in the spring of 1984, LCDC scientists became more actively engaged in AIDS-related work, developing procedures for testing for the presence of the virus and training provincial laboratories in those procedures.

The failure of federal AIDS policy to break with traditional medical models was evident in the establishment of advisory systems within the Ministry of Health and Welfare. In May 1983, when the first Canadian cases were identified, the federal government appointed the Ad Hoc Task Force on AIDS, reporting not to the health minister but to the LCDC, and located within the Department's Health Protection Branch, a unit shaped by traditional regulatory responses to disease.[26] The advisory committee was soon given permanent status and renamed the National Advisory Committee on AIDS (NAC-AIDS), but in its early years it was made up mostly of clinicians and researchers, and maintained a low profile.

Federal institutions fund most Canadian medical research; both the Medical Research Council and the National Health Research Development Program (NHRDP) depend on government grants. In Canada, much more than in the United States, scientific research is greatly reliant on government money, so that the research priorities developed by granting agencies are critically important.

From the beginning, federal policy on AIDS research was reactive. The first funding for AIDS projects, in 1983, was less than $280,000. One official remarked that this was "all that the market would bear"; only twelve research proposals had been submitted of which eight were approved. The perception among Canadian scientists that AIDS research was professionally risky may have been partially rooted in the fear of being identified with a gay-related issue, but it was no doubt reinforced by the slowness of federal granting agencies to entice researchers with major funding. As late as 1986, federal support for research amounted to only $1.9 million. Federal officials still argued that research proposals were not coming forward, pointing out that of the more than three hundred applications sent to the NHRDP in

1986, only eight were AIDS-related. The Medical Research Council had a much larger budget of $129 million, and the relatively modest $1 million share going to AIDS was also said to be a consequence of the small number of applications. But since the grants system did not have a strategic orientation and showed no interest in changing routines for AIDS, researchers with major proposals were discouraged from applying. As the *Toronto Globe and Mail* reported:

> Canadian AIDS researchers are ready to quit. While researchers in the United States are running to join the well-financed and politically popular effort to cure, treat or simply understand the mechanism of acquired immune deficiency syndrome, few Canadians see it as a growth area. In the United States, one federal agency alone provides $120 million [$140 million Canadian] for AIDS research. . . . Several top Canadian researchers say they and their colleagues are on the verge of abandoning their work or going to France or the United States because pleas to provincial and federal officials for special funds for AIDS work fall on deaf ears.[27]

By 1985, officials could see that the spread of AIDS in Canada was following the American pattern, with only a few years' lag. Despite this, federal officials paid little attention to educating the public or to the broader social issues raised by the disease. They felt little need to go beyond the standard operating procedures shaped by epidemiologists and medical researchers, who believed that the most important work was to uncover microbiological facts and trace the spread of disease.

This business-as-usual administrative style was entirely satisfactory to Minister of Health and Welfare Jack Epp, who took office when the Conservatives swept into power in late 1984. Epp was on the right wing of Brian Mulroney's government, especially on issues of sexuality and gender. He was regarded as deeply homophobic by AIDS activists, by a number of health officials at the provincial and local levels, and by some of his own staff.

(There was one exception to this pattern of federal inactivity. In 1985, AIDS Vancouver became the first community group to receive a federal grant. This established a precedent for a full-fledged program that gave strength to community groups across Canada.)

The absence of a significant federal AIDS policy induced activists across the country to form the Canadian AIDS Society (CAS) in the spring of 1985. It would be another three years before the group had office space in Ottawa and a full-time executive director, but CAS did constitute a vehicle through which the agendas of AIDS community groups could be coordinated.

By the mid-1980s, the development of tests to detect HIV antibodies raised a number of policy issues. The question of whether to test the country's blood supply was resolved somewhat later than in the United

States, in part because the blood collection system, based entirely on voluntary donations, was thought to be as good as any in the world.[28] Even the Canadian Hemophiliac Society was reluctant to raise the issue of contamination in public until the evidence about infection of hemophiliacs through blood transfusions became irrefutable. By 1990, 42 percent of Canada's twenty-four hundred hemophiliacs were HIV-positive, and the federal government had agreed to an assistance package awarding $102,000 to every person infected through the blood supply.[29]

The availability of testing introduced the possibility of mass screening for HIV, but the federal government did not institute testing for any of its employees. The armed forces screened only those personnel who enrolled in courses offered by the American military, a requirement necessitated by U.S. regulations. On the other hand, until the spring of 1991, Canadian immigration authorities were empowered to turn away short-term visitors who were HIV-positive or sick with AIDS, although the policy was not vigorously enforced.

The first major budgetary commitment to AIDS came in 1986, when the health minister announced a five-year, $33 million plan. Although most of the funds ($20 million) were targeted for research to be allocated by the NHDRP, $3.4 million was earmarked for national educational programs. The public education program was not mounted directly by the federal government, in part because health administrators believed that AIDS education would be too controversial. Instead, the task was delegated to the Canadian Public Health Association (CPHA), a mainstream professional organization with long-standing ties to the ministry, representing the full spectrum of public health professions. One measure of the CPHA's cautiousness was its view that $3.4 million for health promotion was an enormous sum. As one researcher observed:

> It is important to consider the seriousness with which the need for education could have been perceived when just $600,000 [$700,000 Canadian] was allocated in the first year. Some comparisons are in order. The United Kingdom, with less than half the per capita AIDS problem, devoted the equivalent of about $34.3 million [$40 million Canadian] to education in the same fiscal period. . . . The government of Canada allocated $10.3 million [$12 million Canadian] to educate the Canadian public about its free-trade initiatives. I suggest that the feeble allocation of dollars for AIDS education in Canada demonstrates . . . the lack of political will to deal with a sensitive problem.[30]

The CPHA moved slowly. For example, a draft brochure containing the word "condom" was sent to the health ministry for approval, and only after considerable delay and silence did the CPHA decide to act on its own. Eventually, the CPHA put together a brochure and a video for high school students, but the materials were very tame and came very late.[31] Not all of the delays and caution were the fault of the CPHA itself. In developing public service announcements for television, the CPHA ran into difficulties with television executives and the Canadian Association of Broadcasters, who argued that the general public was not ready for the word "condom." This so delayed matters that a reluctant minister's office was obliged to intervene.

Of the 1986 federal budgetary commitment to AIDS, \$3.4 million was made available to the Health Services and Promotion Branch to fund community groups;[32] but in the Health Protection Branch, where most AIDS policy was developed and administered, there was little inclination to work with these groups. Many officials in that bureau still resisted acknowledging AIDS as a major public health crisis, and disliked dealing with political or social issues, particularly when they involved homosexuality and drug use. Dr. Alastair Clayton, the LCDC director, was disinclined to press administrative and political superiors for a substantially greater budgetary commitment, and was content with a narrow definition of his own mandate on AIDS, arguing for example that human rights issues had nothing to do with AIDS.

Little changed with the establishment of the National AIDS Centre to "coordinate and facilitate AIDS related activities nationally, to perform a policy support role, and to provide recommendations on funding priorities." Significantly, the center was positioned within the LCDC. A few officials in the AIDS Centre and the LCDC were beginning to realize how serious AIDS was, and how multifaceted governmental responses had to be, but the prevailing institutional culture militated against the view. The Federal Centre for AIDS replaced the National Centre in 1987, and it was shifted out of the LCDC. But the new unit remained within the ambit of the Health Protection Branch and was headed by Clayton, who left his directorship of LCDC having established a reputation as a timid administrator unlikely to adopt a broad interpretation of his job.[33]

By late 1986, AIDS activists were intensifying the pressure for the early release of experimental drugs. This issue pitted community groups against the testing and releasing procedures of health officials, which were geared to long-term results and not to the treatment of people currently ill and dying. The Health Protection Branch resisted proposals to liberalize its regulations, partly a result of the scars of having approved Thalidomide in the 1960s. Not even the suggestion that people suffering from acute stages of AIDS sign waivers to prevent lawsuits persuaded the Health Protection Branch staff. It was only after highly publicized demonstrations by people with AIDS in Vancouver that federal officials reluctantly allowed for the release of AZT on compassionate grounds in late 1986, through the emergency drug release program.

Criticism of federal inactivity, which had swelled with the angry resignation of the chairman of the National Advisory Committee on AIDS, peaked at the May 1988 National Conference on AIDS, which saw Epp burned in effigy by AIDS activists. Belatedly, the government recognized the need for damage control on the AIDS front. In June 1988, less than two months after the National Conference, Epp announced that an additional $116 million would be committed to AIDS, spread across a five-year period. Following the federal election in late 1988, he was replaced as minister by Perrin Beatty, who was personally more concerned with the issues presented by AIDS. Beatty was a young politician widely rumored to have prime ministerial ambitions, so had much at stake personally in putting the AIDS house in order. As had previously happened in British Columbia and Quebec, AIDS was now a potential vote winner nationally, and criticism from community groups could jeopardize the popularity of a government. As noted earlier, when Beatty addressed the Fifth International Conference on AIDS, in June 1988, he used the occasion to promise that his department would produce a national strategy on AIDS before the end of the year.[34] This was the announcement that took his department by surprise, and many felt he was caving in to community group demands.

Change also occurred at the Federal Centre for AIDS, which added staff more sensitive to the social and community dimensions of the disease. An expanded National Advisory Committee on AIDS was making recommendations more attentive to the concerns of community groups and people living with AIDS. Early in 1990, Richard Dicerni, a senior official thought to be a troubleshooter and problem-solver, was appointed senior assistant deputy minister in the Health Department, and soon given responsibility for AIDS policy. An AIDS secretariat was established to report directly to Dicerni, its primary objective being to coordinate the various branches and directorates within the ministry working on AIDS, as well as to deal with agencies outside the ministry. Since Dicerni's previous post entailed overseeing the funding of programs for community groups concerned with human rights and minority rights, his appointment signaled that relationships with community groups were to receive a higher priority.

In June 1990, an Ad Hoc Parliamentary Committee on AIDS released its report, "Confronting a Crisis." The committee had no legislative authority, but the fact that many of its recommendations were consistent with community group views added to the push for a national strategy. The report called for greater federal–provincial–territorial cooperation in areas such as public education and drug policies, for more serious attention to AIDS in federal prisons, for a broadening of the mandate of the National Advisory Committee on AIDS, for a national treatment registry, and for the inclusion of sexual orientation in the Canadian Human Rights Code. To pay for these policy initiatives, the report argued for a fourfold increase in federal spending on AIDS. The report was favorably received by AIDS activists, although the health minister was no doubt displeased that it would unrealistically increase expectations about his impending national strategy announcement.

That long-awaited announcement occurred on June 28 at the annual meeting of the Canadian Public Health Association. Some $6 million was directed to establishing a national treatment registry. Other funds were shuffled to limit the reductions in community group funding envisioned by earlier budgets. A Clinical Trials Network was established to induce drug testing by pharmaceutical companies, although in fact the Network had first been announced months before.

A number of AIDS activists and government officials at the provincial and local level expressed cautious approval of the strategy, in part because the language used in announcing it referred to "gay" and "lesbian" people, and spoke warmly of the contributions made by community groups. The optimistic mood was sustained by word that Alastair Clayton was leaving his position as director of the Federal Centre for AIDS. But the absence of significant new funding for AIDS disappointed many. Some observers felt that diverting funds from other AIDS efforts to community groups was a deliberate attempt to temper their criticism of the new policy.

AIDS activists continued in 1991 to protest the difficulty of obtaining new drug treatments as well as the underrepresentation of people living with AIDS and HIV on AIDS advisory boards. Although community groups and progressive health professionals had more influence than ever on the federal policy agenda, the government was still proceeding with considerable caution and modest resources. Still, late in 1991 there was new talk of condom distribution in the federally-regulated prison system, and rumored preparation of federal legislation to prohibit discrimination on the basis of sexual orientation.

There was also talk of administrative reorganization within the Health and Welfare Department. Proposals were being circulated to absorb the functions performed by the Federal Centre for AIDS into various parts of the ministry, with an enhanced coordinating secretariat outside the Health Protection Branch that had so slowed the development of innovative AIDS policy in the past. Such a move toward "normalization" of the disease would apparently not damage existing AIDS programs. But it is unclear whether such absorption would gradually reduce the innovative character of some existing AIDS policy by forcing conformity to pre-existent Health Department practices on disease, or whether it would create incentives to spread innovation beyond AIDS.

AIDS and the Responsiveness of Communities and Governments

Through much of the 1980s, most of the public officials engaged in AIDS-related policy-making and service delivery systems held a narrow vision, rooted in a familiar medical model, of what government should do. The federal agenda was first set by the LCDC, located in the Health Protection Branch, which was committed to retaining the coercive regulatory patterns developed in response to epidemics in the nineteenth century. Those officials saw little need to change well-established structures and routines in responding to AIDS. This view was also widespread in the provincial health ministries and in segments of the medical profession.[35]

Challenging the traditional approach were activists, AIDS doctors, and some public health professionals, who attached more significance to the rights of patients, to the work of community groups, and to the need for high-profile public education programs. Notwithstanding the diversity of community groups, they were united in their critique of traditional contain-and-control public health models that relied on regulation, accentuated the fear of irresponsible behavior, downplayed the role of patients and nonprofessionals in making policy, and focused on protecting the uninfected more than on caring for the sick. They were also critical of the tendency within the medical profession and health bureaucracies to treat AIDS as just another contagious disease, avoiding the peculiar characteristics of HIV and the potential for discrimination against those most at risk. The most influential community groups sought to link concern for gay rights with attention to AIDS, but particularly at the federal level government officials continually sought to narrow the agenda.

While Canadian AIDS policy has emerged out of confrontation between traditional and reformist groups, governments have not been monolithic. There have been individuals at all levels of government who have fought to change the way AIDS policy was handled. Some found considerable flexibility in existing public health procedures and used them to good effect, avoiding publicity for fear that higher-profile AIDS activity would provoke backlash by their political superiors. Most of these health administrators embraced reformist public health perspectives. This has been evident within the federal health ministry's Health Promotion Branch, within some health promotion circles in the Ontario government, and in local health departments in Vancouver, Toronto, and parts of Quebec. This style of reformism has been particularly evident in health administrative units responsible for sexually transmitted diseases and among doctors with large AIDS practices.[36]

As they grew in size, community groups acting in the face of initial government indifference had to learn how to manage large budgets, direct increasing numbers of volunteers, and cope with diversity among their personnel and clients. Tensions were commonplace between directors and staff; between women and men; and, in Montreal, between French and English speakers. There were also tensions between those who favored vocal criticism of government and those who counseled caution, conflict that was exacerbated whenever funding hung in the balance. People with AIDS were often critical of mainstream AIDS groups, in some cases resentful of their status as clients without much influence in shaping organizational policy. Over time, while most community groups provided formal representation to people with AIDS, distinct groups have emerged for people with AIDS: The Toronto PWA Foundation focuses on financial assistance and counseling; the Vancouver PWA Society provides a broader range of services and has developed a more critical political stance. Even these organizations did not serve the political goals of all those with AIDS, and groups like AIDS Action Now! and ACT UP have formed to exert aggressive pressure on governments. They have eschewed government funding, arguing that other groups tempered their criticism of policy for fear of losing financial support. Toronto's AIDS groups have been most successful in containing these tensions and avoiding destructive competition arising from the duplication of services. They have had better access to funding from all three levels of government and therefore more financial security than their Vancouver and Montreal counterparts. They have also maintained connections with the gay and lesbian communities of Toronto.

The proliferation of AIDS organizations in Canada generally came from the diversity of people affected by the disease or from differences of opinion over appropriate tactics. But even in Vancouver and Montreal, there was relatively little difference of opinion over major substantive issues. AIDS activists were wary of HIV testing in its early years, but medical developments gradually induced a shift to a more receptive view. There was never any significant official effort to close the gay baths, and this allowed AIDS organizations and gay political groups to sidestep a politically divisive issue. As more radical groups like AIDS Action Now! and ACTUP emerged, new issues were placed on the policy agenda, but the more established AIDS groups were usually quick to adopt positions roughly in accord with those of the more radical groups.

In its early years, AIDS in Canada seemed almost exclusively confined to gay men and, in Montreal, Haitians. But as the epidemic progressed, the risk to hemophiliacs, IV drug users, prostitutes, Native Canadians, and women became clearer. The prominence of gay-dominated organizations in the AIDS community group networks meant that their efforts focused on issues of particular concern to gay men. Pressure to develop policies for intravenous drug users has tended to come from organizations preoccupied with street youth. Some established AIDS groups have evinced interest in the issue of women and AIDS, but often this has been left to health care professionals or feminists in the field of health. This meant that the AIDS network had to be extended. Government funding played an important role in launching groups or in turning the attention of existing groups to AIDS. With the increase in number of groups involved with AIDS came the formation of formal provincial networks and the Canadian AIDS Society—all dependent to a degree on government funding. This reliance on government invited accommodation by community groups, but this did not generally happen. While CAS's reaction to the 1990 National AIDS Strategy displayed cautious optimism, for example, the organization's leaders still maintained critical pressure on Ottawa.

Physicians were another important group that mobilized in response to AIDS. Primary care doctors with a large number of gay clients saw their caseloads expand rapidly. Since governments and hospitals were slow to respond with support services, their responsibilities to patients often included social work and emotional support, in addition to the research required to keep up with fast-changing treatment information. Getting access to new or experimental drugs required complex procedures for monitoring patients. These physicians, often thoroughly imbued with reformist public health views and sensitive to the human rights issues raised by AIDS, found themselves with an unusually high profile in AIDS policy debates. Although most of their voices were more temperate than those of AIDS activists, they often concurred on issues such as anonymous testing and early drug release.

The earliest government response to the epidemic was undertaken by epidemiologists and researchers, who ascertained the rate and means of spread of AIDS (see Table 2.3). In 1982 and 1983, provincial and federal advisory committees were established, bringing together medical professionals and biomedical researchers to evaluate new scientific findings. The committees were given narrow mandates and were populated by specialists disinclined to open up the full range of policy issues implicated by AIDS. Officials of a more reformist bent were typically situated in positions that lacked influence.

As the number of AIDS cases continued to mount, as public concern increased and routine procedures were found to be insufficient, government officials did not always search quickly for more innovative responses, or for major budgetary commitments to AIDS. In the first half of the decade, the number of Canadians with AIDS was still low enough that the resources of the health care system itself, to which people with AIDS had assured access, were not being stretched.[37] By 1983, enough information was available about the paths of AIDS transmission to allow for preventive public education strategies, but this meant that officials had to confront delicate questions of sexual practice. Conservative politicians believed that to recommend safe-sex practices, whatever the medical merits, was to condone sex outside marriage in general and homosexuality in particular.

One of the first departures from the traditional public health approach came with the provision of funds for AIDS community groups. In 1985, the federal government and the City of Vancouver provided grants to AIDS Vancouver; at about the same time the Toronto and Ontario governments gave money to the AIDS Committee of Toronto. These grants acknowledged the importance of the services delivered by those groups to the ill and the worried, as well as the critical role of explicit safer-sex public education directed at the largest at-risk group. The grants also allowed governments to avoid producing explicit educational materials themselves, and let some politicians continue to keep AIDS issues at arm's length.

As it became clear that AIDS was spilling over into the heterosexual population, pressure increased on provincial and national governments. In 1986, Ontario produced new educational materials for the general public. British Columbia and Quebec launched their first major education initiatives in late 1987; by then, the Canadian Public Health Association was disseminating materials with federal funding. In the fall of that year, Ontario and British Columbia inaugurated AIDS curricula in their school systems. (Quebec introduced an AIDS curriculum only in 1989, and then only at the high school level.) Reliance on groups like the CPHA or advisory groups like Ontario's OPEPA suggested that the AIDS issue was still thought too distasteful, sensitive, or complicated for the regular health bureaucracy.

The widespread availability of HIV tests, beginning in 1985, further broadened the AIDS agenda, opening up more terrain for potential conflict. To traditional public health officials, testing offered the prospect of using established procedures to identify and control the infected. Some public health officials believed that effective control required applying contact tracing procedures used for other diseases, and also felt that some controls were needed for HIV-positive individuals who acted irresponsibly. Among gay-dominated AIDS community groups, HIV testing opened up the threat of discrimination and reinforced their distrust of the government regulatory apparatus. Community groups quickly agreed on the importance of anonymous testing, an idea thought by many officials to be a direct affront to their integrity and to their good record on matters of confidentiality. Still, a number of administrators and medical practitioners supported or acquiesced to anonymity, believing that the spread of the epidemic would be most effectively curtailed if this encouraged more people to take the test.

The intensified concern about discrimination prompted the provision of new rights to those with AIDS or HIV infection. In the middle-to-late 1980s, several human rights commissions at the provincial and federal level took the initiative and interpreted disability provisions to protect people with AIDS or with HIV against discrimination. In that same period, the federal government and the British Columbia government established rules prohibiting discrimination in their own public services, and the Ontario Human Rights Code provided similar protections for provincial employees. Four Canadian provinces (Quebec, Ontario, Manitoba, and Nova Scotia) and one territory (Yukon) have amended their human rights codes so as to extend antidiscrimination protection to lesbians and gays, and the federal government may soon do the same.

The slowness of government to respond to AIDS has been most evident in treatment and testing of new drugs. The federal government has been particularly negligent in failing to encourage research, tacitly piggybacking on U.S. efforts. The National Health Research Development Program and the Medical Research Council did make funds available, but both adopted a "wait-and-see" approach to funding requests, rather than actively seeking out proposals. For a time, the same reactive style dominated the federal government's relationship with multinational pharmaceutical companies, who have been reluctant to market AIDS drugs in the relatively small Canadian market. Only in 1990 did the federal government establish a Clinical Trials Network to facilitate the experiments required to get a drug released; even that network provides fewer inducements than pharmaceutical companies can obtain in the United States.

When drug testing has proceeded in Canada, it has been governed by an extremely restrictive set of protocols. By the late 1980s, those protocols were being challenged by AIDS community groups determined to increase the priority accorded the treatment of the already sick. Sustained political pressure forced the government to stretch the intent of its Emergency Drug Release Program to grant access to drugs, such as AZT, not yet formally approved in Canada. In developing drug testing procedures and mechanisms for exchanging treatment information among medical practitioners, health officials were condemned as too slow and unimaginative, and these accusations were increasingly supported by reformist public health officials and medical practitioners. Although in 1990 the federal government agreed to fund a national treatment registry (an idea spawned by AIDS Action Now! and taken up by the Canadian AIDS Society), the responsibility for identifying promising therapies and sifting through the literature on their effectiveness has until now been left largely to AIDS patients, community groups representing their interests, and doctors with expertise in AIDS.

Canadian governments have tended to respond to AIDS on an ad hoc basis, and their responses have had a crisis character. Although American data on how quickly and devastatingly the epidemic was spreading were available, Canadian provincial and federal governments only established significant programs to deal with AIDS after 1985—in one case, not until 1989. Although AIDS advisory groups were established earlier, their mandates were restrictive, their personnel narrowly recruited, and their budgets small. Except in Ontario, which was a couple of years ahead of other provincial governments and the federal government, that pattern changed only in the late 1980s. By then, AIDS could no longer be viewed as a purely technical problem.

Even though governments in Ottawa, Ontario, Quebec, and Toronto established special administrative units to respond to AIDS, they were not always positioned in ways that allowed them to break from established regulatory patterns of disease control. The federal government, for example, positioned the Federal Centre for AIDS within an administrative division dominated by traditional medical model perspectives and highly resistant to the adaptation of policies to the special circumstances of AIDS. Eventually, even the federal government had to increase the flexibility of its AIDS policy apparatus, installing a more strategically positioned AIDS secretariat.

By the end of the 1980s, federal and provincial governments were under mounting pressure to develop comprehensive strategies for AIDS. Toronto and Vancouver, two of the cities with the largest number of AIDS cases, had already developed wide-ranging plans. To be sure, federal and provincial governments had engaged in a broad range of policy initiatives, but strategic plans would coordinate those activities and signal to the public that these governments were committed to responding to the AIDS epidemic. The National AIDS Strategy is one example: while offering no new funds, it arguably produced greater coherence in federal policy-making.

In a federation like Canada, no single level of government can attack the range of problems posed by AIDS. Developing a coherent policy strategy is particularly difficult in a system with overlapping jurisdictions and responsibilities. And even if decentralization provides an opportunity for provincial governments to learn from one another, rivalries and political differences often limit the amount of learning. The result has been considerable unevenness in governmental response (see Table 2.3).

Although the federal government does have some responsibility to coordinate the activities of federal and provincial governments, little was accomplished in the case of AIDS. The Federal/Provincial/Territorial Advisory Committee was not used to good effect by the federal authorities. Although given a coordinating role as part of its mandate, the Federal Centre for AIDS has done little to engender federal–provincial cooperation. For their part, most of the provinces have not clamored for increased coordination. This has exacerbated the structural difficulties presented by federalism in preparing a coherent national strategy.

Federalism has posed difficulties—and created opportunities—for community groups. On the one hand, those groups have often been overextended in applying pressure to even a single level of government, so the prospect of lobbying several levels has been especially daunting. But federalism has enabled such groups to get around resistance from particular officials or from a single level of government. British Columbia organizations desperately in need of government funding could get some help from federal officials; in Quebec, the availability of money from Ottawa could be used to embarrass provincial authorities into matching those grants.

The jurisdictional complexities of federalism, and the entrenched character of routines for responding to epidemics, have meant that unusual governmental leadership was needed to discern what new approaches AIDS requires. Particularly during the early years of the epidemic, there were few examples of such leadership. One Toronto council member prepared a radically expanded AIDS plan in 1986. A federal cabinet minister helped secure early funding for AIDS Vancouver, establishing a precedent for eventual community group funding across the country. In 1985, Ontario's health minister launched a major public education initiative, and in 1987, together with the education minister, he helped inaugurate the country's first comprehensive AIDS curriculum for schools.

Much of the early responsibility for leadership rested with civil servants. While many clung to narrow professional perspectives, unwilling or unable to break out of practiced roles, others worked to shift governments to more reformist stances. In the first years of the epidemic, some pushed for expanded governmental attention to AIDS, using existing programs to respond to AIDS without raising the ire of provincial politicians and developing programs for funding community groups. Where a champion for reform and flexibility was most needed and most strikingly absent was in the leadership of the Federal Centre for AIDS, the Health Protection Branch, and the Department of Health and Welfare as a whole.

By the late 1980s, AIDS became increasingly difficult for politicians to avoid. The Canadian AIDS Society and groups like Vancouver's PWA Society and AIDS Action Now! had developed considerable political clout in pushing AIDS issues onto the policy agenda. A changed climate of public opinion meant that politicians could attract support in the press and the electorate by announcing progressive policies and increased funding for

AIDS. Health ministers began to speak about AIDS in a way that would have been unthinkable two or three years earlier.

Canada has not been without its incidents of AIDS hysteria. In April 1991, a group of parents in Nova Scotia threatened to set up their own school system if Eric Smith, a teacher known to have tested positive for HIV, was allowed back into the classroom. While the parents recognized that HIV is not spread through casual contact, they objected to having their children exposed to a gay "role model."[38] In 1990, a number of residents in a small Ontario town reacted with fear and anger at the prospect of a retreat's being established for people living with AIDS, and the local medical officer of health was obliged to intervene to calm concerns.[39] Similar panic spread in the Quebec farming town of Martinville when an AIDS hospice was proposed in 1987.[40] These incidents illustrate why large numbers of people with AIDS or HIV infection in Canada live in fear of stigma and discrimination, despite the protections now built into human rights legislation.

Survey evidence suggests that the majority of Canadians oppose discrimination. In a 1988 survey, 69 percent of respondents indicated that they would permit their children to go to the class of a teacher who had been exposed to the AIDS virus, although over half would have some misgivings.[41] Between 74 percent and 82 percent opposed landlords' having the right to discriminate against prospective renters who are HIV-positive.[42] The overwhelming majority of respondents (97 percent) favored educational programs in schools to inform students about the methods of transmission of HIV, and close to 60 percent favored high school students' being able to obtain condoms in their schools.[43]

The results are more unsettling on the question of job screening. The testing of job applicants for HIV was supported by 45 percent in the case of day-care workers, 42 percent for high school teachers, 50 percent for food processing workers, and 73 percent for nurses, despite evidence that respondents generally knew the difficulty of transmitting the virus.[44] The results of other polling add to this disconcerting picture. When asked about whether they approve of homosexuality, most Canadians react negatively: in response to a 1980 survey, 69 percent characterized homosexual relations as wrong, and a 1986 poll of Ontarians found that 62 percent believed that homosexual behavior was not acceptable.[45]

These attitudes do not differ markedly from those of American or British citizens, yet Canadians seem generally less inclined to react in strongly negative ways to AIDS or to individuals with HIV. The Canadian media have been less prone to stereotypes in their coverage of the AIDS epidemic than their American and British counterparts, and fewer public officials have sought to rally the public around the sorts of draconian policies that have been proposed elsewhere. Policymakers have not had to confront widespread panic and well-organized groups raising concerns about the prospects of pandemic and moral decline, and have instead been able to tap popular predisposition to oppose discrimination.

Toward a Consensus

From slow and ad hoc beginnings, by 1990 governments at the federal, provincial, and local levels were forced to address the AIDS epidemic. Even right-wing governments whose representatives had balked at confronting most of the policy issues associated with AIDS were talking of overall strategies and establishing routines for consultation with community groups. Many government policymakers and health care delivery professionals had developed procedures for responding to AIDS that differed from routine reactions to epidemics. Innovative public education campaigns had been mounted, and sexuality was being talked about more honestly in schools. Needle exchanges that could never have been imagined a generation earlier were put in place in Canada's three largest cities. Established drug testing procedures had been challenged to take account of the catastrophic rights of the sick, and a new treatment registry was being set up to speed the dissemination of knowledge about new approaches to AIDS. While all health care facilities in Canada suffered from funding constraints, the Medicare system ensured access to comprehensive health care. A number of hospitals established special outpatient clinics for AIDS, some of them with innovative interdisciplinary teams.

The traditional regulatory practices of public health were challenged in several ways, and so was the previously unassailable authority of medical professionals. For the first time, those affected by the spread of disease mobilized into community group networks. Some community groups began shakily and some remain so, but a good number, including the Canadian AIDS Society, have exercised considerable leverage within policy-making networks. Though most community group activists have applauded recent shifts in AIDS policy-making, they continue to press government to be more aggressive on issues such as public education and drug treatment.

A number of issues are likely to remain contentious in the AIDS policy debate. One is drug testing. People with AIDS and their supporters have raised legitimate questions about the slowness of drug testing in Canada and inattention to the rights of the already sick. They have pushed for the development of more flexible testing, for example using "open arms" for clinical trials and taking better advantage of frontline general practitioners. These suggestions have merit, but so do double-blind trials; in Canada as in the United States, where similar conflicts exist, there is a real danger of losing valuable evidence not easily obtainable through other methods. Drug testing must ensure that fully reliable information is passed on to the next generation potentially affected by AIDS and HIV. Community group activists have until now been arguing that open arms can coexist with double-blind placebo trials, but experience may lead to some rethinking.

A related issue is the reluctance of pharmaceutical companies to test their products in the Canadian market. Not even the generous treatment given to drug companies by federal patent legislation in the 1980s has made those companies more willing to conduct major research in Canada. Governments either must induce drug companies to test their products in Canada, or else must make it easier for drugs to be approved on the basis of foreign testing. A related problem is the continuing resistance of federal authorities to the release of experimental drugs to people with AIDS. Some flexibility was, in effect, forced upon them in the case of AZT, but opposition remains strong among many health officials.

Funding for scientific research is still a serious problem. Despite recent increases, Canadian expenditures still pale by comparison to what is available on a per capita basis in the United States, and backlash is already building among researchers in other fields, who claim that too much grant money has gone towards AIDS funding.

More money is also required for AIDS education. Many of the major decisions—to educate frankly, to use the school system, to distribute condoms—have already been made, but only a minority of sexually active heterosexuals practice safe sex. Even among gay men, still the largest group with AIDS, younger generations are prone to imagine that AIDS is not their problem. The need for continuous, high-profile educational campaigns remains substantial, but until now the budgets for such campaigns have been modest.

An issue receiving greater prominence in 1991 is the testing of doctors and patients for HIV. The news of the infection of patients by a Florida dentist has reverberated through Canadian medical circles and is raising new concerns in policy networks. Despite the absence of a single Canadian case of transmission of HIV from a medical professional to a patient, the Canadian Medical Association's membership appears to be shifting to a position in favor of mandatory testing for all hospital patients, pregnant women, and doctors performing surgery.[46] Some pressure has also been generated on the subject of compulsory testing for prostitutes, although health officials in Ontario and British Columbia have so far rejected the idea.[47]

A harder issue concerns individuals with HIV who knowingly engage in risky behavior. By all accounts, this is a small minority, but the danger being posed to others is real, particularly to those who are not members of high-risk groups. Criminal law remedies are available, but there may be grounds for carefully circumscribed public health legislation to bring irresponsible individuals to rein. While the dangers of such legislation can outweigh the gains, the matter has not been sufficiently debated by community groups.

Federal and provincial governments also must confront the question of human rights. In general, the extension of protections against discrimination to AIDS and HIV has been left to human rights commissions, allowing governments to avoid including explicit protections in human rights codes. This cannot help but send a signal to employers and providers of services and accommodations across the country. Moreover, as long as most of Canada's AIDS cases are associated with homosexual activity, amending the human rights codes that still do not refer to sexual orientation is essential.

Governments in Canada have not coordinated their responses to AIDS. The federal government is particularly culpable in neglecting this function, and in not providing the kind of funding that in the past has induced provinces to act. Federal funding is particularly important for the territories and the poorer provinces.

A final issue has to do with the extent to which the epidemic should be treated as exceptional. Governments at all three jurisdictional levels in Canada have created distinctive administrative units to respond to AIDS, acknowledging that this epidemic poses special issues and dilemmas. But there are now signs that officials in established health bureaucracies would like to reclaim AIDS, absorbing it into their routines. While the culture of cautiousness prevalent in some of those bureaucracies suggests that these strategies ought to be resisted, exceptionalism may not ultimately serve the cause of AIDS or the populations it has most directly affected.[48] Discrimination may arise even more easily from policies explicitly designed to respond to AIDS than from routines developed for all diseases. If one of the positive effects of the epidemic has been to challenge traditional health administration routines, should there not be some attempt to reduce exceptionalism and apply the routines developed for AIDS to other diseases?

In Canada, AIDS has been an agent of transformation. The political ethos and organization of gay and lesbian communities has been radically altered, and in many ways strengthened, by the epidemic. Politicians have been forced to deal with issues of discrimination and sexuality. For the first time, public health bureaucracies, the medical research establishment, and the pharmaceutical industry have had to contend both with a well-organized constituency that learned quickly how to exert political leverage, and with reformist health professionals given newfound voice and strength. Changes in the treatment of the disease combined with such pressures have rewritten the AIDS policy agenda: now it includes legal, ethical, financial, and political issues far beyond the initial policy responses of most governments. The clash between the traditional contain-and-control approach to disease and the cooperation-and-inclusion model has resulted in the traditional medical model's giving ground.

There will be some routinization of policy responses to AIDS in the next years. The consultative mechanisms will probably remain, although grass-roots organizations that depend largely on volunteer labor will have difficulty maintaining their representation on advisory panels and consultative groups. There will be pressure to develop new ways to constrain those who willfully expose their sexual partners to HIV. Policies and procedures to protect against discrimination may well be extended and strengthened.

Whatever public health measures are adopted, the top-down regulatory model run by experts will not go unchallenged. While the toll of AIDS has been heavy, many people with AIDS have resisted acting like victims; they have joined with other AIDS activists in questioning the received wisdom about how best to deal with disease. In doing so, they have permanently altered the Canadian health care system for the better.

Acknowledgments

This chapter owes much to the expertise of community activists, government administrators, and academics in Vancouver, Montreal, Toronto, and Ottawa, who agreed to confidential interviews, and who unfortunately cannot be thanked by name. Many of them will have wanted more detail about the work of their own community group or administrative office, but much of that sort of detail is impossible to include in a chapter destined for an international audience. Apart from interviews, the chapter is also based on a number of published and unpublished documents and papers, most notable among them an extraordinary reference tool produced by the McGill Centre for Medicine, Ethics and the Law called *Responding to HIV/AIDS in Canada*. A number of other documents and press clippings were made available through the Resource Centre of the AIDS Committee of Toronto, arguably the best documentation center for AIDS-related materials in Canada, with an unflinchingly cooperative staff. Additional heartfelt thanks are owed to Gerald Hunt and Lesley Watson for enduring the pressures placed on their partners by the deadlines for this research.

Notes

1. The most recent imposition of federal stipulations on otherwise provincially managed systems was in 1984, when the federal government prohibited the provinces from allowing doctors to bill patients in excess of the provincially established fee schedules.

2. At the time, Quebec's Parti Québécois' government was more socially reformist than the Conservative government in Ontario and certainly more so than the Social Credit government of British Columbia. But Quebec politicians and public health officials generally held to the view that the province's health care system was the most responsive on the continent, and could cope even with the unusual characteristics of AIDS. Quebec had also been the first Canadian province to include sexual orientation in its provincial human rights charter, and many participants in the AIDS policy-making process believed that Quebec society was more tolerant than the English dominated provinces.

3. By 1985–86, the group's budget had grown to $373,000, $197,000 of which came from federal, provincial, and municipal grants. ACT's links to a grass-roots base were not always secure, but several staff members had roots in gay and lesbian political organizing in the city. In 1986, a breakaway faction formed the Toronto AIDS Drop-In Centre, but neither the breakaway faction nor the center has maintained much profile in the city's AIDS community group network, and the divisiveness within ACT has in general not persisted.

4. In Ontario, the provincial Ministry of Health enters into direct negotiations with hospitals and other health-related institutions to determine budgetary allocations. The province also funds provincewide Health Units, over which District Health Councils have some monitoring role. Such bodies have boards made up of professionals and representatives of the general public. They have no regulatory control over health care institutions in their area, but instead are intended to assist provincial officials in planning and coordinating policy. Larger municipalities have Boards of Health with stronger powers that report to city councils. In all parts of the province, responsibility for monitoring public health is delegated to medical officers of health, who lead local departments of health or health units. They monitor the outbreak of disease, data about which is collected and transmitted to the province's chief medical officer of health if the disease is "reportable."

5. One of the consequences of increased funding was that the Public Health Department was able to hire more public health nurses, and to diversify their ranks along the lines of ethnicity, race, and sexual orientation. The provincial government soon committed itself to covering 50 percent of the costs, part of a provincewide funding commitment. Prior to this, the city's capacity to move ahead was partly a function of the large tax base in Toronto and the high profile already established by public health issues. This profile was due to the large immigrant population, to the extent to which other municipal jurisdictions in Ontario turned to Toronto for expertise, and to the extent to which the city's Board of Health had regularly served as a magnet for progressive city politicians.

6. See, for example, stories in *Toronto Globe and Mail* (July 24 and 27, 1991).

7. See David M. Rayside, "Gay Rights and Family Values: The Passage of Bill 7 in Ontario," *Studies in Political Economy*, no. 26 (Summer 1988), 109–147.

8. The program was supported by federal and provincial grants, although in order to obtain that support, city officials had to "repackage" the program.

9. This included major funding for Casey House in Toronto, a hospice for AIDS patients that had been established with the help of well-known writer June Callwood and of a great deal of fund-raising among Toronto's well-to-do. In the view of some policymakers outside Toronto, Casey House was such an expensive facility that it could never serve as a model for any other hospice, in or out of Toronto. Ontario's budget for AIDS also included money for research, for blood screening, and for experimental drugs such as AZT. By 1990, over two thousand Ontarians were on AZT, and over eight hundred on aerosolized pentamidine.

10. "The Role of Public Health in the HIV Epidemic," *Canadian Journal of Public Health*, supplement 1, 80 (May–June 1989), S17.

11. Letter to the *Toronto Globe and Mail* (October 23, 1990).

12. George W. Smith, "AIDS Treatment Deficits: An Ethnographic Study of the Management of the AIDS Epidemic, the Ontario Case," poster presentation at the Fifth International Conference on AIDS, Montreal (June 1989), 2.

13. "An Interview with Philip Berger, M.D.," *Grail* 5 (March 1989), 21–22.

14. *Toronto Globe and Mail* (January 15, 1991).

15. *Toronto Star* (December 23, 1989), 1.

16. "An Interview with Philip Berger, M.D.," 24.

17. "AIDS Activism: The Development of a New Social Movement," *Canadian Dimension* (September 1989), 9–10.

18. Philip Berger, "For AIDS Activists, NDP No Better than Rest," *Toronto Star* (September 30, 1991).

19. Stan Persky, "AIDS and the State," *This Magazine* 22 (March–April 1988), 10–14.

20. As late as 1990, AIDS Vancouver had a budget and paid staff only about one quarter of those of the AIDS Committee of Toronto.

21. In contrast to Toronto, Vancouver decided at the outset that such a program would be best contracted out to a community group, and high usage rates since the beginning have confirmed the wisdom of that decision.

22. Budgetary control is still vested in the Ministry of Health and Social Services, counteracting the decentralization to some degree.

23. There are other institutions at the base of the system as well. Social service centers (CSS) offer counseling and psychosocial services at a regional level (there are three in Montreal), dealing with more difficult or unusual problems than the CLSC can generally deal with. Reception centers (CA) deal with people in need of a protected setting such as a rehabilitation center or a nursing home.

24. As late as 1987, in fact, the minister tried to stop an innovative safe-sex campaign coming out of the DSC–Montreal General because of its explicit talk of condoms. The power of the central ministry over the policy-making units below it was revealed in the process, although in the end a well-orchestrated pressure campaign forced the ministry to organize its own public education campaign.

Between 1985 and 1987, the Health and Social Services Ministry spent a total of $2.2 million on AIDS-related programs

25. There are provisions allowing public health authorities to order someone with a specified contagious disease to undergo treatment, but so far there is no talk of those provisions being invoked for AIDS. In general, the strict controls on confidentiality have the effect of providing official sanction for anonymous testing.

26. One Ottawa official described the Health Protection Branch as having a long-standing paternalistic culture, which "still has an allergic reaction to much of what is going on in AIDS."

27. *Toronto Globe and Mail* (April 22, 1986). See also Colin Soskolne, "A Canadian Retrospective on AIDS: Implications for Future Policy, Economics, Behaviour Modification, and Research," *Tre sactions of the Royal Society of Canada*, Series V, vol. II (1987), 13–39.

28. In 1983, the Red Cross had asked that members of "high-risk groups" voluntarily abstain from blood donation.

29. The package specifically excluded partners of hemophiliacs who were infected through sexual contact, the rationale for supporting hemophiliacs themselves focusing on governmental responsibility for the security of the country's bloo ' supply.

30. Soskolne, "A Canadian Retrospective on AIDS," 23.

31. The most positively received material was a curriculum for elementary school students.

32. The Health Promotion Branch had provided a few community group grants before this, but on an ad hoc basis.

33. The FCA was described by a member of Ontario's advisory committee as having for years "screwed around talking about things."

34. As late as 1990, two senior officials were overhead commenting that AIDS Vancouver's views had nothing to do with public health and only with gay rights, and that it was trying to infiltrate the system as gays had in San Francisco.

35. Through a number of health officials in other parts of the federal ministry, and in particular divisions within health departments at the provincial and local level, did not share quite as restrictive a medical model, for several years even they kept to the view that AIDS should be administered within established routines and kept out of "politics."

36. This was not a perspective much in evidence in the leadership of the Canadian Public Health Association, but even within that quite cautious organization there were critical voices emerging from below.

37. Some critical voices were being raised about the safety of the blood supply, but the blood donor system in Canada was widely respected and not easily challenged.

38. *Toronto Globe and Mail* (April 15, 1991).

39. *Toronto Star* (July 2, 1990).

40. Alberto Manguel, "There Goes the Neighbourhood," *Saturday Night* (June 1989), 33–39.

41. Michael Ornstein, *AIDS in Canada: Knowledge, Behaviour, and Attitudes of Adults* (Toronto: Institute for Social Research, York University, 1989), 65.

42. Ibid., 73. Seventy-four percent oppose discrimination against two men who are infected. The percentage rises to 82 percent in the case of two women.

43. Ibid., 78–79.

44. Ibid., 71.

45. David Rayside and Scott Bowler, "Public Opinion and Gay Rights," *Canadian Review of Sociology and Anthropology* 25 (November 1988), 649–660.

46. *Toronto Globe and Mail* (August 15, 1991).

47. *Toronto Globe and Mail* (July 29, 1991).

48. This is a point made by Margaret Somerville of the McGill Centre for Medicine, Ethics and the Law. Charles Perrow and Mauro Guillen argue that the special units or coordinating bodies created in the United States to respond to AIDS were usually designed to prevent "contamination" of established procedures for dealing with disease, a point which may well apply to Canadian governments at all three levels. "Normalization" of AIDS, for us, is supportable when it challenges established procedures and avoidance strategies. *The AIDS Disaster: The Failure of Organizations in New York and the Nation* (New Haven: Yale University Press, 1990), 140–142.

Chapter 3

Germany: The Uneasy Triumph of Pragmatism

Guenter Frankenberg

The development of a federal AIDS policy in Germany recalls John Locke's statement: "In the beginning of all the world there was America."[1] Whatever one may say about the speed of the German governmental reaction to AIDS, there is no denying that the human immunodeficiency virus was initially considered to be an American disease.

Not until 1983 did the government issue a press release designating AIDS as a national problem. Soon thereafter, the federal Ministry of Health took the unusual step of inviting a task force from San Francisco to deliver, firsthand, information from those who had the greatest experience with AIDS prevention. That visit helped persuade ministry officials to adopt a liberal approach, one that placed the Epidemics Control Act, the traditional public health response to the containment and control of infectious threats, on the back burner.

At the same time, the ministry invited medical experts and representatives from the gay community to a secret meeting to discuss possible methods of AIDS prevention; it set up an informal council, which evolved into the National AIDS Council. Government officials thus tacitly admitted that, faced with such a mysterious, exotic, and dangerous disease, public health authorities were amateurs rather than experts. They had to look for support from those who, in Germany as in many other democracies, do not normally have easy access to governmental agencies.

Viewed from the outside, the ministry appeared to be following a zigzag course. A meeting of medical experts in October 1983 came to the conclusion that "no extraordinary measures were necessary" since the epidemic was limited to certain groups. But a November 1984 press release announced that the Federal Ministry of Health was seriously contemplating a stern, new "Act for the Control of Diseases Transmitted by Sexual Contacts." This legislation was said to call for mandatory medical examinations for potentially infected persons, regulations of infected individuals, a prohibition on blood donation, contact tracing, anonymous reporting, and even non-anonymous reporting of those who refused medical treatment. Medical voices, notably the Society for the Control of Viral Diseases, strongly protested against these plans, and others interpreted this move by the ministry as a provocation designed to elicit calls for a moderate strategy. Ministry officials claim that all they had in mind was a backup strategy, should their pragmatic approach to AIDS prevention be rejected.

Between Minimalism and Maximalism

In West Germany, the political controversy over the correct strategy against the further spread of AIDS has followed a distinct course. The first phase, which lasted through 1985, can be characterized as the incubation period. The responses of public health authorities and nongovernmental organizations were hesitant and restrained. With the notable exception of public statements in the State of Bavaria and the tabloid press, most revealed sympathetic concern, as well as a determination to gather information about AIDS, avoiding panicky reactions.

The second phase began in early 1986, when the public mind had undergone a kind of seroconversion: AIDS was almost omnipresent on the public agenda. Until roughly the middle of 1989, AIDS was often publicly debated and also shaped medicolegal discourse.[2] Controversies took on the appearance of a religious war between the supporters of a moderate strategy pursued by the Federal Ministry of Health and most state ministers of health, aiming at the cooperation and inclusion of those at risk on the one side, and the pro-Bavarian contain-and-control strategists on the other.

This clash reflects a deeper tension in AIDS policy, between one that is committed to a minimalist, cooperation-oriented outlook, and another that is maximalist and control-oriented. Minimalism moves away from the traditional public health instruments and therefore limits governmental controls and interventions. This approach—supported by the organizations and advocates of the so-called risk groups, notably the gay community-based Deutsche AIDS Hilfe, as well as by much of the medical profession—relies on the cooperation of those at risk. Two distinct minimalist approaches have been put forward in Germany. Advocates of a cognitive strategy give priority to information, counseling, and sex education. They support self-help groups designed to initiate a learning process that changes risky behavior, encouraging use of condoms and clean needles, and altering relationships in environments, such as the drug scene, that facilitate the spread of HIV infection. Advocates of a conflict strategy, while not denying the importance of information and education, doubt that public education will induce the desired stable behavioral changes. They aim instead at strengthening the psychological autonomy of individuals in therapy groups, to enable them to deal with the inevitable conflicts between self-preservation and sexual desire, between lust and fear of death.

Minimalists generally assume that coercion will be ineffective because the contexts within which HIV is transmitted typically lie beyond governmental control. They belive that, because of its unique features, AIDS must be treated differently from other communicable diseases. Rejecting the incorporation of AIDS under the Epidemics Control Act (Bundes-Seuchengesetz) or the Sexually Transmitted Diseases Control Act (Geschlechtskrankheitengesetz), they have supported a specific AIDS Act that would grant sex education, the distribution of condoms and syringes, and other "soft" interventions new legal status.

From the beginning, the federal government's Ministry of Health has pursued a strategy that gives preference to sex education, information, research, and support for self-help groups over governmental control and legal sanctions.[3] But because it holds in reserve the possibility of turning to more restrictive measures if the current strategy proves ineffective, this strategy is best defined as "minimalism plus."

Maximalism, by contrast, stresses governmental control and intervention. This approach relies on the classical public health methods—mandatory testing, mass screening, mandatory reporting and notification, surveillance, risk-site regulation, isolation, quarantine, and imprisonment—to identify the sources of infection and to interrupt the chains of infection. Generally speaking, maximalists want AIDS and HIV infection to be treated like any other communicable or venereal disease covered by the Federal Epidemics Control Act or defined as a sexually transmittable disease and to be listed as such in the Federal Venereal Diseases Control Act.

Maximalists claim that all communicable diseases have to be treated similarly. They maintain that only when individuals know their HIV status will they be likely to behave responsibly, and therefore believe that all persons at risk have a duty to know whether they are infected. Legal sanctions for irresponsible behavior are thought to serve the goals of prevention, just as they are thought to deter other antisocial acts. In short, maximalist logic embraces this maxim: The stricter the better.

Because pure maximalism is politically unfeasible, its adherents, notably the Bavarian government, combine it with elements of minimalism such as education and counseling. "Maximalism minus" is a combination strategy that clearly privileges governmental control of risk groups; promotes surveillance of risk zones, such as bordellos and public toilets; and favors coercion over sex education. Thus, maximalist appeals for cooperation of those at risk invariably have a threatening tone, even when they seek to soften the core harshness. Maximalists assume that a contain-and-control strategy and a cooperative strategy can be effectively combined—indeed, that an effective strategy of cooperation is a strategy of contain-and-control.

Minimalists and maximalists have confronted each other with legal arguments: the rights of persons with AIDS or HIV to be protected

Table 3.1. AIDS Cases by Year of Report and Category of Risk Exposure for Germany, 1982–1990

Risk category	1982	1983	1984	1985	1986	1987	1988	1989	1990	Total
Homosexual/bisexual activity	10	42	92	237	429	752	930	1,073	822	4,387
Homosexual/bisexual activity and IVDU					n/a					
IVDU	2	2	7	24	57	131	179	245	174	821
Blood products	1	3	13	26	44	93	90	86	57	413
Heterosexual activity	1	1	7	10	18	25	39	68	91	260
Mother to child	0	0	2	7	7	8	5	5	1	35
Other/unknown	0	1	12	14	27	44	66	89	84	337
Total cases	14	49	133	318	582	1,053	1,309	1,566	1,229	6,253

Source: Federal Health Office, unpublished statistical report (Berlin: 1991).
Note: Data include 28 AIDS cases reported from the five new Eastern states.

against discrimination and to obtain medical care, versus the rights of the healthy to be protected against the threat of AIDS. German discourse on AIDS has made repeated references to the legal regime and reflected constant pressures to prove the juridical legitimacy of the various approaches. The law has not done much in terms of effective prevention, but it has played a critical symbolic role. Especially in its "religious" phase the German AIDS debate drifted toward legalism as the judges, lawyers, and medical professionals encountered one other.[4]

In 1990, a new phase began in the policy debate over AIDS. The fervor of the earlier period all but vanished; the professional battle cries died down. It was as if, after eight years, almost everyone had come to realize that there were no easy answers to AIDS, that law cannot be the source of solutions.

At Risk

AIDS made its appearance in West Germany two or three years later than in the United States. Although one case has been retrospectively diagnosed, the first cases were officially reported in 1982.[5] By the end of 1990, as Table 3.1 shows, 6,253 cases were registered by the Federal Health Office.

Gay and bisexual men, intravenous drug users, and hemophiliacs have constituted the groups most at risk. More than 90 percent of reported cases have been among men.

The number of AIDS cases among gay and bisexual men reported each year has begun to level off, although the total number of cases among homosexual men still continues to rise. This dramatic change reflects the incidence of infection early on in the epidemic and the radical modification in gay sexual behavior that began several years ago. A 1987 survey estimated that between 15 and 40 percent of gay men were infected.

Among hemophiliacs, HIV prevalence is very high. Approximately, thirteen hundred (between 40 and 60 percent of all hemophiliacs) were infected between 1980 and 1984 by HIV-contaminated blood products. Since blood screening began in 1985, this route of infection has been virtually eliminated, although seven hemophiliacs were infected in 1990 by clotting agents that had not been adequately screened.

Drug users appear to be well informed about the risks of needle sharing, which has lessened; but much less change has occurred in their sexual behavior. As a consequence, the prevalence of infection continues to rise. In 1987, between 30 and 60 percent of intravenous drug users were estimated to be infected, although some have suggested a figure as low as 20 percent. Infection is highest in major cities, rising in such cities as Frankfurt to 70 percent.

Prostitution by drug users is regarded as a potential floodgate to the non-drug-using population. Approximately half of female drug users, and between 10 and 20 percent of male drug users, work as prostitutes. Although only 1 percent of registered prostitutes, who undergo regular medical examinations, are infected, the level of infection is much higher among those who are not registered, many of whom are drug users. Despite such fears, little change in the behavior of their customers has been reported. While in a survey of customers of regular prostitutes almost 50 percent reported using condoms, customers of "procurement prostitutes" are more likely to prefer unprotected sex.[6]

Yet heterosexual contacts have not emerged as a major source of transmission of AIDS. In 1987, 82 individuals reported heterosexual contact as the probable source of infection. The figure rose to 126 in 1988, but then fell to 45 in 1989. Most importantly, HIV infection has not spread as rapidly as had been anticipated. As late as 1989, the Federal Health Office (BGA) estimated that the number of HIV-infected persons ranged from 50,000 to 100,000. Based on more recent and more accurate data, in 1990 these estimates were reduced to 30,000 to 80,000. AIDS has remained concentrated in the metropolitan areas: 65 percent of all AIDS cases have been reported from Berlin, Hamburg, Cologne/Düsseldorf, Frankfurt, and Munich, where a little over 15 percent of the former West German population lives.[7]

The Collective Drama

The statistical characterization of the epidemic cannot convey the thousands of personal tragedies produced by the German AIDS epidemic, but it does suggest that, for some groups, AIDS has become a collective drama. A closer examination of the life world of these groups—gays, prostitutes, drug users—helps bring meaning to the devastation that has occurred.

The formation of today's gay movement can be traced to the early sixties.[8] It was preceded and accompanied by developments that reflected a new approach to sexuality—or at least a new rhetoric about sex within West German society. In 1969, the Penal Code was liberalized, leaving only homosexual acts between adult men and minors under the age of twenty-one as a crime, thus ending the era of strict repression of homosexuality.[9]

This legal reform, as well as news of the emerging gay rights movement in the United States, catalyzed gay activism in West Germany. While in the 1960s there was no organizational basis for gay emancipation, in the formative period of the gay movement, between 1971 and 1975, the first gay newspapers and gay groups emerged. Public discussions and demonstrations initially focused on the structures of the homosexual subculture,

Table 3.2. AIDS Cases and Infection Risk for Germany

Risk category	1983	%	1986	%	1990	%
Homosexual/bisexual activity	36	86.0	390	73.2	3,130	70.50
IVDU (male)	2	4.7	33	6.2	392	8.84
IVDU (female)	0	0.0	21	3.9	178	4.01
Hemophiliac	2	4.7	28	5.3	220	4.96
Blood products (male)	0	0.0	6	1.1	51	1.15
Blood products (female)	0	0.0	6	1.1	49	1.10
Heterosexual activity (male)	0	0.0	10	1.9	77	1.74
Heterosexual activity (female)	1	2.3	8	1.5	63	1.42
Mother to child	0	0.0	6	1.1	28	0.63
Other/unknown (male)	1	2.3	20	3.8	223	5.03
Other/unknown (female)	0	0.0	5	0.9	22	0.50
Total cases	43	100.0	533	100.0	4,433	100.00

SOURCE: Federal Health Office, unpublished statistical report (Berlin: 1991).

then celebrated sexual liberation. On an institutional level, the new movement focused its concern on the elimination of the law placing restrictions on homosexual relations between adults and minors. After 1975, two strands of the gay movement became more clearly visible: the integrationists and the radicals. The intergrationists called for the emancipation of the homosexuals in all social contexts. They worked within the trade unions and in the Social Democratic and Liberal parties. The radicals, focusing on gay identity, called for the solidarity with other sexual minorities, one of their goals being the elimination of the entire penal law on sexual offenses.

Under pressure from the gay movement, and with the support of law reformers, the Penal Code was again revised. While sexual acts between males over eighteen years of age with males under that age remained punishable, in such cases, the courts could decline to punish if the "perpetrator" was less than twenty-one years old or if there was some indication that the minor had engaged in solicitation. Recently, there have been initiatives by two state governments and the leading AIDS group, the Deutsche AIDS-Hilfe, to decriminalize homosexual relations between consenting persons over sixteen years of age.

During the 1980s, the gay movement became more institutionalized, as the number of active groups increased from two hundred in 1981 to more than four hundred a decade later. While there is little discussion within the movement about its goals, and a collective gay identity is still more hope than reality, the gay movement is represented in professional organizations for lawyers, doctors, and media professionals, as well as in social institutions such as unions, political parties, schools, and the civil service. The Green party has been noteworthy for endorsing measures advocated by gay spokespersons. It has supported providing benefits for gay couples and has called for the enactment of an antidiscrimination law.

By the time AIDS appeared in West Germany, the gay community, although still split between radicals and integrationists, was sufficiently well organized to reach its members and to influence politics. Buffeted by the threat of AIDS, the movement would be challenged in its capacity to reach inward, to the apolitical gay community, as well as outward to the centers of power.

There are three distinct categories of German prostitutes, and the legal and social situation differs radically among them. Registered prostitutes must have regular medical examinations and are, therefore, obliged to cooperate at least minimally with public health offices. Casual prostitutes are mainly housewives. Unregistered prostitutes work to raise money to pay for injectable drugs.[10] Little is known about the working conditions and number of this last group. The Berlin self-help group for prostitutes, Hydra, estimates that in West Germany there are about four hundred thousand female prostitutes; others suggest a much lower figure.

Although prostitution is not punishable under German criminal law, it is officially regarded as a violation of public morality. Unregistered prostitutes have no way of participating in the full range of insurance protection available to other workers. By and large, they are not protected against the risks of sickness, unemployment, and disability, but must depend on the welfare system in times of hardship.

A wide gulf separates the worlds of registered and unregistered prostitution. Those driven by the desperate need to raise money for drugs are prone to engage in unsafe sexual practices. Registered prostitutes oppose free-lance prostitution, not only as undesirable competition, but also as a dangerous violation of professional ethics. This sense of professionalism is reflected in their efforts to organize and to press for improvements in working conditions, and in their acknowledged status within the social security system.

While the gay community is well organized and has a voice in politics, and while prostitutes have begun to organize, drug users remain entirely unrepresented and unorganized.[11]

Estimates of the number of regular users of hard drugs range from fifty to one hundred thousand; if one includes occasional users, the figure exceeds two hundred thousand. Many drug addicts live in parks and in the streets, their daily existence a struggle for survival. Crime is their desperate answer to an ever-growing need for drugs and to the high price that users have to pay for drugs. The scene is characterized by competition, blackmail, and cheating—a miserable life lived in the shadow of illegality, where only the meanest and fittest can survive even temporarily. Violence and the omnipresent pressure of criminal prosecution erode friendship and partnership. Junkie Associations were founded in several cities, including Frankfurt, Kassel, Bremen, and West Berlin, in the early 1980s, but dissolved within two years. They fell victim to a repressive drug policy that operates on the basis of the Drug Control Act (Betäubungsmittelgesetz), which criminalizes even the small-scale sale and use of drugs. The AIDS epidemic provoked efforts to effect radical modifications in West Germany's myopic and repressive drug policy.

Public Health, Social Security, and the Law: Traditions and Trends

The unique public health demands posed by AIDS compelled political authorities to confront the inadequacy of the legal regime developed almost a century earlier for the control of communicable diseases.

The centerpiece of the government's police power has been the regulation of diseases that endanger public health, an authority that can be traced back to fourteenth-century plague decrees (Pestschriften). This regulation constitutes the basis of a traditional strategy to identify, localize, and control sources of infection through such measures as mandatory reporting, isolation, quarantine of whole areas, and prohibiting immigration from plague-infected regions. The policing of epidemics, focusing on the control of the sick, prevailed until the nineteenth century, when Louis Pasteur, Max von Pettenkofer, Robert Koch, and others laid the groundwork for the causal and rational control of contagious disease through the "battle against germs."

What has been called the conversion to Pasteurism found its legal expression in the Epidemics Control Act (Reichsseuchengesetz) of 1900, which set out the classical methods of epidemic control for diseases regarded as particularly dangerous: leprosy, cholera, smallpox, pestilence, yellow fever, and typhoid fever.

Since then, the development of the legal regime of dangerous and contagious diseases has been marked by two related trends. Epidemic control laws broadened the scope of governmental authority by adding diseases such as tuberculosis to those already covered and by authorizing the regulation of other contagious diseases. Moreover, venereal diseases were singled out for separate and unequal legal treatment. The Venereal Disease Control Act of 1927 had a repressive edge, providing for mandatory reporting, prohibition of sexual intercourse, and strict sanctions if public health regulations were violated.

Both trends—the broadened scope of public health regulations and the differential treatment of venereal diseases—structure the prevailing legal system. Under the 1961 Epidemics Control Act, all communicable diseases come within the authority of the Public Health Service. The Act gives the Service authority to do anything necessary to prevent and control any communicable disease. The law combines preventive measures, such as tracing and locating the sources of infection, with medical examination and surveillance of infected persons and those suspected of being contagious. The authorities may also isolate infected individuals and prohibit the practice of certain professions. Whether these very broad regulations would stand a contemporary constitutional test is an open question, since for three decades the powers confirmed by the Epidemics Control Act have been almost unused.[12]

The Epidemics Control Act's reporting system applies to communicable diseases listed in the act or those added by executive order. It differentiates among three categories of diseases: for the most dangerous, reporting is required, even of merely suspect cases; in the least dangerous category, only death is reportable.

The Venereal Disease Control Act of 1953, like its 1927 predecessor, singles out four sexually transmittable diseases: syphilis, gonorrhea, chancroid, and lymphogranulomatosis. It establishes a regime of strict intervention for these diseases: reporting and notification requirements; the prohibition of professional activities with a risk of infection, sexual intercourse so long as diseases are transmittable, and breast-feeding; and mandatory medical examination and treatment.

Although these regulations mostly have been enforced in the case of prostitutes, it would be misleading to describe the Venereal Disease Control Act as an effort to impose a hygienic utopia or an attempt to enforce bourgeois family values. From the very beginning of the campaign against sexually transmitted diseases, legal regulations were ambivalent: while directed against certain sexual practices, they also served educational purposes and limited the scope of medical and governmental control.

The Venereal Disease Control Act empowers public health offices and vice squads to search out sources of infection. At the same time, the mere existence of such regulations is meant to create awareness about the dangers of infection, and so to have a preventive effect. While the law provides for repressive measures, coercion and legal sanctions are considered legitimate only when curative therapies are available; to apply coercive measures against those whose diseases cannot be medically treated is widely considered inhumane. Yet, efforts to elicit the cooperation of those with venereal diseases in the public effort to control their spread have been thwarted by the stigmatizing effects of coercive measures.

The Basic Law of the Federal Republic of Germany sets out the principle of the welfare state (Sozialstaat), a constitutional obligation to establish a social security system for individuals in need because of sickness, old age, disability, poverty, or unemployment.[13] Its goal, to guarantee everyone a life of human dignity, has been shaped by numerous statutes.

The German health insurance system, which dates from 1883, is designed to protect the working population against the vicissitudes of work life. Today, more than fifty million people are members of the legal health insurance scheme or are jointly insured as family members. The main health insurance institutions are the General Health-Funds (Allgemeine Ortskrankenkassen), work or guild sickness funds, health insurance societies, and rural sickness funds. Workers who earn less than a specified income, the unemployed, students, and recipients of pensions are compulsorily insured. The principle of solidarity means that every member of the legal health insurance system is entitled to benefits including enhancement of health, prevention of illness, early diagnosis, medical treatment, and nursing care.

The controversial Health Reform Bill of 1988 restricted the protection of people needing long-term home care to those incapable of performing the daily routines "in almost every sphere," and only if they had been insured for at least twenty of the past thirty-six months. To avoid hospitalization, members of a legal health insurance plan are entitled to four weeks of home care; long-term home care has to be justified as a necessary substitute for hospital care if it is to be covered by the insurance plan. The provision of insurance benefits also presupposes that no other family member is available to provide the care.

This fragmentary overview of the system of social security in Germany does not answer the concrete questions desperately posed by persons with AIDS or infected with HIV who are in danger of losing their jobs, who are in need of long-term health care, or who simply need insurance. Yet it conveys the extent to which social security and health insurance in Germany is geared toward restoring an individual's ability to work. Long-term unemployment and long-term disability, the familiar experience of those with AIDS, will usually lead from social security to welfare, German society's residual and less generous form of aid to the poverty-stricken.

Public Reactions, Private Feelings: AIDS in the Public Mind

AIDS embodies mystery, sexuality, and danger, and that makes the disease a media natural. After scattered articles in 1981 and 1982 about the "Mysterious Disease Among Homosexuals"[14] and "Dangerous Genes,"[15] intensive and continuous press coverage began in 1983. In the initial phase of "imported panic," which lasted through 1983, most newspapers and TV drew heavily on the American experience: "The evil that comes from America is more lethal than the plague and more mysterious than cancer";[16] "Mysterious Disease AIDS Causes New York to Panic."[17] AIDS became a topic of prime interest once the media could present it as threatening not only marginal groups but also the heterosexual—"normal"— population.[18]

The media often focus on topics that concern a great number of people; topics that are new, controversial, sensational, or—even better—catastrophic, highlighting the aspects of broadest interest. This happened with AIDS in Germany. Coverage has ranged from tearjerking human interest stories about AIDS victims ("The Death of the Innocent Baby") to sensationalism ("How Dangerous Is AIDS? The 'Wanted' Poster of a Killer"; "Canadian Nun Died of AIDS"; "The New Epidemic: Europe Trembles"; "A Kiss Can Do It"), to sober presentations of scientific findings.

The pattern of media responses to AIDS corresponds to the general approach of the particular news outlet. The tabloids, like *BILD-Zeitung* and *Berliner Zeitung,* have focused on human interest stories, present the memorable events—the tale of the first infected German child, the tragedy of an infected pizza baker—and intermittently allude to the mysterious nature of the infection. They deliver sensational tales about Patient Zero, the ominous Gaetan Dugas; the biting criminal; the desperado prostitute; the incestuous father; and, again and again, promiscuous homosexuals and their voracious sexual appetites.

Under the headline "The Sex-Epidemic that Nobody Can Stop," the *Munich Abendzeitung* reported in June 1983:

> George Z. is one of the many young men who love men. Since puberty he enjoyed their company. He loved life, loved love, and treated both lavishly. . . . Today his medical history reads like a classical AIDS case, known from the threatened group of homosexuals with considerable promiscuity: drugs, injected heroin, inhaled popper-drugs (amyl nitrate), many visits to gay meeting places such as saunas, bathhouses, contacts with men from the U.S.A. And one day it all began. . . .

AIDS, the story suggested, was the punishment for George's sexual behavior.

The serious press has reacted quite differently. During the first years of the epidemic, some papers, notably the *Frankfurter Rundschau,* a newspaper with a liberal-social orientation, seemed unable to deal with AIDS at all, ignoring the disease until late in 1983. Other serious newspapers initially gave great emphasis to the biomedical aspects of HIV infection. From the mid-1980s on, such papers became partisans of either maximalism (*Frankfurter Allgemeine*) or minimalism (*Sueddeutsche Zeitung, Die Zeit*).

Despite the generic sensationalism of the tabloid press, and despite sensationalist and homophobic slurs of some of the more serious press, notably *Der Stern,* it is important to note a widespread interest in information-laden reports. Efforts on the part of Deutsche AIDS-Hilfe encouraged such a focus.

Expectations about the relationship between general editorial philosophy and the outlook on AIDS have not always been borne out. *Der Spiegel,* a serious liberal newsmagazine, might have been expected to adopt a minimalist AIDS policy. Yet, *Der Spiegel* discovered AIDS at a very early date, and, unlike other organs of the serious press, called AIDS a "Seuche," a term that translates as epidemic but which in German carries a nastier connotation ("plague").[19] In numerous cover stories, *Der Spiegel* followed the path of the tabloid press and invoked the metaphors of warfare ("The Invasion from the Unknown") against AIDS as a "Seuche," comparable to bubonic plague, cholera, and syphilis, always stressing the lethal outcome of HIV infection.[20] The cover of a 1983 issue announces the "Lethal Epidemic AIDS," which the magazine calls a "modern epidemic," "the lust epidemic (syphilis) of the twentieth century," "homo-epidemic" and "gay cancer" (Morbus Kaposi).[21] *Der Spiegel's* many articles on AIDS describe a dangerously and rapidly progressing enemy.[22] Despite the intermittent presence of articles on virology and epidemiology, and a smattering of pieces criticizing Bavaria's AIDS policy, *Der Spiegel* usually favored the maximalist strategy of search and control.[23]

Yet beginning in 1989, *Der Spiegel* shifted course. The magazine began to lose interest in AIDS, and the articles that did run were not so critical of minimalism. This newfound restraint mirrored the more general mood of the news media regarding AIDS. By 1990, the intensity of the epidemics's religious war–like phase had subsided; the epidemic had become less socially important.

In the epidemic's first years, German public opinion fluctuated between hysteria and indifference. Publicly expressed views about AIDS prevention in general differed remarkably from reactions to AIDS in everyday situations such as schools. Generally speaking, interest in AIDS has declined: in 1988, 41 percent of participants in an opinion poll stated they were "very interested" in AIDS; one year later, only 30 percent.

Opinion polls in 1987, 1988, and 1989 presented a favorable reading of the public consciousness.[24] In the FORSA polls for the Federal Office for Health Education (BZgA), about 65 percent of respondents regarded AIDS as an important health risk, like cancer and heart disease. Not surprisingly, the sexually most active population was most concerned. The fact that many people did not consider AIDS to be the country's prime health problem did not imply that the dangers of infection were underrated. In fact, 75 to 95 percent of the population had precise knowledge about the main routes of transmission; two-thirds knew that the infection is communicable during its asymptomatic phase. More than four-fifths of the younger age groups had a solid knowledge about the more complex problems of AIDS prevention, such as testing. One third of those polled worried about being infected. An increasing number of all unmarried people (from 20 percent in 1987 to almost 60 percent in 1989) claimed to be more careful in sexual matters than before. The number of condom users has steadily increased. In 1988, only 16 percent used condoms: in 1989, 41 percent of those between sixteen and twenty years of age and 30 percent of the persons with multiple sex partners said they used condoms always or often; an additional 35 percent used condoms occasionally. Almost one-quarter of those surveyed had had an HIV-antibody test. A bare majority of the population expressed no fears about contacts with infected persons and indicated they would help them as much as possible. A clear majority favored voluntary prevention and opposed the mandatory testing and isolation of people with AIDS.

On the other hand, in an unrepresentative opinion poll by *Der Spiegel* in 1987, a majority preferred the maximalist approach to HIV prevention: 74 percent favored intensive controls of groups most at risk, 66 percent were in favor of reinforced immigration controls, and 55 percent supported mandatory reporting of all persons with AIDS. Yet only 31 percent thought mandatory screening of the entire population was necessary.[25]

The divergent poll results may be read as an attempt by *Der Spiegel* to buttress its support for maximalism. They might also reflect a shift of public opinion from a more dramatic to a calmer view of AIDS. But all these polls say little about the reaction of people directly confronted by the issue of AIDS, by parents, for example. Numerous incidents of hysteria and discrimination against persons with AIDS or against persons suspected of being "virus carriers" have been reported in kindergartens, schools, prisons, and at the workplace.[26]

The two dominant churches in Germany, the Protestant and the Catholic churches, initially had trouble coping with AIDS. Until 1985, virtually no official statements were issued by either church. Thereafter, one can clearly distinguish two different characterizations of AIDS and views of homosexuality, as well as two different approaches to prevention, guided by sharply differing church doctrines. At the level of practical health care, however, both churches were equally involved and compassionate.

The Protestant Church's statements reflect a determinedly minimalist approach.[27] AIDS is characterized as a dangerous but rare disease. Stressing the importance of avoiding panic, church officials have called for thorough public education and have criticized the concept of "risk groups," denying that HIV infection is a special problem of particular groups.

While some church officials assert a possible connection between personal guilt and disease, between the wrong committed by man and divine justice, the disease is primarily seen as a disruption of God's good creation, an evil that should not be. Like any other sickness, AIDS is accepted as part of human life, the message being "We'll have to live with AIDS." For that reason, the Protestant Church has forcefully opposed discrimination and stigmatization, false moralism and prurience in the public discourse on AIDS:

> Reproaching the sick and the infected with guilt can neither be the first nor the last word, as if in every case there were an immediate causal connection between their disease and misguided personal behavior. In situations of fear Christians have to resist the tendency to name a few scapegoats. They know that every disease represents a sign of the fallen world and of the estrangement between the Creator and his creature. Everyone participates in this estrangement, it does not concern only a few (persons with AIDS). . . . However, a possible connection between personal guilt and the disease must not be denied. The connection between human wrong and God's Tribunal, evidenced by the Bible, cannot be left undecided or be given up altogether. . . . Yet to regard a disease as "God's direct punishment" is a heathen misunderstanding. Jesus contradicted those views. However, they still continue to be felt without explicit religious reasoning, encourage the separation and discrimination of the infected and the sick, and weaken the possible help for those concerned.[28]

By contrast, the Catholic Church (except for one diocese and several more liberally-minded theologians) strictly followed the AIDS policy of the Holy See.[29] AIDS has been characterized as God's punishment; in the exceptional case of innocent victims, particularly children, it is viewed as "God's challenge." "The order established by God cannot be violated with impunity. . . . For many, AIDS is a consequence of an immoral life; others may be infected without guilt, and in such cases AIDS is a trial inflicted on man by God." Mutual sexual devotion according to God's will is based on unconditional faithfulness within a marriage. Sex with multiple partners is considered to violate the divine ethical order. Consequently, the Catholic Church in its public statements and brochures about AIDS has rejected homosexuality, not only because it is not normal but also because it may cause the death of one's partner. Invoking the fate of the Roman Empire, the Conference of German Bishops over and over again has traced the AIDS epidemic back to the sexual revolution in the 1960s, to pansexualism, hedonism, and the maximization of sheer lust. These sins undermine the proper ethics of sexuality, leading to neuroses, depression, and ultimately to AIDS. The Church also delivered its sometimes vicious critique on the "superficial information campaigns" of the federal Ministry of Health.[30] Against the "ideology of the condom," dominant Catholic opinion calls for marital fidelity and, if need be, abstinence:

> With serious worry we have deliberated on the questions that arise in connection with AIDS. The Permanent Council stressed . . . the willingness of the Catholic Church to support the counseling centers and hospitals in helping those concerned and taking steps against their social isolation. At the same time we have pointed out that it is questionable when only technical devices are being recommended for the prevention of an infection. We share the worries of many parents who have turned against the superficial information campaigns. According to our conviction, reference has to be made to binding ethical standards of sexual behavior. According to God's will, the mutual sexual dedication of man and woman is based on unconditional fidelity and the indissoluble bond of marriage. A corresponding change of life-styles and marital fidelity and an ethical order of sexuality are therefore the suitable ways to prevent the further spread of the disease.[31]

These teachings have not hindered local churches from helping those with AIDS. On the level of counseling and health care, the model is not the Pope but Mother Teresa or the Good Samaritan.

AIDS and the Politics of Public Health

In its 1987 Immediate Program, the federal Ministry of Health developed a three-pronged approach: the protection of the population against HIV infection, counseling of and care for persons with HIV infection or with AIDS, and the prevention of discrimination.[32] Implementation of these goals was guided by the principle that information and education should take precedence over classic epidemic control. Measures authorized by the Epidemics Control Act and other laws for the protection of the population would only be deployed against "unteachable" individuals who recklessly violated the health interests of others. Thus the reference to the Epidemics Control Act served as a background threat, even as it protected the strategy against the charge that it might not be comprehensive enough. The main slogan, "AIDS Concerns Everybody" (AIDS geht alle an), gave federal policy a universal ring. Ironically, it ultimately would play into the hands of hard-liners in Bavaria, by overdramatizing and generalizing the threat of AIDS.

It is against the background of this federal strategy that one must understand the repeated calls by Bavaria's Secretary for Internal Affairs Peter Gauweiler for a "closed concept of state measures to control the world epidemic AIDS."[33] His sense that AIDS might be an important political issue, and his direct access to the Bavarian prime minister and power-wielder, Franz-Josef Strauss, enabled Gauweiler to launch a massive campaign against the federal ministry and against Minister of Health Rita Suessmuth. Over and over, at Gauweiler's behest, the Bavarian prime minister wrote to the federal chancellor, urging him to take stricter measures such as testing soldiers and civil servants. From the outset, this approach was embedded in a moral crusade against "national decadence," aimed at "thinning out" sexually deviant groups. The Bavarian government, anxious to distinguish its law-and-order policy from the approach of its more liberal coalition partner in the federal government, treated AIDS as a welcome opportunity to reaffirm the Christian Social Union's conservative profile.

The Bavarian government also tried to recruit other German states to its cause. It sought to push the federal government and Chancellor Helmut Kohl, who had sympathy for the law-and-order aspect of AIDS, towards a maximalist prevention strategy. But the federal Ministry of Health was able to secure the support of the Conference of State Ministers of Health and the liberal coalition partner in the federal government, as well as the Social Democratic and Green party opposition in the federal parliament.

In May 1987, clearly isolated, Bavaria issued its own maximalist catalogue of AIDS measures.[34] The Bavarian program favors classic methods of epidemic control. Characterizing AIDS as a world epidemic and pointing toward the allegedly geometric progression of HIV infection, the Bavarian Government, speaking through Gauweiler, denounced federal Minister of Health Rita Sussmuth as being too soft, not up to the challenge of AIDS.

Bavaria singles out intravenous drug users and prostitutes as risk groups. Anyone identified as a member of those groups is automatically and permanently suspected of contagion and as such subject to investigative measures of the public health authorities. The groups most at risk for HIV infection are referred to as "AIDS-biotopes" that have to be searched out, controlled, and ultimately "extinguished." The Bavarian rules also call for mandatory testing for civil service candidates and foreigners applying for residency permits; they establish the duty of "virus carriers" to warn sex partners and those who provide health care for them. Prostitutes are obliged to use condoms and are forbidden to advertise a negative HIV-antibody test result. HIV-infected persons are prohibited from breast-feeding; from donating blood, semen, and tissue; and from engaging in prostitution. They—and the criminal courts—are instructed that sexual intercourse by an HIV-infected person is punishable under the Federal Penal Code. The police and the aliens' registration offices must report HIV infection to the local administrative authorities. Meanwhile, the

Bavarian approach includes a refusal to offer disposable needles to intravenous drug users or to establish methadone programs.

In Bavaria, information about AIDS is aimed at encouraging people to take the HIV-antibody test, in order to act responsibly. That AIDS prevention evokes profound psychological conflicts seems an alien notion.

Despite the rhetoric of drama, death, and danger, the Bavarian ministry could not fully implement its regime of control. Only civil servants, foreigners applying for a residence permit, and prison inmates were screened; these are the groups most easily accessible to mandatory measures. The results hardly justified the testing. Between 1987 and 1989, only 1 percent of all prisoners tested were found to be infected, although between 75 and 97 percent of intravenous drug users in prisons tested positive. Of the 20,646 candidates for civil service, just one tested HIV-antibody-positive. Of the 24,199 seeking residence in Bavaria, twenty-eight were infected; of 8,613 foreigners resident in Bavaria, just nine were HIV-positive. Between 1985 and 1988, the Munich Public Health Office identified eight male and seven female prostitutes as virus carriers; other Bavarian public health offices reported twelve infections.

As part of the Bavarian strategy, public health agents regulated the meeting places of at-risk groups, ordering the testing of persons suspected of being contagious. Instead of closing the gay bathhouses, public health authorities practiced what might be called risk-site regulation, prohibiting the sale of the stimulant amyl nitrate, prostitution, the showing of pornographic videos, and homosexual intercourse. Bars suspected "of encouraging violations of public morality" were ordered to assure that "the pubic region and the posterior of waiters be completely covered by a nontransparent piece of clothing."[35]

Bavarian AIDS statistics do not specify the prevalence of infection among homosexuals and intravenous drug users, the groups most at risk, and so do not analyze the impact of the maximalist search-and-control program on those in greatest need of care and counseling. Nor can Bavaria identify those at high risk who have been avoiding any contact with the public health authorities since the Munich government embarked on its crusade.

The Bavarian strategy isn't simply symbolic politics. The campaign was intended to punish "deviant groups" and to promote the idea that testing is crucial to the control of AIDS. Bavarian public health authorities applauded judges who sent virus carriers to jail for endangering third parties by engaging in unprotected sexual intercourse. Not surprisingly, the Bavarian strategy stifled the beginnings of a culture of cooperation, a prerequisite for encouraging traditionally stigmatized groups to seek help from the state.

Pragmatism versus Panic

In contrast to the Bavarian maximalist strategy, the program implemented by the federal Ministry of Public Health and all the other state governments is modest and unaggressive. It has relied on education and research—and on a remarkable division of labor between public health agencies and the gay community-based group Deutsche AIDS-Hilfe.

At the end of 1985, the public relations and information agency of the federal Ministry of Health, the Bundeszentrale fuer gesundheitliche Aufklärung (BZgA), began to inform the population about AIDS through the mass media and by supporting the Deutsche AIDS-Hilfe. However, it was not until 1987 that the BZgA allocated considerable funds ($17 to $29 million per year) to launch information campaigns. That year, the campaigns relied on ads, posters and brochures. In the following years, the BZgA also utilized television and movie spots. It focused on informing "multipliers": social workers, teachers, physicians, and politicians. The chief target groups of the government's efforts have been sexually active heterosexuals, health service personnel, adolescents, pregnant women, and, recently, intravenous drug users.

The information campaigns have been intended to inform the population about how HIV infection is transmitted and about how to prevent infection, to further responsible behavior, to overcome and reduce irrational fears, and to enhance solidarity with HIV-infected persons. The information spots stress that everyday social contacts are not dangerous, while pointing out that promiscuity and unprotected sexual intercourse with unfamiliar partners must be avoided. The BZgA has created awareness and a fairly high level of knowledge about AIDS. The greater part of the population seems to have been reached by the AIDS movie spots (70 percent), by newspaper ads, and by TV and radio programs (40 to 60 percent); fewer people have learned about AIDS from doctors or public health offices (1 to 11 percent). But official prudishness, its refusal openly to address risky forms of sexuality or drug abuse, appeared to trivialize AIDS.[36]

Federal funds support counseling services delivered by both the AIDS-Hilfen and local public health offices. More importantly, in 1987 the federal Ministry of Health provided funds for each of the 309 public health offices to hire an AIDS specialist—a physician, psychologist, or social worker—to help the public health offices in AIDS counseling and streetwork, as well as assisting schools in AIDS-related sex education.

Two other poorly funded model programs have been set up in urban areas to provide streetworkers for the particularly endangered persons of the primary groups at risk and to offer consultation and health care for HIV-infected intravenous drug users.

The federal government has opposed mandatory measures in its attempt to seek the cooperation of those most affected by AIDS. As a matter of principle it recommends voluntary HIV-antibody tests, but in fact it supports testing generally. The minister of health suggested in her book *AIDS—Ways out of the Fear of AIDS* that anyone with doubts about his or her serostatus should take the test.

The official message shifted from "AIDS Concerns Everybody" to "Don't Give AIDS a Chance." In a more recent brochure, the ministry states:

> Many people have not yet seriously considered whether they or their partner have been exposed to an HIV-infection risk in particular by sexual intercourse without a condom or by the sharing of syringes and needles. In case one of these risks applies to you, you should seek counseling. A personal consultation can help you to get a clearer picture. An HIV-antibody test can help remove your worries. The HIV-antibody test detects the antibodies the body produces some time after an HIV infection. Since HIV antibodies can only be detected several weeks after an infection, it may be necessary to repeat the test. The test is no protective measure! Only you can take care of your own (and your partner's) protection. Basic rule: as long as you don't know whether or not you are infected, you should use condoms. Especially if you wish to have children, you should seek counseling and, if need be, you should be tested. The public health offices, your doctor, AIDS counseling institutions and AIDS-Hilfen can give you advice. There you can find out where you can be tested free of charge and anonymously.

With advances in therapeutics and the growing recognition that early clinical intervention can be critical, HIV testing has been given even greater emphasis. Federal policy favors anonymous testing and stresses the necessity of pre- and post-test counseling; this has become the strategic centerpiece. Massive propaganda for voluntary testing and the recommendation to test various groups—draftees, pregnant women, and prostitutes—were meant to delegitimize the contain-and-control approach. Once the ministry could claim that its recommendations were heeded, it could suggest that its strategy of building trust and seeking the voluntary cooperation of those affected by AIDS was effective.

The development of drug policy roughly parallels the phases of German AIDS policy generally. Traditional social work in the drug scene was overshadowed by the emphasis on abstinence specified by the Narcotics Act, at least until the mid-1980s. Detoxification, counseling, therapy, aftercare—all had to be oriented toward abstinence. Alternative approaches such as methadone maintenance programs were either illegal or were considered counterproductive. The belief that guided policy was that coercion and suffering help produce the will to live without drugs, once the addict has reached rock bottom. Criminalization was deemed to be pedagogically necessary, an extrinsic motivation for therapy. Yet only 20 percent of drug users ever sought counseling and long-term therapy; less than 6 percent submitted to inpatient treatment, most of them breaking off within the first months.[37]

The threat of HIV infection dramatized the inadequacies of the official drug policy. Yet until the mid-1980s, drug counselors viewed their distribution of needles and syringes as making them the facilitators of addiction, offering freedom from drug use on the one hand while assisting the addiction on the other. Moreover, pharmacists and drug counselors were unsure about the legality of dispensing disposable needles, because some prosecutors claimed that in doing so they would be offering the opportunity for drug use, which was a criminal offense.

In 1983, the Conference of Public Health Ministers took a reformist position on the question of sterile syringes and needles, stating that "the dispensing of one-way needles does not further drug abuse and can be accepted as one of the measures for the control of AIDS." This interpretation of the Drug Control Act was underscored by the federal minister of health Rita Sussmuth, who argued that the "current practice of pharmacies in dispensing one-way needles without prescription does not violate the Drug Control Act, even if the purchaser is a drug addict." Such official pronouncements helped to protect innovative streetworkers from criminal prosecution. Outside Bavaria and its neighbor state Baden-Württemberg pharmacies and drug counselors now make sterile needles available. Drug workers and AIDS-Hilfen have succeeded in establishing a pragmatic approach, including needle vending machines for twenty-four-hour distribution and needle exchange programs.

Even more problematic has been the introduction of methadone programs for heroin addicts. For years, the medical profession resisted the prescription of ersatz opiates. Drug use was considered primarily a social rather than a medical problem, and physicians favored therapeutic measures. Substitution therapy was regarded as merely prolonging the addiction, delaying or even preventing cure. Methadone treatment was also opposed by most drug counselors because it conflicted with the ideology of freedom from drugs. Physicians who delivered substitution treatment were attacked by their colleagues; they came into conflict with the law and with insurance regulations.

AIDS rekindled the methadone debate. While in 1986 the federal government and most state health ministers still strongly resisted substitution programs for intravenous drug users, this opposition weakened with the spread of AIDS and the rise of HIV prevalence among drug users. In March 1987, the public health ministers of all states except Bavaria suggested that methadone treatment was justifiable in special cases and under strict medical control. In the context of the "National Plan for the War on Drugs," the federal government approved of "minimizing damage" by "medically justified [methadone] treatment in single cases and programs for the exchange of syringes," even as it warned that such measures might prolong drug addiction. Although this proposal reflects the overriding goal of achieving a life without drugs, the "single case" rationale of the federal government also corresponds to the changing attitude of the medical profession. In 1990, the federal Medical Council finally declared the provision of methadone acceptable providing that medical supervision was guaranteed, thus ending this aspect of the religious war.

AIDS has also fostered a reorientation of German drug policy, away from the idea of a drug-free life and toward low threshold offers for long-term drug users. Government now funds "contact shops"—refuges where junkies can spend the night, and talk to streetworkers—as well as shelters that offer basic services such as showers and warm meals. In the shelters, drug addicts can try to reduce the amount of drugs they take and experience short drug-free periods. The purpose of the shelters is to support self-healing and to offer a short-term home.

The limited German public health system's reaction to AIDS provoked a number of private responses. The most important and striking has been the Deutsche AIDS-Hilfe (D.A.H.) and its local AIDS-Hilfe chapters, a network of self-help groups unique in the German public health context.[38] In September 1983, a group of gay men in Berlin founded the D.A.H. to organize help for and self-help in the gay community, as well as to fight against AIDS-related discrimination. Two years later, D.A.H. was institutionalized as the parent organization of thirty-two local AIDS-Hilfe chapters in West German cities. Today there are almost one hundred independent local counseling and information centers, coordinated by the D.A.H. and financially supported by the federal government.

The D.A.H. and the local AIDS-Hilfen took over tasks that might ordinarily have been performed by the public health system. But the autonomy of the AIDS-Hilfen, and their institutional distance from the government have been advantageous. These groups speak the language of those they want to reach and serve members of traditionally stigmatized groups who have little confidence in public health authorities. They offer anonymous counseling, free of charge. Yet the AIDS-Hilfe network must depend primarily on government support, which potentially threatens its independence. Conservative politicians have intermittently tried to influence the pro-gay policy of the D.A.H. and to sanitize its AIDS education materials.

Since the D.A.H. and most of the local AIDS-Hilfen were founded by gay activists, they have been widely regarded as a gay interest lobby. However, from the beginning the AIDS-Hilfen tried to reach out to other groups. Since 1987, they have focused particularly on drug users, prison inmates, and prostitutes. Officials in about ninety prisons have called in local AIDS-Hilfen to inform prisoners about safer sex and safer drug use.

More than four thousand people, most of them volunteers, are engaged in the AIDS-Hilfen. The informal division of labor means gay men and lesbians do most of the counseling, care, and educational work with the gay community, while heterosexual men have been more concerned with drug users. Still, there is criticism that the gay-dominated AIDS-Hilfen have effectively colonized junkies, prostitutes, and prisoners, speaking for them instead of enabling them to be their own advocates. AIDS-Hilfen are also contacted by heterosexual men and women, particularly outside the metropolitan areas, where volunteers must deal with "AIDS-phobics."

The D.A.H. information campaigns emphasize avoiding hysteria and AIDS phobia. They also oppose the criminalization of virus carriers. The AIDS-Hilfen assume that it is a social reality that some people are gay or promiscuous, use illegal drugs, or work as prostitutes. This perspective has provoked the charge that the D.A.H. does not take AIDS seriously enough. The quite pragmatic maxim "We have to live with AIDS" has been misinterpreted by some as the endorsement of libertinism and unsafe sex.

Charges made by some within the gay community that the D.A.H. is only playing at Russian roulette express the despair of a group for whom AIDS is a collective tragedy. D.A.H. confronts the difficult task of a semiofficial self-help network that can offer neither a magic bullet nor solutions to the practical, everyday conflicts in the lives of gay men during the era of AIDS. The tensions within the gay community are reflected in varing approaches adopted by different AIDS-Hilfen. The election in 1991 of four HIV-positive members to the board of the D.A.H. represented an effort to respond to accusations that the D.A.H. is unable really to understand the plight of persons with HIV. Such conflicts might have produced organizational paralysis, but the dearth of a practical alternative to the D.A.H. and the effectiveness of its efforts have kept the organization running.

Criticism aimed at the AIDS-Hilfen by the powers that be is potentially even more threatening. The work of the AIDS-Hilfen is under constant scrutiny from AIDS specialists in the federal Ministry of Health and from the homophobic, drug-phobic, and minority-phobic politicians in the ranks of the conservative Christian Democrats. Not surprisingly, some were appalled by the D.A.H.'s championing of needle exchange; they remain astonished by its explicit AIDS prevention posters and by the blunt language of its educational comics. But since the Bonn government has committed itself to this unique division of labor—directing its own efforts at the heterosexual community and leaving the rest of the population to the D.A.H.—such opposition is unlikely to disrupt the work of the AIDS-Hilfen.

The crash program of the federal government, designed and implemented in 1987, was set to run for four years at which time there was to be an evaluation. To prepare such a review and to advise the federal government on AIDS policy, two commissions were instituted: the National AIDS Council (Nationaler AIDS Beirat, or NAB) a permanent committee to advise the federal Ministry of Health and comment publicly on current AIDS issues, and the AIDS Enquete Commission of the Federal Parliament, which submitted its final report in 1990.[39]

The composition of each commission reveals a subtle maximalist-minimalist compromise, reflecting the ongoing Bonn–Bavaria controversy. The federal minister of health originally appointed thirty members to the NAB, most of them medical experts, thus expressing the ministry's approach that AIDS was essentially a medical concern. Most of the experts supported the pragmatic program of Health Minister Heiner Geissler and his successor, Rita Suessmuth. From its inception, the NAB issued statements that endorsed the federal AIDS policy, pointing to the grave consequences of discrimination and criticizing mass screening programs. The NAB was instrumental in legitimizing, if not guiding, federal AIDS policy through the controversies of 1987 and 1988.

The Bavarian Christian Social Union (CSU) was underrepresented on the AIDS Council. When it came to appointing the experts for the Enquete Commission, however, the CSU was granted the right to bring in staunch supporters of the Bavarian program. Yet the moderate Christian Democratic chairperson, and the Social Democratic and Green party members, as well as the experts appointed by both parties limited the impact of the contain-and-control faction. The Enquete Commission's reports provided strong, well-documented support for a cooperation-driven approach to AIDS prevention.

AIDS and the Law

Initially, no one raised an eyebrow when Berlin officials approved the plan of the AIDS-Hilfe to organize group swimming hours for persons with AIDS and HIV infection at the municipal pool. Then the staff of the pool, which had long known about this plan, suddenly had second thoughts and threatened to strike—suddenly it was said that permission had been granted rashly, by an official with no competence in such matters. The district sports councillor then put forward regulations for pools that excluded anyone with a contagious disease from public swimming facilities. The "worries and fears of the personnel" were not to be ignored, he asserted. The AIDS-Hilfe announced a protest swim-in; joining the protest was the wife of Berlin's mayor, a voluntary aide in the self-help organization.[40] Eventually, Berlin's office of the City Councillor for Education and Sports declared that the prohibition would apply only to those diseases that could be transmitted in swimming pools. The General Medical Council of Berlin issued a statement that AIDS could be transmitted only through sexual intercourse or needle sharing, not in swimming pools.

A major city announced that children with AIDS would be accepted in all municipal nursery schools. This policy had been developed in consultation with experts and educators. The medical experts had decided against the social isolation of the children concerned and in favor of their being admitted to regular kindergartens. Nevertheless, those responsible for the program were said to be prepared for protests from the parents.[41]

These incidents did not happen in the first years of AIDS. They were recorded in 1990, after more than five years of information campaigns by the BZgA, the D.A.H. and other organizations attempting to educate the population about AIDS prevention. Other instances of discrimination have been reported. In an upper-class suburb of Düsseldorf, residents successfully resisted the plan of an AIDS self-help group to rent a house for HIV-positive mothers with their children. Prison inmates have been reported to oppose sharing television viewing hours with "virus carriers." In order to avoid contact with HIV-infected inmates, prison officers have asked to be transferred to desk duty. Employees have demanded that an HIV-infected coworker be fired, threatening to quit if their demands were not met. Physicians and dentists have refused to treat persons suspected of having AIDS, and landlords have sought to evict persons with AIDS from their apartments.[42] Despite the widespread knowledge that HIV is not easily transmitted, AIDS has evoked panic. When it comes to personal contacts in everyday life, the spirit of solidarity extolled in public statements often vanishes behind irrational fears of contagion. Discriminatory practices stand in sharp contrast to the opinion polls reporting that an overwhelming majority of Germans would not personally hesitate to care for persons with AIDS.

Although AIDS has enhanced the bonds within the gay community, at times even AIDS activists are unable to confront their families and friends when they themselves have the disease. The stigma that hovers over the human immunodeficiency virus drives some to pretend that they are affected with a different disease, such as leukemia or pneumonia.

Against this backdrop of stigma and discrimination, a strong political drive toward antidiscrimination legislation might have been expected: the National AIDS Council called for measures against discrimination, and gay groups in the Green party made efforts in that direction.[43] Yet no formal proposal has been put forward, perhaps because instances of discrimination have not led to massive exclusions from the workplace. Nor has there been a consensus about how to proceed among the organizations defending the rights of persons with AIDS. Some fear that a specific law protecting those with AIDS would single out such individuals in a way that would be ultimately disadvantageous. There is also no tradition of across-the-board antidiscrimination legislation in Germany. With the exception of disabled persons and women, no other group has ever been granted the legal status of deserving special protection against discrimination. This may have to do with political resistance against governmental intrusions in spheres still considered private and so best regulated by voluntary contractual relations. Finally, a widespread belief exists that adequate protections are already available, reflected in the constitutional principle of equality and in isolated specific provisions that rule out discrimination.

In the absence of an antidiscrimination law, the right to "informational self-determination," which entitles every individual to control the disclosure and use of data about his or her life, has taken on great significance in protecting individuals. Invented by legal scholars and officially recognized by the Federal Constitutional Court in 1983, this right has since been established as a special instance of the constitutional right to privacy laid down in articles 1 and 2 of the Basic Law.[44]

Against the background of modern information technology, the Federal Constitutional Court stated:

> One who does not know what information about him is known in certain areas of his social environment, and therefore has no way of accurately estimating the knowledge of his potential partners of communication, may be restricted in his freedom to plan or decide on the basis of self-determination. A social order and a corresponding legal system, in which citizens no longer know who knows what about them, when, and on which occasion, cannot be reconciled with the right to self-determination. One who is unsure whether deviant behavior is being controlled at every moment and permanently stored, will attempt not to attract attention by such behavior.[45]

Therefore, only a "compelling public interest" can outweigh the right to informational privacy.

In the context of the AIDS debates, the right to informational privacy strengthened the minimalist position. It helped to defeat proposals for mandatory testing and reporting and secret AIDS testing in hospitals. Maximalists were obliged to make a strong argument for the epidemiological gains and preventive impact of mandatory measures that entailed collecting personal data. But the epidemiological advantage of screening, mandatory reporting, and mandatory testing seemed questionable from the very beginning; outside Bavaria, it was rarely regarded as a compelling or fundamental public interest. Even the parliamentary commission of the Bavarian Landtag, in its final report on AIDS and the Bavarian AIDS strategy, concluded that some of the mandatory measures implemented in Bavaria, in particular the screening of prostitutes, had fostered a false and dangerous sense of security among customers.[46]

The right to informational privacy further helped to clarify the terms of hospital patients' informed consent. Patients had been presented with forms that contained broad, vague consent clauses: "Herewith the undersigned consents to all medical examinations deemed necessary by the attending physician"; "I am aware that blood samples may be taken and examined for diagnostic purposes and that such an examination also includes the AIDS test." The influential state commissioner for data protection in Hessen, Spiros Simitis, who was recently appointed a member of the National AIDS Council, publicized the illegal practices of hospitals and specified that after-the-fact consent, global consent on standard forms, and cumulative declarations of consent all violated a patient's freedom to determine which medical examinations to undergo. He convinced the state government to issue guidelines for HIV-antibody testing that call for counseling before and after a test, and developed effective consent forms.[47] The other states of Germany—with the exception of Bavaria— are following Hessen's example.

Because of the German tradition of turning social and political problems into legal problems, courts naturally take center stage. AIDS has been no exception, as all branches of the judiciary have made AIDS-related decisions.[48]

Early in the history of AIDS in Germany, the Federal Constitutional Court had to take a stand in the minimalism versus maximalism controversy. A hemophiliac who had been infected by contaminated blood products claimed a right to risk-free sexuality and criticized what he termed legislative nonfeasance. He asked the court to intervene and grant a temporary injunction. The court dismissed the motion. While expressing sympathy with the fate of the seropositive applicant, the court insisted that the federal government had neither remained inactive nor acted ineffectively.

Following its decisions on legislative nonfeasance and the protection of public health, the court deferred to the judgment of the federal government concerning the most effective strategy of AIDS prevention. More importantly, the court implicitly rejected the maximalist thesis that AIDS must be treated like other sexually transmitted diseases. In striking down the argument for public health symmetry—the claim that because AIDS is a communicable disease, it must come under the Epidemics Control Act or the Venereal Disease Control Act—the court allowed for a distinctive treatment of HIV infection and AIDS.

With the constitutional complaint the applicant calls for legislative measures for the control of AIDS that treat this disease like the diseases listed in the Venereal Disease Control Act, thus reducing the risk of infection and allowing for sexual contacts free of fear without special precautionary measures. The constitutional complaint was not accepted in default of sufficient chances of success.[49]

Unlike the Constitutional Court, lower courts were never asked to judge prevention policy generally, although some felt compelled to cast their vote in the minimalism versus maximalism controversy. The criminal court in Nuremberg gained public attention through its attempt to spell out and juridify the difference between unsafe, safe, and safer sex in a sensational 1987 case. A gay American soldier had active anal intercourse with several partners whose identities were unknown to him at the time, despite knowing about his AIDS infection and despite warnings from his doctor about the risks of unsafe sex. The defendant once had anal intercourse without a condom, which he interrupted to buy a condom and then continued. On another occasion he had oral intercourse, which he ended before ejaculating. Later he tried to have unprotected anal intercourse; then he continued the intercourse with a condom. At the time of the trial, none of the sex partners who testified were HIV-positive. The Nuremberg police searched gay venues quite thoroughly to identify the sex partners, so that they would appear as witnesses.

In a lengthy decision, the Nuremberg court, rejecting the argument that anonymous sex partners act at their own risk and generally do not deserve the protection of the penal law, sentenced the defendant to two years in prison for attempted dangerous physical injury.[50] On appeal, the Federal Criminal Court upheld the conviction but required the regional court to reduce its sentence.[51]

These rulings seem, at first glance, to follow the standard doctrines regarding physical injury. The transmission of infection is treated as the infliction of physical injury; the concept of wrongful intent is held to apply to instances where those with HIV infection have unprotected intercourse. Moreover, common sense seems to suggest that the partner who knows that he or she is infected has superior knowledge, and, according to Federal Criminal Court precedents, such knowledge precludes the claim that the person exposed has acted at his or her own risk.

However, closer scrutiny shows that the two courts had to deny the complex nature of sexual behavior, and then had to ignore the extent to which individuals are aware of the risks of unprotected sex, and, finally, had to stretch extant legal doctrine. It is unrealistic to assume that a virus carrier who wants to have sex necessarily intends to inflict physical injury by infecting the other person. More likely, such individuals hope that nothing serious will happen. Such actions may amount to negligence, but since attempted negligent physical injury is not punishable, virus carriers who cannot be proven to have actually infected their sex partners would go free. To avoid this result and to fill a "punishment gap," most of the roughly two dozen criminal courts that have had to deal with sexual intercourse by a person with HIV infection have interpreted the law on attempted physical injury as "reckless endangerment" or have construed gross negligence as amounting to intentional infliction of harm.

The Nuremberg decision met with a favorable response by the maximalists and protests by a coalition of minimalists, including student groups, liberal criminal law scholars, the D.A.H., and the liberal press.

In contrast to this cause célèbre in Nuremberg, a Hamburg criminal court, which convicted a person with AIDS of dangerous physical injury and sentenced him to two years in prison, proceeded with almost no public notice.[52] The defendant had been involved in a long-standing relationship with a woman. Fearful of losing her, he never told her that he was HIV-positive but suggested that he had leukemia; later, when he fell seriously ill and had symptoms incompatible with leukemia, he spoke of a noncontagious tuberculosis. When the state of his health dramatically deteriorated, the woman finally consulted his physician, who suggested that she take an HIV-antibody test; the result was positive. The court found that he must have infected her during the many times they had had intercourse after he had already known about his infection and the risks of unprotected sex.

In an unusual closing statement, the judge suggested that punishment might be inappropriate.

> The Court does not want its decision to be misunderstood as a remedy for AIDS. It seems as if society seeks refuge against this uncanny, incurable disease in criminal law. Ideas beginning with mandatory testing of the members of risk groups of homosexuals, prostitutes, and intravenous drug users and leading to their isolation obviously tend in that direction. In this context it is striking that society is ready to accept air pollution, dying forests, the poisoning of the soil and drinking water without criminal action and prosecution, whereas human sexuality in case of AIDS is criminally prosecuted. The court hopes . . . that the public does not assume criminal prosecution of AIDS-infected persons to provide even a halfway effective protection against the perfidy of the HIV infection. This can only happen by personal responsibility—a responsibility the defendant was too weak to assume. Therefore it is questionable whether this decision will be suited to serve the goal of enhancing personal responsibility.[53]

Courts in other legal fields received even less attention, although their decisions have more directly influenced AIDS prevention and discriminatory behavior. This is particularly true for the administrative law courts, which are responsible for overseeing public safety and public health.

Their decisions—concerning secret testing and the mandatory testing of asylum seekers, prostitutes, and intravenous drug users; the deportation of HIV-infected foreigners; and the regulation of bathhouses—are full of contradictions. The Munich Administrative Court denied a public health office the right to subject a former junkie to an HIV-antibody test, since the appellant had tested negative three years before, had abstained from intravenous drug use, and had been in therapy ever since. Furthermore, the court believed his assertion that he behaved "AIDS-consciously." On appeal, the higher administrative court overturned this decision, arguing that there was still some slight danger of infection and that mandatory measures specified by the Epidemics Control Act do not depend on the proof of concrete or imminent danger. The decision rested on the questionable maximalist assumption that only those who know, to a certainty, whether or not they are virus carriers will act responsibly.[54]

Another administrative law court had no qualms approving the deportation to the Philippines of the HIV-infected widow of a German national who had died of AIDS, despite the fact that for several years she had taken care of him during his sickness. The court found that the aliens' registration office had acted within its discretion when assuming that "important public health concerns of the Federal Republic of Germany" justified the termination of the residence permit of an HIV-infected foreigner. On appeal, the higher administrative court reversed the decision, criticizing the lower court for not having acknowledged that the woman had been infected by her husband.[55]

Despite all these rulings, legal discourse has had little real impact on the development of German AIDS policy. Government officials claim that both the Nuremberg decision and another ruling prohibiting the distribution of syringes and needles created insecurity in the federal Ministry of Health. Yet even these decisions ultimately did not change AIDS policy. The Nuremberg court, entangling itself in the conceptual thicket of safe, safer, and unsafe sex and the corresponding criminal law doctrines, ultimately failed to delegitimize the minimalist approach. The second decision only led to a revision of the Narcotics Act that made it clear that the distribution of syringes and needles did not represent an inducement to drug abuse.

CONCLUSION: APOCALYPSE CANCELED?

Is it mass murder that the gays are driving toward? For two years the scene has been in the mood for partying; Safer Sex is out. They call it responsibility and officially propagate the right to unsafe sex: Everybody has the right to AIDS. They reject the group norms of Safer Sex and talk about spontaneous sex; the AIDS wards in hospitals are socially accepted. They gossip and sneak but nothing happens in the open and publicly. With the talk of freedom, responsibility, and self-determination more and more are driven to their death, above all because the necessary information is missing. Brochures and elegant Safer Sex posters are of little help. Even under a Safer Sex poster one can fuck quite comfortably.[56]

This diatribe was published in the spring of 1990. While the publisher, *Der Spiegel*, is well-known for its hostility toward the gay community, the name of the author surprised the readers: filmmaker Rosa von Praunheim is well-known for his involvement in the emancipatory gay movement. When defending his manifesto against an outraged gay community, von Praunheim escalated the controversy by stating that Germany needed "many Gauweilers," thus invoking the name of the AIDS hardliner and Bavarian secretary of the interior.

Within a month, and in stark contrast to this wild battle cry, *Die Zeit*, a weekly magazine, carried the headline "AIDS—The Apocalypse Cancelled."[57] Could the AIDS situation have changed so dramatically within four weeks? Who is right, the insider or the experts? The experts from the federal health office talk of a turning point in the epidemiological development of the HIV infection, and of microepidemics limited to certain groups. The insider and gay activist fears that homosexuals will die out unless they overthrow the "prevention bureaucrats" of the AIDS-Hilfen.

Both statements are symptoms that AIDS, unless dramatized, no longer seems to touch the public mind.

In the 1990s, discourse on AIDS has entered a new phase. There is little disagreement about the overall success of federal policy. The report of the Enquete Commission documents a striking consensus, reaching from Christian Democrats to the Greens, that the AIDS policy of the federal government has achieved its purposes.[58] From the Christian Democrats to the Greens, the policy has won at least lukewarm support. The health ministry sees no need to change the direction of its prevention efforts. High-ranking ministry officials express satisfaction that they did not give in to pressures from Bavaria and the tabloids. They welcome the division of labor between the ministry, which addresses the heterosexual population, and groups such as the AIDS-Hilfen, which address those most at risk, in their own language, and at their own meeting places. The ministry has felt vindicated by the epidemiological developments, although high ranking officials are troubled that some have sought to give the "all-clear" signal on AIDS. Recent cuts in the budget of the D.A.H. suggest that the AIDS experts in the Ministry of Health find it more and more difficult to endorse the epidemic's privileged position on the governmental agenda.[59]

While the D.A.H. criticizes the ministry's focus on promiscuity and drug abuse as vectors of the spread of HIV infection, and complains that it receives insufficient resources, the organization also stresses the advantages of the division of labor. The ministry has been credited for interfering very little with the work of the AIDS-Hilfen, well aware that it could not possibly do their job.

It is unlikely that the general course of German AIDS policy will be any different for the Eastern states, which joined the Federal Republic in 1990. HIV prevalence there was extremely low, so that AIDS had not been a significant problem. Pro-Bavarian policy leanings of high-ranking East German public health officials won't prevail: these views are not likely to rock the Federal AIDS policy boat, which after all survived the Bavarian crusade. Yet the gay community and drug users in what was East Germany are being made aware of the mixed blessing of sexual liberation.[60] Information campaigns, ironically echoing the old Communist regime's warnings about AIDS, drugs, and crime in the decadent West, have confronted the newcomers with the collective drama of AIDS.

Notes

1. Strictly speaking, West Germany. The following analysis will only briefly deal with the situation in East Germany, which before the unification in 1990 did not have an "AIDS problem" that was anywhere near as widespread as that in the West.

2. This was the period when the literary production on AIDS/HIV boomed. R. Rosenbrock opened and influenced the further course of the debate on prevention with his book *AIDS kann schneller besiegt werden* (AIDS Can be Defeated Faster) (Hamburg: VSA-Verlag, 1986). In 1985, two publications reflected the development of the maximalist/minimalist confrontation: F. Ruehmann, *AIDS—Wie eine Krankheit gemacht wird* (AIDS—How a Disease Is Being Made) (Frankfurt am Main: Campus Verlag 1985) and H. Halter, ed., *Todesseuche AIDS* (Lethal Epidemic AIDS) (Reinbek: Rowohlt Verlag, 1985). A year later, two books reacted against the symptoms of panic and gay discrimination: S. Dunde, ed., *AIDS—Was eine Krankheit veraendert* (AIDS—Changes Produced by a Disease) (Frankfurt am Main: S. Fischer Verlag, 1986) and M. Frings, ed., *Dimensionen einer Krankheit* (Dimensions of a Disease) (Reinbek: Rowohlt Verlag, 1986). A year later Rita Suessmuth, then federal minister of public health, published her response to the Bavarian call for strict measures: *AIDS—Wege aus der Angst* (AIDS—Ways out of the Fear) (Hamburg: Hoffman & Campe Verlag, 1987). For a comprehensive and fair (if somewhat minimalistically biased) overview of the prevention debates see R. Rosenbrock and A. Salmen, eds., *AIDS-Praevention* (AIDS Prevention) (Berlin: Ed. Sigma Bohn, 1990).

3. The official documents of the Federal AIDS policy and of the Federal–Bavarian controversy are published in G. Frankenberg, *AIDS-Bekaempfung im Rechtsstaat—Aufklaerung Zwang Praevention* (AIDS-Control and the Rule of Law—Education Coercion Prevention) (Baden-Baden: Nomos Verlag, 1988).

4. The legal literature, after a hesitant start, peaked from 1987 until 1989,

and has been on the decline ever since: W. Eberbach, *Rechtsprobleme der HTLV-III-Infection (AIDS)* (Legal Problems of HTLV-III Infection (AIDS)) (Berlin/Heidelberg/New York/Tokyo: Springer Verlag, 1986); G. Frankenberg, *AIDS-Bekaempfung*, note 2; B. Schuenemann and G. Pfeiffer, eds., *Die Rechtsprobleme von AIDS* (The Legal Problems of AIDS) (Baden-Baden: Nomos Verlag, 1988); J. Wolf/S. Mehlem/S. Reiss, *Rechtsratgeber AIDS: Konfliktfaelle im Alltag* (Legal Guide AIDS: Everyday Conflicts) (Reinbek: Rowohlt Verlag, 1988); C. Prittwitz, ed., *AIDS, Recht und Gesundheitspolitik* (AIDS, the Law, and Public Health Policy) (Berlin: Ed. Sigma Bohn, 1990).

5. Cf. Deutscher Bundestag, ed., *Zwischenbericht der Enquete-Kommission des Deutschen Bundestages "Gefahren von AIDS und wirksame Wege zu ihrer Eindaemmung, AIDS: Fakten und Konsequenzen"* (Interim Report of the AIDS Enquete Commission of the Federal Diet) (Bonn: Deutscher Bundestag, 1988—BT-Drucks.11/2495 v. 16.06.1988), and *Endbericht der Enquete-Kommission* (Final Report of the Enquete Commission) (Bonn: Deutscher Bundestag, 1990). Both reports give a very detailed and thorough account of the legal and public health problems of AIDS prevention.

6. Claudia Gersch, Wolfgang Heckmann, Beate Leopold, and Yanne Seyrer, *Drogenabhängage Prostituierte und ihre Freier* (Drug-using Prostitutes and Their Customers) (Sozialpädagogisches Institut, 1989); and Intersofia, ed., *Studie zum Risikoverhalten von Freiern: Abschlußbericht* (Study about the Risk Behavior of Customers: Final Report) (unpublished manuscript) (Berlin: Gesellschaft für Interdisziplinäre Forschung, 1990).

7. Meinrad Koch, "Die Epidemiologie von AIDS," in *Die HIV-Erkrankung: Medizinische und psychosoziale Aspekte zu Beginn der 90er Jahr* (The HIV Disease: Medical and Psychosocial Aspects at the Beginning of the 1990s) (Munich: Ecomed, 1991).

8. A. Salmen and A. Eckert, *20 Jahre bundesdeutsche Schulenbewegung 1969–1989* (Muenchen: BHV-Materialien, 1989); M. Dannecker, *Der Homosexuelle und die Homosexualitaet* (Frankfurt am Main, 1986); the empirical studies of M. Bochow and M. Dannecker in Rosenbrock and Salmen, *AIDS-Praevention.* Salmen and Eckert report that there were thirty-one gay groups in 1972, thirty-five in 1973, and forty-five in 1974.

9. In 1965 over six thousand violations of sec. 175 of the Penal Code were officially registered.

10. H. Bilitewski and S. Klee, "AIDS. Was haben Prostituierte damit zu tun?" *Infodienst der Gesundheitslaeden* 28 (1988), 6–12; Enquete Commission, Final Report, 469ff.

11. Cf. Interim Report of the Enquete Commission, 304ff.; A. Kreuzer, "Besonderheiten von AIDS und Drogenabhaengigkeit," in Prittwitz, *AIDS, Recht und Gesundheitspolitik* 171ff.

12. Very few memorable cases concerning the Epidemics Control Act had to be decided by the Federal Administrative Court. None of the few that reached the court on appeal dealt with diseases transmitted from person to person; cf. *Decisions of the Federal Administrative Court* (Bundesverwaltungsgericht, BVerwGE 7: 257; 12: 87; 28: 233; 39: 190).

13. For a good (AIDS-related) introduction to the German system of social security see Enquete Commission, Final Report, part C, ch. 6. See also M. Dieck, "Long-term Care for the Elderly in the Federal Republic of Germany," in T. Schwab, ed., *Caring for an Aging World* (New York: McGraw-Hill, 1989).

14. *Bild-Zeitung* (December 12, 1981).

15. *Der Stern* (April 15, 1982).

16. *Quick* 29 (1983).

17. *Volksblatt Berlin* (June 5, 1983).

18. See F. Ruehmann, *AIDS—Eine Krankheit und ihre Folge* (AIDS—A Disease and Its Consequences) (Frankfurt/New York: Campus-Verlag, 1985), ch. 2.

19. "The Scare From Abroad," *Der Spiegel* 22 (1982), "An Epidemic which is Only Beginning," *Der Spiegel* 23 (1983).

20. "Die Before Dawn," *Der Spiegel* 39 (1985).

21. *Der Spiegel* 23 (1983).

22. "Face of the Enemy" and "Suicide of the Hosts," *Der Spiegel* 32 (1984); "The Bomb has been Dropped," 45 (1984); "AIDS, An Invisible Network in the Underground," 2 (1988); "AIDS: Took the Hurdle to the Heteros," 8 (1988); "Safer Sex is not Safe," 22 (1987) "The Virus Only has to Learn to Fly," 47 (1987).

23. "AIDS: Sex-Probition for Tens of Thousands?" *Der Spiegel* 3 (1987).

24. FORSA, *AIDS im oeffentlichen Bewusstsein der Bundesrepublik—Eine Wiederholungsbefragung im Auftrag der Bundeszentrale fuer gesundheitliche Aufklaerung* (Bonn: November 14, 1988 and February 27, 1990); see also *Der Spiegel* 36 (1987).

25. *Der Spiegel* 39 (1987).

26. See G. Frankenberg, "Innere Sicherheit in Zeiten der Infektion," in *Kritische Vierteljahresschrift fuer Gesetzgebung und Rechtswissenschaft*, 344 (1988).

27. EKD (Evangelische Kirche Deutschland [Protestant Church of Germany]), *AIDS—Orientierung und Wege in der Gefahr* (Hannover: EKD, 1988).

28. *Ibid.*, 6.

29. See Pressedienst der Deutschen Bischofskonferenz, Dokumentation 2/87, March 13, 1987; Presseamt des Erzbistums Cologne, AIDS: Zeitfragen 41/1987. For a somewhat more liberal view: *AIDS Orientierungshilfen fuer das Bistum Limburg* (Limburg: 1989).

30. Condoms are normally disqualified as "ethically not allowed," technically labeled "not safe," and said to expose "innocent children [to] the path to vice." In some official statements they were even compared to gasmasks.

31. Conference of the German Catholic Bishops. (March 13, 1988).

32. See Frankenberg, *AIDS-Bekaempfung*, 163ff.

33. P. Gauweiler, "Zur Notwendigkeit eines geschlossenen Gesamtkonzepts staatlicher Massnahmen zur Bekaempfung der Weltseuche AIDS," in Schuenemann and Pfeiffer, *Die Rechtsprobleme*, 37ff.

34. Documented in Frankenberg, *AIDS-Bekaempfung*, 179ff.

35. VG Munich, AIFO 1986, 39; Lippstreu, AIFO 1987, 469ff.

36. See FORSA opinion polls, in *Der Stern*, Apr. 15, 1982.

37. See Rosenbrock, *AIDS Kann schneller beseigt werden* and Kreuzer, "Besonderheiten."

38. Three foundations—Deutsche Stiftung "positiv leben," Nationale AIDS-Stiftung, and the Bayerische AIDS-Stiftung (not connected with the Bavarian crusade)—deserve credit for supporting AIDS research and providing nonbureaucratic help in single cases.

39. See Bundesministerium fuer Jugend, Familie, Frauen und Gesundheit, ed., *Voten des Nationalen AIDS-Beirats (NAB)* (Bonn, 1987–88); Enquete Commission, Interim and Final Reports.

40. *Frankfurter Rundschau* (June 11, 1990).

41. *Frankfurter Rundschau* (May 7, 1990).

42. For more examples, see Frankenberg, "Innere Sicherheit in Zeiten der Infektion?"

43. "Entwurf eines Antidiskriminierungsgesetzes," *Die Gruenen* (Bonn: 1987).

44. Decisions of the Federal Constitutional Court (BVerfGE) 65: 1ff.

45. Ibid., 43.

46. Bayer, Landtag, Drucksache 11/134337 (October 23, 1989).

47. See S. Simitis, "AIDS, Massnahmen gegen AIDS und Datenschutz" in Prittwitz, *AIDS, Recht und Gesundheitspolitik*, 63.

48. For summaries and critiques see the primarily pro-minimalism contributions in Prittwitz, *AIDS, Recht und Gesundheitspolitik* and the somewhat maximalist articles in Schuenenmann and Pfeiffer, *Rechtsprobleme*.

49. Federal Constitutional Court, documented in Frankenberg, *AIDS-Beckaempfung*, 169.

50. LG Nuremberg, Neue Jurist. Wochenschrift 2311 (1988).

51. NGHSt, Neue Jurist. Wochenschrift 781 (1989). The Landgericht Nuremberg complied and reduced the sentence to one year.

52. LG Hamburg, AIFO 415 (1989).

53. *Ibid.*

54. VG Muenchen, Strafverteidiger 165 (1988) and VGH Muenchen, AIFO 300 (1988); see also VG Muenchen, AIFO 695 (1988) and VGH Muenchen, Neue Jurist. Wochenschrift 2318 (1988).

55. VGH Mannheim, AIFO (1987).

56. Rosa von Praunheim, in *Der Spiegel* 20 (1990).

57. *Die Zeit*, 25 (1990).

58. See Enquete Commission, Final Report.

59. See *Frankfurter Rundschau* (April 18, 1991).

60. In the gay venues of West Berlin, East Berliners were referred to as "fresh meat" in the months that followed the tearing down of the Berlin Wall.

Chapter 4

Australia: Participation and
Innovation in a Federal System

John Ballard

AIDS was planted firmly on Australia's public policy agenda earlier than elsewhere. Most other industrialized democracies paid limited attention until late 1986, when recognition of the potential for an epidemic spread by heterosexual transmission raised awareness of risk beyond peripheral minorities. Events in Australia required an earlier and more urgent response.

Late in 1984, just two weeks before a national election, the minister for health in Queensland, a state led by the most outspoken conservative opponents of the federal Labour government, announced that three babies had died of AIDS-related diseases after receiving HIV-contaminated blood from a gay donor. Within twenty-four hours, the Queensland Parliament passed legislation imposing criminal sanctions for false declarations by blood donors. Prime Minister Bob Hawke appealed for calm in the face of media hysteria. The leader of the National party in the federal opposition declared that: "If it wasn't for the promotion of homosexuality as a norm by Labour, I am quite confident that the deaths of these three poor babies would not have occurred."[1]

The next day federal Minister for Health Neal Blewett announced a program of urgent initiatives, calling an emergency meeting of state health ministers and pledging substantial federal funds for the production and supply of test kits as soon as they became available. The ministers agreed to coordinate national action on AIDS, adopting a uniform policy banning blood donations by members of high-risk groups and a campaign to attract women donors. A medical working party was reconstituted as the National AIDS Task Force, while a National Advisory Committee on AIDS (NACAIDS), with representatives from government, the medical profession, and community organizations, was established to provide public education.

Apart from political imperatives, the immediate concern in these initiatives was to protect the blood supply and restore public confidence in the transfusion services. The availability of federal funds and federal control of access to American viral-antibody tests encouraged the states to collaborate on matters that lay within their constitutional power over health; but it was also clear that AIDS was seen as political poison, and the states were delighted to leave the problem to Blewett. Over the next few months there was a flurry of organizational activity. The Task Force and NACAIDS made recommendations to health ministers, and Blewett obtained Cabinet agreement to spend up to $4.2 million on AIDS, with the provision that states commit themselves to share costs. (All dollars in this chapter are given in 1990 U.S. dollars.) The AIDS action committees, which had been established in the gay communities in major cities, were reorganized as AIDS councils and were provided with government funding for education and support on the grounds that knowledge of gay culture and practices was essential for realistic and effective programs. While the government of New South Wales (NSW) established a special AIDS clinic in Sydney, the epicenter of infection, the Victoria Department of Health reversed its previous refusal to have any contact with the gay community, enlisting two AIDS council officials as health educators and providing resources for a gay men's community health center.

In January 1985, Blewett and senior officials visited San Francisco, Atlanta, Washington, New York, and London to observe AIDS programs at first hand. During the visit they became aware of the scope of the problem confronting Australia and the need for continued political leadership and coordination of federal and state responses. In Washington they secured agreement for Australia to participate in evaluating antibody testing kits, and Australia's were the only foreign results incorporated into data presented to the U.S. Food and Drug Administration. The Australian results were also used to fast-track regulatory approval in Australia, and by mid-April donations in all states were being screened. At the same time, HIV tests became freely available through designated public hospitals. This involved an extraordinary research and logistic effort, which put Australia several months ahead of other countries in virtually eliminating the risk of further spread of infection through blood transfusion; not a single instance of transmission from transfusion after April 1985 has been identified.

The initiatives and perceptions of this period shaped the Australian response to HIV. Eventually they yielded a complex set of consultative and funding arrangements and ensured community participation in HIV policy-making and programs. This thrust was, however, neither inevitable nor determined by chance. It developed from the institutional culture of health policy in Australia, the political thrust of the Hawke government on health, the state of gay communities in Australia's major cities, and, not least, the personalities involved.

AIDS in Context: Federalism, Interest Groups, and the Public Health System

Under the Australian constitution, adopted when the colonies became a federation and dominion in 1901, responsibility for health remains with the states, but a 1946 referendum extended the Commonwealth's powers to include provision of sickness and hospital benefits and medical services. Since then, the federal government's involvement in health services has been greatly increased through legislation and the allocation of federal funds to states and the private sector. This has provoked disputes between the Commonwealth and the medical profession, state health authorities, and private health insurance and hospital organizations.

The most heavily contested area of health politics since the early 1970s has been health insurance. Australia has long made basic health expense coverage widely available. In the 1970s, a Labour government established national health insurance over strong opposition from a medical profession committed to fee-for-service doctor–patient relations; conservative governments whittled away coverage of the scheme until Labour returned to office in 1983. Under Medicare, the program of universal health insurance in operation since 1984, all permanent residents of Australia are covered for medical services and basic short-term hospital care. There are also subsidies for expensive drugs and for nursing home care, as well as home and community care for the frail aged and chronically disabled.

Other major areas of dispute at both Commonwealth and state levels have concerned the provision of public and private hospital services and the level of medical fees and pharmaceutical benefits, with the medical profession occasionally going on strike to make its point. AIDS arose as a political issue while Labour governments held office in the Commonwealth and in the two most affected states, New South Wales and Victoria, as well as in South Australia and Western Australia. Thus, the Australian government response has been partially shaped by the Australian Labour party's tradition of active intervention in health policy.

Despite the growing presence of the Commonwealth in health matters and a corresponding increase in the staffing of the Commonwealth Department of Health, Australia's six state and two territorial governments retain primary responsibility for providing health services, and substantial variation has developed in the organization, level, and public–private division of responsibility for the provision of services. The 1980s witnessed a tendency to "demedicalize" senior posts within the Commonwealth and state health departments, with generalists replacing administrators with medical qualifications. Some measure of concerted policy and uniform standards is achieved through twice-yearly meetings of the Commonwealth and state ministers of health, and through the National Health and Medical Research Council (NH&MRC) and its many committees, which bring together Commonwealth and state health officials with leaders in medical research. The NH&MRC, which has developed substantial professional autonomy, provides advice across the gamut of health and medical issues and allocates most research funds. This has helped to give the medical research community a higher profile in policy-making on health than that achieved by doctors and public health officials, and that influence is apparent in AIDS policy-making.[2]

Community participation in health policy has also been promoted by Labour governments, initially through the Community Health Program of 1973 and in the beginnings of a women's health movement during the 1970s. Health was not, however, a preoccupation for the gay communities that were to be most affected by AIDS. Although Sydney had a long-established gay community, its public and political mobilization was a product of the 1970s.[3] Following precedents in the United States, the Campaign Against Moral Persecution (CAMP) was organized among gay men and lesbians in Sydney in 1970; it spread rapidly to other cities. CAMP and its radical wing, Gay Liberation, participated in protests and demonstrations against persecution and in favor of law reform through the 1970s. In 1975, the Australian Union of Students adopted a pro-gay policy and sponsored the first annual National Conference of Lesbians and Homosexuals. The first national gay monthly appeared in the same year. Divisions developed between the political gay movement, actively pursuing gay rights, and the larger gay social community, though from 1979 on both supported the Gay Mardi Gras which, by the late 1980s, had become the "largest communal street celebration in any Australian city."[4]

Decriminalization of homosexuality began in South Australia under a reforming Labour government in 1972, and this was followed by the Commonwealth government, legislating for the Australian Capital Territory, and by Victoria in 1980, the only instance of decriminalization by a Liberal government; similar laws were adopted in 1984 in the Northern Territory and New South Wales (NSW), 1989 in Western Australia, and 1990 in Queensland. Only in Queensland was the earlier legislation rigorously enforced during the 1980s. New South Wales and South Australia also adopted antidiscrimination legislation covering sexuality, and the Commonwealth's Human Rights and Equal Opportunity Regulations also cover sexual preference.

With the return of Labour to office under Prime Minister Hawke in March 1983, Neal Blewett, a former Rhodes Scholar and professor of political science, became Commonwealth minister for health with a mandate to reestablish universal health insurance. He was also embroiled in supporting the New South Wales government in a prolonged and bitter dispute over doctors' fees. On both issues he was willing to take controversial initiatives and to confront opposition from sections of the medical profession. He found his department less than fully responsive and began to plan its restructuring, while relying on advice from his ministerial office and consultants. Thus there was, by late 1984, a well-developed predisposition to take initiatives on health matters at the political level.

In his initial briefing from his department, Blewett had been assured that AIDS was a problem confined to a small minority overseas, certainly not arising from a virus. AIDS had received very limited attention in the Australian media, but a few medical specialists and gay activists followed developments through U.S. medical and gay journals and through visits to and from America. Since Sydney, like San Francisco, had a substantial and concentrated gay community, it was anticipated that AIDS would eventually appear there, and in November 1982, a suspected first case was diagnosed, though it was not publicly reported until March 1983.[5]

It was not so much the first cases of AIDS but the issue of blood that stirred public attention. Early in 1983, the problem of protecting the blood supply from infection was being widely discussed in the United States. The Australian National Red Cross Blood Transfusion Committee, a federation of the state services that control all blood donation and supply in Australia, decided to await United States guidelines before acting. However, the director of Sydney's Blood Transfusion Service, after hearing of planned precautions from a visiting American blood bank director, decided to take the initiative in publicly asking male homosexuals to refrain from donating blood.[6] Other blood banks were initially concerned that this would create loss of confidence in the blood supply and among donors.

In June 1983, Professor David Penington, a hematologist who was dean of the Faculty of Medicine at the University of Melbourne and a major power broker in Australian medical science who had been appointed chairman of the National Committee, announced the committee's recommendation that centers not collect blood from "sexually active homosexuals or bisexual men with multiple partners," from intravenous drug users, or from partners of these people.[7]

The announcement of a suspected first case and the Sydney blook bank appeal touched off the first bout of media panic on AIDS in Australia: "U.S. Killer Disease Reaches Australia"; "AIDS—The Killer Disease That's Expected to Sweep Australia"; "The Gay Plague"; together with a spate of stories on AIDS from the United States.[8] Within a short time, some gay men were being refused medical and dental treatment in Sydney. Blewett's first press release on AIDS, in late June, criticized irresponsible media coverage and stated that there were only two confirmed and five suspected cases of AIDS in Australia.

The Sydney blood bank statement, calling for the exclusion of gay men from the donor pool, was the first official labeling of "high-risk groups" in Australia. It served as a catalyst for gay activists in Sydney, who had been politically divided and frustrated in their attempts to persuade NSW politicians to follow other states in decriminalizing homosexuality. When the blood bank director refused to meet with them to discuss alternative means of deterring donors, a small gay group picketed the blood bank for a day. Following the picket, a public meeting of gay groups was held to discuss the threat from AIDS and from further stigmatization. An AIDS Action Committee (AAC) was formed for educational and lobbying purposes, while the Gay Counselling Service was given responsibility for services to people with AIDS. In its first weeks the AAC persuaded the New South Wales minister for health to establish an AIDS Consultative Committee, with membership from the Department of Health, medical specialists, and the AAC. It also organized a forum, attended by 450 people and addressed by Penington and by Sydney medical specialists, at which a prospective study monitoring gay men's health was launched.

AIDS Action Committees were also active by mid-1983 in Melbourne, Perth, and Canberra. Many of the early mobilizers of the AACs had been active in the 1970s in radical gay politics, where they had learned their organizing skills, and a substantial network of contacts was based on the generation which had been active in the Australian Union of Students in the mid-1970s. Differences of view between those who were concerned with political issues and public policy, and the wider nonpolitical gay social community who provided fund-raising, care, and support services, were a feature of early AIDS groups.

Among the issues that initially preoccupied the AAC and the medical Working Party on AIDS, established by the National Health and Medical Research Council in early 1983 and chaired by Penington, was the setting of clinical criteria for defining cases of AIDS. In view of media speculation on the number of AIDS cases, the AACs were concerned to have the restrictive definition of the U.S. Centers for Disease Control (CDC) adopted and to ensure official control over the release of numbers of cases. The Working Party established three case categories relating to AIDS, AIDS-related conditions, and (when such a determination became possible) asymptomatic infection. The first, based on the CDC definition, became compulsorily notifiable without any public protest in all states during 1983 and was reported nationally, while some states later made all categories notifiable.

Despite the development of expertise on AIDS issues within the AACs, Penington saw them as primarily concerned with defending gay interests and believed that their participation in official and medical committees would compromise "scientific" advice to governments. He opposed requests for AAC representation on the Working Party and advised state governments against AAC representation on AIDS medical advisory committees, which were established at the Working Party's behest to prepare facilities for care and infection control. Blewett agreed with this position and offered as an alternative a liaison committee between the AACs and his department officials.

The trauma of the initial reaction to AIDS abated, and for a year, until mid-1984, the media paid it little attention. Government health departments were preoccupied with other issues; in the absence of certainty about its viral origin, AIDS was seen as a low-priority problem confined to a self-contained minority group. The AACs and gay periodicals, together with sexually transmitted disease (STD) clinics, were responsible for almost all public AIDS education during this period. Awareness within the gay community in Sydney, where by October 1984 there were fifty reported cases of AIDS, led to some behavior change and to the formation of gay support organizations to raise funds and provide services for people with AIDS. Meanwhile, the first AIDS cases raised fears among hospital staff and other workers, and a few trade union officials began organizing education programs and drawing up policies for occupational safety and against discrimination.

The lull in public attention ended in late July 1984 with confirmation of the first cases of AIDS contracted through blood transfusion.[9] This raised media speculation about the spread of AIDS beyond stigmatized communities to "the general public." The gay community was blamed for the spread of AIDS to "innocent" victims; and the leader of the Sydney Festival of Light, a fundamentalist religious group, proposed a quarantine of all homosexuals. The Blood Transfusion Services tightened control over donations, replacing earlier notices about risk with a donor declaration denying membership in a group at risk. At the same time, evidence of infection in blood products for people with hemophilia led to a decision to provide heat treatment for Factor VIII, produced by the Commonwealth Serum Laboratories. Serological testing by immunofluorescence assay was already available, and this permitted both the tracing of the first cases of transmission by blood transfusion and the testing of the cohort of one thousand gay men in the Sydney prospective study,[10] with test results creating much greater awareness of risk within Sydney's gay community. While most research in the United States was focused on the end stages of AIDS, ready access to public clinics through Medicare and collaboration between research teams and gay cohorts in Australia provided information on early stages of infection and led to the identification of the acute illnesses associated with HIV seroconversion.[11]

This, then, was the situation at the time the Queensland minister of health announced the deaths of three babies through transfusion of infected blood. A few medical specialists and the gay communities were already paying attention to AIDS, but serious risk to public confidence in the blood supply had only begun to focus the minds of health departments on the new disease. The threat that AIDS might become a political issue in the midst of a federal election ensured that policy would not be left to bureaucratic and professional policy-making, but would be given strong political direction.

Contending for Policy Control, 1985–1987

In Australia, male homosexual and bisexual contact continues to account for five cases in six (see Table 4.1). Intravenous drug use has not emerged as a significant category. The incidence of AIDS, which increased rapidly between 1984 and 1989, appears to have leveled off in subsequent years.

But demography does not dictate policy, and the institutional framework for AIDS programs established in November 1984 left considerable scope for political differences. One area ripe for dispute lay in two implicit models for programs, a medical contain-and-control model and the community cooperation model, one stressing professional medical determination through traditional public health controls, the other education and peer support. Those who sought a wider role for testing fell back on the traditional medical model. In the absence of a treatment for the virus, however, education for individual and community awareness of transmission risks and for behavior change was promoted by others as the appropriate priority. Testing and education thus came to be seen by some as rival rather than complementary approaches. As Blewett's office and department became fully committed to education as the primary method of prevention, those asserting a major role for testing were cast in the role of attacking the Commonwealth government.

The conflict was embodied in the two national advisory committees. While the AIDS Task Force, which superseded the NH&MRC Working Party, was composed of medical specialists, NACAIDS was broadly representative in its membership. Penington, who had borne the brunt of countering public fears about AIDS, was well established in the media and among state governments as the authoritative voice on AIDS issues; he controlled the agenda of the Task Force and dominated its proceedings. By contrast the chairperson of NACAIDS, Ita Buttrose, a prominent editor and publicist, was totally new to AIDS issues; she chaired a disparate committee that included Penington and other doctors and officials as well as the presidents of the NSW and Victorian AIDS Councils. While the Commonwealth Health Department's small AIDS Coordinating Unit served merely as secretariat for the Task Force, it played a much wider role in shaping the early work of NACAIDS and in promoting the activities of the AIDS councils and other voluntary bodies. Both the AIDS Coordinating Unit and Blewett's office became firm defenders of NACAIDS in the conflicts that developed.

Differences quickly arose. In December 1984, the Task Force rec-

Table 4.1. AIDS Cases by Year of Report and Category of Risk Exposure for Australia, 1982–1990

Risk category	1982	1983	1984	1985	1986	1987	1988	1989	1990	Total
Homosexual/bisexual activity	1	4	33	100	197	322	463	497	510	2,127
Homosexual/bisexual activity and IVDU	0	2	1	1	11	8	16	15	9	63
IVDU	0	0	0	0	2	2	11	12	10	37
Blood products	0	0	12	17	14	26	14	19	22	124
Heterosexual activity	0	0	0	1	0	6	8	8	14	37
Mother to child	0	0	0	1	0	0	1	1	3	6
Other/unknown	0	0	0	2	2	7	9	16	23	59
Total cases	1	6	46	122	226	371	522	568	591	2,453

Source: National Centre in HIV Epidemiology and Clinical Research, *Australian HIV Surveillance Report*, vol. 7, Supplement 3 (July 1991).

ommended strengthened legislative controls through notifiability of antibody-positive test results, penalties for false donor declarations, and closure of gay bathhouses. (On the latter point, health ministers accepted the NACAIDS argument that this would merely drive parts of the gay community underground and make education campaigns more difficult.) Penington stated that irresponsibility on the part of some homosexuals had led to contamination of the blood supply, while the AIDS councils argued that the misleading specification of "multiple partners" in the donor exclusion guidelines was to blame.[12] There was further disagreement over Penington's proposal that Sydney's Gay Mardi Gras be abandoned and over a Task Force estimate of 50,000 infected Australians, an extrapolation from San Francisco figures. (In the absence of any reliable base for estimates, the figure of 50,000 continued to be cited, even by Blewett, as late as mid-1987, whereas the government's national strategy of 1989 adopted an estimate of 15,000.)

Conflict arose between the Commonwealth Department of Health and Penington early in 1985. The department's representative on the Task Force proposed that its work be carried out within the department, but Penington mobilized support in the states against what was portrayed as a Commonwealth political takeover. The department backed down, agreeing to the appointment of representatives of all states as corresponding members of the Task Force, and conceding Penington's right to consult on all AIDS matters and power to recommend allocation of AIDS research grants. Nonetheless, at their May 1985 conference the state health ministers endorsed a National Health Strategy for AIDS Control drafted by the department, which stressed education progams and social as well as medical research. This rare statement of health priorities remained effectively intact for the next three years. The state ministers also agreed to match Commonwealth funding for state and territory programs, while any additional costs for hospital AIDS inpatient services would be incorporated into the Medicare agreements with each state and territory. All states except conservative Queensland agreed to help fund the AIDS councils.

By mid-1985, with HIV testing in place, opinion on the need for legislative controls had changed. Medical and community groups united in opposition to the proposal by the premier of New South Wales for compulsory notification of antibody test results and criminal penalties for knowing transmission of the virus. The proposal was a reaction to the final spate of media hysteria, brought on by the first case of AIDS infection in schools, a brief airline ban on passengers with AIDS, and a Sydney doctor's claim (never substantiated) to have seen the first case of transmission from a female prostitute. The panic was also fueled by news of Rock Hudson's terminal illness and predictions of a world plague.[13] The immediate result of the proposal to legislate was a sharp reduction in the number of those seeking antibody tests, since compulsory notification created fears concerning confidentiality. Although the NSW legislation was eventually enacted with several mitigating features, doctors refused to comply with the notification requirements.

During the latter months of 1985, a dispute between strategies based on testing and on education began to surface. The chief protagonists initially were the Albion Street Clinic in Sydney, which argued that knowledge of antibody status was the best inducement for changing individual sexual behavior, and the AIDS councils, which promoted education to move community norms toward safer practices regardless of antibody status, and which opposed testing as providing no personal benefit but raising problems of confidentiality and discrimination. Confrontation between the two approaches was avoided at the first national conference on AIDS in November; but in February 1986, Penington criticized "safe-sex" education as inadequate and proposed testing high-risk groups.[14] The new Australian Federation of AIDS Organizations (AFAO), which had been established by the state AIDS councils at the national conference, issued its own guidelines, and public exchanges between Penington and the AFAO threatened to politicize the issue.

Blewett intervened by calling a "summit" meeting with the protagonists. Rival submissions argued for the medical and community approaches for reducing transmission; but the meeting was not held until July 1986, by which time Penington and others had attended the second international conference on AIDS in Paris. There it was generally agreed that an effective scientific response to AIDS was not foreseeable and that preventive education programs were the only practicable response. At Blewett's summit, Penington, Buttrose, and representatives of the AIDS councils agreed that testing should remain voluntary and take place only in the context of informed consent and counseling.

Meanwhile Blewett insulated debate on AIDS issues from partisan politics by establishing and educating a Parliamentary Liaison Group drawn from all political parties. He also rejected Penington's proposal that responsibility for planning on AIDS legal and social issues be allocated to the Task Force, awarding them instead to NACAIDS, which established working parties on issues such as insurance, prisons, and care facilities. A month after the summit, Penington asserted that, since a NACAIDS working party on Aboriginal communities was to be chaired by a gay doctor, it would inevitably oppose surveillance testing. The Queensland, Northern Territory, and Western Australian health departments were considering antibody screening of Aboriginal communities, and Penington bypassed the Commonwealth department in advising them. He also approached the Commonwealth Department of Aboriginal Affairs (DAA) with his concern that the NACAIDS working party would only provide advice "which would not upset the white homosexual community," and suggested that the Task Force advise the DAA on its own program.

The 1986 Paris AIDS conference had signaled to Western governments the risk of heterosexual transmission of HIV, and most began their first major intervention programs in a matter of months. Penington had returned from Paris to warn Blewett of the urgent need to alert Australians to the risk of heterosexual transmission, and NACAIDS was given responsibility for devising a national education program aiming beyond "high-risk groups" to the "general community."

A steering committee chaired by Buttrose negotiated with media and advertising agencies a television advertisement, "The Grim Reaper." In it, black-cloaked figures in a misty bowling alley sent human tenpins flying. This major investment of resources on a potentially divisive issue required Cabinet approval, and the secrecy accompanying a political media project like the Grim Reaper campaign brought a major departure from the open policy-making that had characterized the AIDS community. It also meant a break in the tradition of collaboration with health education programs in the states. Nevertheless, the campaign, launched in April 1987, alerted the public to the threat of heterosexual spread, and mobilized school programs and the churches and other inactive groups. But essential follow-up programs intended to provide explicit instruction on ways to avoid contracting AIDS were shelved when the federal election campaign began a month later. There were many who disagreed with the tone of the Grim Reaper and the content of the backup messages, from which reference to anal sex was timidly deleted for political reasons. The Grim Reaper damaged the trust that had developed between the AIDS councils and the Commonwealth department, and it stirred a noisy public controversy.

A leading columnist, Philip Adams, led an attack on the campaign, arguing that HIV was spread almost exclusively through anal intercourse among gays. Penington publicly criticized Buttrose's claim that two million Australians were at risk and called for the Grim Reaper advertisements to be withdrawn.[15] Shortly afterward the leading Melbourne newspaper published a long commentary on the Grim Reaper campaign, questioning the reality of heterosexual transmission, citing Penington's criticisms and quoting an anonymous Task Force member: "The committee that Ita Buttrose chairs is dominated by the gay community, and what the advertisement is designed to do is to take the pressure off and to say AIDS is everyone else's problem. They don't want it identified as a gay problem."[16] In response it was pointed out that while six out of fourteen NACAIDS members had medical qualifications, only two represented gay interests. The secretary of the Commonwealth department exchanged strongly worded letters with Penington and attended a Task Force meeting to argue the irresponsibility of undermining education on heterosexual risk.

Table 4.2. Public HIV/AIDS Expenditures in Australia (in millions of 1990 U.S. dollars)

	1984–85	1985–86	1986–87	1987–88	1988–89	1989–90
Education/prevention[a]						
National education	.56	.28	2.33	3.04	3.27	2.83
Community groups	.009	....	.69	2.23	2.41	2.22
State/Commonwealth matched funding	1.01	3.26	3.21	5.45	8.61	12.49
Other	....	....	.44	.48	1.07	.98
Treatment, services, care						
State/Commonwealth matched funding[b]	1.01	3.26	3.21	5.45	8.61	12.49
Medicare HIV/AIDS dedicated[c]	....	....	....	.84	13.02	18.63
Other[d]	....	....	.86	NA	NA	11.31
Research	....	.59	1.09	2.45	3.03	4.05
Testing						
National Reference Lab	.28	.30	.39	.52	.68	.81
Blood screening[b]	5.22	3.25	3.14	4.56	4.88	5.26
Other	.48	.37	2.44[e]	.28	.34	....
Total	8.56	11.32	17.80	25.30	45.93	71.06

SOURCE: AIDS Policy and Programs Branch, Commonwealth Department of Health, Housing and Community Services.
[a]Blood supply screening listed separately below.
[b]Includes both State/Territory and Commonwealth components.
[c]General Medicare hospital funding applicable to HIV/AIDS not included (est. $4.42 million in 1986–87).
[d]State-only expenditure—supplied only for 1989–90.
[e]State administration (identified by commissioned study for 1986–87 only).

By this time Penington had been appointed head of the University of Melbourne and had made known his intention of stepping down from the Task Force. This provided an opportunity for restructuring the advisory committees. Rather than amalgamate the Task Force and NACAIDS, Blewett proposed to maintain both groups and to create a third body, an Intergovernmental Committee on AIDS, to resolve issues between the Commonwealth and state governments. The Task Force had served as a forum for the airing of state grievances, and Penington, referring to Blewett's proposals as "the height of folly," asserted that the removal of state government representatives would emasculate the Task Force.[17] He won the support of the NH&MRC, but the state health ministers accepted Blewett's proposals, while retaining two state officials on the Task Force. Blewett's nominee, a prominent Sydney immunologist not previously active on HIV issues, succeeded Penington as chairman of the Task Force.

Penington announced that he had succeeded in saving the Task Force. A *Sydney Morning Herald* editorial in June 1987 hailed the result as a Penington victory, claiming that Blewett's proposals were based on a gay agenda leading to a single national advisory committee.[18] A month later, on election day, the *Herald* gave headline prominence to Penington's claim that gay lobby groups had manipulated the federal government into pursuing an inappropriate AIDS campaign "to protect their fast-lane lifestyle" and threatening to end the Task Force. "There are people in the leadership positions in Australia who, without it being known, are gay or bisexual and have a firm commitment to aligning themselves with the gay community. I believe the minister is getting advice from these people."[19] Months later, Penington maintained this position in a long interview with *Australian Penthouse* magazine.[20]

With the reelection of the Hawke government, Blewett had Community Services added to his Health portfolio and was raised to Cabinet status. Institutional politics, which had become an increasingly personal conflict between Penington on one side and Blewett's advisers and department, NACAIDS and the AIDS councils on the other, did not disappear with the departure of Penington. Tensions between the medical and community models remained but were primarily expressed through debate over policy detail. This dispute lost much of its interest for the media, which had helped politicize AIDS policy by accepting a simplification of issues in institutional and personal terms, dramatized with heroes and assumed vested interests. Penington's successor chose not to adopt a high public profile, and others with clinical experience became the media authorities on HIV issues.

One of the aims of the shock tactics of the Grim Reaper had been to create the basis for a substantial increase in funding for AIDS prevention and treatment. This proved successful, and the considerable growth in funding in the 1987–1988 budget (shown in Table 4.2) was allocated through a formula based on each state's population and its number of AIDS cases and IV drug users, with funds to be equally divided between prevention and treatment programs. Under this formula, New South Wales received a massive increase, while others dropped slightly or received negligible increases. The chief program beneficiaries were education, especially through community organizations, and research, with funds allocated primarily through a new Commonwealth AIDS Research Grants Committee. AFAO and the AIDS councils, particularly those in New South Wales and Victoria, were able to multiply their staff and undertake a broad range of new programs within and beyond the gay communities, and they became much more widely recognized as professional service organizations.

Ita Buttrose, who had been working full-time on NACAIDS for the previous year, stepped down early in 1988 to become editor-in-chief of a Sydney tabloid newspaper (and later launched her own monthly women's magazine, *Ita*). Blewett seized this occasion to reduce the potential for conflict among the advisory bodies by establishing a single national committee. After much negotiation, and with the approval of state health ministers, he appointed an Australian National Council on AIDS (ANCA), replacing the Task Force and NACAIDS but leaving intact the Intergovernmental Committee on AIDS. ANCA was chaired by Professor Peter Karmel, a prominent government adviser on education who had recently retired as head of the Australian National University. ANCA's fifteen members, seven medical and eight nonmedical, included leading members of the previous advisory bodies. An additional eighteen members were appointed to a broader National AIDS Forum where a wide range of community and professional interests were represented.

Strategic Planning in a Federal System, 1987–1990

For two years after the July 1987 election, national policy-making on HIV was focused on the process of developing a long-term strategy that would lock the states—and particularly the non-Labour governments of Queensland and Tasmania—into compliance with Commonwealth policy and provide a rationale for long-term commitment of Commonwealth resources. Consultative arrangements for developing policy involved the preparation of a discussion paper as the basis for nationwide consultation and eventual adoption of a national strategy White Paper.

This paper, "AIDS: A Time to Care—A Time to Act," was finally issued in October 1988. It gave strong priority to preventive education and care. It was discussed in the state parliaments as well as the Commonwealth Parliament, and Blewett and his colleagues briefed state politicians, officials, and community groups. Six working panels—on Aboriginal people, discrimination and other legal issues, education and prevention, treatment and care, intravenous drug use, and testing—were appointed by Blewett's office, with members drawn primarily from Parliament, ANCA, and community groups. Each panel held public hearings early in 1989 and presented reports much more substantial than the anticipated window dressing.

Throughout the period of consultation the greatest controversy centered on the effort on the part of those who, like Penington earlier on, sought to reestablish medical control over AIDS policy and who believed that it had been a great mistake to treat AIDS differently from other threats to the public health.

At the 1988 National Conference on HIV/AIDS, an aggressive Liberal party shadow minister for health, Wilson Tuckey, momentarily broke the long-standing bipartisan approach to HIV issues by insisting that HIV had been given special treatment and should be brought into line with traditional public health controls.[21]

> I have got to say to you as a political observer that those promoting the political position of the homosexual community and of those associated with the AIDS problem have been surprisingly successful, extremely successful. But I wonder whether that has been for the proper and best reasons. . . . We have very strict quarantine and isolation laws for contagious diseases. The public has accepted that and you have been very successful politically in isolating AIDS from that point of view. . . . I think the accent to date is a little too much on protecting people from themselves when in fact we must take more of an attitude that we have a public health problem on our hands, we must address it as such and we must look to the way we have treated others in the community when they have become a public risk or a risk to people's livelihoods as they have in drunk driving and other areas such as that, and we are hypocritical if we believe there is a difference.[22]

These widely reported comments elicited a strong homophobic response on call-in radio programs and in letters to the press.

Tuckey was quickly replaced as shadow minister at the insistence of several politicians from his own party and his successor would ultimately strongly support the national strategy. But the following months saw a mounting campaign within the medical profession against Blewett and for greater medical control of HIV policy. At the 1988 conference, the Australian Medical Association had called for the "medicalization" of AIDS or "mainstreaming" within conventional health planning and programs.[23] The issue of surgeons' rights to test elective surgery patients for HIV became the focus of this controversy. In testimony before the National Strategy Working Party on Testing, several hospitals and nursing groups advocated universal precautions against infection and argued that the testing of patients lowered adherence to infection control procedures.

Surgeons, on the other hand, were adamant in insisting on their right to know the HIV status of elective surgery patients.

In March 1989, a Melbourne hospital announced its refusal to admit patients with HIV; although it was quickly brought into line by the state government, this touched off a spate of media commentary on the risks to health care workers. Bruce Shepherd, a leading Sydney orthopedic surgeon, organizer of the doctors' fees dispute of 1983–1984, and head of the NSW Australian Medical Association (AMA), repeated Penington's allegations. He accused Blewett of allowing HIV policy to be dominated by pressures from a gay lobby. Shepherd used his Doctors' Fighting Fund raised during the previous dispute to organize a "medical summit" on the risks of HIV for doctors and the need for compulsory testing of patients, inviting Dr. Lorraine Day, an American campaigner on the issue, for an extended visit. To counter this, the Inter-Governmental Committee on AIDS and the moderate national AMA leadership, with the aid of Australian Federation of AIDS Organizations expertise, mobilized a case against the routine mandatory testing of patients. Their evidence was presented persuasively by Blewett and his scientific adviser at Shepherd's conference; a speech by the AFAO executive director, which indicated that most patients accepted testing and that the remainder could readily be dealt with by infection control, served to defuse the issue temporarily. Yet medical opinion remained unconvinced. A majority of doctors favored mandatory testing of elective surgery patients, compulsory for "high-risk groups," and aggressive contact tracing.[24]

Despite these considerable pressures, the government's White Paper, presented by Blewett in August 1989, rejected the effort to impose a regime of tight medical control over AIDS. The National HIV/AIDS Strategy committed the Commonwealth government to a set of ten guiding principles:

> 1. Transmission of HIV is preventable through changes in individual behavior; education and prevention programs are necessary to bring about such changes.
>
> 2. Each person must accept responsibility for preventing infection through sexual intercourse or the sharing of needles and for preventing further transmission of the virus.
>
> 3. The community as a whole has the right to appropriate protection against infection.
>
> 4. The law should complement and assist education and other public health measures.
>
> 5. Public health objectives will be most effectively realized if the cooperation of people with HIV infection and those most at risk is maintained.

6. Specific informed consent should be obtained before any test is performed to diagnose a person's HIV infection status. The result should remain confidential, and appropriate pre- and post-testing counseling should be provided.

7. People infected with HIV retain the right to participate in the community without discrimination, and have the same rights to comprehensive and appropriate health care, income support, and community services as other members of the community.

8. Professional care-givers have a duty to care for infected individuals; governments, employers, and unions have a responsibility to provide working conditions and training programs that minimize the risk of occupational transmission.

9. Research into the epidemic is essential to the management of the epidemic.

10. General principles of public health, service provision, and the legal system should be applied to the HIV epidemic; special measures or services require justification.

The most controversial areas covered in the White Paper concerned prevention. The objective, it declared, was "to eliminate transmission through the use of preventive measures such as safer sexual and drug using practices, testing with counseling, removal of legal impediments, and education to prevent the infection of people who care for infected individuals."[25] To that end it advocated the extension of existing needle distribution programs, which existed in most states either with or without legislative sanction, to the entire country; voluntary partner notification, though with special arrangements for warning of potentially endangered third parties in exceptional circumstances; mandatory testing for immigrants seeking permanent residence; provision of condoms, needle sterilization equipment, methadone programs, and education in prisons, and compulsory testing of prisoners at the time of release; universal infection control in hospitals rather than mandatory testing of patients; review of all public health and privacy laws for conformity with the White Paper; and decriminalization of homosexuality, prostitution, and needle and syringe possession.

The White Paper adopted a position already endorsed by the state health ministers and the national AMA, requiring informed consent to testing and confidentiality. In view of the political consensus mobilized behind the White Paper, these provisions received only pro forma opposition. Penington dismissed it as a "political document designed not to offend the homosexual lobby or the community at large,"[26] but he no longer attracted media attention.

Commonwealth contributions were planned to rise from $30,950,000 in 1988–1989 to $67,885,000 in 1992–1993. Over 55 percent of the projected increase would consist of growth in Medicare payments for hospital care, but substantial growth in prevention, treatment, and research programs was provided for. The most controversial funding provision was an attempt to direct state expenditure through detailed specification of the formula for allocation of matched funding among specific program areas, and particularly an attempt, later abandoned, to earmark percentages to be allocated through the AIDS councils to intravenous drug users, homosexual and bisexual men, and sex industry workers.

After the period of consultation leading up to the National Strategy, Blewett's office and ANCA played a less active role. The initiative lay instead with Commonwealth and state officials and with the AIDS councils. Coordinating implementation of the White Paper fell to the AIDS Policy and Programs Branch of the Commonwealth department, by now with a staff of thirty-five, and to the Intergovernmental Committee on AIDS (IGCA), which had become an effective policy forum on issues lying within the authority of the states. During 1990, IGCA began collaborative planning on the difficult areas of HIV programs in prisons and schools and among youth and Aboriginal communities, while an IGCA legal working party began developing recommendations on law reform in each of the areas specified in the White Paper. Individual states also responded: Western Australia with a parliamentary select committee report; the new Tasmanian Labour government with a proposed omnibus public health law on HIV, which sought to win support for the legalization of homosexuality and needle exchange by conceding the mandatory testing of elective surgery patients and the compulsory testing of prisoners; other states with piecemeal measures.

In February 1990, the Hawke Labour government was elected to a fourth term of office. Blewett, who had held the health portfolio for almost seven years, longer than any previous Commonwealth minister, was appointed minister for trade negotiations. He was replaced by Brian Howe, the leading representative of the Labour Left faction in the Cabinet, who had established a strong reputation through restructuring social security and who took over in a period of economic stringency. HIV held a lower priority than economies in Medicare and community services, but one of Howe's first tasks was that of reappointing advisory bodies. He chose to abolish the National AIDS Forum and to reconstitute ANCA under Karmel's continuing chairmanship. Although it was agreed that specific interests and groups should not be directly represented on ANCA, the former executive director of AFAO was appointed to its executive and the minister accepted ANCA's request that a person living with HIV be added to its membership.

The issue of medicalization remained alive under Howe. At the 1990 annual conference of the Australian Medical Association, Shepherd, the surgeon who had been so critical of Blewett's strategy, defeated moderate candidates for the national presidency. Penington's keynote address reasserted the demand for medical ownership of HIV policy:

> In the AIDS debate, much has been driven by the social ethic on the basis of equity and civil rights. A high level of control of policy has been achieved by those suffering from the infection or likely to be infected, with inevitable distortion of the policies and their depiction to the community. The HIV epidemic is a public health issue and the principles of public health must take priority if spread of the infection is to be contained. As with any other epidemic, identification of those infected and strategies to minimize the risk of them infecting others must be the central issue rather than policy being driven by the image of the responsibility primarily resting with the uninfected community, an approach which has engendered fear and anxiety and achieved little to control spread of the virus. Testing for HIV infection prior to major surgery must, on any grounds, be seen as logically mandatory in this day and age because of the very finite, tangible risk to health care workers when dealing with persons carrying the infection if this fact is unknown.

The issue of testing surgical patients for HIV simmered. Though the proposal failed to win support from governments, hospitals, or nursing associations, it served as a trigger for other professional frustrations for the NSW Resident Medical Officers' Association, which threatened to strike if patients were not tested.

State-level Politics

The political impact of HIV in the states has been most obvious within their departments of health and in community groups, particularly the AIDS councils, which have become broadly representative rather than restricted to gay men. Commonwealth funding provided a substantial injection of resources for state HIV programs, and in the first years these were often used to remedy deficits in existing state health programs. It proved much easier to spend money on programs already in place than to establish new and innovative projects; hence, it was easier to reinforce hospital infection control than to gear up for education or to negotiate the setting up of hospices or the distribution of condoms. During the early years the emphasis of programs depended in part on which health bureau had AIDS as a responsibility. In New South Wales, South Australia, and especially in Queensland, the only health department where doctors had not been replaced by generalist administrators, AIDS was assigned to medical staff that worked primarily under a medical model of response to AIDS issues. In Victoria and Western Australia, primary responsibility was assigned to health education divisions that were disposed to work through community-based programs. Just as the national response to AIDS depended heavily on the political determination by Blewett and his advisers to proceed with electorally unpopular policies and to break through entrenched bureaucratic practice, so the response of the states depended on the exercise of political will. In no area was this more evident than in the forging of collaboration with the AIDS councils, which received both state and Commonwealth funding through the states.

Although New South Wales had the great majority of cases, it was Victoria that set the model for innovation in AIDS programs in the mid-1980s. In the absence of other service organizations within the Melbourne gay community and with a much smaller number of AIDS cases, its AIDS Council was able to mobilize a large number of volunteers within an integrated program. The Victoria minister for health initially refused contact with the council, but after the national blood transfusion crisis of November 1984, he gave his director of health promotion free rein to deal with AIDS matters. The director recruited two Victoria AIDS Council (VAC) officials to her health education staff, and arranged funding for a Gay Men's Community Health Centre as the focus for VAC's health and education programs. VAC took the initiative among the state AIDS councils in framing policy, favoring safe-sex education programs and opposing antibody testing early in 1985, and it sponsored the first national conference on AIDS, held in Melbourne. Blewett's office and department and NACAIDS supported the initiatives of VAC and the Victoria Department, and they promoted their collaboration as a model for other states.

In New South Wales, successive Labor ministers of health were generally uninterested in the difficult and politically unattractive problems raised by the epidemic. Consultation with the AIDS Council of New South Wales (ACON) was left to public servants who worked under the medical model, and to the Albion Street Clinic, which was often in rivalry or conflict with ACON. The Commonwealth health department had greater difficulty in obtaining information and cooperation from New South Wales than from other states. In 1986, a new minister of health undertook the first political effort at innovative planning on HIV issues, establishing an AIDS Bureau with substantial staff, a Ministerial Advisory Committee with a broad range of expertise, and a Cabinet sub-committee, each with a clear mandate to resolve outstanding issues. After the election of a Liberal–National coalition government in January 1988, these initiatives were maintained, and resources for the development of HIV programs were increased.

From its start in January 1985, ACON was a federation within which service organizations retained their separate identities. The division of politics and education from services reflected in part the long-standing difference in focus between the radical gay movement and the nonpolitical gay community. There were also divisions over leadership style, which led to coups within ACON's governing board against successive presidents in 1986 and 1987. During 1987, after the recruitment of an experienced executive director, ACON matured into a professional body, with seventy paid staff members by mid-1990. ACON took the lead among national AIDS organizations in developing policy on issues such as HIV testing, access to treatments, and legal reform. The availability of resources and the development of expertise in both ACON and the state AIDS bureau from 1987 on made New South Wales the driving force for planning and innovation in education and care, perhaps the equivalent of San Francisco's role in the United States. Apart from educational initiatives with gay men, beginning in 1987 the Australian Prostitutes' Collective in Sydney was funded to provide AIDS education in brothels and among street sex workers. Needle exchange services from buses visiting major drug-trading venues were pioneered in Sydney and Canberra, without substantial public reaction.

Political support for these initiatives was given its most severe test when, in July 1989, a television channel broadcast interviews with an HIV-infected intravenous drug user, a prostitute named Charlene, who admitted to continuing unprotected intercourse without informing clients of her HIV status. The New South Wales health minister, under heavy political pressure to act, labeled Charlene "a walking time bomb" and detained her for some time in a hospital, as a threat to public health. In collaboration with ACON, the AIDS Bureau worked out guidelines for the control of people assessed as continually putting others at risk. These involved stage intervention, with education, counseling, and formal warning preceding the imposition of court-monitored sanctions, and community participation in all stages of assessment and control. Similar guidelines have been adopted in other states.

If Victoria and later New South Wales provided useful models for state programs, from the Commonwealth's viewpoint, right-wing Queensland was (as on many other issues) a model of what *not* to do. Sodomy remained illegal, and gay men were frequently prosecuted in Queensland during the seventeen years of John Bjelke-Petersen's regime. The minister for health refused to have any contact with the predominantly gay Queensland AIDS Council (QaAC) as well as with NACAIDS programs, while Queensland's Department of Health continued to assert the primacy of a traditional medical model for dealing with epidemics.[27] Aboriginal and prison issues were dealt with as medical problems, doctors were recruited to offer AIDS education in Queensland schools, and AIDS Control Queensland programs were based entirely on interdepartmental consultation. Public education on AIDS was left to QuAC; it received no state support, only Commonwealth funds funneled through the Sisters of Mercy.

The appointment of Mike Ahern as minister for health early in 1987 produced a change in direction and challenges to Premier Bjelke-Petersen, over sex education in schools, needle exchange programs, cooperation with QuAC, and the availability of condom vending machines at universities. The latter, remarkably, became the subject of an acrimonious state Cabinet debate.[28] AIDS turned into a focal point of division within the Queensland National party[29]—a division that ultimately led to Ahern's displacing Bjelke-Petersen as premier in December 1987.

During 1988 and 1989, a royal commission investigating government and police abuses in Queensland implicated key figures of the Bjelke-Petersen regime. This paved the way for election in November 1989 of a Labour government, despite Conservative campaign threats that the state would be flooded with gays and AIDS. Under the Labour party, massive reform of government administration included the overhaul of the police and the Department of Health, to which were appointed several senior officials from elsewhere in Australia with AIDS policy experience. However, the new government, determined to establish its legitimacy in conservative Queensland country towns, proved cautious on social reform; a carefully orchestrated campaign by gay law reform groups was needed to achieve decriminalization of homosexuality in 1990. Young gay men who sought more radical change staged a local version of Sydney's Gay Mardi Gras, while QuAC was able to embark on adventurous safer-sex education programs, which had elsewhere been under way for several years.

In Western Australia and South Australia, with only a few AIDS cases, collaboration between Labour governments and AIDS councils raised few problems. South Australia had an exceptionally strong minister of health, who took advantage of the November 1984 crisis and the Grim Reaper campaign to extend the reach of HIV programs beyond his department. In Tasmania and the Northern Territory, with conservative governments, weakly organized gay communities, and few AIDS cases, there has been reluctance to consider AIDS a serious problem and difficulty in mobilizing continuous activity by AIDS councils. The election of a Green party–supported Labour government in Tasmania in 1989 offered the possibility of a fresh approach with decriminalization of homosexuality and needle exchange part of omnibus AIDS legislation, but the conservative state senate balked at decriminalization.

Organizations and Personalities

At several critical junctures in the development of Australia's AIDS policy, events were shaped by individuals, and the capacity of interests for mobilization depended heavily on the political, professional, and community cultures that shaped those interests.

Within the medical profession, there was a substantial contrast in attitudes between leading figures in scientific research and those concerned with clinical treatment of people with HIV. Neither David Penington nor his successors as chief Commonwealth scientific adviser on HIV/AIDS had clinical experience with HIV. But they all made pronouncements in line with the medical model on a broad range of policy issues and were seen by Blewett and his department as unsympathetic with the thrust of Commonwealth policy. By contrast, many clinicians working with people living with AIDS were sympathetic to community education, and those based at the two hospitals with the largest AIDS caseloads, St. Vincent's in Sydney and Fairfield in Melbourne, worked closely with the AIDS councils. It was vital for the public credibility of government programs that they were firmly supported by noted clinicians such as immunologist Professor Ron Penny, and Dr. David Cooper, both of St Vincent's. Penny, who served on both the Task Force and NACAIDS, was appointed chief Commonwealth education advisor on HIV/AIDS and became a primary source of media comment on HIV issues after Penington's retirement.[30]

While AIDS was a relatively peripheral issue for the well-established structure of the medical profession, it was a reshaping force for the gay community in Australia. The differences of view between those who were concerned with public policy and the wider nonpolitical gay social community, which provided the base for care and support services, was a central feature in the early years of the AIDS councils, which tended to displace other gay community organizations. These differences receded as the councils became better funded and more able to recruit experienced staff, but tensions developed between staff members, seen as bureaucrats, and the volunteers, who often dominated council boards.

The Australian Federation of AIDS Organizations (AFAO) also developed professional expertise after the establishment of its Canberra office in 1986. Under Warren Talbot, its executive director from 1986 until 1989, AFAO won recognition from the Department of Health as a significant policy contributor; Talbot was later appointed to the steering committee for the White Paper. AFAO received an annual grant from the Commonwealth for its operating expenses, set at $375,000 in the National Strategy, in addition to grants for specific projects. Collaboration did not eliminate differences between AFAO and the Commonwealth, and there was substantial friction on issues of treatment, funding, and AFAO's right to representation on ANCA and other appointed bodies.

The AIDS councils and AFAO served as models and godparents for other groups affected by AIDS. People living with AIDS, encouraged by the Commonwealth government and AFAO, gradually developed their own voice, particularly on treatment issues. By 1990, ACTUP provided a still more radical voice of protest to complement the councils, which were seen by some as compromised by their close relationship with government programs. The extension of council activities beyond the gay community became feasible with the expansion of government funding, beginning in 1987. In most states, collaboration had already been established with drug use services and prostitutes, and the Health Department encouraged AFAO's sponsorship of separate but affiliated groups at both national and state level. This led, in 1988 and 1989, to the foundation of the Australian IV League among intravenous drug users, the Scarlet Alliance among prostitutes and the National People Living with AIDS Coalition (NPLWAC, pronounced Nipplewhack), each accorded membership in and support from AFAO. Councils were also active in promoting education in prisons and schools and among health care workers, and their skills in community education became widely recognized. This extension of activities led to the loss of gay identity in some councils and to tensions over an AIDS rather than gay focus in some programs. After the 1990 National Conference on AIDS, gay council activists argued that the gay community was the only group not given attention.[31]

The only other organization in the AIDS arena accorded status comparable to that of AFAO and the councils in the early years was the Haemophilia Foundation. This was established in 1980 as a federation of state associations and was heavily dependent on the energies of its executive director, who pursued the issue of potential infection of Factor VIII during 1983–1984 and then, as an active member of NACAIDS and ANCA, the wider implications of education and care programs. The foundation's yearly operating costs were funded by the Commonwealth at $156,000; and the issue of compensation to people with hemophilia infected by HIV was resolved shortly before the 1990 national election, when the Commonwealth established a trust fund of $10.3 million. This was clearly aimed at avoiding potential electoral damage, but it raised surprisingly little public discussion of the equity of compensating only one category of persons with AIDS. Those who had been infected by blood transfusion pursued damages through litigation; early in 1991, the largest compensation award in Australian history was made in a case where negligence in changing hemophilia medication was conceded.

In addition to the medical profession and the community groups, the third group closely involved in shaping AIDS policy were Blewett's staff and the Commonwealth health department. Blewett himself was courageous in taking a high profile on a politically unpopular issue. His commitment to broad participation in health policy extended well beyond AIDS issues, as is evident from his strong support from the Public Health Association, the Community Health Association, women's health programs, and a new Consumer Health Forum. His chief advisers played particularly significant roles in determining the direction and shape of AIDS policy and in guaranteeing community participation in policy-making. Others, such as David Penington and his successors, and key officials in AFAO, in the AIDS councils, and in the health departments of New South Wales and Victoria, were equally significant for the content of policy. But Blewett's advisers had entrepreneurial skills essential for innovative policy-making on the wide range of new issues raised by AIDS.

The adoption of the National Strategy in 1989 marked the end of an era of federal entrepreneurship in AIDS policy. Scope for further radical development of policy and institutions was limited, and AIDS was not seen by the new minister and his staff as an issue requiring substantial innovation. Most initiatives continued to arise from ACON and AFAO, which had a greater capacity for policy development than that of other groups. In the absence of other centers of power, the head of the AIDS Policy and Programs Branch of the Department of Health became the Commonwealth's primary focus for relations with the several committees. In this sense, AIDS policy was no longer characterized by exceptionalism, but became absorbed into more familiar bureaucratic structures and routines.

The Articulation of Policies and Programs: The 1990s

Australia's early start on AIDS policy-making, its strong emphasis on community participation and government commitment of resources all meant that education, prevention, and care programs became increasingly detailed and were targeted at increasingly specific local groups after 1984. Programs were organized directly by state governments or through nongovernment organizations, so a wide range of groups became involved in AIDS projects.

Education for prevention and community care services were already established within the gay communities when government funding became available in 1985. The problems confronted and the messages deemed acceptable varied state by state, and the individual AIDS councils developed many of their own programs, with matched funding allocated through the states. However, it was a 1987 NACAIDS working party on gay and bisexual men that set out a systematic proposal for funding peer education programs. Thereafter, AFAO and its monthly *National AIDS Bulletin* served as a clearinghouse for innovations by AIDS councils. AFAO itself initiated and ran training programs. Considerable research was devoted to evaluating the effectiveness of AIDS council programs and the reasons for behavior change. It became clear that, within the gay community, substantial modification in sexual behavior had occurred.[32] As a result of the perceived success of the AIDS councils and the Haemophilia Foundation, community-based programs for other groups—Aboriginal, non-English-speaking communities, youth, and prostitutes—received Commonwealth funding and support under the National Strategy.

Community education programs, particularly those of the AIDS councils, became increasingly explicit in their messages about safer-sex practices and innovative in their means of conveying these messages. Occasionally they encountered opposition. The Tasmanian AIDS Council came under political fire for distributing pamphlets on safer-sex techniques that had been produced and distributed in Victoria without hindrance. In 1990, a Victorian AIDS Council poster of two young men kissing, aimed at encouraging adolescents' recognition of the legitimacy of homosexuality, was attacked by religious groups and banned from newspapers and magazines by the state advertising council.

Some state education programs were also innovative. The New South Wales AIDS Bureau not only negotiated appropriate safe-sex messages with many different ethnic groups; it also commissioned peer educators from a wide variety of communities to develop education and prevention programs within their own cultures. Programs directed to Aboriginal people began during 1986, triggered by the first Aboriginal case of AIDS and by awareness that health conditions and services in Aboriginal communities and settlements, especially for people with sexually transmitted diseases, were generally much poorer than for other Australians. Nonconsensual HIV screening of Aboriginal communities was proposed by some states and favored by the AMA, following exaggerated claims of high rates of infection among Aboriginal groups, but this was discouraged by the Commonwealth. Later screening of some Queensland communities was undertaken only after negotiated invitation by community councils, and in mid-1989 this revealed a number of cases in one island community. Many communities were encouraged to design their own programs; this led to the widely circulated Condoman poster. A Northern Territory Aboriginal health educator popularized condoms through her community presentations of a large dildo known as Black Rambo.

One of the Working Panels preparatory to the 1989 White Paper held hearings on HIV issues relating to Aboriginal peoples. It noted risks created by high rates of alcohol consumption and imprisonment and the tendency of doctors and hospitals to notify those with sexually transmitted diseases among Aboriginal people more readily than they did in other cases. It recommended community control over all HIV programs and their integration with STD and primary health care services and with alcohol and drug programs. The White Paper specified priority in community education grants, HIV care and support models for Aboriginal communities.

By contrast, the Commonwealth government's national campaign, which received funding equal to that of all the Commonwealth's matched funding for education and prevention programs in the states, relied primarily on national media and focused rather tamely, after the Grim Reaper, on condoms and needles. Thus, while the community programs celebrated diversity of sexual expression, the national campaign reinforced the standard authorized discourse of penetrative heterosexual intercourse. Not until 1991 did the national campaign deal with homosexual safe sex.

One group that was difficult to reach and lacked an organized community was intravenous drug users. Because of the rise in drug use and associated crime after the Vietnam War, official inquiries proliferated during the 1970s; between 1981 and 1985, law enforcement powers were increased in most states and territories. In April 1985, after a "Drug Summit" involving federal and state leaders, a distinction was drawn between illegal drug sale and illegal drug use, with the latter considered as a "health problem" rather than one of "moral vice." Although there had been a long-standing debate on the possible decriminalization of the use of prohibited drugs, particularly in the case of marijuana, no moves were made to legalize the nonmedical use of any prohibited intravenous drugs. In 1986, the federal government launched a National Campaign Against Drug Abuse. The largest portion of its budget was still allocated to the enforcement of drug-related criminal laws, but a new emphasis was placed on public education aimed at discouraging the use of both legal (alcohol and tobacco) and illegal drugs. The National Drug Abuse Information Center estimated in March 1988 that there were between thirty and fifty thousand heroin addicts and between sixty and ninety thousand recreational, nonaddicted users.

Evidence of widespread HIV infection among intravenous drug users in the United States and Britain raised awareness of the risk in Australia. Needle and syringe exchange programs were begun in 1987 in Sydney and Canberra, with government sanction and funding. Subsequently, needle exchange programs have been established in every other state except Tasmania. In Victoria, a different initiative was launched in 1987 with the funding of a community AIDS education group for drug users, called VIVAIDS. This also attracted support from the Commonwealth department, which encouraged participation by intravenous drug users and People Living With AIDS at the 1988 national conference. This provided an opportunity to develop national associations from the state delegations present. In other states, local groups were difficult to maintain. Surprisingly, in Queensland the strong Drug and Alcohol Dependence Services organized an education group on intravenous drug use, and pushed through Australia's first legislation decriminalizing possession of drug paraphernalia in 1989. Proposals for the legalization of heroin supply to people with HIV, though floated by some professionals since early 1988, have received no official support.

The National HIV/AIDS Strategy has given priority to the prevention of HIV transmission among drug users, although it reflects the long-term commitment to cessation of drug use. "Promoting abstinence from drug use is the Government's primary aim in initiatives such as the National Campaign Against Drug Abuse. This is a goal which may be achieved only in the long term and must be complemented by otther strategies to reduce transmission of HIV among IV drug users. Education messages should reflect as a matter of priority reduction of harm from the sharing of needles and syringes, and from practicing unsafe sex." In 1989, the national media campaigns of the National Campaign Against Drug Abuse and the National AIDS Education Program were brought together in the Commonwealth's Department of Community Services and Health; the National AIDS Education Campaign for 1990 emphasized the risk of AIDS infection to and from intravenous drug users through needle sharing and unprotected sex.

School education programs on HIV were slow to start; they received considerable impetus from the Grim Reaper in early 1987. The only public discussion of the appropriateness of explicit school-based education on AIDS took place during the following months. By the end of 1987, each state had prepared a curriculum for use in the higher levels of secondary schools, usually as part of health education or personal development programs. In Queensland, where social science education, especially sex education, had been a major political issue in the late 1970s, AIDS programs in schools were sanctioned only if taught by doctors. The National Strategy called for the development of appropriate programs and coordination through the national curriculum center, and the Intergovernmental Committee on AIDS determined in 1990 that one of its highest priorities was the development of school programs on sexually transmitted diseases and AIDS at all levels of education.

Efforts to prevent HIV transmission in prisons have provoked some of the most intractable questions, in large part because of the closed culture of prison systems. Although seroprevalence studies conducted in prisons have shown low levels of infection, there has been pressure within the prison systems for compulsory testing of inmates. Compulsory testing of all prisoners is undertaken in the states that have had conservative governments—Queensland, Tasmania, and the Northern Territory—as well as in South Australia, with compliance obtained through the use of "correctional sanctions." Testing is repeated after three months in South Australia and Tasmania, while in Queensland those prisoners assessed as "high-risk" are retested at yearly intervals. In Victoria, all prisoners are offered testing on admission, and reluctant prisoners are counseled and encouraged; the compliance rate is about 98 percent. In Western Australia, testing is voluntary and few volunteer to be tested, but those assessed as "high-risk" may be compulsorily tested.

In New South Wales, with the highest rates of HIV infection among prisoners, testing has been voluntary; segregation of those who are infected under inferior conditions effectively discouraged voluntary testing. In 1990, the Liberal minister for correctional institutions, against the advice of his colleague, the minister for health, announced that the state would compulsorily test all prisoners on admission, but he ended segregation because of the cost of operating a very small unit for infected inmates. South Australia also integrated those with HIV infection. By contrast, Western Australia and the Northern Territory segregate seropositive prisoners, while Victoria and Queensland segregate them together with intravenous drug users.

The range in prison practices adopted by the states demonstrates the gulf between Commonwealth policy and implementation in the Australian federal system. The National HIV/AIDS Strategy condones voluntary testing on admission and at intervals and calls for testing only at the time of release, with appropriate counseling. It also advocates wider prison education programs and access to condoms (which no state prison system presently provides), bleach or disinfectant for drug paraphernalia, and methadone programs (provided in New South Wales and Victoria). The Intergovernmental Committee on AIDS has given high priority to these discrepancies and has opened discussions with the national body of state corrective institutions.

For other groups, the issue of mandatory testing has continued to be a central focus of policy. Late in 1987, the chief medical officer in the Defense Forces proposed compulsory testing of all members of the armed forces. Negotiations with the Department of Community Services and Health resulted in a revised scheme: HIV-antibody testing of all recruits was to be carried out on a one-year trial basis. No antibody-positive cases were found, but the "trial" has remained intact indefinitely. The National HIV/AIDS Strategy omitted reference to the armed forces, apparently in an attempt to avoid allowing Cabinet discussion to freeze the current practice.

When some life insurance companies began asking questions of policy applicants in 1986, a NACAIDS working group undertook a year's study and proposed a voluntary code of practice. This code, adopted in April 1988, eliminates sexual orientation as a basis for refusing coverage and sets out specific conditions for HIV testing and confidentiality.[33] Pension funds then became involved in extended negotiation with the Commonwealth government concerning a comparable code of practice but were unable to reach agreement, and in 1991, the government was considering new legislation.

Anonymous and nonconsensual testing of selected populations for general surveillance purposes was hotly debated in 1988 when an ANCA working party proposed a program of blinded screening of hospital patients and pregnant women in which samples stripped of identifiers could be tested for HIV without consent. Venereologists successfully argued against such surveillance because they believed that the sample for screening a low-risk population would need to be of a vast and costly scale to produce valid results; meanwhile, more useful and still unprocessed information was held in sexually transmitted disease clinics. While the National Strategy did not rule out anonymous nonconsensual screening, it presented strong arguments in favor of voluntary testing in all situations.

Since the first cases of AIDS were identified, the gay community has provided resources for care and support. Volunteer support groups, established in 1983 and 1984, draw on volunteers from all sectors of the society. Much of the counseling for people with AIDS is carried on by the AIDS councils, usually in close collaboration with counselors attached to clinics and health centers. With substantial resources available after 1987, councils also began to provide limited accommodation for needy people living with AIDS. The Queensland AIDS Council, limited by state policy in its education programs, developed sufficient care resources to provoke complaints by the state government that it could not maintain the same level of care through mainstream services.

From 1986 to 1989, those living with AIDS in Australia were able to keep roughly abreast of the United States in their access to treatments. AZT became available for people with AIDS through hospitals very quickly after its clearance in the United States. After considerable pressure from ACON—including the first major AIDS demonstration in November 1987—the Commonwealth agreed to make AZT available under Medicare. But two years later, with the development of a much more complex range of treatments and agreement on the fast-tracking of official approval of therapeutic agents in the United States, access for Australians fell behind. While Australia's health system and collaboration between researchers and the infected made it attractive for clinical trials, pharmaceutical companies were deterred by Australia's slow and cumbersome system for approving the testing and licensing of therapeutic agents. ACON's research potential was brought into play through a working group, which made information on new treatments widely available. Late in 1990, an ANCA subcommittee produced detailed recommendations for the reform of drug approval and for community-based drug trials. Pressure for reform also came from the effective mobilization of state and national People Living with AIDS and their more radical offspring, ACT UP, which followed American precedents in demonstrating for better access to treatments. As the cost of treatment increased, it was inevitable that questions would be raised about the appropriate level of funding for AIDS prevention.[34]

The demand for the mainstreaming of specialized AIDS programs, and for the reintegration of prevention programs into generalized health promotion and AIDS services into standard arrangements for treatment and care, arose in 1988 both from the medical profession and from hospitals. Such mainstreaming seems to be supported by the White Paper, which includes among its guiding principles the proposition that "General principles of public health, service provision and the legal system should be applied to the AIDS epidemic; special measures or services require justification." Nonetheless, the National Strategy itself was an exercise in justifying AIDS exceptionalism. Queensland could be said to have insisted on "normalizing" AIDS; and some mainstreaming began to take place in New South Wales in 1990, with the decentralization of AIDS programs to regional health offices and the consequent reductions in the state's strong AIDS bureau. With increasing economic recession, the budgetary commitments of the National Strategy have also come under heavy pressure.

Will there be any enduring impact of AIDS on the Australian health system? In 1988, the secretary of the Commonwealth Department of Health described AIDS programs as a model for community participation in future public health policy:

> Gradually, all governments came to accept that people from the high risk groups had to be involved in all aspects of program delivery, from prevention and support through to treatment and research. This often followed deep challenges to the cultural, social and moral values of decision-makers themselves, and involved overcoming the view that health care delivery was the province of health care professionals alone. It meant sharing power, along with responsibility.[35]

Confronting the AIDS epidemic has provided a point of entry for those concerned about reform in education, prisons, and law, and changes in social values as well. It has enlisted an increasing number of officials, educators, and volunteers, who have received a practical education in the redefinition of health and social reform. This is part of the enduring legacy of AIDS in Australia.

Notes

1. *The Australian* (November 17, 1984).
2. For a discussion of the historical dominance of the medical profession, see Evan Willis, *Medical Dominance: The Division of Labour in Australian Health Care* (Sydney: Allen and Unwin, rev. ed., 1989).

3. For its history see Garry Wotherspoon, *City of the Plain: History of a Gay Sub-Culture* (Sydney: Hale and Iremonger, 1991).

4. Dennis Altman, "The Emergence of Gay Identity in the USA and Australia," in *Politics of the Future: The Role of Social Movements* ed. Christine Jennet and Randal G. Stewart (Melbourne: Macmillan, 1989), 47. Altman's essay is the best available discussion of the background of gay politics and culture in Australia. His *Homosexual: Oppression and Liberation* (Sydney: Angus and Robertson, 1972) had a major impact on the development of gay identity in Australia.

5. *Sydney Daily Telegraph* (March 1, 1983).

6. *Sydney Morning Herald* (May 10, 1983).

7. *The Age* (June 3, 1983).

8. *The Bulletin* (May 10, 1983); *Sydney Daily Mirror* (May 26, 1983); "60 Minutes" (television program) (May 29, 1983).

9. A. I. Adams, "AIDS and Blood Donors," *Medical Journal of Australia* 141 (1984), 588.

10. Sydney AIDS Study Group, "The Sydney AIDS Project," *Medical Journal of Australia* 141 (1984), 569–573.

11. D. A. Cooper, P. Maclean, R. Finlayson et al., "Acute AIDS Retrovirus Infection: Definition of a Clinical Illness Associated with Seroconversion," *Lancet* 1 (1985), 537–540.

12. *Campaign* (February 1985); Terry Goulden, "Promiscuity Error," *Australian Society* 4 (2) (1985), 39.

13. Evan Whitton, "AIDS! The Media, Paranoia and the Wrath of God," *Sydney Morning Herald* (August 17, 1985).

14. *Canberra Times* (February 13, 1986). There was, in fact, evidence of substantial behavior change in the fall in the incidence of anal gonorrhea at Sydney STD clinics, but this was not made available until much later. See B. Donovan and B. Tindall, "Behavior Change in Sexually Transmitted Disease Patients" in *AIDS and Other Sexually Transmitted Diseases*, ed. R. Richmond and D. Wakefield (Sydney: Harcourt Brace Jovanovich, 1989), 23, and B. Donovan, T. C. Harcourt, I. Bassett, and C. R. Philpot, "Gonorrhea and Asian Prostitution: The Sydney Sexual Health Center Experience," *Medical Journal of Australia* 154 (1991), 520–521.

15. *Sydney Morning Herald* (April 18, 1987).

16. M. Gawenda, "AIDS: Reaping Responsibility," *The Age* (May 2, 1987).

17. *Sydney Morning Herald* (June 5, 1987).

18. *Sydney Morning Herald* (June 8, 1987).

19. *Sydney Morning Herald* (July 11, 1987).

20. G. Hunter, "Penthouse Interview: David Penington," *Australian Penthouse* 8 (12) (1987), 95–100, 109.

21. In Australia, the Liberal party is the ideological counterpart to the Conservative party in Britain.

22. Wilson Tuckey, M.P., "The Politics of AIDS," in Department of Community Services and Health, *Living with AIDS, Toward the Year 2000: Report of the Third National Conference on AIDS* (Canberra: Australian Government Publishing Service, 1988), 739–741.

23. Bryce Phillips, "The Role of the Australian Medical Association," in Department of Community Services and Health, *Third National Conference* (Canberra: Australian Government Publishing Service, 1988), 641.

24. David I. Grove and Jon B. Mulligan, "Consent, Compulsion and Confidentiality in Relation to Testing for HIV Infection: The Views of WA Doctors," *Medical Journal of Australia* 152 (1990), 174–177.

25. Department of Community Services and Health, *National HIV/AIDS Strategy: A Policy Information Paper* (Canberra: Australia Government Publishing Service, 1989), 25.

26. *News Weekly,* (September 16, 1989).

27. Ken Donald, "Priorities in Allocation of Resources for AIDS Programs," in Commonwealth Department of Health and Department of Health Victoria, *Meeting the Challenge: Papers of the First National Conference on AIDS* (Canberra: Australian Government Publishing Service, 1986).

28. Evan Whitton, *The Hillbilly Dictator: Australia's Police State* (Crow's Nest: Australian Broadcasting Commission, 1989), 130.

29. Andrew Stewart, "Queensland Nationals Divided on AIDS," *Canberra Times* (May 15, 1987).

30. For example, Ron Penny and Marcia Neave, "AIDS: A Carefully Selected Course," *The Bulletin* (April 24, 1990), 42.

31. Adam Carr, "Out in the Cold in Canberra," *OutRage* 89 (October 1990), 60–61.

31. G. W. Dowsett, "Reaching Men Who Have Sex with Men in Australia. An Overview of AIDS Education: Community Intervention and Community Attachment Strategies," *Australian Journal of Social Issues* 26 (1990), 187–198.

33. Department, *Third National Conference,* 221–245.

34. Adam Carr, "The Age of Hard Choices," *OutRage* 93 (1991), 20–23.

35. Stuart Hamilton, "The Role of Government in Health Development," in *Health Development: Whose Baby?* (Canberra: National Centre for Epidemiology and Population Health, 1989), 11.

Chapter 5

Spain: An Epidemic of Denial

Jesús M. de Miguel and David L. Kirp

Spain sits at the fringe of Europe, separated (together with Portugal) from the rest of the continent by a ruggedly forbidding mountain range. The country's isolation is not simply geographic. Until recently, Spain has been a bit player in the Western European theater. Democracy came late to Spain, restored only after the death of Generalissimo Francisco Franco in 1975, and as recently a quarter of a century ago, Spain was poor enough to be classified as part of the second world, a western Czechoslovakia.

But in recent decades Spain has made giant strides toward economic and political integration into the European mainstream. Its economy began taking off in the 1960s, and the pace of modernization picked up with the end of the Franco era. The swift transition from dictatorship to democracy culminated with a progressive new constitution, adopted in 1978, which describes a federation of states each possessing more power than states in most other European nations. Significantly, the new constitution also incorporates a bill of rights, which guarantees legal protection against discrimination on a variety of grounds, including sexual preference.

Developments in the technologically advanced democratic world have often come to Spain late and in transmuted form. This has been true of AIDS, which until the mid-1980s was widely regarded as someone else's disease, belonging to the United States and then to northern Europe.

Not until the end of the decade—a time when the era of AIDS exceptionalism was elsewhere drawing to an end and AIDS was being reintegrated into existing institutions of public health—did AIDS panic strike Spain with full force. Then, widespread popular fears that schoolchildren could spread the disease prompted schools in several parts of the country to bar HIV-infected children, and there were broadsides against prostitutes, who were thought to be transmitting AIDS to the general population.

Nor was AIDS panic confined to an unsophisticated populace. On November 30, 1990, the eve of World AIDS Day, Rafael Najera, director of the Carlos III Institute of Health, where most of Spain's AIDS research is carried out, proposed quarantining everyone with the AIDS virus. "If the advance of AIDS is not stopped in the 1990s, health authorities may have to isolated HIV-infected persons."[1]

Around the globe, there had been murmuring about the idea of quarantine in the epidemic's earliest years. But it is startling for so prominent a national official to be making such inflammatory statements so late in the day. If this threat were ever to become policy, it would turn Spain into another Cuba, the only nation that isolates its HIV-infected population. Yet among Spanish AIDS policymakers, talk of quarantine was just another exercise in symbolism, another non-response to the realities of the epidemic.

Meanwhile, even as the threat of AIDS is lessening throughout western Europe, the disease continues to gather force in Spain.[2] The composition of the AIDS caseload is importantly different as well: in Spain, most of those who have contracted AIDS are not gays but intravenous drug users, their sexual partners, and their children—the most marginal members of the society. Even as AIDS policy-making remains more symbolic than substantive, Spain offers a picture of things to come in the demographics of the epidemic. The linkage may not be coincidental.

Demographics, Democracy, and Distrust

At the end of 1990, Spain had recorded 7,198 cases of AIDS. With 171 cases per million, it ranked second among European nations, behind only Switzerland, and accounted for one-sixth of Europe's AIDS cases. More alarmingly, the AIDS caseload has increased 2.25 times annually. Because case reporting in Spain tends to be slower than in other European countries, these figures understate the incidence of the disease (see Table 5.1).

It is somewhat surprising that AIDS should be so significant an epidemic in Spain. Elsewhere, AIDS has been associated either with prosperity and liberation (as in the United States) or with poverty and traditional sexual practices (as in Africa). But Spain has a low rate of homosexual contacts, a weak and divided gay community, strong social control over sexual mores, and a public health system—revamped in 1986—that offers free medical care to almost everyone.[3] In these respects, it resembles the Eastern European countries, yet the AIDS rate in Spain is many times higher.

The incidence of AIDS in Spain, unlike most European countries, is concentrated in the lowest social classes. Two-thirds of those with AIDS are intravenous drug users—that is more than double the proportion in Europe. And while elsewhere almost half the AIDS cases have been recorded among homosexuals, many of them middle-class, gays account for just one-sixth of the cases in Spain. (Three percent are both gay and drug users; the data suggest that drug use is the primary causal factor in most of these cases.) Among the industrialized democracies, only Italy shows a similar pattern. The proportion of women with AIDS is slightly

Table 5.1. AIDS Cases by Year of Report and Category of Risk Exposure for Spain, 1981–1990

Risk category	1981	1982	1983	1984	1985	1986	1987	1988	1989	1990	Total
Homosexual/bisexual activity	1	1	4	10	35	77	188	297	384	206	1203
Homosexual/bisexual activity and IVDU	0	0	1	2	11	25	30	42	66	44	221
IVDU	0	1	4	16	83	233	540	1,236	1,503	941	4,557
Blood products	0	2	4	13	18	45	59	99	89	33	362
Heterosexual activity	0	0	0	0	2	12	34	61	117	80	306
Mother to child	0	0	0	1	4	19	25	61	56	22	188
Other/unknown	0	0	1	4	6	12	33	88	136	81	361
Total cases	1	4	14	46	159	423	909	1,884	2,351	1,407	7,198

Source: *Publicacion Oficial de la SEISIDA*, Vol. 2, no. 3 (March 1991), 170–171.
Note: Data as of December 31, 1990; Centro Nacional de Epidemiologia, Instituto de Salud Carlos III.

higher in Spain than in other European countries, and it appears that the pediatric AIDS case rate is substantially higher (although underreporting is most blatant for pediatric AIDS). As in other nations, AIDS cases are concentrated in the more developed regions of the country; Madrid, Catalonia, the Basque Country, and the Balearic Islands.

The first known AIDS case in Spain occurred in 1981, when a gay man developed Kaposi's sarcoma, but was not diagnosed as having had AIDS until after his death two years later. In 1981, there *was* an epidemic of death commanding widespread attention in Spain—but it was not AIDS.

That year, some 650 inexplicable deaths and 25,000 reported illnesses—what came to be called the Spanish Toxic Syndrome—stirred popular concern that lingered through the decade.[4] Eventually, tainted cooking oil was blamed for the tragedy, but even after a formal inquiry in 1990, doubts persisted about the real cause of these deaths. Meanwhile, AIDS made its first appearance in Spain, largely unnoticed.

There are some similarities between AIDS and the Spanish Toxic Syndrome. The impact of both was concentrated in the lower classes and Spanish Toxic Syndrome galvanized reform of the health sector, even as AIDS sparked some reformist strategies. Yet, while the experience with the Spanish Toxic Syndrome might have taught the nation useful epidemiological lessons that could be applied to AIDS, instead it kept interest focused elsewhere.

In the mid-1980s, as other nations were seeing rapid increases in AIDS cases and were increasing their AIDS budgets exponentially—partly in response to the fear that the disease would reach the general population in sizeable numbers—Spain did little to combat AIDS. Officials ignored the fact that Spain was not immune from AIDS but merely lagged behind its northern neighbors by a few years. As a result, Spain missed an opportunity to take the kinds of aggressive public health measures—among them, widespread education about AIDS prevention, support of gay groups' efforts, prison reform, and distribution of syringes—that could have minimized the impact of AIDS.

The system of public health in Spain is built on reforms brought about by wars and epidemics, from the 1855 cholera epidemic to the Spanish Toxic Syndrome. The General Health Law, first proposed by the social democratic government of the Spanish Socialist Workers party when it took power in 1982 and implemented four years later, provides for free and universal health care, some three-quarters of which is publicly financed.[5] The Ministry of Health estimates that AIDS care costs about $200 million (in 1990 U.S. dollars) annually, which is 2.5 percent of the national health budget and as much as the country spends on its national drug program.[6]

In providing health care, cost containment has not been a significant concern. While prenatal and perinatal services have expanded considerably since the new health legislation, on other fronts there has been more planning than action; political squabbling and economic difficulties have impeded implementation.[7] Relatively little is spent to treat chronic illnesses and in the context of AIDS, this means that life-prolonging drugs like AZT have not been made widely available.[8] As one AIDS patient movingly wrote in the influential daily *El País*:

> I have AIDS. I'm dying, but the administration thinks I have to be even nearer to death before they will give me AZT. My doctor thinks it's the only thing that can help me but his supervisor won't allow it for reasons of cost. There are very costly programs to prevent cancer, but nothing for those who are sick with AIDS. . . . How much would [AZT] cost: Listen, sirs, I'll pay for it. You say it's not fair for the rest of the sick ones. Well, don't blame me. . . . Please, help me! I need AZT, at whatever price.[9]

Spain's social democratic government has been much more secular in orientation than its predecessors, more socially progressive on such matters as homosexuality and the liberalization of drug laws, more anxious also to develop systems for protecting the populace: all this has brought Spain into the modern age. But the complex allocation of governmental responsibilities in Spain, coupled with the tendency of Spanish bureaucracy to rely on delaying tactics rather than problem-solving, has undermined development of a coherent national health strategy.

As in other nations with federal systems, much policy-making and all direct responsibility for patient care is left to the states. But Spain is distinctive because its states are semisovereign entities: autonomous regions, as they are called, some with their own languages and cultures. Only for limited purposes do they recognize the authority of Madrid. Liberation movements are most evident in the Basque Country and Catalonia, where the major proportion of the AIDS caseload is concentrated. While across Spain many of the states and major municipalities are governed by progressively inclined governments, their wealth varies widely, and so too does their capacity to provide social and health services.[10]

The national government in Madrid has responsibility for collecting epidemiological data, conducting medical research, and managing the major AIDS education campaigns. It has made AIDS, but not HIV status, a reportable condition, with a special registry maintained for just this purpose. On other matters, including confidentiality, HIV testing, and regulation of insurance, no national policy exists.

Power over national AIDS policy has been highly concentrated, with an elite (widely referred to as The Three Rafaels) centered at the Juan Carlos III Institute. The institute manages the data collection, conducts the research, organizes the conferences, and determines who will represent Spain at international meetings. The effect of such concentration has been to discourage innovation. Some researchers resent this concentration of effort; others oppose spending on AIDS research even at modest levels. In August of 1990, a contingent of prominent Spanish scientists publicly complained that too much was being spent on AIDS research, to the detriment of more worthy causes.[11]

Until 1987, the national government devoted little attention to AIDS, only establishing a small working commission to track cases and running one modest education campaign. Currently the more substantial and more visible National AIDS Project carries on this epidemiological job and also offers scientific and technical counsel; it organized the first national congress on AIDS in 1991.[12] Provincial and city officials are responsible for delivering health care, and they make most policy decisions.

Most impressive have been the efforts of officials in the Basque region, which has almost double the national rate of AIDS cases. A state strategy for AIDS prevention and treatment was developed in 1987. Among the innovations, an AIDS hotline was installed, and a campaign to encourage condom use was launched. Programs were developed to educate schoolchildren about the disease and to combat the by-then visible discrimination against those with AIDS. For a time, the Basque government sold, at cost, an "Anti-AIDS Kit" that included a condom, a syringe, a container for disposing of the syringe, and an AIDS pamphlet aimed at intravenous drug users. Special AIDS clinics were founded at public hospitals and infectious disease units were installed. The country's first hospices for AIDS patients were also opened.[13]

Catalonia has also been active, particularly on the AIDS education front. It operates an AIDS hotline and has distributed more than half a million copies of its straightforward written pamphlet "For a Future without AIDS: Don't Be Ignorant."[14]

Doctors have not sought to dominate discourse about AIDS; Spain's medical association, the College of Physicians, has had almost nothing to say about the disease. The trend of the public health system is to integrate AIDS care with ordinary primary care. This is also the view of the federation of AIDS groups, which asserts: "Every primary care physician should treat any citizen who presents with any AIDS-related problem. AIDS is a health problem. As such it should be treated within the general health network as just another health problem, avoiding the creation of 'special services.' "[15]

Four decades of Franco's repressive rule have left a legacy of popular distrust in Spain, not only toward the national government but toward officialdom generally. Government is them, not us, and its advice is often greeted with suspicion. Those most affected by AIDS, intravenous drug users and gays, have had only the most modest influence on policy. Even though some high-placed AIDS policy-makers are known to be closet gays, none have come out (a concept untranslatable into Spanish). Officials with AIDS responsibilities have sometimes felt obliged to meet with gay organizations and, less frequently, with others—intravenous drug users, delinquent youth, prostitutes and convicts—especially hard-hit by AIDS. But at the national and state levels, policy-making remains firmly in official hands.

Both gays and drug users were subject to harsh repression during Franco's reign. While homosexuality was legalized in 1978 (two of Europe's biggest gay havens, Sitges and Ibiza, are situated in Spain), and subsidized needles provided by the government a decade later, social attitudes have changed more slowly than the law. Even in postliberation Spain, opinion polls report, homosexuality and drug use are still condemned as sinful (though by lesser majorities than a decade earlier). The influential Catholic Church reinforces this view through its preachments and school curriculum, while social conservatives conflate AIDS and homosexuality. In August of 1990, Barcelona professor Alfonso Balsells wrote in *La Vanguardia* that AIDS is a "punishment of nature, which has been injured, and of men, one to another and on themselves. . . . We are paying the consequences of the hackneyed sexual liberation, of gay pride . . . of the initial tolerance of 'soft' drugs which will be followed by the 'hard' ones."[16]

This perception is internalized by many Spaniards with AIDS, who believe the disease dishonors them. In many democracies, people with AIDS have made their presence noisily felt, but in Spain gays are said to be "afraid to speak up and say they are scared of AIDS."[17] "AIDS is lived with guilt or as revenge, as a threat or a punishment. . . . It is lived as a disgrace, as a loss of honor."[18]

Gays initially believed that the epidemic wasn't their concern, a view they held longer than did their counterparts elsewhere. As Alberto Cardin and Antonio de Pluvia noted in their influential 1985 tract, *AIDS: Biblical Curse or Deadly Disease?*: "It has been at least two years since concern spread throughout the European gay milieu. . . . The predominant Spanish [gay] attitude is one of absolute indifference if not ridicule."[19] Through the mid-1980s, Spanish gay groups dismissed talk of AIDS as fomenting repressive hysteria—an export of the "neoconservative politics" of the United States.[20] Even as attitudes have changed in the face of the mounting death toll, no organizations have been formed by gay health workers to deal specifically to deal with AIDS; indeed, there are no openly gay doctors or public health officials in Spain.

Homosexuals have been active behind the scenes, however, writing the best of the AIDS books, drafting the reports that tackled intolerance and discrimination, manning the AIDS hot lines set up in the Basque region and Catalonia, and caring for the sick. Support groups for people with AIDS are also largely staffed by gays, although these are euphemistically referred to as civic organizations or citizens' associations. While there are numerous gay groups on the landscape, they are small and poorly organized. Their biggest policy accomplishment has been symbolic: in 1990, official AIDS terminology substituted reference to risky behavior for talk of risk groups, with its connotation of blame.

Others significantly affected by AIDS are essentially voiceless. In some states, notably the Basque region, parents of intravenous drug users have organized to press for treatment; and Project Hombre, a lay group linked to the Catholic Church, works with intravenous drug users. Those organizations helped push through the National Drug Program in 1985. While that program relaxes legal sanctions and subsidizes needle distribution, its promises of better care remain mostly words on paper.

Although in Spain there are as many women with AIDS as gay men, this fact has received almost no notice. "The nonalarmist message, the message that reduced the problem of AIDS to the 'risk groups,' encouraged the spread of AIDS in women. Even some experts dared to say that heterosexual AIDS wasn't proven or was more or less exceptional. . . . As is habitual, truth was evaded and prostitutes and female heroin addicts were made into the most dangerous groups."[21] Similarly, only modest attention has been paid to the widespread problem of the transmission of AIDS from mother to child. Abortion has not been officially encouraged for HIV-positive women, as it was elsewhere in Europe; officials urge only that pregnancy be "delayed." The reason for this non-policy is the Catholic Church's staunch and vocal opposition to abortion: while abortion is legal in the largest states, it is not officially encouraged. While only 189 cases of AIDS transmitted from mother to child were recorded by the end of 1990, a proportion of the AIDS cases just slightly higher than elsewhere in Europe, epidemiologists estimate that there actually may be ten times as many HIV-infected children.[22]

Shifting Fears

Spanish AIDS policy has passed through five distinct stages. Until 1984, indifference prevailed. AIDS was regarded as a rarity and a foreigners' disease; government undertook only to keep count of the cases. For the next three years, as the incidence of AIDS increased, the modest bureaucratic innovation of a national commission was adopted. Policy remained passive by design: the intent was to act with prudence, in order not to sound alarmist. The framework for national policy concern was imported from other European nations. It presented AIDS as a gay plague, despite the fact that in Spain, as early as 1985 there were more intravenous drug users than gays with AIDS.

The policy perspective began shifting from "a conviction that AIDS was only the heritage of the designated 'risk groups' "—especially gay men—when the number of new cases substantially exceeded projections. In some circles, this prompted "the apocalyptic idea of a twentieth-century plague."[23]

From 1987 until 1990, as fears of an AIDS pandemic were widely voiced, there was a tendency to define the epidemic in moral terms, to separate the "guilty"—gays, prostitutes, and drug users—from the "innocent" sufferers of AIDS, hemophiliacs and those who received contaminated blood in transfusions. While in Madrid the working commission was replaced with the more authoritative-sounding National AIDS Project, still no adequate apparatus existed to address the disease on the federal level. Most recently, as it has become plain that AIDS is primarily a disease of the most powerless, interest has slackened. There are renewed demands to divert resources to less "dishonorable" diseases. AIDS has once again become a back-burner topic and a hardship duty, for which health professionals are demanding extra pay.

In most countries, it was fear of a contaminated blood supply that initially commanded attention. Gays were discouraged or prohibited from making blood donations, raising fears in many places about their stigmatization and exclusion from the social mainstream. In 1985, when a test for the AIDS antibody became widely available, the blood question was reduced to a largely technical problem.

Concern was also voiced in Spain about contamination of the blood supply. But antibody testing came very late: although the screening of plasma for blood products started in the fall of 1985, whole blood screening did not begin until 1987. And while blood was supposed to be tested, lack of adequate facilities led to violations of a kind not encountered elsewhere among developed nations.

In one notorious case, Barcelona's Bellvitge Hospital's blook bank obtained more than six thousand donations and carried out more than two thousand transfusions of untested blood. In lieu of tests, hospital administrators relied on donors' personal appearance, refusing to accept blood from men with earrings or tattoos. Consequently, several patients became HIV-positive; hospital directors were later tried and imprisoned for their criminal negligence. In 1991, after another Barcelona hospital was found to have given a transfusion of contaminated blood to a patient who later died of AIDS, Catalonia's health department was ordered to pay $250,000 in damages.[24]

More litigation is anticipated, especially lawsuits by hemophiliacs, some 60 percent of whom are HIV-positive because of having received an AIDS-tainted blood-clotting product. The question of blood became a way of distinguishing guilt and innocence, as hemophiliacs have been at pains to distance themselves from others with AIDS. "We hemophiliacs refuse to [be] lumped . . . with those groups that are themselves responsible for spreading AIDS. . . . [W]e are innocent victims. . . ."[25]

In the mid-1980s, the development of an AIDS antibody test also encouraged some politicians to advocate mandatory testing of "risk groups," including foreigners (especially Africans), prisoners, intravenous drug users, couples planning to marry, prostitutes, as well as people in particular professions involving potential safety concerns, such as airline pilots. While concerns about privacy and confidentiality, which in other countries inflected the testing debate, were seldom voiced in Spain, there was little official enthusiasm for mandatory testing. To the new generation of public health officials, this seemed inconsistent with the social democratic ethos of inclusion and cooperation.

When gay-dominated organizations, led by the Citizens' Anti-AIDS Movement, lobbied against it, the proposal quietly disappeared—this despite the fact that 88 percent of the population, when surveyed, favored testing people in these "risk groups."[26] In addition to concern about the use of coercion, limited resources also played a role in shaping testing policy. The health minister insisted that, while the HIV test should be made widely available, it could not be offered universally, "due to the natural scarcity of resources." At present, HIV testing is hapazardly done and no systematic national surveillance survey has been mounted. This is a policy response that serves to illustrate a more general disorganization in the public sector.[27]

Popular opinion has generally been less informed and less progressive than public health admonitions. According to a 1987 national opinion poll conducted by the Center for Sociological Investigation, half the population thought AIDS could be contracted by kissing, and a quarter believed that it could be contracted by sitting on a toilet or drinking from a glass used by someone with AIDS. One in six Spaniards believed that AIDS could be contracted by living with an afflicted person.

Support for control-oriented public health measures has been strong. Nearly nine Spaniards in ten favored testing risk groups; 61 percent believed foreigners with AIDS should be kept out of the country; nearly half felt AIDS patients should be quarantined; one-third supported requiring people with AIDS to carry some form of identification.

AIDS education campaigns were not undertaken by the government until 1986. Meanwhile, the most useful sex education material on AIDS was prepared by a gay group in Barcelona, with substantial American input.

The pamphlet, "Enjoy Life, Avoid AIDS," explains the techniques of safe sex in clear language. Its message—hot, erotic, safe—was calculated not to preach but to change behavior. Yet intravenous drug users, who most needed advice on how to avoid AIDS, did not receive it. When it did emerge, the government-produced material generally "suffered from vague slogans and imprecise instructions."[28] "Use condoms whenever possible. . . . You have to take into account that there are many ways of expressing sexuality," was the Polonius-like advice of the Health Ministry.[29]

The national government sponsored three more AIDS education campaigns between 1987 and 1990. The first showed cartoon figures engaging in various behaviors, some risky and others safe. "Sí-da, no da" was the label, a play on SIDA, the Spanish acronym for AIDS. A 1989 campaign was partly targeted at intravenous drug users. It declared: "Don't shoot up, or AIDS will hook you"—a variant on "Just Say No." To the general public it urged: "Don't get infected with fear." In 1990, the government adopted its most ambitious effort to promote condom use. The slogan of the $6 million campaign was: "Put [a condom] on yourself! Put it on him!"

The best publicly produced education material is an AIDS pamphlet developed in 1988 by the Catalan Program for the Prevention and Control of AIDS and distributed as a Sunday supplement to *La Vanguardia*. Its theme: AIDS is a challenge, but one that can be met. It argues, in straightforward language, not only for individual precautions but also for social tolerance, "the adoption of . . . an attitude toward infected and sick people that . . . does not add to their rejection and segregation. . . . Not only is there no health justification for isolating those affected by AIDS, but marginalization and exclusion are, from a strictly public health point of view, totally inappropriate for limiting the spread of the epidemic."[30]

Meanwhile, the mass media have approached AIDS timidly. There has been little sensationalism in the press, but little information either. While advertisements state that "the most dangerous thing about AIDS is not knowing anything about it," specifics have rarely been published. The tone of commentary swings between anxiety and optimism: "Being a carrier is not the same as having AIDS." One consistent theme has been the need for tolerance toward those with AIDS. Only rarely have there been editorials or TV shows calling for measures of containment such as mandatory testing, and quarantine has received no media support.

Neither the government's campaigns nor the media coverage of AIDS prevention techniques explains the relatively slow spread of AIDS in the gay community (except in the Balearic Islands, a favorite gay vacation spot). The experts fumble for theories about this non-event.

Sociologist Oscar Guasch contends, on the basis of substantial interviewing, that AIDS is not treated as a "serious topic of concern about which [gays believe] they should take effective preventive measures."[31]

Gay men regard condoms with disdain, as "an object that heterosexuals have to put up with, having to do with procreation, a strange thing that interferes with possibilities for pleasure. Gay groups . . . jealous custodians of the conquests of the sexual revolution that cost so much to win, [have regarded] a condom as a straitjacket."[32] Guasch argues "that the basically romantic tendency of the Spanish homosexual subculture hasn't permitted the limitless spread of high-risk sexual activities."

Alternatively, Dr. Alfonso Delgado Rubio has asserted that because "AIDS fortunately had a somewhat delayed arrival in Spain, [this] permitted us to learn from the experience of other nations . . . which would explain the slower spread of AIDS among Spanish homosexuals."[33] Yet this claim is based more on supposition than evidence: the country's forty gay bathhouses remain open and anonymous sex is still common.

The 1990 federal AIDS education camapign, which emphasized using condoms, provoked the ire of the Spanish bishops. They quoted Pope John Paul II's assault on "spiritual AIDS" as "immunodeficiency of existential values," and also attacked "morally illicit means and remedies that humiliate the dignity of the human being. . . ."[34] Advising youth to use condoms merely encourages promiscuity, the bishops insisted, and so encourages AIDS and death. Amidst the controversy that the bishops' statements generated, little notice was paid to the fact that the campaign hadn't worked: there was no reported change in sexual behavior among the youth at whom the initiative was directed. As Manuel Carballo Macano, then deputy director of the World Health Organization's AIDS prevention program, observed: "The campaigns carried out in the mass media . . . are of very short duration and don't always reach those who need them most. Often they have increased public uneasiness . . . in those who are least at risk, while those most at risk . . . don't want to hear [the message] or . . . don't understand it."[35]

That the prevention campaigns focus on youth and gay men is remarkable, since intravenous drug users—estimated to number one hundred thousand in Spain—constitute nearly half of the country's cases.[36] The government's strategy amounts to an unthinking preference for the northern European AIDS model over the Spanish facts of life, an emphasis on condoms when clean needles would matter much more. Rafael Najera, director of the Carlos III Institute of Health, restates the conventional wisdom when he argues that "the condom must enter our culture as a hygienic necessity, as commonplace as brushing one's teeth or drinking purified water."[37]

To be sure, there have been efforts at both the national and the provincial levels to encourage intravenous drug users to use disposable needles. The national government has made it easier to purchase disposable syringes, which are now available in all pharmacies without prescription at the cost of fifty cents. The syringes are sold in an envelope containing the instruction, from the Health Ministry's General Office of Pharmacy and Health Products, to"Use it and break it," and on the syringe itself there is the admonition: "Use once and destroy. Shared use constitutes a risk of infection." The policy is admirable. But practical difficulties—the cost of the syringes, pharmacists' attitudes—as well as the hard-to-break tradition of solidarity that makes needle sharing the cultural norm, have hindered the effort.

For a short time, the Basque authorities distributed syringes, together with condoms and an AIDS information brochure. However, the pilot effort ended abruptly and with no evaluation, in the face of apparent resistance from addicts on the street. Later, the government opted to promote condoms but not syringes, a tactic that evaded the problem.

The best data on the incidence of HIV among drug users come from prison studies. A 1989 national survey, mandated by the Director General of Penal Institutions and carried out without the prisoners' knowledge or consent, found widespread seropositivity among prisoners. Overall, more than a quarter of Spanish prisoners are seropositive or have AIDS. In prisons in Madrid and Catalonia, the seropositivity rate approaches 50 percent. And at the Center for Youth Detention in Madrid, the rate is a staggering 63 percent.

Heroin use is tacitly tolerated by prison officials because it pacifies inmates, and heroin is widely available. As one prison official declared, when drugs get scarce "you know that something is cooking . . . the prisoners are upset because no drugs have arrived for a week. . . . You tremble in your guts."[38] Thus, the policy dilemma: the condition of Spain's prisons makes heroin use functional, and heroin use is likely to mean HIV infection. Efforts in some of the states to supply syringes and bleach to prisoners have been sporadic and widely condemned by the Right. There is no evidence that these efforts have slowed the spread of AIDS. As the Federation of Civic Anti-AIDS Committees reported in 1988: "The majority of inmates lack information on [AIDS] and don't have the necessary means of preventing contagion (condoms, syringes). . . . It is not enough to distribute pamphlets and give talks in the jails."[39]

Spanish inmates have been vocal about the lack of medical attention for those with AIDS. During the summer of 1990, there were three prison demonstrations. Five Barcelona prisoners with AIDS climbed up to the prison roof and stayed there for fifty-two hours. Their concern wasn't to promote reform of the prisons but the more culturally familiar desire for a good death. "We want a dignified death in a hospital, not in a prison," they insisted. An embarrassed government finally arranged hospital admission, over the opposition of hospital administrators—only to transport the inmates to another prison four days later.

In a Barcelona women's prison, three hundred convicts protested when a woman running a high fever was kept isolated in her cell for nine days. Although prison doctors diagnosed her condition as tonsilitis, an autopsy revealed that she had AIDS. The media attention these demonstrations received angered prison officials, who accused the press of "making a sounding board of these incidents and of inciting inmates elsewhere."[40] Meanwhile, prison policy did not change. Prisoners with AIDS are generally not hospitalized until the last stages of the disease; instead they are placed in isolation cells or transferred from one prison to another.

Given the demographics of AIDS in Spain, the challenge—one that no country has satisfactorily met—is to develop strategies for mobilizing drug users, nurturing information networks, encouraging the use of clean needles, and combating the ethos of solidarity that encourages drug users to share their "works." Differences of opinion exist on the most sound course for policy. Basque administrators still support the idea of needle exchange, despite having abandoned the program. In Catalonia, official policy is to oppose drugs while promoting the use of clean needles among addicts. That way, advocates say, "the person who despite everything continues to use drugs is, at least, protected from suffering infections," while opponents make the familiar argument that this approach encourages drug use.[41] But the debate is more rhetorical than real, since little has been done to reach out to this most marginal of social groups.

One consistently voiced theme expressed both by private groups and by government officials has been a call to protect people with AIDS against discrimination. The Federation of Civic Anti-AIDS Committees and Commissions of the Spanish State came together to "denounce any possible violation of rights of those affected with AIDS . . . in the school as well as the workplace, in medical help, in the treatment of AIDS in the mass media, in housing, and elsewhere."[42]

In 1987, Minister of Health Julian Garcia Vargas delivered the first address on AIDS by a national politician. His emphasis was not only on disease prevention but also on preventing discrimination. "The challenge is to inform the entire population of how to prevent this disease. We must provide elaborate information and support systems. . . . This challenge will put our social and health services to the test. Above all, it is already putting to the test tolerance, solidarity, and rationality in our society."[43] Three years later, meeting with the National Health Commission of the federal Senate, he pleaded for help in the struggle against discrimination.[44]

But despite constitutional language that is meant to guarantee a wide range of freedom, AIDS-based discrimination has gone largely unchecked. This has been most visible in the schools. Shortly before Garcia Vargas' speech, a boy in the Basque city of Durango had been barred from a Catholic school when officials discovered that he was seropositive. Then, at a state-subsidized religious institution, the boy was kept out by a council of parents and administrators. Two months later, in the city of Santander, two HIV-positive children, both girls, were barred from school. Similar stories were reported in 1991.

Health Minister Garcia Vargas tried to calm popular fears by appearing on television, holding one of the Santander girls in his arms. On a second occasion, the health minister brought his own son along with one of the HIV-infected children. Still these youngsters remained out of school— and unlike in the United States, where Ryan White became a national hero after being sent home from the Kokomo, Indiana, schools, in Spain there was no groundswell of support for the youngsters. Nor, despite urging from the health minister, did the federal government move to bar discrimination against those with AIDS.

Into the 1990s

AIDS has challenged the social traditions of Spain, and some of the changes it has wrought have been for the good.[45] The advent of the disease has prompted fuller discussion of drug use and sex (including male responsibility for contraception) and somewhat greater attention to the plight of the most marginal groups.

The policy response is another matter. "This society has more or less clarified the rights of sick people," writes Hector Anabitarte, "but not the right to avoid illness. The health network did not hesitate to administer sophisticated treatment to incurably ill patients, but it wavered on publicity campaigns. . . . AIDS remains a challenge, a provocation."[46] But whether AIDS can encourage the development of more effective public health strategies in Spain remains to be seen.

Acknowledgements

Thanks to Daniel Wohfeiler of the Stop-AIDS Project in San Francisco, who has worked extensively with the Catalonia Health Ministry. In Spain, Josep-Lluis Bimbela, Omar Garcia Ponce de Leon, Mauro Guillen, Albert Jovell, Josep Rodriguez, Andreu Segura, and Joan Villalbi critiqued an early draft of this manuscript. Jose Garcia at Columbia University tracked down needed additional information. Daniel Sparler speedily and admirably translated an early draft of this chapter into English.

Notes

1. *El Diario* (November 30, 1990), 15.

2. While the 1990 figures show fewer new AIDS cases, this is most likely an artifact of delays in reporting, not an indication of declining incidence.

3. Joseph Rodriguez and Louis Lemko, "Health and Social Inequities in Spain," *Social Science and Medicine* 31:3 (1990), 351–358. OECD ranks the Spanish health care system as comparable to Western Europe generally. See OECD, *Measuring Health Care 1960–1983: Expenditures, Costs and Performance* (Paris: OECD, 1985).

4. See generally World Health Organization, *The Cooking Oil Syndrome: Massive Food Poisoning in Spain* (Copenhagen: World Health Organization, 1984); Andreas Faber Kaiser, *The Pact of Silence: The Concealment of the True Cause of the Toxic Syndrome Impeded the Recovery of Thousands of Spaniards* (Barcelona: Compania General de Letras, 1988); Lluis Botinas, "Toxic Syndrome, A Revealing Court Ruling," *El Correo del Sol: Suplemento de la Revista Integral* 118 (October 1989), 6–7.

5. On the health system generally, see Jesús M. de Miguel and Miguel Guillen, *The Spanish Health Crisis* (Oviedo: University of Oviedo Press, 1987).

6. *El País* (November 4, 1990), 27.

7. *El Paíus* (May 16, 1991), 34.

8. Rodriguez and Lemkow, "Health and Social Inequities," 351–358.

9. *El País* (December 1, 1989), 35.

10. Rodriguez and Lemko, "Health and Social Inequities," 351–358.

11. *La Vanguardia* (August 30, 1990), 16.

12. For a discussion of central government's early role, see Ricardo Usieto et al., *AIDS: A Problem of Public Health* (Madrid: Diaz de Santos, 1987).

13. Javier Alonso et al., "Some Social Aspects of AIDS in the Health Field," *Health Notebooks*, volume 2 (1989), 85–95.

14. Jordi Casabona et al., "Characteristics of the Demand for a 'Hot Line' Service and the Influence of Mass Media Campaigns" (Barcelona: Generalitat de Catalunya (mimeo) (1988).

15. Andreu Segura, *AIDS: A Manageable Challenge* (Barcelona: *La Vanguardia*, Guia numero 3, 1989), 26.

16. Alfonso Balcells, "El SIDA," *La Vanguardia* (August 29, 1990), 12.

17. Hector Anabitarte, "Indifference and Challenge," in *AIDS: A Public Health Problem*, ed. Ricardo Usieto (Madrid: Diaz de Santos, 1987), 268.

18. Ricardo Lorenzo and Hector Anabitarte, *AIDS: A Burning Topic* (Madrid: Editorial Revolucion, 1987), 56.

19. Alberto Cardin and Antonio deFluvia, eds., *AIDS: Biblical Curse or Deadly Disease?* (Barcelona: Laertes, 1985).

20. See generally Oscar Guasch, *The Pink Society* (unpublished Ph.D. dissertation) (University of Barcelona, School of Public Health, 1990).

21. Lorenzo and Anabitarte, *AIDS: A Burning Topic*, 78.

22. Joseph Lopez, "The Children of AIDS, the Sad Consequence of a Disease," *La Vanguardia* (March 7, 1990), 4–5 ("Health and Quality of Life" supplement).

23. Federation of Civic Anti-AIDS Committees and Commissions of the Spanish State, *AIDS Information Notebook* (Madrid: Federación de Cómites Ciudadanos Anti-SIDA, 1988), 4.

24. *El País* (January 21, 1991), 13.

25. Quoted by Anibararte, "Indifference and Challenge," 263.

26. Federation, *AIDS Information Notebook*, 2.

27. See generally Jesús M. de Miguel, *The Myth of an Organized Society* (Bacelona: Peninsula, 1990).

28. Oscar Guasch, "The Medical Construction of a Stigma, *Luego*, 16–17, (1990), 87–99.

29. See Ministry of Health, *AIDS Reports* (Madrid, Ministry of Health, 1989), 61.

30. Segura, *AIDS: An Assumable Challenge*, 7. See also Alberto Cardin, "The Stigma in the Shadow: The Atypical Marginality of Homosexual AIDS Carriers," *El Pais* (November 2, 1989), 10.

31. Oscar Guasch, "AIDS and Spanish Homosexuals," *Jano* 32:772, (1987), 91–95.

32. Anibatarte, *"Indifference and Challenge,"* 266.

33. Alfonso Delgado Rubio, *AIDS Manual: Medical and Social Aspects* (Masdrid: Organizacion Medica Colegial, 1987), 66.

34. *El País* (November 24, 1989), 12.

35. Quoted in *El Médico* (May 19, 1990), 77.

36. Carlos Gonzales et al., *Rethinking Drugs* (Barcelona: Grupo Igia, 1989); see also Ramon Bayes, "Drug Dependencies, Psychology and AIDS," *Community and Drugs*, vol. 12, (Fall 1989) 203–210; Ricardo Usieto, ed., *Scientific Symposium on Drugs and Society* (Madrid: Universidad Internacional Menendez Pelayo, 1989).

37. *El País* (November 4, 1990), 21.

38. *El País* (July 29, 1990), 2.

39. Federation, *AIDS Information Notebook*, 10.

40. *El País* (July 29, 1990), 18.

41. Segura, *AIDS: A Manageable Challenge*, 29.

42. Federation, *AIDS Information Notebook*, 2.

43. Quoted in Ricardo Usieto et al., eds., *International AIDS Conference* (Madrid: Universidad Internacional Menendez Pelayo, 1987), 24.

44. *El País* (November 4, 1990), 21.

45. See Albert Jovell, "The Social Dimension of AIDS" (Sociology Department, Autonomous University of Barcelona, 1990) (Mimeo).

46. Anabitarte, "Indifference and Challenge," 270.

Chapter 6

Britain: Policy-making in a Hermetically Sealed System

John Street and Albert Weale

British AIDS policy has mixed the untypical with the predictable. Politicians have been typically cautious, fearing the effects of shocking their constituents, while civil servants have sometimes been untypically willing to embrace innovation. The tabloids have been predictably hysterical about AIDS, while popular opinion has been remarkably sanguine. The moral right has, unsurprisingly, seen AIDS as divine retribution for depravity, while television has presented a generally responsible public health message. The style of policy-making has been predictably elitist, even as spending on services for people with AIDS has been untypically generous and the process of implementing policy has been unusually participatory.

In short, the contradictions that mark British political and social life are echoed in AIDS policy. "The British response to AIDS ha[s] been shaped as much by the nature of the British policy making system as by the nature of the epidemic."[1] AIDS policy reveals the tensions within the policy process, and for this reason, many competing interpretations have been advanced. We emphasize the highly centralized and exclusive character of the policy process, while others have placed more stress on the pressure politics behind AIDS policy and the influence of such gay groups as the Terrence Higgins Trust.[2] Our argument is not that these are unimportant, but that they are not decisive in the political process that has forged and defined British AIDS policy.

Three moments are pivotal. In autumn 1986, government policy was transformed in a matter of weeks. Instead of being a backwater issue confined to the policy agenda of the Department of Health (DoH), AIDS became the focus of a high-profile political campaign. A special cabinet committee was created. There was a massive budget increase and the promise of a major national publicity program. Every household received a leaflet on AIDS and how to avoid it; this was supplemented by the first in a series of television advertisements about the dangers of AIDS. For the first time, Parliament debated the issues raised by AIDS.

Since this moment, AIDS policy has been an explicitly political issue, subject to direct political interference. Three years later, after lengthy

185

Table 6.1. AIDS Cases by Year of Report and Category of Risk Exposure for Great Britain, 1983–1990

Risk category	1983	1984	1985	1986	1987	1988	1989	1990	Total
Homosexual/bisexual activity	25	93	245	538	1,032	1,634	2,288	3,234	9,089
Homosexual/bisexual activity and IVDU	0	0	0	6	19	31	38	61	155
IVDU	0	0	2	9	19	39	80	161	310
Blood products	0	3	19	35	94	162	216	295	824
Heterosexual activity	0	7	13	18	44	88	135	268	573
Mother to child	0	0	0	3	13	19	23	36	94
Other/unknown	6	5	1	1	6	21	50	43	133
Total cases	31	108	280	610	1,227	1,994	2,830	4,098	11,178

SOURCE: Public Health Laboratory Service, Communicable Diseases Surveillance Centre, *Reports*, 1984–91; Department of Health, *On the State of the Public Health* (London: HMSO); AIDS Unit, Department of Health, *AIDS Briefing Note*, (London: Department of Health).

negotiations among government departments, research bodies, and other agencies, it was decided to launch a national survey of sexual behavior, to gather crucial evidence for the future development of AIDS policy. The survey's research director promised "a truly comprehensive and reliable picture of the distribution of sexual activity throughout the whole population. It will pinpoint the social location of higher-risk activity and allow accurate prediction of the cause of the disease over the next decade and beyond."[3] Not everyone shared this enthusiasm. The proposed survey was held in abeyance for ten months. Then Prime Minister Margaret Thatcher expressed her disapproval, insisting that the survey would be an unwarranted intrusion into people's privacy. Suddenly, support for the survey fell away. This moment seemed to signal the end of the government's interest in AIDS policy, and the special cabinet committee was wound up at the same time. But following Mrs. Thatcher's sudden resignation in November 1990, her successor, John Major, quickly reversed the government's policy on compensation for hemophiliacs who had contracted HIV from contaminated blood products.

These three moments raise critical questions about AIDS policy in Britain. Why did AIDS policy become a central political issue in the autumn of 1986? How have political interests and values shaped its course? The moments of political decisiveness have to be set against the more routinized but no less important process by which the bureaucracies implemented AIDS policy, as well as against the broader social and political context. Among the relevant influences are the efforts of the media to shape popular perceptions of AIDS and of gay groups to fight prevalent stereotypes—a fight made all the more urgent when the Thatcher government secured legislation that curbs the rights of homosexuals. In sum, British AIDS policy emerged in the interaction of very different policy processes, in which divergent criteria, interests, and actors intersected.

HIV and AIDS in Britain

The first recorded death from AIDS in Britain was in 1982. By the end of 1990, 4,098 people had contracted AIDS, of whom 1,789 had died (see Table 6.1).

The same pattern applies to the prevalence of seropositivity. By the end of 1990, there were 15,166 people known to be infected with HIV. This figure underestimates the prevalence of HIV, but it has been difficult to obtain a more accurate count because of the government's reluctance to introduce systematic anonymous testing.[4] Not until January 1990, after considerable political argument, did the government approve limited anonymous testing of pregnant women and those who visited sexually transmitted disease clinics.

While these numbers do not explain the nature of the political response to the disease, they do reveal the concentration of cases among homosexuals and the proportionately rapid spread among drug users and heterosexuals. Both aspects of the prevalence of AIDS have influenced AIDS policy.

While most people with AIDS have been treated in the London area, this does not mean that AIDS is a localized phenomenon. AIDS resources and expertise are concentrated in London, and London draws people because it offers the possibility of anonymity and because it is the center of British gay life. While the bulk of sex-related AIDS cases are in England, Scotland (Edinburgh in particular) is where most drug-related cases are to be found.

The Emergence of AIDS as a Political Issue

Politically, the "problem" of AIDS emerged from two different sources: public opinion and official practice in the health care system. In the watershed of November 1986, public concern and official policy were joined in the decision to make AIDS an explicit part of the government's political agenda. A special cabinet committee was established to coordinate policy and distribute the new funds for education, research, and treatment. To understand how this happened, it is necessary to sketch a portrait of politics in Britain.

Britain's political system is hermetically sealed. Although the country is formally a parliamentary democracy, real power lies with the executive, elected politicians sustained by party discipline. Since M.P.s depend on the party for their fortunes, for members of the governing party there is little incentive to challenge the government except when electoral futures are at stake. Representatives of the opposition have the incentive to challenge but not the voting power.

The executive is largely untouched by arguments it is not disposed to hear. Its privileged position is reinforced by an administrative system that is secretive and uncoordinated. Each department competes with all the others for resources; each chooses the advice it receives and structures it within a close-knit advisory system whose primary goal is corporate consensus. In such a system, change comes from within; external factors serve to expedite, rather than to cause, change. With respect to AIDS, popular concern has been a necessary but not sufficient basis for policy to emerge. The same is true of interest group activity, since access to power is selective. In the case of AIDS, medical interests have been present in the policy process, while gay interests have been largely excluded.

Although gay groups in Britain have a long history, they have not been able to get their concerns onto the political agenda or to insinuate themselves into the corridors of power. The explanation resides in the homophobia that pervades British culture and in the legal restraints upon homosexuality. It is illegal, for example, for men under twenty-one to have sex with one another. Gay groups have not benefited from the patronage of the major parties, nor has their cause been taken up by the administrative structure. There are few platforms for gay politics generally, and gay political activity has been confined to fighting specific acts of legislation—notably the infamous Clause 28, introduced by the Thatcher government, which requires withholding funds from local authorities that "promote homosexuality." Although AIDS is of profound concern to gay people, it has not provided a focus for gay politics. There was no argument over the closure of bathhouses, because there were none to close; groups like ACT UP, visible in several European countries and Australia as well as the United States, are noticeably absent. By contrast, the medical profession, a significant force since the founding of the National Health Service after World War II, has had enviable access to and influence on the political system.

AIDS reached the political agenda through two routes: heightened public concern, translated into electoral pressure, and internal administrative pressure.

AIDS Becomes News

Public concern was crucially shaped by mass media concern over AIDS in the mid-1980s. While the first news of AIDS was carried years earlier in the gay press, which focused on the advent of AIDS in America at the beginning of the decade, AIDS received little attention, either from the mass circulation tabloids, with their standard diet of sex, scandal, and right-wing views, or from the more serious press.

The first front-page story devoted to AIDS appeared in 1983, when *The Mail on Sunday*, a respectable tabloid, focused on the heterosexual spread of the disease. When the tabloids began to feature AIDS in 1985, they gave it their most lurid attention. For several months, "hardly a day would pass without it receiving national press coverage."[5] Stories played upon the homophobia that was part of the papers' staple diet, with frequent references to the "gay plague," "gay menace," and "gay killer." Stories about the spread of AIDS described the "dark corners" and "twilight world" of homosexuals.

The event that galvanized this attention was the death from AIDS of a prison chaplain, Gregory Richards: this was "one of the most significant domestic factors [affecting] government policy in the early years."[6] Tabloids like *The Sun* and *The Sunday Mirror* described the chaplain's "double life." "After finishing work at Chelmsford prison, Essex, he regularly slipped off to London for secret meetings with male companions." *The Daily Star* reported how medical staff refused to treat him, and *The Sun* claimed that when he was cremated he was "burned for five times longer than normal."[7]

Television often follows the lead of the press, but in the case of AIDS it began its coverage in 1983, just as the first popular newspaper reports surfaced. Its tone was very different. Unlike the press, broadcasting is bound by a legal requirement to be fair and impartial, to educate as well as to entertain. While the tabloid press fueled public fears of AIDS, television focused on policy; and AIDS received "unprecedented [TV] coverage" during the two months before the November 1986 watershed.[8] "Broadcasting was expected to respond at the point when the virus threatened to leak into the general population." and television has subsequently become an agent of the government's policy, conveying its public health messages and reinforcing preconceptions about who represents the threat and who is threatened.[9]

Public service broadcasting took a particular view of the public—as entirely heterosexual. It also remained uncritical of government's role, and this stance created a climate in which the government could more readily respond to AIDS. As one cabinet minister commented: "Just as it would have been unthinkable to fit children with gas masks until the Second World War made it acceptable, so steps to stop AIDS spreading could be tolerated only if public opinion was mobilized beforehand."[10] By taking the lead provided by TV coverage, the government was able to steer a middle course between the policies advocated by the right-wing moralists of the tabloid press, on the one side, and by the gay activists, on the other.

Health Policy-making and the Emergence of AIDS

In Britain, popular concern is not sufficient to force change; that has to come from within the policy process. Before AIDS became a political issue, it was already a practical reality for the system of health care delivery. The model of AIDS care was being developed while political changes of another kind were being put in place. During the 1980s, the health service was under considerable pressure: from the voters, who retain a deep commitment to the public health service, there was pressure to see that it was preserved and protected; from the political leadership, there was economic pressure to cut public expenditure and political pressure to introduce market efficiency, both derived directly from Prime Minister Margaret Thatcher's political ideology.

But while Thatcherism set the context in which AIDS policy was being made, it did not determine its form. Although other parts of the health service suffered cuts, AIDS services flourished—and heralded new health care practices, in which patients played an active role in determining the form of care. How this happened can only be understood by looking in more detail at the making of health policy.

The potential for political intervention in health policy, while always present, is somewhat attenuated. Formal responsibility for health policy is lodged in the Department of Health (DoH). The political head of the DoH is the secretary of state for health, a cabinet minister who is at the center of party political power.[11]

The day-to-day running of the health service is divided into two sets of institutions: the health authorities for hospital care and the family practitioner committees (now Family Health Service Authorities) for primary (ambulatory) health care. Fourteen regional and 190 district health authorities manage the hospitals in England and Wales.

The discretion of the health authorities is limited by the centralized political structure and by the politically sensitive question of National Health Service (NHS) resources. Approximately 85 percent of the National Health Service's expenditure is funded from direct taxation. The Department of Health participates in the annual public expenditure round of negotiations with the Treasury; the final form of its allocation is a budget agreed upon at the cabinet level. Throughout the 1980s, and arguably since the NHS's inception in 1948, funding has been politically controversial. Expenditure control is tight, usually leaving little opportunity for the health authorities to secure increased funding when new health needs emerge. Before there was any explicit political commitment, the initial response to AIDS was constrained by the resource limitations under which the authorities worked.

The authorities' capacity to cope depended partly on the fact that they were not typically pressured by patient demands. The style of policy-making and decision-making in the NHS is patrician. There is little stress upon patients as bearers of rights; a good deal of emphasis, however, is placed upon professional codes of conduct, for example in relation to the confidentiality of patient records. There is little malpractice litigation and a great deal of professional autonomy.

AIDS policy has emerged in close conjunction with policies for sexually transmitted diseases.[12] Individuals who attend special Genito-Urinary Clinics are referred to by numbers only. Their names and addresses are kept on a confidential record, used only when others are deemed to be at serious risk. As a result, contact tracing depends on the cooperation of the patient and the willingness of named contacts to be examined. A similar practice has evolved for AIDS: the clinics, which play a central role in testing for HIV, follow the same guidelines on confidentiality and contact tracing. AIDS, like venereal disease, is not a reportable disease; there are no requirements for quarantine or public notification. While AIDS is covered by infectious disease regulations, which theoretically enable the authorities to confine people with AIDS in hospitals, to order a person to be examined for AIDS, and to restrict the movement of a person with AIDS, in fact, these options have been left unused.[13]

Prevention through health education is the other key element of the policy response. This has included commissioning TV advertisements and creating school information packs. The responsible agencies have themselves been the subject of political conflict and control, as has the character of their campaigns. In 1983, the Gay Medical Association drafted a fact sheet for general practioners, but it was scrapped at the behest of the Department of Health on the grounds that it was too graphic.[14]

Early in the epidemic, health education was primarily the responsibility of the Health Education Council (HEC), with limited resources and power. A new institution, the Health Education Authority (HEA), took responsibility in 1987; it became much more closely tied to the political and economic structure of the National Health Service. While it is funded by the DoH, the responsibilities of HEA have been left ill-defined, obliging the authority to pay close heed to the political winds. In 1987, the HEA also took over responsibility for public education about AIDS; its special AIDS unit was disbanded in 1990, amid speculation that political pressure was being brought to bear and tighter control being demanded.

The general structure of health policy-making makes direct political control possible. It also permits initiatives to be taken by local health authorities and health education agencies. The structure does not, however, allow for active political participation by outsiders, whether patients or other public servants such as social workers or housing officials. The only real impact such groups can have is in implementing policy locally; they play little part in designing national strategies. Before the dramatic political intervention of 1986, AIDS policy was formulated on an ad hoc basis, through the initiatives of the various constituents in the health policy apparatus.

AIDS Policy-making before the 1986 Watershed

Initially, AIDS policy essentially concerned treatment, although some attempts were made at prevention through education. Relatively little policy about treatment was made centrally; detailed policy strategies evolved in the field. In England, the main responsibility fell upon London's health authorities, which looked after half of all the people with AIDS in England.

St. Mary's Hospital in the Parkside district houses the largest genitourinary unit in Europe; since 1982, it has been developing services for AIDS patients. In its own AIDS strategy document, issues concerning contact tracing and the segregation of AIDS patients from other patients under care are settled without any reference to departmental guidance.

Regional strategy classified the key issues as prevention, on the one hand; and diagnosis, treatment, and support on the other. The emphasis on prevention meant that accurate monitoring and surveillance, as well as initiatives to raise levels of awareness, enabled people to adopt behaviors that minimize the risk of infection. One such initiative occurred in Parkside, where education aimed at the young took the form of a play, produced in conjunction with the Royal Court Theatre, that encouraged safe sex.

The role of the health authorities during the early days of the AIDS epidemic was not an unmitigated success. Since these health authorities were not well adapted to working with other agencies like the social services or to involving other interested parties, the full range of treatment services was not always developed. Since health authorities did not generally see prevention as an important part of their job, these efforts got relatively little attention.[15]

At the time, the central government did not recognize the AIDS problem as a policy issue in its own right, and AIDS services had to be developed within the existing health budget. Competition for resources means new medical developments require committed champions. So it was with AIDS; medical specialists devoted a great deal of energy to persuading policymakers of the importance of this new disease.

Also critical in the early days of AIDS policy were groups whose membership is mostly gay, organized specifically to help people with AIDS, most notably Body Positive and the Terrence Higgins Trust (THT).[16] During a time when politicians played a marginal role, these groups formed alliances with key physicians and health officials. They introduced the buddy system of emotional support in Britain, set up counseling services, and raised funds for AIDS hospices. They were also successful in getting access to new treatment regimes and drugs, even before these were fully tested. The AIDS groups contributed, too, to the official definition of safe sex and to the vocabulary in which policy documents and related material was phrased. Concepts like advocacy, which do not normally find a place in NHS policy documents, were introduced when discussing how to respond to AIDS.

The influence of these voluntary groups, though, was largely confined to the early years of AIDS. After November 1986, they were pushed to the margins of the policy process.

The Political Takeover of AIDS Policy

In the autumn of 1986, the structure and character of AIDS policy-making changed dramatically. Prime Minister Thatcher's government assumed direct control. Instead of leaving matters with the Department of Health and the local health authorities, the government put a special cabinet committee in charge; more importantly, it was given a large budget to distribute $50 million as compared with $5 million the previous year. This reorganization joined health service concerns and growing public concern about AIDS. To understand why the government took on this responsibility, committing resources to AIDS while pursuing a policy of financial stringency elsewhere, it is essential to know why the government had *not* acted earlier. The explanation includes uncertainty about the nature of AIDS, the political incentives to act, and the institutional processes that envelop any policy initiative.

It was only in 1981 that the syndrome that came to be called AIDS was first identified. The 1983 DoH report *On the State of Public Health* announced that "the cause remains unknown, but is likely to be a viral agent transmitted by sexual contact, transmission of blood and certain blood products . . . [but] there is no conclusive proof that this is so."[17] For that reason, the DoH recommended only that those "at risk" should not donate blood. Meanwhile, evidence about variations in susceptibility to the disease, about the percentage of people who were antibody-positive who would develop the full-blown syndrome, and about the precise course of the disease seemed constantly to shift.

This medical uncertainty was compounded by ignorance about the prevalence of AIDS. The least reliable data concerned the number of people who were HIV-positive. In 1988, the official estimate was fifty thousand; others put the figure at one hundred thousand.[18] Little was known about people's sexual habits. It was said that medical science knew more about the molecular structure of the HIV virus in a lycocyte than it knew about human sexual behavior in the bedroom.

Such ignorance, even if partly fostered by the government itself, furnished an excuse for hesitation. Politicians still faced a familiar dilemma: whether to act before all the facts were known and risk criticisms of overreaction, or to wait until the evidence was clear and risk accusations of complacency.

The scale of the AIDS problem, as represented by deaths per year, was small compared to that of other causes of death. AIDS did not look like a major epidemic, at least in the short term. The long-term scenario did, however, suggest the need for action, and there were experts making this point. The College of Health, a well-respected group campaigning for reform in the health service, argued in 1986 that spending on AIDS should increase thirtyfold in the next two years.[19]

Disagreements about the character of the disease meant that less scientific factors could assume prominence. If an excuse was needed, here was a place for prejudice and ideology to shape the problem as the government viewed it.

Popular press discussion of AIDS portrayed the disease as a threat posed by gays, an unpopular group in British society. Where popular opinion is thought to be conservative, politicians are reluctant to promote radical change. There were few votes to be gained in fighting AIDS, irrespective of what the future brought. This inclination toward inaction was reinforced by the social construction of the problem. Because the initial attention paid to AIDS stressed its links to homosexuality and drugs, the disease was not seen as a threat to society at large—a common problem like the Blitz—but instead as an affliction of fringe groups that elicited little public or political sympathy. It was possible to portray people with AIDS as responsible for their condition; AIDS was a matter of personal, not governmental, responsibility. Such a reaction was made plausible by the way hemophiliacs with HIV could be presented as the "innocent victims" of AIDS. Others, by implication, were responsible for their own infection and were "guilty" of passing it on. The government tacitly embraced this view. While it was prepared to make ex gratia payments of $49 million (in 1990 U.S. dollars) to the Hemophilia Trust for hemophiliacs who acquired HIV from contaminated blood products, no such offer was made to anyone else with HIV. Officials who spoke of the broader threat of AIDS risked sharp criticism. The medical adviser of *The Sun* wrote in 1987: "The only people really at risk are promiscuous homosexuals and drug addicts. The Department of Health and the British Medical Association have drummed up hysterical campaigns designed to scare heterosexuals and put us all off sex."[20]

The urgency felt by regional and district health authorities did not guarantee AIDS a place on the national policy agenda. The tendency in health policy is to diffuse responsibility through a network of advisory committees, with little strategic thinking or policy coordination. The dominant ethos of health policy-making favors a noninterventionist strategy, since it assumes that individual behavior cannot be directly affected.[21] Partly because of the dominance of the medical profession, health education continues to receive relatively low priority within the DoH. The general approach of government helped those who favored caution—who saw AIDS not as a public issue but as a consequence of private life, wrongheaded behavior.

Despite these barriers, AIDS did land on the national political agenda in November 1986. One simple explanation is the growing danger it was seen as posing: the threat of death can be a powerful incentive. In describing government's response to an earlier epidemic, historian William McNeill writes: "To do nothing was no longer sufficient; old debates and stubborn clashes had to be quickly resolved by public bodies acting literally under fear of death."[22] But in Britain in 1986, the chance of dying from AIDS was very small; what really mattered was the longer term. It was this vision that Norman Fowler, the health department minister who presided over the 1986 policy transformation, brought back from a visit to San Francisco, where he saw firsthand the impact of the epidemic. But while Fowler's trip made AIDS policy more salient, it did nothing to change the basic policy framework.[23]

The knowledge gleaned from the United States coincided with a shift in the DoH's perceptions of who was potentially affected by AIDS. All along, it had been acknowledged that AIDS was not confined to homosexuals, but this fact now took on political significance. Chief Medical Officer Sir Donald Acheson stressed the possibility of heterosexual spread, both because that risk was not being taken seriously by the general population, particularly the young, and because it was a way of extracting money and forcing action.

Moreover, 1986 saw the publication of some telling data on the financial demands incurred by AIDS.[24] The total economic and medical cost of just the five hundred existing cases of AIDS was put at $240 million; treatment alone was expected to increase nearly 100 percent by the end of the decade.[25] This may well have led the Treasury, a key part of the policy process, to press the Department of Health and the Cabinet for more decisive action. The very political ideology that previously worked against a major initiative now worked for it. Sir Nicholas Bonsor, speaking for Conservative M.P.s who wanted the government to do more about AIDS, argued that treasured values and institutions were threatened. "Obviously there is substantial drug-taking and homosexuality," he observed, "and we have to decide how we can protect people from the undesirable activities of their neighbors."[26]

A comparison between the reaction to AIDS and to another serious illness, malignant melanoma, shows the influence of such fears. In the early 1980s, specialists were warning about the spread of melanoma. Melanoma causes 85 percent of all deaths from skin cancers. There were 1,318 cases of primary malignant melanoma of the skin between 1979 and 1983, and the incidence of skin cancer rose 2.5 percent each year in this period.[27] In 1987, the incidence of melanoma in Scotland was 5.2 per 100,000 for men and 9.0 per 100,000 for women.[28] Comparative studies of the United Kingdom and Sweden revealed that vulnerability to melanoma was connected to one's life-style.[29] While cancer specialists argued for intensive public education campaigns to aid early identification, they went unheard. Both AIDS and malignant melanoma have life-style connections, present new medical and policy problems, and are increasing in incidence. But, critically, melanoma is not infectious; nor does it touch upon the fears raised by sex, drugs, and deviance. AIDS was more easily constructed as a crisis which could be captured in political terms; there were groups to be "protected," moral points to be scored.

Yet even taking this exceptionalism into account, AIDS funding was remarkably generous. The health service was not the only institution under financial pressure. Since 1979, the Conservatives' strategy had been to hold down public expenditure in order to finance tax cuts. Moreover, these tight fiscal controls were accompanied by a fiercely expressed insistence that social problems could not be solved by throwing money at them. Yet beginning late 1986, money *was* being thrown at AIDS. One possible reason is that although AIDS spending was out of line with general norms, there were other favored initiatives; public spending on various job creation schemes, for example, increased considerably during this period. Another view, held by some health service administrators, focuses on bureaucratic needs to explain public generosity: providing AIDS money was a tacit way of responding to the funding crisis in London teaching hospitals, which could not be dealt with openly for fear of upsetting the momentum towards the general redistribution of public resources from central London. It is also probable that key policymakers, genuinely panicked by some of the more apocalyptic futures envisaged for the AIDS epidemic, suspended their normal disbelief in the efficacy of money to cure social ills.

Getting Advice on AIDS

To get a fuller understanding of what led the government to take charge of AIDS policy, we need to look more closely at the machinery that shaped the government's perception of the disease, and the information that reached key decisionmakers. Information is always a vital political resource, but it has been peculiarly important to AIDS policy. There are two dimensions to the advice that led to the government's AIDS policy: technical advice about what ought to be done, and political advice about *whether* it ought to be done.

The core executive knew little about AIDS as late as the mid-1980s. Such ignorance generally leads the executive to depend heavily on selective external experts for advice; so too with AIDS.[30] Two features distinguish the system by which the central executive accumulated information and advice about AIDS policy: the relatively small role assigned to the voluntary groups such as the Terrence Higgins Trust and the dominance of medical expertise.

A key actor in the history of AIDS policy is Chief Medical Officer (CMO) Sir Donald Acheson. The CMO, not a career civil service post, is given to someone working professionally in the academic medical world. The role is ill-defined and its authority limited; the CMO answers to the health minister whom he advises, and so straddles the medical and political realms. Acheson describes his job as providing "a source of unbiased objective advice on scientific matters related to medicine and health. . . . It is for Ministers to decide how to use it."[31] Power lies in the CMO's ability to persuade, and Acheson has managed his role with exceptional skill, delicately pressing reluctant or ill-informed ministers into action.[32] Because he is an epidemiologist, his expertise has been strategically useful in promoting AIDS policy. He has utilized a number of advisory committees, whose advice he has drawn upon in negotiations with ministers.

The first major attempt to collect knowledge about AIDS was the Expert Advisory Group on AIDS (EAGA), formed in February 1985 at Acheson's initiative. The EAGA was responsible for persuading the government to reject "the notion of a central register of AIDS patients, contact tracing and the disclosure of an AIDS patient's details without specific consent."[33] This counsel reflected the experience of people who understood the value of confidentiality in the treatment of sexually transmitted diseases, and who thought patient trust and easy access to care were more important than centralized monitoring.

The EAGA was selected not for its representativeness but for its expertise, defined in medical-scientific terms. It did not include social scientists or those working with AIDS outside the official health service structure. Indeed, the definition of expertise was not broadened until 1988 when law professor Ian Kennedy was appointed to help sort out the ethical questions raised by the issue of anonymous screening.

By then, however, EAGA's influence was on the wane. The advisory group had been launched to push the Department of Health into action. Once AIDS had acquired a political momentum and machinery of its own, EAGA's functions were usurped. There were also political reasons for the decline of EAGA. The group's recommendations were increasingly subjected to ideological scrutiny, since the higher profile accorded to AIDS had increased the political capital attached to it, and EAGA members were made aware of the limits to which policy could be expected to go.

The Health Education Advisory Group (HEAG) was set up by the CMO in 1985 to advise on AIDS prevention policy. It included Tony Coxon, a sociologist who specializes in research methodology and a member of the Gay Research Group. HEAG contained representatives of AIDS pressure groups, Body Positive, and the Terrence Higgins Trust, as well as a member of the Gay Medical Association.

HEAG undoubtedly made an impact in the early days of AIDS education. The Department of Health was initially uncertain about how to proceed in informing the public on AIDS. When Chief Medical Officer Acheson proposed that the message should be "avoid London" and "avoid male prostitutes," HEAG persuaded him to drop these irrelevant slogans, pushing the department to make its AIDS campaigns more explicit and to give greater prominence to the use of condoms. But HEAG's influence was inversely proportional to the political interest taken in its work. As political responsibility grew, expertise became more selectively chosen, and groups like the Terrence Higgins Trust were pushed to one side.

The character of HEAG's advice also diminished its impact. HEAG was not offering hard science; its suggestions were grounded in the study of individual and social behavior, a kind of knowledge widely viewed in Britain as mere common sense. As Professor Coxon remarks: "The feeling I have, particularly, was that there was a very strong mix of concern and expertise which, in the event, was not actually used and that whilst in particular medical skills were being called upon and used and respected, other sorts of nonmedical skills were being ignored."[34]

EAGA and HEAG were departmental creations that drew together experts, not representatives. Apart from a limited role in HEAG, people with AIDS have played no part in policy formulation. Organizations like THT were used by government, rather than influencing it. They received government support to help establish the infrastructure and central organization of these bodies, not to provide services; that was the business of health authorities (see Table 6.2).[35]

These figures need to be put in context. In 1986, the Trust's printing bill for nine months equaled the government's grant allocation for the entire year; its 1990 budget was nearly five times larger than the government's grant, the rest of its funds coming from private sources. And because the THT's work was done largely by unpaid volunteers, the financial support was even more marginal.

The policy role played by the THT has been largely defined by the Department of Health. Norman Fowler, the health minister who presided over the 1986 watershed, had few dealings with the Trust and rarely spoke of it in his public pronouncements, while one of his successors, David Mellor, visited the Trust's headquarters and was willing to acknowledge its importance to the government's overall strategy. The THT acted, Mellor said, "to update and deepen my awareness of AIDS."[36] But the THT was used as a conduit for communication from the government to the client groups, notes a policy initiator; it was part of the government's plan, according to health minister Mellor, "to have good links with key groups in the community."[37]

The THT has nonetheless been closely involved with the HEA, building upon the close relationship forged with health authorities in the early days as well as the network of groups organized around the National AIDS Trust and the Network of Voluntary Organizations in AIDS/HIV (NOVOAH). It has representatives on two London Regional Health Authorities, and, along with other groups, it has delivered services funded from health authority resources. Hospice care provided by London Lighthouse and

Table 6.2. British Government Grants to the Terrence Higgins Trust, 1985–1989 (in 1990 U.S. dollars)

Year	Amount
1985–86	58,261
1986–87	182,099
1987–88	578,850
1988–89	739,217

SOURCE: AIDS Unit, Department of Health, *AIDS Briefing Note* (London: Department of Health); also Z. Schramm-Evans, "Responses to AIDS: 1986–1987," in *AIDS: Individual, Cultural and Policy Decisions,* ed. P. Aggleton, et al. (London: Falmer Press, 1991), 221–232.

Mildmay Mission, for example, was funded as part of the care strategy of health authorities.

The British Parliament has embraced a generally consensual AIDS policy. Among Labour M.P.s there are those who argue for more radical, state-directed policies, and some Tory backbenchers advocate a more repressive, moralistic approach, but these voices carry little weight. Both the Select Committee on the Social Services and the All Party Parliamentary Group on AIDS have advocated greater coordination at the center, curbs on discrimination, and more explicit AIDS education campaigns.[38]

Their success can be measured not in policy change but in the character of debates about AIDS. In 1986, Conservative M.P.s argued for compulsory national screening and blamed the spread on homosexual promiscuity.[39] Under-Secretary of State for Scotland John Mackay told Parliament in April 1986 that "AIDS is a totally self-inflicted illness, and it is so much more morally reprehensible when it is inflicted on children. . . . It is moral question which comes down to people reviewing their living habits."[40] The 1989 debate showed considerably greater expertise and sensitivity; the barely suppressed prejudices of the earlier session were entirely absent.

But these different groups were just bit players in a larger political drama. Policy advising has been strictly controlled by the central administrative machine, reinforced through the medical profession, which has served not only as a source of knowledge but also as an establishment. For example, Professor Michael Adler, a leading clinician, has been involved in almost all the key AIDS policy discussions, whether these involve research, public education, prevention, or treatment.

The Department of Health has used its advisers to counter prejudice. When doubts were raised in the press about the heterosexual spread of AIDS in 1989, the DoH organized a symposium on the current state of knowledge. This was a deliberate attempt to counter homosexual complacency and to reinforce the hand of the political leadership within the DoH, and the resulting media coverage reasserted the official policy.[41]

The creation of the special AIDS Cabinet committee in 1986 removed some of the power from the department, and in doing so further marginalized outside advice. "Once the government itself started intervening in AIDS, the [Terrence Higgins] Trust gradually lost influence and relations became more formal."[42] Dr. Mukesh Kapila, deputy director of the HEA's AIDS program, summed up the effect of greater political involvement:

> U.K. government leadership has been an important driving force to get things going and, in general, our politicians have made wise decisions. But it is also true that in countries in which political expediency dictates social policy, the personalities and personal beliefs of key individual politicians and civil servants have profound influence on how programmes evolve, including their tone, credibility, public and professional acceptability and ultimately their impact.[43]

While creating an ad hoc cabinet subcommittee is a standard device for high-level decision-making, it received unusual publicity. Such committees are traditionally official secrets, but the formation of the AIDS committee was announced to journalists outside 10 Downing Street. With that development, greater emphasis was placed on political calculations and Prime Minister Thatcher's influence became more apparent. This cut two ways. There was an incentive for politicians to be seen to be acting, a factor that favored high-profile public education campaigns, but ministers were also aware that their political fortunes rested largely with a prime minister wary of the implications of AIDS.

Margaret Thatcher represented the moral right, whose views had been mostly excluded from the policy process. AIDS, Thatcher said, was not something the government could stop. It was a matter of individual responsibility and a moral issue on which the Anglican Church should speak.[44] More generally, Thatcher stressed the importance of the traditional family, the market, and individualism: this also was a reason for government to act cautiously with respect to AIDS or not to act at all.

The conjunction of media attention and treatment policy before 1986 led to decisive intervention by an essentially elitist government apparatus. How did these processes find expression in substantive AIDS policies?

The Policy Strategy

The British government's policy strategy stressed four elements: stemming the spread of HIV infection, increasing scientific understanding of the disease, helping those affected, and fostering informed and caring social attitudes. The increases in expenditure shows how these objectives generally translated into policy (see Table 6.3).

Table 6.3. Funding of Policy and Allocation per Case for Great Britain, 1985–1990 (in millions of 1990 U.S. dollars)

	1985	1986	1987	1988	1989	1990
Research[a]	0.6	3.5	5.7	7.7	9.8	14.3
Dollars per case	2,253	5,741	4,615	3,541	3,477	3,483
Treatment[b]		51.48	125.1	144.5	230.5	231
Dollars per case		3,582	55,599	47,295	51,109	56,380
Prevention[c]			7.7	19.9	20.7	20
Dollars per case			6,303	9,871	7,321	4,789

SOURCE: Cabinet Office, *Annual Review of Government Funded Research and Development* (London: HMSO; Department of Health, *On the State of the Public Health* (London: HMSO); Medical Research Council, Annual Report (London: MRC); Health Education Authority, *Annual Report* (London: HEA).
[a]Based on MRC grants for AIDS-directed research.
[b]Allocation on RHAs by DoH.
[c]Based on central government grants to HEA.

Public education was perceived by policymakers as the only way to stem the spread of HIV infection. This has also been the most visible aspect of AIDS policy and so has carried the greatest short-term political implications. Norman Fowler remarked that "public education is the only vaccine we have"; and successive ministers of health have put education at the forefront of their policy pronouncements.

The Department of Health recognized that "we frankly don't have time to rely on changing the moral climate."[45] It sought "a way of telling people what the risks are and what they should do without shocking them so much that they switch off entirely."[46] This strategy was criticized—by Prime Minister Thatcher, most notably—and other departments have been more moralistic. The Department of Education and Science, for instance, demanded the pulping of AIDS material prepared for the schools because it lacked a suitably strong moral message about sex within marriage, as well as about the "immorality" of homosexuality.[47]

The Health Education Authority mostly avoided preaching. Its aim was to "to create and sustain an informed climate of opinion around HIV and AIDS."[48] This has meant telling people how AIDS is transmitted and how to prevent transmission primarily through safe sex, with occasional reference to monogamy. But these messages have been subject to closer political scrutiny since 1986. Right-wing critics have demanded more explicit moral declaration, while leftist critics claim that the HEA has played on an implicit Puritan moralism, relying too much on fear—"behind every beautiful person there is a potential carrier of HIV"—to get its lesson across.

The HEA claims that its campaigns owe more to market research than to any particular ideological line. Its aim is to reach those groups who are not changing their behavior; the message is merely a function of its target. The phases of the information campaign fit this general strategy. While the first two campaigns, run in 1986, were largely directed at the general population, some subsequent initiatives have been more precisely focused on the young and on intravenous drug users. Almost all the campaigns have been directed at heterosexuals, with no notice paid to homosexuals—proportionately, the major risk group—until 1989. In this sense, the choice of target groups reflects the political focus of AIDS policy. But it also reflects the fact that, through the Terrence Higgins Trust, there had already been extensive publicity aimed at gay groups. When the HEA started paying attention to gays in 1989, it relied upon established gay groups to help reach this audience (see Table 6.4).[49]

The initial AIDS advertisements, which cost $170,000, gave an accurate, if undramatic, account of current wisdom. One, headed "AIDS. NEED YOU WORRY?" opened with an injunction to "Please read this carefully" and was signed by the chief medical officer. It explained what AIDS is, how it is spread, and how it can be avoided: "Using a sheath can

Table 6.4. The Themes of AIDS Publicity Campaigns

Date	Audience/location	Theme
March 1986	National press	Information
Dec. 1986 to Feb. 1987	TV, press, posters, leaflets to all homes	Don't die of ignorance
Feb. 1988	TV, youth magazines (men and women)	You know the risks; the decision is yours
Summer 1988	Posters in airports, ports, stations, etc.	Holidays
Dec. 1988 to March 1989	National press	You're as safe as you want to be
March 1989	Gay press	Men who have sex with men
April 1989 to June 1989	Young women's magazines, young women's ethnic press	Young women
Summer 1989	Posters at airports, ads in inflight magazines	Holidays
Dec. 1, 1989	Ads in national daily, Sunday, and ethnic press	World AIDS Day
Dec. 1989 to March 1990	Ads in youth press (men and women), radio	Young people
Feb. 1990 to March 1990	TV, national press	Experts on HIV and AIDS

SOURCE: HEA, *Strategic Plan 1990–1995.*

help reduce the risk of catching AIDS. So can cutting out casual relationships." The only illustration was a picture of another AIDS leaflet. Later advertisements in this series continued this pedantic approach. One had a schematic representation of HIV, another an illustration of how the virus is transmitted: "Virus attacks T cells and multiplies."

The second advertising campaign was both more direct and more extensive. It too used the newspapers, but it added national hotlines (previously available only through voluntary organizations like the Terrence Higgins Trust), poster and billboard advertising, and TV and radio slots. Leaflets were mailed to every home in the country. This campaign was also much more expensive, costing more than $17 million. Its intention was to encourage safer sex: "stick to one partner" or at least "use a condom."

The newfound willingness to make use of television and radio was part of a more general government trend. While in the past public service announcements have typically warned of dangers on the roads or in the home, the Thatcher government transformed this tradition. The Department of Industry employed contemporary advertising techniques to promote its policies, just as other departments used advertisements to sell shares in the government's privatization program. What distinguished AIDS was the government's interest in the wider coverage given to the disease. For example, the Department of Health encouraged the advertising of condoms—albeit without showing the product and late at night. Meetings between the chief medical officer and senior television executives led to a media "AIDS Week."[50] The health education campaign linked official strategy to the ethos of public broadcasting, with its commitment to balance and moderation.

The first television advertisements, shown in January 1987, were coy. Their intention was not to discuss AIDS but to notify the public of the leaflet being distributed nationally and the new national AIDS hot line. Directed by Nicholas Roeg (maker of the film *Don't Look Now*, among others), the ad featured the words "AIDS" being carved into a block of stone. Its message was "Don't die of ignorance." But while the TV campaign was elliptical, the AIDS leaflet spoke directly about the risks entailed in anal and oral sex and about the use of condoms.

Department of Health officials originally wanted the TV campaign to be as explicit as the leaflet. But they were dissuaded from this approach because of the concern, expressed by Prime Minister Thatcher among others, that people might be offended. In fact, a majority of people would have accepted more explicit language.[51] The government received only 187 letters of complaint about the AIDS leaflet, half from people who had not even opened the offending document.

Intuition initially guided the education campaign. But through the use of expert advisers and market research, the DoH gradually became more sophisticated, employing numerous research organizations to look at the impact of its initiatives. The first campaign was at best a mixed success: while it did not change behavior significantly, it did increase awareness— although at the expense of increasing prejudice against homosexuality and encouraging the view that people with AIDS only had themselves to blame. The weakness of this campaign did not surprise advertising executives. "We are talking about changing a way of life. There is no point buying one page in a paper to discourage permissiveness when the other 24 promote it."[52] But while the first campaign had little effect on general sexual behavior, it did rouse the worried well: between September and November 1986, requests for HIV tests rose by 300 percent.[53]

The second TV campaign was more effective at influencing its audience.[54] In January 1987, 69 percent of people surveyed said they had seen the advertisements; 73 percent now reported they knew how to avoid the disease. Among heterosexuals there was a major increase in knowledge about AIDS but little change in behavior; only among gays did behavior change significantly. Young heterosexuals were the most resistant to influence. A March 1987 poll of eighteen to twenty-four-year-olds revealed that, while 15 percent said that they had given up casual sex and 36 percent said they favored monogamy, only 2 percent said they used condoms.[55] While it prompted people to seek tests for HIV, those doing so were not in the primary target groups. Of the people asking to be tested, the figure rose by 191 percent among homosexuals and bisexuals, by 138 percent among drug users, and by 352 percent among those with no known risk factor.[56] The public has been "informed but not yet adequately educated."[57]

In early 1990, a series of advertisements was run for six weeks on prime-time TV. Its format was a single talking head, as AIDS experts, including Sir Donald Acheson and Professor Michael Adler, each delivered a simple statement. Chief Medical Officer Acheson said: "We know for certain that HIV, the virus that causes AIDS, can be spread by sexual intercourse from man to man, man to woman and from woman to man. It is also spread by sharing infected needles and syringes during drug abuse."

This low-key approach partly reflected a changing perception of the problem: AIDS was no longer seen as an immediate crisis but rather as part of long-term health policy. There were also more direct political causes for the change of tone. There had been renewed media interest in AIDS shortly before the ads appeared, but this time it took the form of skepticism, borrowed from the United States, about the risks to heterosexuals. The *Sunday Times* serialized Michael Fumento's *The Myth of Heterosexual AIDS*,[58] and a television documentary publicized University of California at Berkeley Professor James Duesberg's claim that HIV was not the cause of AIDS. This new skepticism coincided with reports that the HEA was scrapping its AIDS unit.[59] Moreover, the dramatic decline in the political fortunes of the Conservative government made the leadership sensitive to anything that might detract futher from its popularity, which was built around the family and morality. It was in this political climate that the HEA devised the "experts" campaign, informed as much by the politics of the day as by the epidemiology of the disease. It was designed to maintain the credibility of the HEA and to deliver information in an unsensational fashion.

The government has also tried directly to counter the spread of the disease. Since October 1985, all blood donations have been tested for HIV. Two years earlier, the Department of Health had requested that all "high-risk groups" not give blood. In Britain, unlike in some other countries, this request did not provoke an outcry from those affected, and when AIDS took on a high political profile, the key issue was not blood donations but HIV testing.

Once tests were commercially available, the Department of Health consistently encouraged voluntary testing. The Terrence Higgins Trust opposed this: it argued that, without an available treatment, knowledge of one's HIV status was of little value and that attention should focus instead on the need for safe sex. The Trust also pointed out the danger that those who were HIV-positive would be vulnerable to discimination.

The expert advisory group was less interested in encouraging testing than in obtaining accurate figures for the incidence of HIV, and for that reason it advocated a system of national anonymous testing. This controversial view was backed by the chief medical officer, the All-Party Parliamentary Group on AIDS, the British Medical Association, the Royal College of Physicians, and the Imperial Cancer Trust. Arrayed against them were the Parliamentary Select Committee, the Public Health Laboratory Service, and the Royal College of Obstetricians and Gynecologists, who argued that costs, practicality, and confidentiality prohibited any such scheme. In June 1988, the government ruled against anonymous screening, preferring instead to ask for volunteers, but six months later, with a new health secretary, the government declared that the scheme would be launched in January 1990.[60] Once again, political actors played the decisive role.

Beyond screening blood and issuing guidelines to "do good," the Department of Health engaged in little detailed strategic thinking and planning about prevention. As before, important policy questions concerning isues such as confidentiality and contact tracing were left to professional bodies or to the health authorities. And when the government was urged to do more—to encourage the use of condoms and the implementation of needle exchanges—it resisted. While the Labour opposition advocated free distribution of condoms, the government said no. Some hospitals and family planning clinics distribute condoms but doctors cannot prescribe them, as they can with all other forms of contraception.[61] The government declined to distribute condoms in prisons, on the grounds that this would only encourage dangerous sexual practices, which are, in any case, illegal in prison. It also refused to monitor condom production or to insist on new condom safety standards, and there has been little effort to destigmatize the condom. This too has been left to retailers, manufacturers and their advertisers, and voluntary bodies. Although the HEA has occasionally injected a note of sensuality into some of its advertisements, this has been most effectively achieved in ads aimed at gays, prepared by the Terrence Higgins Trust and Body Positive, neither of which is subject to official government control.

A similar exercise in non-decision-making has characterized policy on the provision of free needles and needle exchanges. Although the chief medical officer and the Advisory Council on the Misuse of Drugs (ACMD) advocated a national needle exchange scheme, the government balked. In 1986, it introduced a number of pilot needle exchange schemes, with $1.7

million to counsel drug users; pharmacists were encouraged to support the policy through the sale of syringes. But implementation was left to local authorities. Where there was a strong local anti-drug policy and little desire to promote needle exchanges, as in Edinburgh, the spread of HIV increased markedly; where a more relaxed drug policy operated, as in Liverpool and Glasgow, the incidence of HIV was relatively low. Two years later, needle exchange remained an "experiment" even as health ministers were voicing concern about its effectiveness and its potential political costs.[62]

Needle exchanges in prisons were ruled out by the Home Office, which is responsible for the management of the prison service. It argued that the incidence of intravenous drug use in prisons was small and that distributing free needles would just exacerbate the problem.[63] While the incidence of HIV in prison is low—in January 1989, there were fifty-seven HIV-positive prisoners—unofficial reports suggest that needle sharing is common.[64]

It was only in 1988 that any move to a national policy on AIDS and intravenous drug use was made. Once more, political factors held the key. The government was caught in an awkward dilemma: while it was committed to countering the spread of AIDS, it was at least as determined to stamp out drugs. The dilemma was made all the more difficult because each side was represented by a powerful state institution. The goal of the Home Office is elimination of drugs through the use of tough law enforcement; the Department of Health is less concerned with preventing drug use, more anxious to hinder the spread of HIV through shared needles. The DoH has stated that "HIV is a greater threat to public and individual health than drug misuse."[65]

The government came eventually to accept the need for a policy of needle exchanges, to prevent the spread of HIV. A key element in this change of mind was the report "AIDS and Drug Misuse," produced by the Advisory Council on the Misuse of Drugs. It recommended that more effort be put into preventing the sharing of needles and into informing users about how to minimize the risk of infection. This meant "a change in professional and public attitudes to drug misuse is necessary, as attitudes and policies which lead to drug misusers remaining hidden will impair the effectiveness of measures to combat the spread of HIV."[66] These recommendations won the support of the chief medical officer, and, unexpectedly, received considerable public attention. Ruth Runciman, the chair of the responsible working group, decided that going public was necessary if the government was to be persuaded to act, and so she made sure the press and Parliament were fully briefed.

Even with considerable publicity, Health Minister John Moore was fearful about appearing to condone the use of hard drugs. He delayed three months before publishing the report and only saw Runciman after being goaded into a meeting. While the government gave the report a grudging endorsement, it avoided accepting its main message. Needle sharing

> presents a grave threat . . . [but] it is self-evident that if people do not start using drugs in the first place then they do not put themselves at risk of infection through this route. We remain therefore determined to prevent the misuse of drugs, both through tough law enforcement measures to reduce the supply of illicit drugs, and through effective education and information to make it less likely that young people will be tempted to try them.[67]

A similar attitude was expressed towards needle exchanges: "Ministers believe that there is as yet insufficient evidence about the benefits or otherwise of syringe-exchange schemes to recommend expansion of schemes."[68]

Not until Moore was replaced at the Department of Health by David Mellor was decisive action taken. In September 1988, the department made $5.1 million available to health authorities to reduce the spread of AIDS among drug users by expanding services and by informing pharmacists and GPs about needle exchange schemes. "Drug misusers," said David Mellor, "must be encouraged to come forward for help."[69]

Behind the prevention and education campaigns has lain a general if vaguely stated assumption that the response to AIDS depends, in the long run, on generating better understanding of the disease through research. How this understanding has been defined and what research has been funded further reveals the impact of political values on AIDS policy. Both before and after the 1986 watershed, almost all the funding has gone to medical research. But social science research has attracted political attention, with Prime Minister Thatcher giving vent to her general dislike of social science and her particular dislike of "intrusive" surveys.

Research funding comes from the central government through the health service and general science budgets, and both have been subject to severe restraints. Clinical researchers in teaching hospitals have been in the forefront of investigating AIDS, but they have increasingly found themselves having to provide treatment rather than doing research. Professor Adler, a leading AIDS researcher and clinician, described the situation in his hospital:

> There are seven clinical academic staff in my department who do academic sessions. They, I would submit, shore up the NHS department; they paper over the cracks, so that the cracks that we are beginning to see would have appeared much earlier if it had not been for the injection of academic hands, clinical hands, hands on the pumps. That is very unsatisfactory

because it pulls my staff away from research, which is very important in this area, but it also, I am afraid, gives the false impression that the NHS can cope.[70]

Two institutions are responsible for the funding of AIDS research, the Medical Research Council (MRC) and the Economic and Social Research Council (ESRC). The MRC and ESRC are underwritten by the Department of Education and Science. They allocate resources on the basis of individual grant applications and also promote directed research, with a long-term commitment, for a predetermined research program.

Initially, little money was made available for AIDS research; after the 1986–1987 watershed, the sum was dramatically increased. In 1985–1986, $732,700 was allocated to the Medical Research Council (MRC) for six projects on AIDS. In 1987, $24.65 million—a thirtyfold increase—was made availabe for three years' work; $17 million a year was proposed for subsequent years.

Politics prompted the increase. The MRC AIDS working party, until then a key actor in the allocation of awards, was not consulted about the proposal, which went instead to the Special AIDS Cabinet Committee. Three years earlier, the government had argued that AIDS research should be funded out of the MRC's existing budget.

> Just before the [1987] election, and a day before a by-election, the government announced that it was giving $24.65 million to the Medical Research Council specifically for a "directed program" of scientific research into AIDS. It was a welcome sweetener for the Council, which could not remember the last time that the British government had given medical research all that it had asked for.[71]

For all its generosity, the government preferred to freeload on the French and American research. The government was also hesitant about the scope of inquiry. Not until 1987 was there any support for research into the sexual behavior of homosexuals. The one previous study, conducted by the Public Health Laboratory Service, was not published in the government pamphlet "Health Trends," at the insistence of the Health Minister, because it was thought to be politically problematic. This sensitivity to political values has continued to frame the activity of the various institutions that shape AIDS research.

That the Medical Research Council has been dominant in AIDS research funding is hardly surprising, since AIDS has been portrayed as essentially a medical problem. The MRC established an AIDS working party as early as 1983. In 1986–1987, the total allocation for science research was $1045.5 million, of which $217.6 million (21 percent) went to the MRC. Of this, $3.4 million was allocated for AIDS research in basic science or clinical trials. The MRC approved seven epidemiological studies, and these were funded, at a cost of $510,000, by the Department of Health.

The history of social science research funding is a less happy tale. The MRC has consistently seen behavorial and social-epidemiological research as being outside its brief.[72] At the same time, it has funded innovative social science projects on male and female prostitution, sexual knowledge among teenagers, and sexual behavior among bisexuals and drug users. The Economic and Social Research Council was a late entrant into the funding of AIDS-related research, because of the politics within the ESRC and the nature of research funding in Britain.

A number of social scientists, who formed the Gay Research Group, sought to investigate the incidence of HIV among homosexual and bisexual men. The research began as a privately-funded pilot survey, but was broadened into a more ambitious project—SIGMA (Socio-sexual Investigations of Gay Men and AIDS)—for the ESRC.[73] The ESRC rejected this proposal, claiming that the project had "no policy or priority relevance to ESRC." The project was then offered to the MRC, which after two years' procrastination approved it in 1987, funding it in collaboration with the Department of Health and Social Services.

The ESRC began funding AIDS research in late 1988. It made available $3.2 million "to create the strategic research base from which an effective program of health education, health policy and intervention strategies can be developed."[74] While the ESRC explained its apparent tardiness in addressing AIDS by saying it had received few applications for AIDS-related research funds, this is disingenuous, since the council could have encouraged research on AIDS. The more plausible explanation is that, at a time when its work and funding were under close political scrutiny, the ESRC was not disposed to launch major projects that might be ill-received by its political masters.

When the political agenda on AIDS changed in 1986, just such a program of research was initiated, but the commitment proved to be evanescent. It was expected that more funds would be forthcoming to broaden the first, predominantly epidemiological, phase of research, yet this has not happened. The explanation may lie in the ESRC's experience with the National Survey of Sexual Behavior, promoted by the council but abruptly canceled by Prime Minister Thatcher. Critics complained that the ESRC accepted the political decision too meekly and without considering alternatives; the ESRC responded that it lacked the resources to continue without government support.

Treatment policy also changed in 1986. There were substantial infusions of funds for specific services. The government requested new facilities to prevent the spread of HIV: genitourinary clinics, drug clinics, and the like.[75] It also provided for new methods of treatment, in particular the costly drug zidovudine (AZT). The expansion began in the fiscal year 1987–1988, but gathered pace in the two subsequent years. At first the money came in uncoordinated packets, but by 1988–1989 it amounted to $50.77 million, rising to $61.62 million in 1989–1990 and $64.68 million in 1990–1991. To set these sums in perspective, that year Parkside Hospital alone allocated $16.5 million for AIDS; and the operating budget for a single hospital, St. Mary's, was $102 million.

The new money meant AIDS services could develop at a time when the health service generally was under considerable pressure to cut costs. Capital investment went ahead, not only for the wards where AIDS patients were being treated but also for the genitourinary service generally. Public money, supplemented by voluntary donations, made it possible to care for AIDS patients in buildings furnished and equipped more lavishly than would be found in a typical National Health Service hospital.

Traditionally, the genitourinary services had been poorly organized and inadequate. Clinics for sexually transmitted diseases only opened for brief hours, were located in second-rate buildings, and reflected the military ethos that had launched them. They were designed to punish and discipline, rather than to aid prevention or cure, and their impoverished character reflected their low status within the health service. The need to monitor the course of AIDS meant that change was necessary. Patients were given more attention and greater privacy. The clinics dealing with sexually transmitted diseases were integrated into services concerned with drug treatment and psychiatric disorders.

More important were new care strategies, particularly the development of more wholistic forms of treatment, sustained by the higher level of funding provided for AIDS. Parkside Hospital funded a home care team, whose job it was to ensure that the social, psychological, and domestic needs of patients were met; the team also included a welfare rights officer to look after social security, housing, and discrimination concerns. Hospital space was also provided to practitioners of alternative or complementary therapies.

While the ability to develop new services stood in stark contrast to the problems that elsewhere plagued the system, problems nonetheless remained. Funds were provided on a nonrecurrent basis, which made planning difficult. The formula for the allocation of funds, based primarily on the number of AIDS patients, was fixed—but the amount allocated according to the formula varied unpredictably. The increase from 1988–1989 to 1989–1990 not only allowed for inflation but also provided for real growth of nearly $8.5 million, while the following year the government provided only for inflation-driven increases; these were calculated at 5 percent, significantly less than the actual rate. Whereas individual coping strategies for AIDS were based upon the need for a stable context within which to plan for uncertainty, ironically, the health service itself provided an unpredictable context within which to cope with financial uncertainty. In practice, street-level policymakers adopted an incrementalist approach, assuming that the next year's allocation would approximate the present year's.

Even as specific AIDS services benefited from the government's generosity, other related services suffered. In 1989–1990, the Family Planning Association, one of the few agencies to distribute condoms, was cut back. And the allocation of funds for AIDS patients in different health regions revealed considerable diversity (see Table 6.5). The explanation for these disparities is not discrimination among regions but the ad hoc character of allocation. Although the Department of Health is spending more money on AIDS, because of the emerging political interest it has operated an inefficient distribution network, which maintains the structural status quo.[76]

The formal intention of AIDS policy has been to keep the epidemic from becoming a source of fear and prejudice. There have been sporadic reports of HIV-positive people having their houses set on fire by their neighbors, and more frequent cases of discrimination. The government has confined its reports to well-intentioned injunctions and a reliance on existing legislation, which in a country with no bill of rights gives little true protection.[77]

The Department of Health, in a report on health care workers, argued against testing patients before surgery, but surgeons in Scotland have adopted their own testing scheme. No national legislation has been introduced to prevent discrimination against those who are HIV-positive. The Department of Employment's pamphlet, "AIDS and Employment," says that dismissals based on HIV status would be unfair under existing legislation, but that claim has gone untested in court.

The lack of explicit legal protection against discrimination has meant that people suspected of being HIV-positive are refused insurance. Insurers, for their part, argue that they have a right to determine who they cover. Mr. R. Zamboni, the chairman of the Life Insurance Council, the industry's regulatory body, told the House of Commons Select Committee on AIDS: "We are not turning people down just because they are homosexual, but there is usually a medically related factor that comes in."[78] No one, Zamboni said, was refused insurance simply because he had been tested for HIV. But the Association of British Insurers, the insurers' trade representative, has no enforceable industrywide policy on this issue, and companies are free to impose "their own particular underwriting philosophy and standards. We are not in a position to say to a member that he has refused a case incorrectly."[79] Thus the insurers claim that they are not

Table 6.5. Allocation of Funds per Person with AIDS, by Regions, 1989–1990
(in 1990 U.S. dollars)

Region	Allocation per patient with AIDS
Yorkshire	89,250
Trent	98,600
East Anglia	127,500
Oxford	123,250
Mersey	84,150
Lothian (Scotland)	34,000

SOURCE: A. Maynard and K. Tolley, "The Economic and Social Challenge," in *AIDS: Can We Care Enough?*, ed. V. Beardshaw (London: Kings' Fund, 1989), 22–26.

making judgments on the basis of sexuality but on grounds of risk, even as they insist there are no formally imposed criteria for deciding who gets insurance. The predictable result is discrimination against people with HIV.

The Parliamentary Select Committee for the Social Services criticized the insurance firms and called on the government to outlaw the asking of AIDS-related questions by insurers. The government, however, was willing only to discuss the matter with industry representatives. This was a mere gesture. The government announced its belief in "the need of the insurance industry to find out relevant information before providing life insurance," a view consistent with the Thatcher government's enmity to intervening in the market.[80] Meanwhile, an increasing number of people have refused to be tested for HIV, fearing the effect a positive test result might have on their insurance status.[81]

Thatcherism and the Politics of AIDS Policy

The first decade of AIDS in Britain was dominated politically by the presence of Margaret Thatcher at Number 10 Downing Street, and she directly affected AIDS policy. Talk of Thatcherism assumes, first, that a single ideology pervades all aspects of policy, and second, that the driving force behind policy was Thatcher herself, but the British response to AIDS suggests that both assumptions require some qualification.

Prime Minister Thatcher made few public comments on AIDS and did not take part in the parliamentary discussions of AIDS. While she headed cabinet committees when issues concerned her directly, the AIDS cabinet committee was assigned to her then deputy, Lord Whitelaw, and subsequently to a more junior minister, before being dissolved in 1989.

But while Thatcher did not initiate AIDS policy, she influenced its course both directly and indirectly. Thatcher pushed to modify the language of the advertising campaigns and to cancel the National Survey of

Sexual Behavior. "The Prime Minister's veto on public money [for the sex survey] appeared to derive from an instinctive distaste for invasion of heterosexual privacy—although homosexuals were fair game. Her decision was never explicitly defended. It simply happened, without a public rationale and without the relevant minister, in possession of the scientific facts, feeling able to challenge it."[82]

This decision was consistent with Thatcher's vision of normality and decency, which she saw herself as personifying. The cancellation of the survey was also provoked by businessman Godfrey Bradman, who was influential with the prime minister. Bradman contributed to a variety of causes, AIDS among them. He used a privately commissioned poll to draw Thatcher's attention to the potential unpopularity of the survey, and this finding accorded with her general instincts.

Thatcher's sudden departure from office in November 1990 signaled a change in AIDS policy. One of the first steps taken by her successor, John Major, was to provide $71 million in compensation to hemophiliacs with AIDS, a reversal of Thatcher's policy that was supported by most members of Parliament, whom the Hemophiliac Society had long cultivated.

Conclusion: Politics and Policy

AIDS policy in Britain has only rarely been the result of individual initiative or grass-roots politics. Instead, it has been primarily shaped by elite political interests and existing institutional structures. The elitist character of the process has not necessarily disadvantaged those directly touched by AIDS. The exclusion of gay groups conceivably dampened prejudice within the government, and the narrow base of the consultative process also worked to minimize the impact of right-wing groups. Even after the takeover of AIDS policy by the political leadership, the principal administrative actors have been the health authorities, especially those in the London area, and while their activities depend on central government, they are not under its direct control. Health authorities have received generous but unpredictable funding. A lack of central policy control has meant that politics takes precedence over planning, and expediency substitutes for rationality.

The role of politics in AIDS policy varied with the nature of the policy being shaped. Because education was most publicly prominent, it was subject to the most political influence; interest groups had only marginal involvement. By contrast, treatment had a lower political profile, and this allowed for greater local and interest group participation, as well as for relatively generous funding. Prevention fell between these two extremes. Drug policy at the national level was subject to Home Office pressure, and hence to a variety of political concerns; at the local level, it has assumed both liberal and repressive forms. The scope of research was also determined by a mixture of political and institutional pressures. Medical research either was untouched by or benefited from political pressure; by contrast, social science research was very sensitive to hostile political forces. In all these respects, the AIDS policy process follows the familiar British pattern of proceeding incrementally, allowing interest groups a very limited role.

Whatever the particulars of policy, its formulation has not diverged greatly from established patterns of departmental corporatism and fragmented central control. This accounts for the lack of coordination and the influence of political factors. It also makes predictions about the second decade of AIDS policy difficult. The shift in political leadership may signal a return to the pre-Thatcher tradition of granting substantial autonomy to the health authorities and the Ministry of Health. But at the same time, radical changes to the Health Service being implemented in 1991 may force reductions in treatment for people with AIDS, and may afford even less influence for agencies like the Terrence Higgins Trust.[83] If this happens, the best days of British AIDS policy will be history.

Acknowledgments

Our thanks to the various people who helped us throughout the research on this chapter: Zoe Schramm-Evans, Mildred Blaxter, Professor Steve Smith, Mike and Linda Stephens, Dr. Mukesh Kapila, David Painter, Sheila Adams, Ruth Runiciman, Chris Smith, M.P., Professor Ian Kennedy, Professor Tony Coxon, Dave Bailey, Ailsa Butler, and Helen Christophers. Our editors gave much detailed and helpful guidance. Invaluable data has been provided by the Department of Health, the Health Education Authority, the King's Fund, the University of East Anglia, and the Norwich and Norfolk Hospital libraries.

Notes

1. R. Klein and P. Day, "Interpreting the Unexpected: the Case of AIDS Policy Making in Britain," *Journal of Public Policy* 9 (1990), 352.

2. V. Berridge and P. Strong, "No One Knew Anything: Some Issues in British AIDS Policy," in P. Aggleton et al., *AIDS: Individual, Cultural and Policy Dimensions* (London: Falmer Press, 1990), 233–252; Z. Schramm-Evans, "AIDS: Responses 1986–87" (unpublished Ph.D. thesis) (1990); see also, "Responses to AIDS: 1986–1987," in Aggleton et al., *AIDS: Individual, Cultural and Policy Dimensions*, 221–232; A. Coxon, "Towards a Sociology of AIDS," *Social Studies Review* 3, no. 3 (1988). For an alternative view, see D. M. Fox, P. Day, and R. Klein, "The Power of Professionalism: Policies for AIDS in Britain, Sweden,

and the United States," *Daedalus* 118 (1989), 93–112; or J. Street, "British Government Policy on AIDS: Learning not to die of ignorance," *Parliamentary Affairs* 41 (1988), 490–508.

3. A. Marsh, "The ESRC AIDS Programme," *ESRC Newsletter* 62 (June 1988), 24.

4. In 1989, the official estimate was that at least 20,000 were seropositive; on this basis it was calculated that by 1992 there would be 13,000 AIDS cases in Britain. Later, these figures were revised downward, following the publication of the Day Report, which suggested that only 12,250 people were seropositive. Day had more recent data, used newer evidence about incubation periods and about the effects of AZT, and assumed longer survival times.

5. W. Naylor, "Walking Time Bombs," *Medicine in Society* 11 (1985), 5.

6. Schramm-Evans, "AIDS: Responses 1986–87," 4.

7. Quoted in Naylor, "Walking Time Bombs," 9–10.

8. R. Garland, "AIDS–the British Context," *Health Education Journal* 46 (1987), 50–52.

9. K. Alcorn, "AIDS in the Public Sphere," in *Taking Liberties: AIDS and Cultural Politics*, ed. E. Carter and S. Watney (London: Serpent's Tail, 1989), 193–212.

10. *The Guardian*, November 12, 1986.

11. In Scotland, the relevant government institution is the Scottish Home and Health Department (SHHD). This means that both hospitals and prisons fall within the same institution, and as a result there is a more coherent set of policies for dealing with AIDS in prisons. Scotland also has a different legal system, which has implications for drugs policy. However, the role of the DoH is complicated by the allocation of power to the various territories of the United Kingdom. The Scottish system, for example, is quite different from that elsewhere. We confine our remarks largely to England and Wales.

12. Although predecents can be found in the nineteenth-century Contagious Diseases Act, the key developments occurred in the aftermath of the 1914–18 World War. The spread of syphilis among the British troops prompted the government to provide state-backed pathology laboratories, to provide free medicines to doctors, and to encourage the creation of special clinics in general hospitals. See J. Weeks, *Sex, Politics and Society* (London: Longman, 1981), 215.

13. V. Daniels, *AIDS* (Lancaster: MTP, 1986), 13–14.

14. *General Practitioner* (January 20, 1984), 4.

15. V. Beardshaw, "Blunted Weapons," *New Statesman and Society* (December 1, 1989), 24–25.

16. M. Kapila and K. Wellings, "The UK Public Education Campaign," (draft chapter) (London: HEA, 1989), 2.

17. DHSS, Briefing, 83/166 (September 1, 1983).

18. Department of Health (Cox Report), *Short-term Predictions of HIV and AIDS in England* (London: HMSO, 1988); N. Wells, *The AIDS Virus: Forecasting its Impact* (London: Office of Health Economics, 1986).

19. College of Health, *AIDS and the Government* (London: College of Health, 1986).

20. *The Sun* (October 20, 1987).

21. W. H. McNeill, *Plagues and Peoples* (Harmondsworth: Penguin, 1979).

22. *Ibid.*, 249.

23. *The Guardian*, (January 22, 1987).

24. N. Wells, *The AIDS Virus: Forecasting its Impact* (London: Office of Health Economics, 1986).

25. *Ibid.*, 38–39, 48.

26. J. Lewis, "AIDS Policy," *The Lancet* (May 14, 1988), 10.

27. R. M. Mackie et al., "Malignant Melanoma in Scotland, 1979–83," *The Lancet* (October 19, 1985), 859–862.

28. R. M. Mackie et al., "Personal Risk-factor Chart for Cutaneous Melanoma," *The Lancet* (August 26, 1989), 487–490.

29. D. Vagero, A. J. Swerdlow, and V. Beral, "Occupation and Malignant Melanoma: A Study Based on Cancer Registration Data in England and Wales and Sweden," *British Journal of Industrial Medicine* 47 (1990), 317–324.

30. L. Keliher, "Core Executive Decision Making on High Technology Issues: The Case of the Alvey report," *Public Administration* 68 (1990), 61–82.

31. T. Prentice, "The Top Doctor's Dilemma," *The Times* (November 7, 1985), 10.

32. *THS Health Summary* 11 (1985), 1.

33. Schramm-Evans, "AIDS: Responses 1986–87," 11.

34. Social Services Select Committee, *Problems Associated with AIDS*, vol. ii, 35.

35. D. Mellor, *DoH Press Release*, 89/398.

36. *HC Debs.* (January 13, 1989), col. 100.

37. Social Services Select Committee, *AIDS* 202 (London: HMSO, 1989), 12.

38. The Select Committee is a means of scrutinizing, albeit with limited powers, the activities of the executive and administration. The All Party group is a more informal parliamentary grouping, which seeks sponsorship from inside and outside the House of Commons. Each has given a platform to a wide variety of opinions and expertise on AIDS.

39. *House of Commons Debates* (Hansard) (November 21, 1986), cols. 812, 820–821.

40. *HC Debs.* (April 30, 1986), col. 992.

41. Health Education Authority, *AIDS and Sexual Health Programme* (London: HEA, 1990), 7–8.

42. Berridge and Strong, "No One Knew Anything," 242.

43. M. Kapila, "AIDS Prevention Through Public Education: The Work of the Health Education Authority," *Royal Society of Medicine: The AIDS Letter* 15 (October/November 1989), 3–4.

44. *The Guardian*, (December 13, 1986).

45. *The Guardian*, (November 22, 1986).

46. *The Guardian*, (November 17, 1986).

47. *The Observer* (June 19, 1988).

48. HEA, *AIDS Programme: First Annual Report*, Aids Programme Papers 4 (1989).

49. D. Wiseman and D. Bodell, "Sustaining Safer Sex," *AIDS Dialogue* 4 (1990), 3.

50. K. Alcorn, "AIDS in the Public Sphere," 193–212.

51. J. E. Campbell and W. E. Waters, "Public Knowledge about AIDS Increasing," *British Medical Journal* 294 (1987), 893.

52. *Media Week* (November 21, 1986).

53. E. Beck et al., "HIV Testing," *British Medical Journal* 295 (1987), 193.

54. M. Kapila and K. Wellings, "The UK Public Education Campaign— Evaluation and Evolution" (draft chapter) (London: HEA, 1989).

55. Department of Health and Social Security, *AIDS: Monitoring Response to the Public Education Campaign* (London: HMSO, 1987).

56. *The Lancet* (1987), 1429.

57. Nutbeam et al., "Public Knowledge and Attitudes to AIDS," *Public Health* 103 (1989), 205.

58. M. Fumento, *The Myth of Heterosexual AIDS* (New York: Basic Books, 1990).

59. HEA, *AIDS and Sexual Health Programme: Summary of Second Annual Report* (London: HEA, 1990), 7.

60. *New Scientist* (June 2, 1988), 22; (December 3, 1988), 24.

61. *The Independent* (July 23, 1990).

62. Department of Health, Press Briefing, 88/102 (March 29, 1988).

63. Department of Health, *AIDS: Response by the Government to the 7th Report from the Social Services Committee Session*, Cm 925, (London: HMSO, 1989), 8–9.

64. Britain's notoriously overcrowded jails provide a challenge to which policy-makers have failed to rise. In part this is due, once again, to the division of responsibility between the DoH and the Home Office. However, the Prison Service, which is responsible for the day-to-day operation of the prisons, has been sluggish in response. Although joint meetings have been held between health authorities and the Prison Medical Service, there was little understanding between the two sides, and the meetings have not been followed up. In Scotland, relations between the health side and the prison side have been better, not least because policy is organized in the same department (the Scottish Home and Health Department in Edinburgh).

65. Advisory Council on the Misuse of Drugs, *AIDS and Drug Misuse*, Part 1 (London: HMSO, 1988), 1.

66. ACMD, *AIDS and Drug Misuse*, Part 1, para. 2.3.

67. DHSS Circular, HC(88)26 (March 1988).

68. *Ibid.*

69. DoH, Press Release, (September 27, 1988).

70. Social Services Select Committee, *Problems Associated with AIDS*, vol. i (182–I) (London: HMSO, 1987), para. 24.

71. S. Connor and S. Kingman, *The Search for the Virus* (Harmondsworth: Penguin, 1988), 23.

72. F. Mort, *Dangerous Sexualities* (London: Routledge, 1988), 216, and MRC, *AIDS Research 1990* (London: MRC, 1990).

73. Coxon, "Coping with the Threat of Death," in *AIDS: A Moral Issue,* ed. B. Almond (London: Macmillan, 1990), 143–152.

74. A. Marsh, "The ESRC AIDS Programme," *ESRC Newsletter* 62 (June 1988), 21.

75. *HC Debs.* (January 13, 1989), cols. 1106–1107.

76. A. Maynard and K. Tolley, "The Economic and Social Challenge," 22–26.

77. A. Orr, "Legal AIDS, Implications of AIDS and HIV for British and American Law," *Journal of Medical Ethics* 15 (1989), 61–67.

78. Social Services Select Committee, *Problems Associated with AIDS,* vol. ii (182–II) (London: HMSO, 1987), 261

79. Ibid., 262.

80. Social Services Select Committee (1989), *AIDS* (London: HMSO, 1989), 202, para. 19.

81. *Parliamentary AIDS Digest* 3 (Summer 1989), 2.

82. H. Young, *One of Us* (London: Pan, 1990), 548.

83. C. Bentley and M. Adler, "Choice Cuts for Patients with AIDS," *British Medical Journal* 301 (1990), 501–502.

Chapter 7 **France: Social Solidarity and Scientific Expertise**

Monika Steffen

In July 1988, Dr. Leon Schwarzenberg, a well-known professor of medicine, was named minister of health by the Socialists, who had just been returned to power in France. Nine days later, he was dismissed from office. AIDS policy was the reason for his political demise.

Just days after his appointment, Schwarzenberg had held a press conference at which he announced sweeping new policies. His AIDS program was a mix of radical departures from past public health practices and authoritarian elements of the traditions of disease control. Schwarzenberg's agenda included the government-sponsored distribution of drugs to addicts, compulsory HIV testing for all pregnant women and surgical patients, and the protection of patients' rights to know the nature and prognosis of their illness. It was a bold program—not surprising from a man who had in the past taken courageous and heterodox positions on social questions—which provoked the ire of both the political left and right. Announced without consultation with other members of the government, the program met with general criticism from medical and social welfare professionals, from all the major political parties, including the Socialists, and from the opposition. The presidents of three medical and ethical bodies, when consulted, approved the dismissal of Schwarzenberg. His nine-day term was the briefest tenure of any cabinet minister in the Fifth Republic.

Four months later, a special report commissioned by Claude Évin, Schwarzenberg's successor as minister of health, decried the government's failure to provide anything approaching the financial and administrative support necessary to face the challenge of the AIDS epidemic. Despite the fact that AIDS had been proclaimed a matter of great importance, a "national cause," only five full-time staff members (including clerical staff) had been committed to AIDS work in the Ministry of Health.

Only in 1989, eight years after the first reports of AIDS in France, did the government allocate substantially increased resources to fund the battle against AIDS. Yet once France decided to act, it proceeded swiftly. Just a year later France had emerged as an example of a country with a successful liberal AIDS policy that protects the rights of those with HIV infection in accord with the principle of human rights and extends the support of medical and social welfare services to those victimized by the epidemic in an expression of the philosophy of solidarity.

The evolution of AIDS policy in France has passed through three phases. During the first minimalist era there was little official interest and only the most modest commitment of resources. The second agenda-setting period witnessed the enunciation of a set of principles covering the rights of persons with AIDS, the importance of prevention, and the necessity of extending care to the sick, but the allocation of resources to fight the epidemic remained quite limited. It was only during the third phase of institutionalization that resources became available, implementing policy commitments made during the prior period.

The very lengthy period of relative government inaction cannot be explained by the epidemiology of AIDS in France, since it has recorded more cases of AIDS than any other European country. Only Switzerland, a small nation profoundly affected by its special international character, has more cases per inhabitant. Figures from 1987, the turning point for public AIDS policies in many European countries, as well as more recent data, illustrate the discrepancy between government action and the epidemiological situation (see Table 7.1). In Great Britain and Germany, where the burden of the AIDS epidemic was far smaller than in France, governments moved earlier to launch aggressive programs directed at AIDS prevention.

The tardiness of the French government in confronting AIDS reflects the changing political climate in which policy was made: there were three changes in government during the period, and these correspond directly with the policy epochs. The policy decisions and the shape that policy ultimately took, however, show the influences of essential characteristics of France's health care system: a strong tradition of social solidarity institutionalized in the social security system; the weak position of public health within the administrative hierarchy, making a modest governmental response more likely; the privileged position of physicians and scientific experts in health policy-making; and the weakness of organized interest representation for patients. The inaction of the early years of the epidemic is also symptomatic of the difficulties French policymakers encountered when faced with an unexpected challenge, in a situation characterized by scientific uncertainty about the risks involved and political uncertainty about how society should respond.

Deciding on a national AIDS policy in France involved a protracted process, since public policies traditionally emerge from an alliance between a segment of the elite public administration and a professional group. Before new policies could be formulated, new actors had to

Table 7.1. AIDS Cases in Selected European Countries

	December 31, 1987		December 31, 1990	
	Total number of reported cases	Per million inhabitants	Total number of reported cases	Per million inhabitants
France	3,073	55	13,145	234
West Germany	1,669	27	5,612	71
Great Britain	1,227	22	4,098	71

SOURCE: World Health Organization, European AIDS Center, Paris.

emerge and establish their authority within the administration and the relevant professional groups. The inevitable clash of perceptions among those touched by the epidemic necessitated arbitration on the part of the state, involving outsiders as well as the familiar band of insiders to secure the needed consensus that would legitimate public policy.

The French National Context of AIDS Policies

This process of consensus-building was shaped by the institutional networks and processes of the national policy-making system.

The Health Sector

The national health insurance scheme covers almost 99 percent of the entire French population.[1] It is financed by compulsory contributions from all work-related income. Health insurance in France is based on principles of social solidarity; there is no risk selection. The amount contributed by any individual depends entirely on income; the size of the family is irrelevant. A recently instituted program for those without independent income provides for automatic health insurance coverage. Only a handful of marginalized individuals find themselves without financial coverage for medical care, but even they cannot be denied treatment by hospitals, which must fulfill their special mission of public service.

Patients are free to choose the physician who will provide them with treatment as well as the hospital within which they will receive care. In the ambulatory care system, where physicians, pharmacists, and paramedical staff are self-employed, and in private clinics, the national health insurance program reimburses patients for 60 to 80 percent of expenses. There is no reimbursement for drugs classified as nonessential.

Most French citizens are members of nonprofit mutual societies, which provide protection against the unreimbursed portion of medical expenses. Like the compulsory health insurance program, mutual societies may not engage in risk selection. The principle of solidarity means that no grounds exist for HIV screening. This broad, unquestioned commitment to social solidarity has deep historical roots in France; it dates to the tradition of mutual aid societies at the end of the nineteenth century and the creation of the current social security system in 1945, influenced by British Labour principles.

Health insurance covers up to 100 percent of the cost of maternity-related care, expensive care such as highly technical examinations or therapy, hospitalization exceeding thirty days, and illnesses that are officially recognized as being lengthy and costly to treat. At the end of 1986, AIDS was added to the list of illnesses with 100 percent coverage.

Nonetheless, there are critical shortcomings in the French health system stemming from the dominance of the medical model of illness and the central place of the representatives of public hospitals in heath politics. Both are of immediate relevance to the French response to AIDS. Alternatives to traditional hospital care, especially efforts to combine hospital and ambulatory services into a continuum of care, have been difficult to promote, even when there is a political willingness to engage in reform.[2] The initiation of such changes must confront established professional hierarchies; it requires a shift in power from the public hospitals to the ambulatory medical services.[3]

Prevention and public health services are the stepchildren of health care policy, in part because of the dominance of the medical leadership, in part because of a widely held belief that the right to health, guaranteed by the constitution, means the right of access to medical services. Nevertheless, it has become abundantly clear that the dominant medical paradigm is ineffective in fields like drug and alcohol treatment, the care of those with sexually transmitted diseases, suicide prevention, and the care of the chronically ill. Effective policies in these fields require close coordination between medical and social services and a redirection of public expenditures, away from acute therapy to less medicalized services. They also necessitate the enhancement of the professional status of physicians working in public health, who presently occupy the bottom rungs of the medical hierarchy.

The strong liberal tradition that most French physicians share emphasizes the therapeutic relationship between patients and their doctors and the protection of confidentiality. As a consequence, French physicians do not readily accept public obligations, such as reporting their activities, especially if they would require named reporting of those with infectious diseases. Nor do they welcome efforts to limit their freedom to prescribe medication.

An anecdote illustrates the strength of the individualistic professional ideology. During the 1983 annual meeting of a national medical association, a physician declared that he had never reported a single case of infectious disease as required by regulation or law, because he considered himself to be at the exclusive service of his patients; he felt that he was not bound by ministerial rules that did not have a directly beneficial impact on those for whom he cared.

The special characteristics of French health policies and medical traditions have provided solid grounds for a liberal approach to AIDS care. But these same values have limited efforts to launch collective prevention strategies and to promote the public health sector, also crucial to fighting the epidemic.

The Importance of the Central State and of Scientific Legitimacy

France has a highly centralized system of government. The scope available for policy initiatives by government at the regional or local level is extremely limited, despite decentralization reforms, adopted in 1983–84, that primarily affected the provision of social services. Decision-making in the medical sector has become increasingly centralized, under the tutelage of the ministry of economy and finance, which keeps careful watch on the rising costs of the social security system.

In comparison to the situation that prevails in the United States or Germany, interest group organization is weak. Organizations representing general consumer interests do not exist in the health sector, although some mutual aid societies have attempted to expand their influence beyond the provision of reimbursements for health care expenditures. There are specialized associations of patients organized around particular diseases, but they are dominated by physicians, who also exert great influence over service-providing institutions.

The general weakness of interest group organization and popular representation has historical roots dating back to the French Revolution, when intermediate associations—mainly the guilds—were abolished. From the perspective of the Revolution, neither group identity nor organized group interest were to be permitted; these might interfere with the new principles of national interest and the equal rights and obligations of all citizens.

During the Third Republic, from 1870 to 1940, secularization and a belief in science were promoted as a basis for social progress and democratic government. Social problems were to be resolved on the basis of scientific knowledge by professional experts like teachers, doctors, social workers, urbanists, and engineers. This rationalist approach still influences public action and the policy process.

Initiatives for new policies typically originate from senior officials of the state elite, who encourage the development of social organizations that support the proposed policy changes. National policies for the elderly and the handicapped adopted in the 1960s and the 1970s provide examples of this model of change. Thus initiatives seldom arise from society, and when they do emerge, they must find support in the political-administrative apparatus. The result is a closed policy system that tends to reproduce existing conditions and to resist reforms.

The economic growth of the 1950s, 1960s, and 1970s has permitted France to face new social problems and demands by creating new services and increasing expenditures, with each new system grafted onto existing ones without reorganizing the whole. Thus, social policy has grown by a process of "sedimentation," and only rarely do organizational innovations occur.[4] Such innovations may, however, occur when they are promoted by the state as "grand national projects," especially in industry and technology.[5] The electrification of France, the nuclear power program, the Concorde jet, and the high-speed train are examples of such grand projects that have become national priorities. When AIDS was declared a "national cause" in 1987, a similar logic was introduced into the health sector.

The Political Context

Major political changes occurred in France during the first decade of the AIDS epidemic. National elections were unusually frequent, and the ruling majority changed several times. These shifts were consequential: conflict-laden reforms were undertaken, and major ideological transformations occurred. In the 1981 presidential elections, the Socialist party came to power for the first time in nearly fifty years, and the general elections gave an absolute majority to the leftist alliance formed by the Socialists and Communists. Two years later, though, the left-wing alliance splintered, and the Communists departed from the government. The Socialists then abandoned their long-held commitment to nationalization, public service, and social expenditure and began pursuing policies oriented toward economic efficiency, private enterprise, and the free market.

The 1986 general elections returned the liberal and conservative parties to power in the legislature, while the presidency remained in Socialist hands. As a consequence, for two years important policy initiatives were stymied and decisions delayed in expectation of forthcoming elections.

During this period, the political landscape underwent major changes. The Communist party lost almost all its influence. The conservative party bloc split into competing groups; an extreme right movement, the National Front, directed by Jean-Marie Le Pen, gained considerable electoral influence—as much as 30 percent in some areas, notably in the southeastern region of the country. The National Front's focus on insecurity, immigration, and national decline attracted some support from many segments of society; it was especially welcomed by those hardest hit by the economic transformations of the 1970s and 1980s: workers in traditional industries, shopkeepers, the unemployed, and retired pensioners. The National Front also drew support from individuals who favored limiting divorce and abortion, restoring capital punishment and the legal prohibition of homosexuality, isolating AIDS patients in special institutions, and halting the construction of mosques for Muslim immigrants.[6]

In a climate of growing politicization, AIDS became yet another contested topic. As old partisan boundaries and beliefs weakened, allegiances became even more personalized, prompting a general critique of the political elite. Nevertheless, the reelection of President Mitterand in 1988—after a campaign based on the broad themes of solidarity, liberty, and equality—provided a renewed social consensus and reinforced the government's legitimacy. For the struggle against AIDS, this meant that seven years after the epidemic was first reported, infusions of substantial resources first became possible.

At Risk

France was the first European country to establish an epidemiological surveillance system for AIDS: thus, AIDS not only appeared early but also quickly became visible. When the reporting of an AIDS diagnosis become obligatory in June 1986, statistical evidence of the course of the epidemic was already available.

Table 7.2 shows the steady increase in diagnosed AIDS cases. (There is an artificial decrease for 1990, because of delays in reporting. Adjusting for such delay, the Ministry of Health estimates that 14,760 cases of AIDS had been diagnosed by the end of 1990.) Although the law requires physicians to make an anonymous report for each diagnosed case, no enforcement mechanism exists. The rate of underreporting is estimated by the ministry as between 10 and 20 percent. Hence, the actual number of cases at the end of 1990 was probably closer to 17,700.

There is no requirement that seropositive but asymptomatic cases be reported, and consequently the extent of HIV infection in France remains undetermined. Since systematic testing of representative samples was disapproved early on, because of scientific concerns about the validity of the sampling, there was little objective basis for choosing among competing estimates and no objective way of confronting the political manipulation of the seroprevalence debate. In 1986, some suggested that as many as half a million individuals were infected. In 1990, the first systematic analysis, using alternative epidemiological methodologies, concluded that at most there were 200,000 cases of HIV infection in France, with 150,000 cases the most probable figure.[7]

In France, as in other economically developed countries, AIDS disproportionally affects a population of young male adults: two-thirds of all reported cases are concentrated among those between ages twenty and forty. The proportion of reported cases among gay or bisexual men has declined over the decade, as the number of cases among women and

Table 7.2. AIDS Cases by Year of Report and Category of Risk Exposure for France, 1978–1990

Risk category	1978	1980	1981	1982	1983	1984	1985	1986	1987	1988	1989	1990	Total
Homosexual/bisexual activity	2	1	3	20	54	142	369	729	1,210	1,493	1,657	1,242	6,922
Homosexual/bisexual activity and IVDU	0	0	0	0	2	5	18	44	56	39	59	21	244
IVDU	0	0	0	0	0	8	42	141	322	599	802	657	2,571
Blood products	0	0	0	1	6	15	36	106	208	246	259	124	1,001
Heterosexual activity	2	2	3	7	24	37	68	114	197	313	373	299	1,439
Mother to child	0	0	0	0	3	9	9	18	60	49	45	17	210
Other/unknown	1	1	2	1	1	11	20	51	112	165	200	193	758
Total cases	5	4	8	29	90	227	562	1,203	2,165	2,904	3,395	2,553	13,145

Source: Bulletin Epidémiologique Hebdomadaire (B.E.H.), No. 7 (1991).

heterosexuals has increased. Contributing to this change has been the growing importance of intravenous drug use as a vector of HIV transmission. Despite this epidemiological picture, state-run AIDS education and prevention campaigns have focused on those least at risk: the general heterosexual population.

There are important geographical differences in the distribution and nature of the epidemic. In metropolitan France, AIDS is concentrated in two regions: Île-de-France (Paris and its suburbs); and the southeastern Mediterranean coast, including the urban centers of Marseilles, Cannes, and Nice. A third center of the epidemic is situated in the overseas departments of the Antilles Islands and Guyana. Each center has its own dominant mode of transmission (see Table 7.3).

In fact—and quite uniquely—France is faced with three different AIDS epidemics. The northern European pattern of initial homosexual transmission obtains in the Paris area; the southern European pattern, where transmission by intravenous drug use, concentrated among especially disadvantaged segments of the population, characterizes the southeast of France; and a heterosexual pattern of transmission, typical for Third World countries, clearly prevails in Guyana and the Caribbean islands.

In metropolitan France, apart from Paris, the highest proportion of gays and bisexuals among reported AIDS cases is found in Lorraine, in Poitou-Charente, and in the North. Each of these three regions has a low proportion of intravenous drug users among its AIDS cases, despite the fact that they are confronted with significant unemployment and youth problems. Michael Pollak has attributed the relatively high level of homosexual transmission in provincial areas to the fact that since small or medium-sized towns cannot provide the basis for gay social life, homosexuals turn to Paris, with its high seroprevalence among gay men, more frequently than do those living in cities that support an autonomous gay social life.[8] In these cities, infection appeared later and has spread less rapidly.[9] Despite these distinct and disparate patterns of epidemic spread, French AIDS prevention policy has been homogenous. It takes little account of the epidemiological data and so fails to acknowledge the special needs of regions with divergent epidemiological patterns.

The Policy Process

French AIDS policy has passed through three phases. During the period of "problem diagnosis," from 1981 to 1984, the new epidemic was ignored by established elites. Marginal groups played an essential role as they accumulated the scientific evidence necessary to substantiate their claims and began to put forward proposals for a practical response. The second policy initiation phase, from 1985 to 1988, was marked by serious government

Table 7.3. Regional Distribution of Reported AIDS Cases in France as of December 31, 1990

Region	Number of cases	Per million Inhabitants
Metropolitan France		
Ile de France	6,771	658.6
Provence-Alpes-Côte d'Azur	1,809	438.1
Aquitaine	509	186.4
Languedoc-Roussillion	343	165.9
Midi-Pyrénées	339	142.7
Corse	29	117.4
Rhône-Alpes	537	103.4
Haute-Normandie	157	92.1
Limousin	65	88.6
Poitou-Charentes	132	82.9
Champagne-Ardennes	108	79.5
Basse-Normandie	101	73.0
Picardie	129	72.5
Alsace	116	72.1
Lorraine	166	71.3
Auvergne	93	70.0
Bourgogne	110	68.2
Franche Comté	73	67.1
Pays de la Loire	201	65.8
Bretagne	175	63.2
Centre	141	60.2
Nord-Pas de Calais	166	42.2
Overseas departments:		
Guyane, Guadeloupe, Martinique	511	699
Réunion (near Madagascar)	45	87.2
Others		
French citizens living abroad	288	. . . .
Non-identified	31	. . . .
Total	13,145	234.1

SOURCE: Bulletin Epidémiologique Hebdomadaire (B.E.H.), No. 7 (1991).

attempts to implement new policies, but these interventions were limited by electoral disturbances and the concomitant uncertainties of French political life. The third phase, institutionalization, dating from mid-1988, witnessed important decisions to increase AIDS resources and institutional innovations that permitted the more rapid implementation of policies centered on the previous commitment to support public information, scientific research, and social solidarity.

The Period of Problem Diagnosis

The earliest information about the new disease that would ultimately be called AIDS reached France in June 1981, when the U.S. Centers for

Disease Control's *Morbidity and Mortality Weekly Report* (MMWR) published an article on five cases of Kaposi's sarcoma in homosexual men. At that time, Dr. Willy Rozenbaum, a Paris physician familiar with the *MMWR* article, saw a gay patient presenting the same clinical syndrome; soon there were other patients with similar clinical manifestations. Like physicians in the United States, Rozenbaum and his colleagues were confronted with the challenge of understanding the etiology of the illnesses with which they were faced. While homosexuality figured in all the accounts, such life-style–based explanations did not correspond to French scientific thought, which is shaped by rational Pasteurian influences. The French public learned about the new disease only six months later, in January 1982, when the first articles on the mysterious symptoms that had affected American gay males appeared in the daily press.[10]

Late in 1981, an informal group was constituted to discuss new cases and to review relevant literature. Quickly, the group was transformed into a structured working unit, with regular meetings and participation from representatives of the public administration. Physicians represented a majority of this working group: clinicians recruited from various specialties, among them infectious and tropical disease and venereology, who were caring for the first hospitalized AIDS patients, as well as two general practitioners who worked with gay men. Researchers, mainly immunologists, also participated, as did two representatives of the health ministry, one responsible for general prevention and environment, the other for sexually transmitted diseases. A physician-epidemiologist, Jean-Baptiste Brunet, played a crucial role in the group's work. It was Brunet who proposed the creation of a surveillance system that could determine whether the small number of cases in France—five or six at the time—presaged developments similar to those occurring in the United States.

The participation of officials from the health ministry in the working group made this task easier. In March 1982, the Department of Health allocated $10,000 to finance a special leave for Dr. Bruent to conduct this study. Recalling this initiative, Brunet has noted:

> It was extraordinary that the ministry agreed to finance an epidemiological study of a totally unknown disease when only a handful of patients in the entire country had been diagnosed, when the proposal for such a study had come from a working group that had homosexuals among its members! This would have been unthinkable had not two participants from the ministry been active participants. They knew how to present the proposal.[11]

The provision of funds represented a clear sign that public authorities recognized the new problem. The commitment of public funds also gave the working group an official status and linked doctors and researchers who had been studying the new disease.

The composition of the working group remained fluid, as virologists joined the group in early 1983. A psychiatrist with links to the gay community, who would ultimately found an organization that provided apartments with medical support to individuals with AIDS, also joined the group. Still, participation by gay community representatives remained weak. Linkages were attempted with the only established gay militant organization, the Emergency Committee Against Homosexual Repression (CUARH), as well as with the just-created Gay Medical Association, but these proved rather unproductive. On the other hand, useful contacts were made with researchers from the prestigious Pasteur Institute. When the lymph node of one of Dr. Rozenbaum's patients was transmitted for analysis to Luc Montagnier's research team at the Pastuer Institute, the AIDS virus was rapidly isolated and identified; in March 1983 it was named LAV.

The discovery of the virus led the working group to divide into two autonomous structures; one focused on epidemiology, the other on clinical and scientific research. Montagnier assumed the leadership of the latter group, which was transformed into a formal association, Association pour la Recherche contre le Sida, known as ARSIDA (Association for Research against AIDS), dedicated to raising research funds. Brunet was granted an extended leave by the Ministry of Health so that he could continue his surveillance of the epidemic. In November 1984, the World Health Organization and the French government agreed to establish the European Center for the Epidemiological Monitoring of AIDS in Paris under Brunet's leadership.

Almost one hundred cases of AIDS had been reported by the end of 1983. The overwhelming majority were among gay men living in Paris, half of whom had traveled to the United States, Haiti, or Central Africa. During this initial period, the health authorities made two modest efforts to prevent the spread of AIDS. To prevent transmission and anxiety in medical settings, health care workers were reminded of the necessity of following precautions when handling potentially infectious materials. The second set of recommendations focused on the protection of the blood supply. Mirroring the U.S. approach, they called on blood collection and transfusion centers to use interviews and questionnaires in order to screen out potential donors who were homosexual or bisexual, intravenous drug users, individuals of Central African or Caribbean origin, and their sexual partners. These recommendations were not welcomed by the blood centers, which feared that such inquiries might discourage potential donors. They were denounced by CUARH as a return to racist scapegoating, which was socially dangerous and medically ineffective.

The low profile adopted by the French authorities in this period was partly rooted in the lack of scientific consensus about the etiology of AIDS. Two hypotheses competed for dominance. The first viewed AIDS as an infectious disease caused and transmitted by a viral agent, the retrovirus isolated by the Pasteur team. But from a contrasting perspective, AIDS was viewed as an immune deficiency, the consequence of a multiplicity of assaults on the body's disease-fighting capacity. Most immunologists, oncologists, and virologists, among them the most eminent and well-known specialists in their fields, defended the immunity hypothesis. The retroviral hypothesis was supported by a minority of less-known researchers.

Open conflict between these two constituencies ensued when research funds from the National Institute of Medical Research (INSERM), the Foundation for Medical Research and the Ministry of Research and Technology, were made available in late 1983. Each side organized international working sessions on AIDS in Paris that winter. Commenting on the dispute a year later, Professor Jean-Paul Levy, the president of the National Agency for Research on AIDS (ANRS), recalled the history of medical science and the relationship between cancer, retroviruses, and the immune system, which had been known since the beginning of the century.[12] This was a call for interdisciplinary collaboration and for a coordinated national research program on AIDS.

The Policy Initiation Period

Technical developments led to the resolution of the scientific controversy and paved the way for policy initiatives.

In early 1984, the Pasteur Institute perfected its first blood test for the antibody to the AIDS virus. At the same time Margaret Heckler, the Secretary of the U.S. Department of Health and Human Services, announced the discovery of the AIDS virus, called HTLV-III, by Robert Gallo. Heckler's refusal to acknowledge the achievements of Luc Montagnier galvanized the French authorities and press. The ensuing scientific war suddenly transformed AIDS into an issue of national importance for France. The expansion of the epidemic in Africa, where branches of the Pasteur Institute are well established, and the discovery by the Pasteur group in early 1986 of a second virus, named LAV2, which was linked to the African epidemic, reinforced the growing consciousness that French national interests were at stake.

AIDS also became a media event. Famous people had died of AIDS, most notably Michel Foucault, who died in June 1984; well-known gay Parisians actively sought to mobilize the media in order to promote more research funding and to oppose group-specific measures for controlling the epidemic. France also became an international point of reference for those afflicted with AIDS. Famous patients, most notably Rock Hudson, arrived from abroad seeking advanced treatment in French hospitals.

Reflecting both the pressure to assert French interests and the role that had been assumed by the media in this period, the Socialist party's Minister of Social Affairs and Health Georgina Dufoix, used the context of a press conference to announce a major therapeutic advance in the care of AIDS patients. After a brief trial with cyclosporine on a very small number of patients, she declared that French physicians had made "major progress in curing AIDS." Her move was premature and unwarranted and provoked an embarrassing disavowal by the entire scientific community.

The development of a blood test capable of detecting the AIDS antibody, and the capacity to produce it in large quantities, constituted the starting point for significant public intervention. The availability of the test posed two urgent practical problems, requiring decisions on the highest government level. Since France has a national health insurance system, large-scale testing for purposes of prevention would entail significant public expenditures. At a time when cost containment dominated health policy discussions, any decision that required new outlays had to be made at the interministerial level. In addition, with the signing of an agreement between France and the United States concerning the patent for the antibody test—a temporary truce in the Montagnier–Gallo wars—strategies to govern the production and marketing of the French test kits were needed.

The first compulsory testing measure was published in July 1985: All blood donors, and by extension organ and sperm donors, were to be tested.[13] Three months later, a government circular added that seropositive donors were to be personally informed of their status.[14] In February 1986, all AIDS virus antibody tests prescribed by physicians became fully reimbursable by the national health insurance plan. These actions had been called for by a group of specialists from the National Transfusion Society, the National Commission on Transfusion, the National Committee on Ethics, and of course, the first AIDS experts. They also opposed the very idea of a registry of the infected, because they feared that such a list would discourage voluntary blood donation.

Hemophiliacs, the institutions that served them, as well as their physicians all had a long-standing commitment to an ethic of social solidarity and equity. Voluntary donation and the provision of blood products from national sources were viewed as assuring a safe blood supply. They initially hesitated to endorse the importation of foreign heat-treated products, which would be available—some argued—in limited quantities only to a fortunate minority.

The decisions on blood screening might have been made earlier; the United States had recommended screening half a year before. But since blood collection and transfusion is a public service in France and must meet a common safety standard, no testing could begin until the Pasteur Institute could provide test kits in sufficient quantities and at a competitive price to all of the country's centers.

Although France was among the first countries to mandate the testing of blood donors, the rate of infection has been high among hemophiliacs and those receiving transfusions: together these groups account for more than 7 percent of reported AIDS cases. According to the National Association of Hemophiliacs, more than 1,200 hemophiliacs—about 40 percent of those with the severest form of the disease—are infected with HIV, and nearly two hundred have developed AIDS. As is true elsewhere, the infection of hemophiliacs who depend upon the regular administration of a blood-clotting compound provoked sharp disagreement over whether the public health authorities had moved quickly enough to protect those whose very survival was at stake.

AIDS specialists believed that the blood-clotting factor could have been made safe as early as February 1985. But physicians from institutions responsible for the blood supply argued that such efforts would disrupt the care of hemophiliacs, a disruption with dire clinical consequences. Concerns were also voiced about the cost of discarding the existing untreated stock. In this instance, the still emerging community of AIDS specialists was unable to overcome the entrenched leadership of the blood transfusion establishment. As a consequence, hemophiliacs continued to be exposed to the risk of a lethal virus until October 1985, when the use of untreated clotting factor was prohibited.

This issue ultimately resurfaced when France confronted the question of whether to compensate individuals infected through blood products. Only in 1989, after repeated refusals to do so, and the burning, in protest, of the automobile of the Director of the National Blood Transfusion Center, did the government establish a special fund to provide an indemnity to infected hemophiliacs—and then only if they agreed to forego lawsuits against public authorities. This stipulation provoked new and even more important controversies during 1991, leading to an ambitious project— now under way—for the reform of the entire blood transfusion and indemnity system.

But as blood testing began, yet another policy issue seized center stage. As data on the prevalence of infection among blood donors accumulated, a passionate debate took shape over the significance of these findings in estimating the level of HIV infection in the French population. One in a thousand blood donors was infected; if this figure were extrapolated to the entire population of France, that would mean that fifty thousand individuals were already infected in 1985. Some argued that this was a low estimate because those at risk, notably homosexual and bisexual men, were being screened out by questionnaires. Others argued that the estimate represented an exaggeration, since those who feared that they might be infected were using the blood centers to determine their HIV status. It was during these epidemiological debates that the idea emerged of creating special centers to provide information about AIDS and anonymous blood tests.

As the French government confronted the range of issues surrounding the blood supply, it also established the principles that would guide AIDS policy: the provision of public information, emphasis on personal responsibility, and social solidarity. As in most other democratic nations, compulsory measures were rejected. The issue of whether to close the gay bathhouses, which caused so fierce a debate in the United States, was never a matter of serious consideration. There was to be no mandatory screening except in cases of blood, organ, and sperm donation. All public institutions that dealt with people who might be HIV-infected—hospitals, drug treatment centers, prisons—were told not to introduce testing without individual consent.[15] These regulations included technical advice about how to manage AIDS patients medically and how to treat them in a humane manner. A circular issued by the government in July 1985, addressed to all hospitals, stipulated that patients with HIV infection or AIDS could not be denied inpatient or outpatient care.[16] These institutions were to be responsible for the appropriate treatment of patients by medical personnel; they were to establish procedures for protecting their personnel from risks of infection. No specialized AIDS units were to be created. Guidelines were issued on how physicians should communicate with HIV-infected patients, and a year later similar instructions were issued to all French physicians. The guidelines underscored the necessity of recommending the use of condoms by the infected, and proposed psychologically appropriate ways of communicating this information.

But two crucial issues went unresolved at this time: whether the law prohibiting the advertisement of condoms should be abolished; and whether the sale of syringes to drug users should be legalized. In early 1986, just prior to the general election, the Socialist government was reluctant to press for such changes. It feared that conservatives would use such reforms to tar the already vulnerable governing party with the charge that it was engaged in a leftist program on social and moral issues. During this period of policy indecision, AIDES (the French word for support and help, as well as a play on the English term AIDS), an organization founded at the end of 1984, began to agitate for new policies on condoms and syringes. AIDES activists distributed condoms at gay meeting places, and with the encouragment of AIDS-conscious officials in the Ministry of Health, who could not themselves give public voice to the need for reform, they organized conferences urging the sale of syringes.

AIDES took the initiative during this period of government instability—the Socialists were defeated in March 1986, ushering in the era of political "cohabitation"—to press for broad policies to protect the medical and social interests of the HIV-infected. Together with the national association for continuing medical education, it published a book for doctors that included information on the epidemiological, clinical, and social dimensions of AIDS. In 1987, together with the the humanitarian medical association Médicins du Monde, it issued a "Bill of Rights of AIDS Victims and Seropositive Persons." With the government too paralyzed to act, AIDES sharply criticized the state for its inactivity and incapacity in the face of an epidemic threat.

The Institutionalization of AIDS Policy

Just prior to the 1986 general election, a working group attached to the Ministry of Health, including those inside and outside government who had been working on AIDS since it first struck France, prepared an internal document, the Rapin Report, on the challenge of the epidemic. This report not only described the scientific and social problems posed by AIDS, but also detailed the need for reforms and new resources. It was passed on to the policymakers in the new conservative government and provided the blueprint for the measures undertaken by Michelle Barzach, the minister of health appointed to the cabinet of Prime Minister Jacques Chirac.

Barzach moved more forcefully than might have been expected. Relying upon the recommendations of the first expert group on AIDS, the central elements of the French legislative and regulatory position on AIDS were enacted in 1987. Quickly, AIDS was added to the list of diseases reportable without the identification of the patient[17] and to the list of chronic disease fully reimbursable by the national health insurance program.[18] In sharp response to fears of contagion and calls for measures to prevent the spread of AIDS across national boundaries, the government rejected arguments for prohibiting air travel by people with AIDS.[19] In early 1987, Parliament enacted legislation permitting the advertisement of condoms for the prevention of sexually transmitted diseases, but not for the purpose of contraception. The sale of syringes by pharmacies was also legalized, although opposition from pharmacists delayed its formal approval until 1988.[20]

Most important was legislation that made the central government exclusively responsible for setting AIDS policies.[21] Each administrative district was provided with a center for free, anonymous blood testing. AIDS was thus de-coupled from the legal regime governing sexually transmitted diseases. In so doing, the government sought to protect AIDS policy from the influence of local politicians—a special concern since the extreme right-wing National Front had gained considerable influence in southern France.

This was the authority relied on by Barzach when she prohibited officials in southern France from conducting a research project that would have required registering patients by name in order to gather extensive epidemiological data on those treated for AIDS and HIV-related symptoms. This was not a health or scientific project, she declared, but instead a matter that pitted the local authorities against the central government.[22] This centralized power was not always so wisely used, however. Earlier, Barzach had bowed to conservative pressure when she sided with the Catholic bishops and parents in Britanny who protested sex education in the schools. Despite the fact that the previous Socialist government had endorsed such efforts, she removed the officials who initiated the venture.

The second International Conference on AIDS, held in Paris in 1986, provided Barzach an unparalleled forum for announcing her program. AIDS was made a "national cause." New policies covered all major issues raised by the epidemic: international collaboration, directly related to the French–American scientific controversy; the promotion of funding of research on treatment and vaccines, which was to be supervised by a special research council; the nomination of Professor Alain Pompidou as "Monsieur AIDS," the AIDS coordinator attached to her cabinet; the creation of Comité de Reflexion, a group to advise the health ministry on social and ethical questions related to AIDS; the promotion of medical care and testing facilities; and the undertaking of large-scale public information campaigns. For the first time a major infusion of funds was promised: $18,300,000 for research for two years; a $6,600,000 supplementary budget allowance for Paris hospitals; a subsidy of $80,000 for the private organization AIDES. Twenty-three special AIDS centers were established during 1987, and eighty-eight more for the provision of information, treatment, and prevention services.

The first AIDS media campaign, in the spring of 1987, was cautious and indirect. Its message was conveyed by the picture of a rising statistical curve being broken by an elegant young woman who declared, "AIDS will not pass through me." The public was invited to call a special number for further information.

Regulations establishing at least one free anonymous HIV testing center in each district were published. Nearly 120 such centers were operating by the end of 1988 paid for by the state (30 percent) and the national health insurance program (70 percent).[23] In January 1988, the Ministry of Education was charged with the responsibility of running AIDS education campaigns in the schools, as part of general education on sex and the prevention of sexually transmitted diseases.

In this period, regulations formalizing the prohibition of involuntary testing by hospital and drug treatment programs were issued,[24] and the confidentiality of test results was emphasized in a decree prohibiting the notification of families providing homes for recovering addicts of their serological status.[25] Technical norms for the quality of condoms were established after a campaign by consumer associations, which led to the withdrawal from the French market of five brands deemed unsafe.[26]

This remarkable series of reforms provoked debate as well as opposition by both the National Front and a number of professional groups.

The National Front denounced the "conspiracy of silence," accusing the government of hiding the truth of the extent of HIV infection in France. According to Dr. François Bachelot, the party's self-declared medical expert, AIDS could be transmitted by casual contact. The Front's leaders called for banning those infected with HIV from entering France, compulsory testing of entire segments of the population, and isolation of AIDS patients and HIV carriers in closed institutions they called "sidatoriums." With rather anti-Semitic intentions the party invented the term sidaïque—rhyming with judaïque (Jewish)—to refer to those infected with HIV. The High Commission on the French Language declared that the newly coined term did not comply with the rules of French grammar, and was "un-French." Only the term "sidéen" can now be used.

The Front's assault on French AIDS policy was part of its broader campaign against the "problems of society": it denounced the national moral and demographic decline, immigration of "undesirables," growing insecurity, and criminality. Its attempt to redefine the AIDS epidemic in political, rather than scientific, terms caused it to split with other conservative parties. In May 1987, the government publicly condemned the National Front's position on immigration and AIDS.

But the National Front was not alone in opposing the government's refusal to embrace contain-and-control measures. Demands for systematic testing of patients arose also from professional groups, in 1986 and early 1987, initially supported by trade unions. Such demands were rooted in fear of accidental infection. A year later, well-known hematologists and oncologists joined the call for systematic testing of specific groups: pilots, railroad engineers, bus drivers, those planning to marry, and pregnant women. For the oncologists, it seemed appropriate that the nation's cancer institutes serve as the sites for such screening. Without doubt, the rapidly expanding field of AIDS had attracted the attention of the medical elite, who saw the epidemic as an opportunity to extend their influence.

To each of these calls for policies of containment, officials responded with the strategy of inclusion, encouraging voluntary testing and public education to induce individuals to assume personal responsibility for preventing the spread of disease. They responded to the calls for extraordinary measures by asserting that routine approaches were adequate to the challenge. Thus, although Health Minister Barzach initially supported mandatory premarital and pregnancy testings, she ultimately reversed herself, calling upon physicians to "systematically propose voluntary HIV tests." The government responded to the fears of hospital workers by asserting that normal infection control measures provided adequate protection. In case of accidental needle sticks, those exposed were to be offered an HIV test immediately following the exposure and a subsequent test three months later. Workers who felt unable to deal with AIDS patients were offered the option of transferring. The government responded to the concerns of employers by providing an example of nondiscrimination. It rejected the option of screening applicants for employment and sought to protect those with AIDS who were employed, following established procedures for workers with medical handicaps. Trade unions and employer associations were invited to establish working groups with public authorities, in order to resolve problems in the private sector. The laws that protected the employment rights of those with handicapping conditions governed such efforts. The dismissal of such individuals could only occur when an employer could prove that repeated absences disrupted the functioning of the enterprise. And when a lawful dismissal did occur, social security benefits became available.

This period of national debate gave shape to the societal consensus on the appropriate response to AIDS. For the Catholic Church, however, the emphasis on condom use, so central to that consensus, was problematic. The bishops ultimately rejected efforts to portray AIDS as a divine punishment and expressed their solidarity with the sick, but used the occasion to reassert the claims of sexual morality. In assuming this posture, the bishops distanced themselves from Catholic fundamentalists who had maintained links with the National Front. In 1988, the French Protestant Church, which had remained silent during the first years of the epidemic, approved the public advertisement of condoms.

Regrettably, Barzach had neither the time nor the resources fully to implement her program. Her efforts were also hampered by the public health system's administrative apparatus, which remained poorly staffed and subject to intermittent power struggles.

The 1988 elections, which returned the Socialists to power, were accompanied by a period of extraordinary turmoil caused by the appointment and speedy dismissal of Leon Schwarzenberg as health minister. Nevertheless, his replacement, Claude Évin, moved quickly to further the effort against AIDS, calling upon Professor Claude Got to prepare a report on the epidemic. Got was known for his expertise on both public health and public administration. His report, which was completed by October and published immediately thereafter, was the first official and public document on the epidemic.[27]

The Got Report reaffirmed the principles of French AIDS policy—its stress on public education, its rejection of compulsory testing, its reliance on well-established norms, its rejection of the creation of special AIDS policies and rules. It was sharply critical of the failure of the administration to give meaning and bite to these principles. The health department had lost nearly 10 percent of its staff since 1980—precisely at the moment when AIDS was making demands for greater administrative capacity. At a minimum, the report estimated that twenty staff positions were necessary for AIDS, a quadrupling of the effort.

The Got Report was equally severe in its criticism of the government's failure to recognize the potential importance of funding clinical and pharmaceutical research. A trebling of the allocation for research— from $8,300,000 to at least $25,000,000 a year—was called for. Even more important was the proposal to launch an independent national research agency, which would not only distribute special funds but also coordinate and evaluate all public AIDS-related research in France. In an effort to infuse the research program with flexibility—a particularly difficult challenge given the structure of French research—the report called for funding doctoral and postdoctoral grants and engaging researchers on time-limited contracts.

The French campaign of public information and education, a pillar of AIDS policy, was also subjected to withering criticism. The use of condoms was a priority for AIDS prevention, Got argued, and this required a radical transformation of French attitudes and mores. Previous campaigns were not up to the job: their serious style was no more appropriate than the technical approach adopted by some other countries. Publicity about condoms had to be made vivid, even humorous. It had to be sensitive to the life-styles of the groups to which it was targeted, especially young people. It had to pay attention to the realms of love and sexual relationships into which condom use would be integrated.

The demands imposed by the AIDS epidemic also required a fundamental change in educating youth. Reflecting both the preeminence of French rationalism and a commitment to the legitimacy of central power, the report asserted that it was unacceptable for a modern state to yield to local politicians who mobilized parents to oppose effective education, thus sacrificing the health of schoolchildren on the altar of ideology.

The prevention of AIDS and the care of those already infected and sick required a major infusion of funds, the report noted. Resources for information and other preventive efforts would need, at a minimum, to be four times the $5 million provided in 1988. Supplementary budgets were essential for institutions that provided care.

Finally, Got insisted that the broad social and ethical challenges of AIDS required a revitalized, expanded advisory system. The role of the Comité de Reflexion attached to the office of the minister of health had to be enhanced by the creation of a new ethical committee on AIDS, comprised of individuals drawn from a broad range of disciplines and named by the prime minister. Such a committee would provide crucial advice to the government that should "not be left alone with the AIDS situation."[28]

The Got Report's general strategy was to argue for policies compatible with prevailing approaches to similar problems and, if this were not possible, for new policies that could be extended to cover other related matters. There was to be no AIDS exceptionalism in France. This posture is reflected in the report's analysis of a number of issues.

The report expressed reservations about the demand for a special indemnity for hemophiliacs infected through the clotting factor, asserting that since indemnity had never been paid to those who became ill because of pathogens transmitted through blood transfusion, the question had to be examined in the broader context of iatrogenic illness. On the matter of whether insurance companies should be permitted to test for HIV infection, the report noted that well-established norms of underwriting required medical examination for the determination of risk—although it suggested that screening be restricted to large policies. To face the challenge of all those unable to obtain insurance because of increased health risks, the report proposed that a publicly subsidized insurance scheme could be created.

The analysis of AIDS in the prisons was particularly critical. Got observed that the health care provided to inmates was inadequate, sexual activity among prisoners was winked at, and condoms were provided by prison doctors under the cover of medical confidentiality. The entire system was rife with "official hypocrisy." Only a willingness to improve general prison health care and to acknowledge the sexual needs of prisoners through regular conjugal visits could improve the situation.

The report also addressed the complex legal and policy questions of how to respond to cases involving the knowing transmission of HIV infection from an individual to an unsuspecting partner from the anti-exceptionalist perspective. Existing juridical categories—such as poisoning, physical injury, or attempted murder—were deemed to be inappropriate, since by definition they assumed an intent to inflict harm and required proof of such intent for successful prosecution. Instead of efforts to force AIDS cases into these categories, the report proposed a new juridical category centered on the concept of "risky behavior regardless of the health consequences to others." Such an offense would not require proof of "intent to harm." Instead, it would require only a showing of an awareness of the risks entailed, would cover a range of behaviors, including reckless driving and the contamination of food with harmful products as well as the careless transmission of infectious disease.

Since so much of the critique contained in the Got Report centered on the failure of the state apparatus to provide effective coordination of the various governmental agencies that had to cope with AIDS, it is not surprising that the major administrative innovation proposed entailed the creation of a "committee on governmental action in AIDS," which would coordinate the work of all the relevant ministries. While linked to the Ministries of Health, the committee would be located, strategically, in the office of the prime minister. The committee, proposed as an alternative to the visible figure of "Monsieur AIDS," would possess broad ministerial authority and also oversee international AIDS issues; it would serve as a single source of credible information on the epidemic, thus minimizing the manipulation of public opinion through distorted characterizations of AIDS and its risks.

Many of the recommendations of the Got Report were implemented with astonishing speed. Funds for prevention were quadrupled, rising from $5 million in 1988 to $20 million in 1989. In November 1988, Minister of Health Claude Évin announced his National Plan Against AIDS, asserting that AIDS was no longer a disease of particular groups "but concerned everyone."

The first condom promotion campaign aimed at normalizing their use began three weeks later. The message: Condoms ("préservatives" in French) "protect [literally, preserve] you from everything, even from appearing ridiculous." A second campaign repeated the message, this time asserting that condoms protect you from everything "except from love." The third campaign conducted stressed the universal risk of HIV infection: "Everyone can meet the virus."

Administrative changes also occurred soon after the release of the Got Report. Parliament established its first working group on AIDS in December 1988. Two months later, a National Agency for Research on AIDS was launched and placed under the joint aegis of the National Institute for Medical Research and the Ministry of Research, rather than being attached to the office of the prime minister, as Got had proposed. That same month, an ethical advisory panel, the National Council on AIDS, was launched; its chair, an anthropologist, was appointed by President François Mitterand. The council endorsed a national survey of sexual behavior, despite the opposition of AIDES; on the other hand, the panel barred insurance company inquiries about private behavior. More recently, it has begun to consider the ethics of medical responsiblity in providing medical information to the public.

Finally, a National Agency for AIDS Prevention was created in January 1989, charged with the responsibility of developing mass education campaigns and other prevention efforts, in collaboration both with the newly created AIDS Division of the Department of General Health and with AIDES. In an unusual step, the agency was given the status of a private association but was linked to the Ministry of Health. This granted it some formal autonomy and permitted the government to appear distanced from issues involving AIDS.

Unlike the new research agency, which moved quickly to assume its responsibilities, it took the prevention agency a full year to get off the ground. Its first director, Dominique Coudreau, who had headed the national insurance fund for ten years, resigned after a year, but only after he had developed a two-year plan. Coudreau was replaced by Dominique Charvet, a former official from the Ministry of Justice who had worked on issues affecting minority groups. The career trajectories of the two directors underscore an important point about the French administrative elite: it is a shared culture that permits easy transition among posts with responsibility for a wide variety of substantive matters. That shared culture provides the foundation for elite consensus on important social issues, including AIDS policy.

Two recent measures concerning the rights of those with HIV infection reflect the continuing influence of the early commitment to social solidarity and the recommendations of the Got Report regarding the importance of embedding the resolution of issues involving AIDS in broader policy perspectives. Article 187 of the penal law, which prohibits discrimination on the basis of nationality, race, sex, and religion, has been extended to include medical handicaps. It is now illegal to exclude individuals from employment; public places; and public and private services such as transportation, housing, shops, and restaurants on the basis of health status alone. Associations representing patients or handicapped persons have been authorized to initiate lawsuits on behalf of those who believe they have been victimized by discrimination.

Early in 1991, the government proposed a new policy concerning insurance. Now, questions about the private lives of those seeking insurance are prohibited; requests for HIV tests are permitted only if they are part of a general medical examination and only for policies in excess of $165,000; those who are infected are to be insured along with people with cancer and other chronic diseases as "increased health risks," for whom a higher premium may be charged.

AIDES, the Civil Partner of the State

Although AIDS policy-making and implementation have been largely an affair of the administrative and political elite, it would be impossible to portray the scope of the response to the epidemic in France without underscoring the role of AIDES, the largest and most active private association concerned with the epidemic in France. AIDES attempts to represent the interests of all HIV-infected persons, although most of its members, staff, and leadership are gay. Despite its all-inclusive mission, the fact that AIDES is dominated by gays has hindered collaboration with hemophiliacs; it has been difficult for AIDES to engage drug users because of their social isolation.

The association works closely with public authorities and parapublic agencies, such as the National Agency for AIDS Prevention. Its remarkable success can be traced to the philosophy of its founder and first president, Daniel Defert, a sociologist who was the intimate companion of the late philosopher Michel Foucault. Defert, shocked by the circumstances of Foucault's death, was strongly motivated to make AIDS his cause:

> I was confronted with the death of Michel Foucault and the way doctors dealt with it. They simply were not on the level! It was totally unacceptable. . . . We did not know much about AIDS and its symptoms [at the time], but I had doubts; I had to inform myself by reading in medical libraries. When I questioned the doctors, they told me: "If he had AIDS, we would have examined you as well." It was only on the death certificate that I discovered that my friend had died of AIDS.[29]

As a disciple of Foucault, Defert viewed medical practice—in particular the silence of physicians—as characteristic of the network of invisible "mirco-powers," the examination of which had constituted the focus of Foucault's work. From this perspective, the domestication of the body, and the inhibition of sexuality and speech, were the essential means to oppress the individual.

During the 1970s, Defert and Foucault had initiated social movements or "information groups" in such institutions as prisons and psychiatric hospitals. Groups of this type were also created in the battle for abortion rights. Unique to their stratgey was the attempt to bring together specialists and lay persons to analyze and reconsider the foundation of standard practice, initiating reforms under the pressure of public debate and internal institutional rebellions.

These experiences informed Defert's understanding of AIDS. His approach centered on the patient. All ill persons facing a lonely death had to be supported humanely; the impersonality of hospital services had to change. In order to preserve the rights of patients, it was crucial to engage lay people in the effort to break the isolation, the silence, and the hegemony of the professionals.

Defert brought together lawyers and ethicists to support his enterprise; he set up a scientific council to make it easier for AIDES to influence hospital practices. From his earlier experiences as a Maoist militant, Defert retained two lessons: the need to inject special issues into more general movements, and the importance in political work of resolving everyday problems.

That is why AIDES has sought out alliances with all citizens' groups concerned about AIDS. Working in schools, in professional organizations, and in gay settings, it has made the dilemmas of AIDS socially visible, experimenting with new solutions to those problems and promoting successful experiments through existing institutional networks.

AIDES also delivers specific services. It provides public information through pamphlet material and a hot line, it offers psychological and social support from volunteers at home and in the hospital, it makes available legal advice, and it organizes discussion groups. AIDES has promoted home care—the poor stepchild of the French health care system—to maintain the social connections of those with AIDS.

AIDES presently has local chapters in every large town, although it has come to some cities late in the epidemic. Only recently did it establish itself in Lyon, a major medical center, where medically dominated AIDS-related associations had previously been created by physicians in leading hospitals.[30] All local AIDES groups are now affiliated through a national federation.

The success of AIDES is all the more striking because there has been virtually no organized gay movement or community in France. After the election of socialist President François Mitterand in 1981, the old law prohibiting homosexuality was abolished. Some gay organizations emerged to promote this cause, but the gay community was linked primarily through the gay press and in gay meeting places. None of these nascent community structures mobilized to confront AIDS during the first years of the epidemic. Indeed, the gay community was divided over the risk posed by AIDS. Was it a new threat to liberal tenets and sexual emancipation or, instead, a public health problem that first struck gay men? Gay physicians made no collective commitment to the challenges that were plainly emerging. As late as 1985, Defert had to introduce the topic of AIDS as the subject of a working group at the gay community's annual summer university, since the subject had not been included in the initial program.

It was in this context that AIDES confronted the profound questions posed by the epidemic. The development of an HIV-antibody test and advances in therapeutics made possible a break with the fatalism characteristic of the epidemic's first years. Not only did the initial opposition to the HIV test begin to lose its rationale, it also became clear that the needs of those who were seropositive—a group much bigger than those with acute AIDS—had to be met. Large-scale prevention and service programs required government intervention and funding as well as institutional support. Activists in AIDES were thus forced to redefine the organization's attitude towards the public authorities. They opted for close links with the state, while holding firm to their philosophical opposition to government intrusion into matters of sexuality and rejecting the posture of a supplicant seeking only financial assistance. "AIDES is not an organization promoting claims on the State," said Defert. "It relates to the public authorities on the basis of equal partnership." But the role of equal partner is itself problematic. Will AIDES be able to collaborate with the authorities while mobilizing those touched by the epidemic and representing their special interests? AIDES leaders have begun to acknowledge the possible need to define two separate components in their organization: one, committed to the provision of services by professionals and financed through contracts with the public authorities; and a second, devoted to political mobilization, which would remain in the hands of volunteers. Defert left office in 1991. His successors will have to resolve this issue.

A Policy of Solidarity and Its Price

Despite the political changes faced by France during the 1980s, governments on the right and left have pursued a common strategy on AIDS, one centered on the principle of social solidarity. This persistence might surprise those who are more aware of the passionate ideological debates that characterize French political life than of the traditions of liberty and social solidarity that inform public policy. Since 1985, rapid developments in scientific understanding, as well as achievements made possible by the capacity to identify infection through serological testing, have provided the foundations for a broad consensus on AIDS policy. Contain-and-control strategies such as systematic screening, the registration of virus carriers, segregation, and discrimination all have been rejected. Instead, the importance of public education and of providing care to, and solidarity with, the epidemic's victims have been embraced.

Opposition to this consensus came only from marginal groups, political extremists, and professionals with narrow interests. Over the past three decades, French social policy has continually extended the realm of individual choice and responsibility, in fields ranging from medical care to abortion and divorce. The good of society and the protection of individual rights have increasingly been seen as mutually reinforcing. The AIDS policies adopted by France must be viewed in this light. The attempt by the National Front to define the challenge of AIDS as one that pits the legitimate claims of society for security against the interests of infected persons has been accepted neither by the political elite nor by the broader society. If modern democracy can be viewed as an attempt to defend both individual and public interests, then the failed efforts of the National Front must be viewed as part of its antidemocratic project.

But broad consensus on the principles that ought to undergird policy is not enough. New policy tools had to be developed that would prove effective in the unexpected and quite special case of AIDS. This has meant delays in policy formulation and implementation, as government sought to adapt existing policy principles to new circumstances. The normalizing process reflected in AIDS policy-making, as well as the newly invented institutions that gave life to those policies, nicely illustrate the welfare state's capacity to deal with unexpected social dangers and new social problems.

The policies pursued by the French government have produced mixed results. Public information campaigns were more effective in preventing fear and panic than in promoting safer sex habits in the general population.[31] Condom use remains low in France, and in the period from 1984 to 1989, the sale of condoms increased only 56 percent.[32] The voluntary, free, and anonymous testing facilities have eased anxious people's fears, thus undercutting those seeking to manipulate these fears for political ends.[33]

France has provided access to medical care for everyone with AIDS. According to AIDES, from whom the most critical evaluation of the prevailing situation might be expected: "The principle of social integration and solidarity was prefectly adhered to by the public authorities. . . . There is no problem with [access to] medical care in France." This characterization more accurately describes the situation that confronts those with AIDS than those who are seropositive but have not developed full-blown AIDS. Little difference appears to exist in the extent to which gay men and intravenous drug users receive acute medical treatment. But social inequalities persist in the care of those who are not acutely ill.[34] Although there have been no reports of large-scale refusals to treat people with HIV, there have been some instances, notably involving dentists. The courts have had to intervene in order to remind these clinicians of their professional responsibilities.

The epidemic has promoted changes in the health care system that had earlier been unachievable. The burden of having to treat growing numbers of AIDS patients has led to the rapid expansion of ambulatory care. The day hospital has become the central feature in the provision of care, and "hospitalization at home" is an important element in the continuum of AIDS care.

There are also indications that, in the case of AIDS, the independence of French physicians has been effectively challenged. Thus, only hospital based physicians can write an initial prescription for AZT; the Ministry of Health now wants to limit the number of HIV tests ordered by general practitioners, preferring instead that such tests be performed at anonymous test sites, where the rate of positive findings is higher.

The achievements rooted in the commitment to social solidarity, as well as the limits of such a commitment, can also be seen in the strategy of prevention. How was the public to be warned about the risks of infection without stigmatizing those groups known to be at risk? The solution adopted in France was to dissociate AIDS from homosexuality: against all epidemiological evidence, AIDS was presented as a threat to everyone.[35] This political choice was informed not only by the principle of solidarity but also by the traditions of limiting state intervention in private matters and rejecting official recognition of special group identities. These historic factors—rather than any particular sense of decency or discretion—may best explain why French public education campaigns have avoided moralistic references to marriage, faithfulness, or the norm of heterosexuality.

Finally, French AIDS policy has borne the imprint of the emphasis placed on the consensus of the community of experts. Where agreement has existed, it has been possible to act; where agreement has not been obtainable, the strategy has been to restrict disagreements to internal debates among the elites. Hemophiliacs, prisoners, and intravenous drug users have paid a heavy price for this conservatism. While the infection of those dependent upon clotting factor constituted a starting point for public policy on AIDS in Britain, French hemophiliacs were compelled to pursue legal avenues in seeking redress against the state.[36] AIDS policy in prisons and institutions caring for intravenous drug users has remained largely limited to prohibiting involuntary screening.

The strengths and failures of French policy on AIDS reflect French policy-making more generally. In a sense, AIDS was a unique challenge, a cause pushed by outsiders, which prodded the system to adopt new policies. But the pattern of change has followed one of the characteristic models in innovation in the French health sector, as scientific and professional experts ultimately developed links with the public administration. Those policies that have emerged do not represent a rupture with the core values of solidarity and liberty, but instead reflect them. The question that remains unanswered is whether these approaches have best served the goal of meeting the challenge of interrupting the spread of HIV infection, especially among those at risk because of intravenous drug use.

Acknowledgment

This chapter results from ongoing research on AIDS policies in four European countries, financed by the ANRS (Agence Nationale de Recherches sur le SIDA, Paris).

Notes

1. J. Y. Delanoë, "Bilan de la politique de santé 1981–1986," *Revue Française des Affaires Sociales* 1 (1987) 65–90.

2. M. Steffen, "Entre le social et le médical, quelles alternatives?" *Prévenir* 14 (1987) 11–21.

3. B. Jobert and M. Steffen, "Décisions et non-décisions en matière de politique de santé," Congress of the Société Française de Santé Publique, Lyon, France (May 16–17, 1988).

4. B. Jobert, "Mode de médiation sociale et politiques publiques: le case des politiques sociales," *L'Année Sociologique* 40 (1990), 155–178.

5. J. J. Salomon, "Le gaulois, le cowboy et le samouraï; la politique française de la technologie," *Economica* (Paris, 1986); J. Zysman, *L'industrie française entre l'État et le marché* (Paris: Edition Bonnel, 1982) (first English edition: *Political Strategies for Industrial Order: State, Market and Industry in France*, Berkeley and Los Angeles, Calif.: University of California Press, 1977).

6. SOFRES inquiry, Figaro-RTL, April 1990.

7. "Incidence et prévalence de l'infection par le VIH en France," Action Coordonnée no. 6, in *ANSR-Information, Bulletin de l'Agence Nationale de Recherches sur le SIDA* 4 (December 1990), 11–17.

8. M. Pollak, *Les homosexuels et la SIDA; sociologie d'une épidémie* (Paris: Éditions A. M. Métailié, 1988).

9. J. P. Brunet, A. Laporte, A. Messiah, M. Pollak, "From Paris middle classes to small towns and blue collar workers; socio-demographic trends of the AIDS epidemic among French homosexual men," Communication presented at the Fourth International Conference on AIDS, Stockholm (1988).

10. *Libération* (January 6, 1982); *Le Quotidien de Paris* (January 6, 1982); *Le Monde* (January 27, 1982). For a detailed anlaysis of the French press reports on AIDS, see C. Herzlich, J. Pierret, "Une maladie dans l'espace public; le SIDA dans six quotidiens français," *Annales ESC* 5, 1109–1134.

11. Personal interview.

12. *Le Monde* (April 25, 1985).

13. *Arrêté* (July 23, 1985).

14. *Circulaire* (October 20, 1985).

15. *Circulaire* (July 18 and 26, 1985) for institutions dealing with drug abuse; (October 2, 1985) for prisons.

16. *Circulaire* (July 26, 1985).

17. *Dicret* (June 10, 1986).

18. *Dicret* (December 31, 1986).

19. *Circulaire* (June 3, 1986).

20. *Dicret* (August 24, 1988).

21. Law of July 30, 1987.

22. M. Pollak, "AIDS policy in France: Biomedical Leadership and Preventive Impotence," in *Action on AIDS; National Policies in Comparative Perspective*, ed. B. A. Misztal and D. Moss (Westport, Conn.: Greenwood Press, 1990).

23. *Dicret* (January 18, 1988); *Circulaire* (January 20, 1988).

24. *Circulaire* (October 23, 1987).

25. *Circulaire* (December 4, 1987).

26. *Arrêté* (November 23, 1987); *Circulaire* (January 25, 1988).

27. C. Got, *Rapport sur le SIDA* (Paris: Flammarion, 1989).

28. Ibid., 125.

29. Personal interview.

30. P. Duty, D. Welze-Lang, and P. Pelège, "Dispositif de lutte contre le SIDA à Lyon," Communication at the conference, "SIDA et Homosexualités," Groupe de sociologie Politique et Morale, MSH, Paris, April 13, 1991.

31. J. P. Moatti and C. Serrand, "Les sciences sociales face au SIDA: entre silence et trop parler," *Cahiers de Sociologie et de Démographie médicales* 3 (1989), 231–261.

32. *Le Monde* (May 30, 1990).

33. N. Licht, "Événements, entourage et motifs de dépistage," *Écologie Humaine* 1 (1990), 61–67.

34. Y. A. Flori, Y. Souteyrand, and A. Triomphe, "Les filières de soins des patients VIH; les interrelations médecine de ville et de médecine hospitalière," Communication at the First French Seminar on Health Economy (Dijon: 1990).

35. A. Jobert, "SIDA: prévenir l'exclusion par la communication; construction et gestion du consensus sur la prévention," Thesis for the DEA Diploma "Politiques sociales et société," University of Paris I (1990).

36. R. Klein and P. Day, "Interpreting the Unexpected: The Case of AIDS Policy Making in Britain," *Journal of Public Policies* 9, 3 (1989) 337–353.

Chapter 8   # The Netherlands: AIDS in a Consensual Society

Jan K. van Wijngaarden

In 1987, at the fortieth anniversary celebration of the founding of the Dutch Society for the Integration of Homosexuality (NVIH/COC), the Dutch minister of welfare, health, and cultural affairs, a Christian Democrat, gave the major address on behalf of the government, and in the name of Queen Beatrix presented one of the organization's founders with a royal honor. Three years later, the government agreed to support legislation that would ban discrimination against gay men and women, capping years of discussion over how to balance the constitutional rights to religious freedom and equal treatment. When formally adopted by Parliament, the act will represent the achievement of formal equality long sought by the Dutch movement for gay emancipation.

In Amsterdam there exist almost two hundred coffee shops and similar venues where marijuana and hashish are sold freely, the quality and price of the drug being determined by the market. This policy of toleration represents an expression of the Dutch policy toward drugs, which since 1985 has sought to normalize the problem of drug use through a commitment to harm reduction rather than to the chimera of abstinence.

The policies toward sexual minorities and drug users are rooted in the social history of the Netherlands, a history characterized by the coexistence of minority religious cultures. The importance of finding a political accommodation to such complexity imposed upon the Netherlands the necessity of developing cultural and political norms that stressed tolerance and accommodation. Those values and their institutional expressions would have a profound impact on how the challenge posed by AIDS would be confronted.

At Risk

The first Dutch patient with AIDS was diagnosed in April 1982 in Amsterdam.[1] By the end of 1990, 1,531 people had been diagnosed. Reporting of AIDS cases is voluntary and anonymous. Thus physicians report only the presenting disease, the date of diagnosis, the age, sex, and risk group. In order to prevent double counting, the initials and date of birth of the patient are also reported. Detailed small-scale investigations have revealed no significant underreporting (see Table 8.1).[2]

The vast majority (93 percent) of AIDS cases are among men—80 percent of cases among homosexual men. Those between forty and forty-nine years of age constitute 29 percent of the reported cases, followed by those thirty-five to thirty-nine years of age. About 8 percent are intravenous drug users. The number of persons who have contracted AIDS as a result of heterosexual contact has more than doubled since 1988. Fifteen children with AIDS have been diagnosed. Most persons with AIDS come from Holland's three largest cities—Amsterdam, The Hague, and Rotterdam— which together account for 69 percent.

There are no data on the overall prevalence and incidence of HIV infection in the Netherlands. Two ongoing cohort studies and a study among pregnant women provide some indication of prevalence and seroconversion rates.

- A study of gay men begun in 1984 showed an initial prevalence of 33 percent and a seroconversion rate of 8.8 percent.[3] Soon this rate dropped considerably, and in 1987 it was virtually zero, reflecting considerable behavioral change (comparable to that which has been reported by the participants in the major multi-city studies undertaken in the United States).[4] These changes have been confirmed by a considerable decline in the incidence of other sexually transmitted diseases among gay men in the same period. But in 1989 the seroconversion rate again began to rise, reaching 3 percent in 1991.
- A cohort study among intravenous drug users, started in 1985, revealed an initial HIV prevalence of 31 percent among those tested.[5] The current seroconversion rate of 4.3 percent represents a small decline over the last three years. Although 52 percent reported participating in the Dutch needle exchange system, a large proportion still share needles regularly.
- Infection among blood donors has remained constant between 1985 and 1990, at the very low level of 0.003 percent.[6] A study of pregnant women in several Dutch hospitals has revealed an infection rate of 0.1 percent, although these results may reflect the distortion of participation bias.[7]
- Close observation by social nurses who specialize in sexually transmitted diseases reveals no indications of measurable secondary transmission among young people.

The total number of HIV infected persons in the Netherlands is estimated at between nine thousand and twelve thousand persons, mostly gay men from Amsterdam.[8]

Table 8.1. AIDS Cases by Year of Report and Category of Risk Exposure for the Netherlands, 1982–1990

Risk category	1982	1983	1984	1985	1986	1987	1988	1989	1990	Total
Homosexual/bisexual activity	2	17	29	58	117	186	250	300	264	1,223
Homosexual/bisexual activity and IVDU	0	0	0	1	2	6	7	2	1	19
IVDU	0	0	0	1	6	16	32	32	29	116
Blood products	2	2	1	3	3	8	9	12	9	49
Heterosexual activity	0	0	1	1	4	17	14	26	25	88
Mother to child	0	0	0	0	0	1	3	1	2	7
Other/unknown	1	0	0	0	4	5	6	9	4	29
Total cases	5	19	31	64	136	239	321	382	334	1,531

SOURCE: Department for Infectious Diseases of the Office of the Chief Medical Officer.

The Molding of Consensus

As was true elsewhere in Europe, the first few cases of AIDS in the Netherlands were considered isolated events, the consequence of extensive homosexual contacts with Americans.[9] But concern mounted in the latter part of 1982 and early 1983, as Dutch observers monitored international medical and epidemiological literature, and as those who attended meetings on AIDS in Europe and America returned home.

In May 1982, shortly after the first patient with AIDS had died in Amsterdam, a medical symposium on the new disease was held. On that occasion, Dr. James Curran of the U.S. Centers for Disease Control (CDC) declared: "If I were a gay man, I would refrain from any sex." Members of Amsterdam's gay medical group, which had established a private sexually transmitted disease clinic for gay men, began wondering whether statements about the unmitigated pleasures of gay sex could be sustained. For a few years, some members of this group, with the financial support of the Ministry of Welfare, Health, and Cultural Affairs (WVC), had published a booklet about the medical problems that could result from gay sex. The central message was that virtually all sexually transmitted diseases could be cured or prevented. But with the growing stream of articles in the medical and American gay press about parasitical bowel infections, hypersensitivity reactions to amyl nitrate, and the new, as yet unnamed, syndrome, it was decided that additional information had to be provided to the gay community.

Some members of the group started to publish articles about AIDS in the gay press.[10] In "Be on Guard But Don't Panic," two gay health care workers thus wrote:

> In many papers it has been suggested that the [new] syndrome would exclusively strike gay men, giving all the publicity a rather nasty aftertaste. Of course, homosexuality per se can never be the cause of a disease and any [such suggestion] recalls the period of deplorable interference of medical science with gay men. However, certain life-styles do carry with them an increased risk of disease . . . the group [that] runs the greatest risk [engages in] many sexual encounters [has] extensive use of [many different] drugs and [has] a history of many STDs. Clear guidelines cannot be given [and each person should] conclude for himself how far his behavior should be influenced by available information. On the other hand, we are dealing with a serious syndrome. . . .[11]

At the same time, public health officials specializing in infectious diseases and officials from national organizations responsible for the quality of the blood supply soon realized the potentially infectious nature of the new syndrome, the possibility of a long incubation period and the implications for the safety of the blood supply.[12]

Reports from the the CDC in late 1982 documented the possibility of transfusion-associated AIDS. Alert to the debates then occurring in the United States, Dutch blood bank authorities decided in January 1983 to prohibit blood donations from gay men and sought to exlude them from the donor pool. It was clear, however, that such restrictions would create an uproar in Dutch society, in which the homosexual community holds a relatively strong position and in which there exists a public aversion to unwarranted discrimination.

To face this crisis, the director of the Central Laboratories for Blood Transfusion (CLB) asked Dr. Roel Coutinho, head of the Department of Infectious Diseases of the Municipal Health Service of Amsterdam, to mediate.[13] Coutinho was in a good position to do so. He headed the two municipal sexually transmitted disease clinics frequented by gay men and had a reputation for imaginative and aggressive leadership. Alarmed by the rapidly rising incidence of sexually transmitted diseases, he had organized outreach activities for gay men in venues where anonymous sex was commonplace, performing blood tests in back rooms of bars and bathhouses, to check for seromarkers of syphilis and hepatitis B. Coutinho had also studied hepatitis B in a cohort of sexually active gay men and had undertaken the only hepatitis B vaccine trial among gay men outside the United States. As a consequence, he and his staff had established informal contacts with the Amsterdam gay medical group.

As a result of Coutinho's efforts, representatives of gay organizations, public health authorities, the bloood banks, and the Dutch Hemophilia Association met for a period of three months. In April 1983, a compromise was reached. An information campaign would be organized to persuade gay men to refrain voluntarily from donating blood.[14] To those who had participated in the successful process of resolving the controversy over the blood supply, this was to serve as a model for the future, one based on the avoidance of confrontation, one that would stress inclusion and negotiation.

The campaign was organized by a committee of three gay men. It was chaired by the director of the Amsterdam Municipal Health Education Office, who was later to become chairman of the National AIDS Policy Coordinating Team. The second member of the Committee was a paid staff member of the Dutch homosexual organization. The third member of the triumvirate, who represented the gay medical community, was later to become the national AIDS policy coordinator and head of the office of the National Commission on AIDS Control. The budget of the campaign was $50,000, mostly provided by the blood banks and the Ministry of WVC.[15] Before donating blood, every blood donor received a leaflet that included information about AIDS and urged those who belonged to a group at risk to "seriously consider refraining from donating blood."[16]

At the same time an extensive campaign was organized to inform gay men about the risks of blood donation and about how to avoid the new disease. Leaflets were distributed in gay bars all over the country. Information was published in Dutch gay media, including porn magazines, and discussions were also organized in gay bars.[17] Because the gay community had been involved in this process from the start, there was little opposition from those who might otherwise have interpreted the plea for withdrawal from the donor pool as an act of unacceptable discrimination.

Those who came together to evaluate the campaign to protect the blood supply—leaders of the gay community, as well as public health officials—formed the nucleus of what would become the National AIDS Policy Coordinating Team. They recognized the importance of effectively facing the new challenges that might emerge, as well as of the importance of creating a forum for the harmonious resolution of such issues.

The Welfare Ministry provided a small grant for the appointment of a national AIDS policy coordinator to prepare the meetings of the Coordinating Team, monitor developments in the United States, and disseminate information among the gay community.[18] Over the next several years, the staff of the Coordinating Team would grow larger, and in 1986, a separate office was established, which also housed the national AIDS hot line.

The Infectious Diseases Act, which classifies diseases in terms of their potential threat and requires, among other things, the reporting of suspected cases of fatal contagious illnesses, gives the chief medical officer a crucial national role in the control of infectious diseases. This official has great authority and is automatically consulted if a major problem arises. And so it was that Dr. Henk Bijkerk was called on by the blood banking authorities in the first encounters over AIDS. From the beginning, he was a member of the national AIDS Coordinating Team.

Although this group was self-appointed and without any official or legal status, Bijkerk's membership provided de facto authority. Another important contribution to the rather informal structure of policy-making was made by the decision of Bijkerk not to classify AIDS as a notifiable infectious disease, relying instead on a system of voluntary anonymous reporting of cases by individual physicians.[19] By making this decision, he acknowledged the concerns of gay men about the issue of privacy and underscored a position central to Dutch AIDS policy: transmission occurred in the context of consenting relationships.[20] Thus, AIDS was not like those conditions, the mere presence of which posed a public hazard, since individuals could protect themselves. The alarm that took hold among gay men when the initial studies of the prevalence of HIV suggested that one-third were infected created a strong motivation for sustaining a cooperative relationship with health experts and precluded the emergence of the denial that in some countries provoked suspicion about the public health focus on AIDS.

The personal commitment of Bijkerk, and the consensus among the main interest groups that was maintained in the years to follow, enabled the welfare ministry to leave virtually all policy-making to an unofficial group until 1987.[21] Indeed, the Ministry had nothing more than observer status in the Coordinating Team. This arrangement was not unusual for the Netherlands, where reliance on consensus between experts and interest groups may replace independent ministerial action.

Paralleling the unofficial Coordinating Team was the Standing Committee on AIDS, established in 1984 by the National Health Council, an organization that provides scientific advice on medical matters to the government. This committee prepared numerous reports on specific issues related to AIDS.

There was substantial overlap between the membership of the Coordinating Team and the Standing Committee; and in several respects their work was complementary. The Coordinating Team concentrated on information, education and psychosocial matters, the Standing Committee on scientific and clinical matters. The Coordinating Team dealt with practical and organizational matters, the Standing Committee limited itself to reviewing the scientific literature and to formulating recommendations for the government. The Coordinating Team made quick decisions, mostly forced by circumstances; the Standing Committee then advised on the same issue, after deliberating somewhat longer on all aspects of the problem. Thus, for example, when it became clear after officials visited the United States in the summer of 1984, that serological testing for HIV would become feasible within several months, the Coordinating Team decided that an extensive information campaign would be necessary to warn the gay community of the lack of any clinical benefit of testing, and the potentially damaging consequences of a positive test result.[22] A year later, the Standing Committee endorsed this posture on scientific grounds.[23]

Based upon its observation of the course of events in Europe and especially in the United States, the Coordinating Team set itself four broad tasks: to assure that all involved and interested individuals, groups, and organizations were given adequate, uniform, and reliable information; to identify gaps in existing AIDS policy and to make sure that appropriate and timely action was undertaken to fill the gaps, primarily by stimulating existing organizations to take action; to strive to maintain consensus, primarily by creating opportunities for different parties to meet; and to coordinate public information by keeping the number of spokespersons very limited.

On a regional and local level, the establishment of parallel AIDS Coordinating Teams was encouraged, almost always with the municipal or regional health service. By 1990, forty-four of these teams were in existence in Holland, providing an infrastrucure for implementing national policy on a local and regional scale.[24]

The collaboration of the Coordinating Team and the Standing Committee on AIDS of the Health Council was effective in forging and sustaining a broad policy of consensus. Indeed, when the Dutch Parliament considered both the substance and structure of the government's AIDS policy, it received unanimous approval. The extent of the consensus is best demonstrated by the position adopted by the Christian Democratic party, the dominant political force in Dutch politics. The party occupies the center of the political spectrum, and has held at least one-third of the seats in Parliament since the beginning of this century. Its participation is thus crucial to any effort to form a government. Rejecting any suggestion that AIDS should be viewed as the consequence of a failure to abide by norms of behavior sanctioned by Christian dogma, the party instead stressed the imperative of caring for and solidarity with the victims of disease. AIDS, said the party, is a public health problem that demands resources adequate to the challenge. This perspective enabled the party to shape policies that paid for educational activities at a crucial moment in the history of the Dutch epidemic. In so doing, the Christian Democrats also contributed to the depoliticizing of AIDS in the Netherlands.

But despite its successes, the informal structure of policy-making that emerged from the first challenge of seeking to protect the blood supply in 1983 could not sustain the pressures generated by increasing concern about the potential impact of AIDS on Dutch society. After the Second International Conference on AIDS, which met in Paris in the summer of 1986, concern mounted that AIDS could reach the general population. Because of the emerging picture of the AIDS epidemic in sub-Saharan Africa and the Caribbean, all persons with multiple sexual partners had to be considered potentially at risk.[25] AIDS then became a major issue which received much media and political attention, the tenor of which was captured by the important weekly magazine *Haagse Post:* "Russian Roulette: One Hundred Thousand Dutch Infected in 1990. How AIDS is Spreading Within the Hetero-World."[26]

The shifting perception of the scope of the problem contributed to major changes in the organizational structure of AIDS policy-making in the Netherlands. In March 1987, the newly appointed state secretary for health convened a meeting with key persons in the health care system: politicians, chairpersons of the main advisory bodies, leading public health officials, and representatives of the national AIDS Coordinating Team. Although this meeting endorsed the policy based on cooperation, consensus and the rejection of coercive measures, it concluded that a formalized structure of decision-making was necessary because of the epidemic's threat to society at large.[27]

In October 1987, the Coordinating Team was replaced by an official ministerial committee, the National Commission on AIDS Control (NCAB).[28] The commission members consisted of experts rather than organizational representatives; although gay groups were not displaced in the process, they clearly lost influence. A former deputy director-general of the Ministry of WVC was appointed chairperson, introducing experience with government administration in the new structure. But because there was no change in the principles that had guided Dutch AIDS policy for five years, the transition was carried out without much disruption. Continuity was also assured by the appointment, as staff members, of the staff of the Coordinating Team and, as members, many from the Coordinating Team itself. Thus Roel Coutinho, secretary of the Coordinating Team, was made vice-chairperson of the Commission; Hans Moerkerk, chairperson of the Coordinating Team, was made its secretary.

The change from an informal and personalized structure to a formal and bureaucratized one ended a critical phase that was decisive for the formulation of the principles that would shape AIDS policy. It also represented a kind of normalization of the AIDS problem. Nevertheless, the broad outlines of policy that emerged out of the first efforts on the part of public health officials and gay organizations to forge a consensus with broad political and social support would remain a critical legacy.

Policies of Inclusion

The cornerstone of Dutch policy on AIDS education has been the belief that AIDS can be avoided. Prevention is each individual's responsibility.[29] Only if the norms governing behavior in the social milieu of the individual supported such change would individuals respond. From this perspective, close cooperation with the organizations representing target groups was crucial.

The first education campaign, undertaken in the summer of 1983, was aimed at gay men and blood donors. It was dominated by the urgent need to safeguard the blood supply. Activities aimed at gay men gradually expanded, making as much use of gay organizations as possible.[30]

The commercial sector generally cooperated. Bars, bathhouses, and other enterprises with a gay clientele permitted the distribution of leaflets and the prominent display of posters and, when requested, served as settings for meetings to convey information. In Amsterdam, these efforts built on a tradition, dating from the late 1970s, of close contact between the owners of the most important bars and bathhouses and public health nurses of the Sexually Transmitted Disease Department of the Municipal Health Service.[31] This cooperative relationship prevented the confrontational atmosphere that ultimately emerged in cities like San Francisco, where pressure built to close the bathhouses.[32] Since Amsterdam attracts large crowds of gay tourists from all over Europe and the United States, these collaborative relationships were deemed crucial to AIDS prevention efforts.

Much attention was given by the gay members of the Coordinating Team to the way information was to be conveyed. Straightforward presentation of what was scientifically known, rather than speculation, was emphasized. Most striking was the decision to emphasize abstention from anal intercourse.[33] Condom use, the centerpiece of AIDS prevention efforts in other countries, was not promoted. By calling for this behavioral change, and by "allowing" virtually all other forms of sexual contact, it was hoped that there would be only a minimal disruption of the culture of the gay community. The consequence, it was believed, would be the rapid adoption of a change crucial to AIDS prevention.

The constant flow of information toward the gay population was made possible by the publication of a monthly magazine, *AIDS INFO,* which appeared for the first time in 1984. Published by independent editors but paid for by the government, *AIDS INFO* was a cooperative effort between the largest gay magazine in the Benelux countries and the national gay organization. Distributed free of charge every month, *AIDS INFO* is inserted into major gay magazines.

A different educational strategy was used in trying to reach intravenous drug users, the second largest group at risk. The message was straightforward: Do not share needles, make use of the officially sanctioned and funded needle exhange programs. There was initial resistance, on the part of drug counselors and those involved in the methadone maintenance program, to undertaking AIDS education, because they saw it as beyond the scope of their already too demanding jobs. Since drug counselors reached large numbers of intravenous drug users—estimates in Amsterdam suggested that 60 percent of such individuals were in contact with the system—it was crucial to modify such reluctance. Special training programs were organized, and the counselor's resistance was ultimately overcome.

A second focus was the Junkie Unions, another phenomenon unique to the Netherlands. For a number of years, government support has been given to the National Federation of Junkie Unions, an alliance of groups of users and ex-users that sought to protect the rights of those involved with hard drugs. Such funding enabled this federation to undertake the distribution of sterile injection equipment and to sponsor activities that were beyond what the public authorities could do directly, such as the organization of "safe shooting workshops."[34]

Until 1987, educational policy towards the general public was termed "passive-active."[35] This rather cryptic expression was meant to characterize a policy that ensured the availability of information for the general public without active confrontation. Thus, the AIDS hotline staff was prepared to answer questions with a set of standard responses.[36] This policy changed when the potential for the spread of HIV infection through heterosexual contact became a matter of concern in mid-1986. In addition, public pressure had begun to mount for a broad-based campaign of AIDS prevention, like those launched in other Western European countries.

Since the Netherlands was late in coming to such an effort, it was possible for Dutch experts to evaluate AIDS campaigns elsewhere before designing their own. Three types were identified: those that sought to evoke fear (United Kingdom), those that were factual (Switzerland), and those that took on a lighter tone (Norway). The subcommittee on information and education of the Coordinating Team, which prepared the Dutch campaign in cooperation with a major advertising agency, chose the third strategy.

The goal of the campaign was to make heterosexuals realize that they too could be at risk for HIV infection. Given the unpleasant and frightening nature of the epidemic, the campaign had to attract attention without scaring people away or fostering denial, and without blaming gay men or intravenous drug users for the disaster.[37] The resulting effort, launched in 1987, consisted of a short television spot shown during prime time almost daily for several months, urging people to get a free leaflet available in post offices and libraries; the leaflet itself; and a series of four advertisements— "Additional Course on Sex Education"; "Foreplay New Style"; "We Should Talk Seriously, John"; "Spoiling the Game?"—in the daily newspapers.[38]

The television spot designed to warn about the dangers of casual sexual encounters used the old story of the bumblebee and the flowers as a metaphor for sex, depicting the bee flying from flower to flower—and then dropping dead. The bee on the flower remained the trademark of official AIDS educational activities for several years. In contrast to the educational efforts aimed at gay men, which had focused on the risks of anal intercourse, this campaign stressed the risks of unprotected sex with multiple partners. To mark the launching of the campaign and to underscore its seriousness, an unusual decision was made to donate five hours of Dutch television to the issue of AIDS.

In the fall of 1987, a second campaign organized by the Sexually Transmitted Disease Foundation was launched, to enhance the acceptability of condom use. A third campaign, focused on the risk of AIDS in the workplace, had a dual message: AIDS is very hard to get, but in some cases precautions are necessary. Further campaigns have been aimed at different groups in society or have repeated the main message to the general public, in order to emphasize that AIDS has not gone away.

Generally, the reponsibility for communicating about safer sex is deemed too sensitive a matter to be dealt with by the government, and so has been given to nongovernmental sexually transmitted disease organizations. Uniformity in the messages and consistency with public policy goals have been secured by the de facto monopoly of the Coordinating Team, and later of the NCAB, in advising the government on funding such efforts.

Little religious opposition has been provoked by these initiatives. Although the conservative denominations, the Catholic Church and some of the more orthodox Protestant churches, reject condom use as a preventive measure, stressing monogamy and abstention, they recognize publicly that the state has the responsibility to reach out to all its citizens, adapting particular educational messages to group norms.[39] Recognition of the principle of the separation of state and church and the acknowledgment of the differing responsibility of each in the realm of education has created the space necessary for peaceful coexistence in the field of AIDS.

Even in the Netherlands, with its tradition of tolerance and its well-established gay organizational structure, AIDS was viewed by gay men as posing a threat of renewed repression. To preclude this possibility, those involved in creating the Coordinating Team decided in 1984 that they would determine who could be called upon by the media for authoritative statements about AIDS. All requests from the media were to be channeled to the office of the national policy coordinator.[40]

Media policy has been governed by three principles: always provide information; give accurate information; do not deny what is true. For the Coordinating Team this policy served the function of avoiding confusion. For journalists this restrictive posture made it possible to know where to turn for accurate and timely information. Collaboration was also fostered by the fact that in a small country like the Netherlands only a few newspapers have medical editors. Over time they developed personal relationships with members of the Coordinating Team. Those ties reinforced the more abstract norms of candor in shaping their interactions.

The spirit of cooperation has also been sustained by the fact that in the Netherlands there exists virtually no tabloid press. Daily newspapers are all rather serious. An eye for social wrongs and misery among minority groups is accompanied by a general aversion to sensationalism. From the beginning, therefore, AIDS coverage was characterized by sobriety. Journalists generally refrained from recounting the sometimes spectacular sexual histories of some of the first patients. By stressing journalistic responsibility, a norm emerged that imposed upon newspapers the importance of covering AIDS in the "correct" way. In the absence of a distrustful press, or one that sought to provoke alarm as a way of increasing circulation, the spirit of consensus was reinforced.

Unlike public health officials in the United States, those responsible for AIDS policy in the Netherlands have never embraced testing for HIV as a central element in the strategy of fostering behavioral change. Thus those who belong to groups at risk have never been encouraged to undergo testing. Members of the Coordinating Team were aware of reports from the United States about the potentially catastrophic consequences of being told that one had tested positive for the antibody to HIV. Thus, as preparations were made in 1985 to initiate screening in blood banks, a campaign was undertaken to urge gay men to think twice before undergoing testing.

In addition to the concerns about the psychological burdens of testing, the Coordinating Team and the public health authorities believed testing had little role to play in effecting behavioral change. All individuals who were at risk had to be encouraged to change their behaviors: those who were negative, for purposes of self protection, those who were infected, to protect their partners. Thus one's serological status was irrelevant. The Dutch position on testing was also informed by the belief that avoiding infection is the responsibility of both parties in a sexual encounter. Regardless of either one's serostatus, both individuals have the responsibility to avoid sexual acts that could result in HIV transmission. Despite this negative evaulation of the role of testing, the Dutch government established three sites where individuals could be tested anonymously, a move that replicated efforts in the United States to protect blood banks from the risks that might accompany the large-scale use of blood centers by those who wanted to know their serological status.

The special nature of HIV testing, as well as the more general Dutch political and constitutional commitment to the protection of the "integrity of the body," resulted in a policy that placed great emphasis on obtaining the informed consent of any individual before any testing could be undertaken. This was true of testing for clinical or diagnostic purposes as well as in other social settings. It was within the context of this principle that the response to an effort to undertake screening by Philips, a Dutch-based multinational electronics company, one of the largest in the Netherlands, must be understood. Following the example of some firms in the United States, Philips introduced a policy of asking job applicants during their medical examinations whether they had been tested for HIV infection. For those who had tested positive, Philips ordered a new test for purposes of confirmation. Those who proved to be infected were refused employment.[41]

The public outcry that developed after this policy became known illustrates Dutch attitudes toward testing. Editorials in every major newspaper rejected the Philips policy as an instance of unacceptable discrimination and as an intolerable violation of privacy.[42] In the face of public opinion and political pressure, Philips rescinded its policy.[43]

Before AIDS became a critical issue in Holland, Amsterdam had already sought to meet the public health, medical, and social problems associated with intravenous drug use through a well organized program founded on the principle of harm reduction. Although a number of organizations were involved in providing therapeutic services to drug users, the Municipal Health Service played a critical role in its easily accessible system of methadone distribution. Methadone buses traveled the city twice daily, providing the heroin substitute to addicts. Prisons and hospitals were routinely visited to assure that addicts received an appropriate dose of methadone. A network of neighborhood health stations provided low-threshold interventions to drug users. This full range of efforts was intended to establish ongoing contact with those drug users least inclined to modify their behavior. These were the individuals who would also be at greatest risk for HIV infection.

The sharing of injection equipment by drug users has long been recognized as a source of disease transmission. As early as 1982, talks were initiated between those who provided services to drug users and the local authorities in Amsterdam about creating a system of free needle distribution to prevent the spread of hepatitis B, but these talks failed to reach any consensus.[44] At the end of 1984, after deliberations within the municipal health service, it was decided that a needle exchange system should be created—a move dictated by the refusal of a number of pharmacists to sell syringes to drug users at bulk prices. The system proved an instant, although hardly universal, success. In 1986, 100,000 needles were exchanged, and although the estimate by some that over 90 percent of used needles were exchanged is probably an exaggeration, the number of reported needle-stick incidents on the streets of Amsterdam has not risen substantially.[45]

The introduction of the needle exchange system in Amsterdam did not provoke much public discussion, nor did it attract much media or political attention. There was simply no resistance. This is in striking contrast to the response in other European countries and in the United States, and can be explained only by the broad-based acceptance of the philosophy of harm reduction in the Netherlands—a philosophy that made it possible to conceive of needle exchange as reducing, rather than exacerbating, the drug problem.

Opposition to repressive measures is also reflected in the Dutch response to the risk of HIV transmission by prostitutes. Consonant with the commitment to the belief that the transmission of HIV involves two parties, efforts to control prostitutes who might be infected was deemed particularly inappropriate, since it was often their clients who pressed for sex without condoms. Instead, education was viewed as necessary both for prostitutes and their customers.

Information campaigns have been targeted towards prostitutes, organized by the Sexually Transmitted Disease Foundation.[46] Special material has been developed to promote safer sex. Even towels with appropriate messages have been made available. Additional efforts have been made to reach drug-addicted women who rely on prostitution to raise money to pay for their habits. Some are young, work the streets, and have sex with their customers in their cars. To assist these women, who the Dutch believe represent a threat of secondary HIV transmission, special facilities have been set up. In these settings, open through the night, young women can relax, receive food and drink, and exchange used injection equipment.[47] Counselors use the opportunity to encourage prostitutes to use condoms and not to share needles.

The Quality of Care

Virtually the entire Dutch population is insured against the standard as well as extraordinary costs of medical care and, as a consequence, limitations on care for AIDS and HIV-related diseases because of ability to pay are unknown in the Netherlands. The health insurance system is a complex one. For those whose income is below $30,000, there is a compulsory insurance scheme through "sickness funds," which charge income-based premiums. For those who earn more than $30,000, coverage is voluntary and premiums are set by the insurance companies themselves. In case of high medical risk, the cost of protection can be rather expensive. Supplementing this system of protection against standard medical costs is the national Exceptional Medical Expenses Act, which covers the entire population against extraordinary costs. Ambulatory or inpatient mental health treatment and nursing home care are among the services covered by this act.

During the first years of the epidemic, the provision of care to patients with AIDS was centered in Amsterdam, mirroring the concentration of AIDS cases there. Such care was available from a few primary care physicians with large gay caseloads, in clinics that had a long tradition of dealing with sexually transmitted diseases and at the University of Amsterdam's Academic Medical Center (AMC).[48]

The most important institution for somatic care of those with AIDS has remained the AMC. From 1982 on, an increasing number of gay men reported to its clinic for infectious diseases with anxiety or with symptoms related to the new syndrome. Typcially, patients at the clinic were seen first by interns. But because of the sensitive nature of the syndrome—related as it was to gay sex and drugs—and because it was initially a deadly disease of unknown etiology, the physician heading the clinic decided to see this group of patients himself. Increasingly intrigued by AIDS, he soon emerged as the clinical expert on the new syndrome. To the public, he became the "AIDS doctor."

The AMC started a special clinic for immune disorders in 1984, and a year later a separate AIDS ward was opened, modeled after the example of Ward 5A of San Francisco General Hospital.[49] From 1985 on, the AMC attracted specially trained nurses, who gave patients emotional support and organized home care, but who also served as consultants for frightened nurses throughout the country.[50] On the basis of a 1988 recommendation of the National Health Council, ten hospitals throughout the Netherlands have been designated as special centers for the care of patients with AIDS and have been given resources for AIDS clinics and wards.[51]

In 1984, the Schorer Foundation, established to provide psychological support to gay men and women, began to develop a volunteer "buddy" system, based on the experience of the Gay Men's Health Crisis in New York. Notwithstanding a readily accessible and almost free system of home care in the Netherlands, the foundation believed that buddies could be very helpful. Volunteers with special training would understand the special needs of those with AIDS, many of whom were young, lived alone, and were psychologically unprepared to die. The buddy system has expanded and is currently available throughout the Netherlands.[52]

The Schorer Foundation also launched the first self-help group for persons with AIDS in 1985. Soon thereafter it launched groups for asymptomatic but infected individuals, as well as for the worried well. Based on the experience gained from these efforts, the NCAB developed a plan to incorporate a system for psychosocial support of those with HIV infection and AIDS into existing regional organizations for ambulatory mental health care.[53]

In a remarkable reflection of the adequacy of the network of psychosocial support and of the effectiveness of the efforts on the part of municipal housing authorities in Amsterdam to assure that all individuals with AIDS had suitable housing, a hospice especially designed to meet the challenge of AIDS closed because of a lack of demand for its services.

Virtually all funds for AIDS-related activities, outside of direct patient care, are provided by the Welfare and Health Ministry. Private funding of education, psychosocial care, and support and research is virtually unknown, although one foundation has raised private funds to support research and to provide individuals with support for such things as washing machines, which may be crucial to home care. This system of predominantly public funding reflects the Dutch tradition of meeting public challenges with public resources.

From the start of the epidemic through 1990, the government has increased its allocations for AIDS to meet growing demands. The threatening character of the epidemic dictated such a response: the needs, as defined by the consensus arrived at by the Coordinating Team and the Standing Committee of the Health Council, were met almost automatically by the Welfare and Health Ministry. The sharp increases in funding in 1988 and 1990, noted in Table 8.2, reflected concerns about the possible spread of HIV to the general population, and hence a need to expand the scope of education. Only in 1987, when the focus of AIDS policy shifted to the general population, did the staff at the ministry take on a more active role in shaping the allocation of resources.

Consensus about matters involving resources was almost self-sustaining. The groups that came together initially to resolve the challenge of protecting the blood supply recognized the advantages of cooperation. The legitimacy accorded to the Coordinating Team by the government and the chief medical officer reinforced its capacity to dominate the field. It became virtually impossible to challenge the consensus without running the risk of being cut off from governmental funding, which was tantamount to losing the capacity to function.

Conflict in the Face of Consensus

Despite an almost total consensus about the appropriate course of AIDS policy in the Netherlands, there were voices calling for the government to restrict those with AIDS, but they were rare and inconsequential. This consensus was expressed in the decisions of the Coordinating Team and its successor, the NCAB, by the absence of virtually any conflicting media coverage; and by the unanimous support in Parliament for the AIDS policy of the government. It stands in striking contrast to the nasty conflicts that have arisen elsewhere. Framing the consensus has been a broadly shared view of the role of the state and the importance of protecting individual rights.

Two principles have guided Dutch AIDS policy from the beginning, at first implicitly and eventually explicitly: the social benefits of any measures that might place restrictions on individuals had to be demonstrated before they were imposed, and the least restrictive alternative that could achieve the desired social benefit had to be given priority.[54] Such principles have been endorsed by commentators in other countries,[55] and reflect not only a commitment to the rights of privacy but the unhappy experience of seeking to control sexually transmitted diseases with coer-

Table 8.2. Public Resources Devoted to AIDS for Prevention, Psychosocial Services, and Research in the Netherlands, 1984–1990 (in 1990 U.S. dollars)

Year	Amount
1984	39,211
1985	55,251
1986	1,042,730
1987	1,136,061
1988	9,196,897
1989	9,623,334
1990	16,308,932

SOURCE: Ministry of Welfare, Health, and Cultural Affairs.

cive measures.[56] What is unique about the Netherlands is that these broad principles have generated consensus on policy itself.

Yet even the existence of a general consensus cannot eliminate controversies. Strikingly, the conflicts that did occur over Dutch AIDS policy were relatively short-lived and contained.

As was true in the United States, the question of how to respond to the gay bathhouses required deciding whether the public health demands imposed by AIDS justified either restricting the behavior that occurred within them or outright closure. In 1985, Roel Coutinho, who from the outset had been a central figure in AIDS policy discussions, argued for the closing of the gay bathhouses and backrooms in Amsterdam. From previous epidemiological studies on sexually transmitted diseases and the relatively high (more than 30 percent) seropositivity rate in his gay cohort study, Coutinho concluded that a substantial number of sexual contacts in those venues would increase the spread of HIV infection. Furthermore, since Amsterdam is a very popular stop for gay tourists, he feared that gay American travelers, among who he assumed, the level of infection was also high, would increase the level of infection among Dutch men with whom they would have sexual contact. For Coutinho, unconvinced that the gay community would voluntarily undertake the changes in behavior necessitated by the epidemic, it was crucial to send a message about the dire implications of AIDS. The repressive nature of closure, its dramatic departure from the generally liberal stance of Dutch society toward homosexuality and the open tolerance of bordellos in Amsterdam's red light district, was its attraction: Coutinho hoped to create a shock wave through the gay community.

Given the startling character of this option, the board of the Coordinating Team decided to commission two papers—one from Coutinho and the other from Rob Tielman, head of the Interdisciplinary Gay and Lesbian Studies Department at the University of Utrecht—to make the strongest case for and against closure. Tielman was opposed to closure. Central to his argument was the belief that this strategy would merely drive sexual behavior to other settings, such as parks and toilets, where safe-sex education would not occur. Equally important was Tielman's concern for how bathhouse closure would affect the relationships between gay men and the broader society. "From a *political* point of view it is obvious that the gay movement will see the forced closure of public meeting places as an attack on their struggle for emancipation. From a *medical* point of view, closure may result in breaking the relationship of trust between gay men and the health care system which [will be] detrimental to public health."[57] The policy coordinator prepared a summary paper laying out the arguments both for and against closure, concluding that closure was not called for "at this moment."[58] The members of the Coordinating Team, including the public health experts, unanimously agreed with the Coordinator's conclusions. Because the entire debate took place behind closed doors, there was no media attention. The public posture of consensus was not disrupted.

Just as AIDS represented a threat to the public health, it also entailed a potentially dramatic challenge to the health of clinicians who cared for patients infected with HIV. After decades of relative safety, health care workers were confronted with the possibility that they might contract a lethal disease as the result of their work. Surgeons felt this risk most acutely. After the U.S. Centers for Disease Control reported the first HIV transmissions from patients to care-givers following needle-stick accidents, concern intensified, especially among surgeons who performed open-heart surgery.[59] Some physicians began to suggest that every patient should be tested routinely for HIV before surgery, enabling their doctors to take special precautions in the case of infection.[60] There were also reports of unconsented-to testing.[61]

The deputy chief medical officer responded by issuing a statement confirming that serological testing could be done only after informed consent,[62] thus rejecting routine preoperative screening. But a very vocal and well-known anesthetist used the Dutch media as a forum to express his support for routine presurgical testing.[63] He went further, asserting that, in AIDS policy, too many concessions had been made to the gay community, thus endangering the lives of "innocent" people. Other physicians joined the call for presurgical screening.[64]

For the first time, there was an "AIDS story" to report in the media: a dissenting voice from someone outside the "AIDS Mafia" had broken the controlled flow of information. Because of his professional stature, he could speak with some credibility and received widespread coverage.

At first, an attempt was made to resolve this problem through the tried-and-true method of quiet diplomacy within the medical and gay communities. After some probing, a solution seemed within reach. It would have stressed the voluntary disclosure of the possible risk of infection by individual patients thus providing surgeons with the opportunity to take special precautions regardless of whether permission for testing was granted. But the hoped-for compromise was shattered when it was prematurely made public on the day before a scheduled parliamentary debate on AIDS. The government's opposition to unconsented-to testing was unanimously endorsed by the Parliament. The government also made it clear that it would not provide the funds to support an educational campaign to inform patients and physicians about the importance of the voluntary disclosure of risk prior to surgery. The government's position was further strengthened by a report of the Standing Committee on AIDS of the Health Council, which stated that preoperative serological screening was unnecessary given the small risks involved.

In the months following this controversy, emphasis shifted to the protection of surgeons through the adoption of procedures that would reduce even further the risks of HIV transmission. Armed with data from the CDC which demonstrated very low levels of risk of infection after needlestick injuries, the government convinced virtually all surgeons that hazards could be minimized by modifications in their practices. This brought the move toward unconsented-to testing to an end.

Testing was also at the center of a controversy involving access to life insurance, but in this instance efforts at persuasion and mediation have failed to produce a broadly accepted solution—this matter remains an ongoing dispute in the Netherlands. In 1987, life insurance companies insisted that they should be able to test individuals at increased risk for HIV infection before providing coverage.[65] From the perspective of the companies, such a policy represented a straightforward extension of sound underwriting principles. After all, they risked substantial financial losses because of the premature death of persons belonging to high-risk groups and faced the prospect that individuals who knew themselves to be infected would be disproportionately inclined to take out insurance. Furthermore, Dutch firms were being required by international reinsurance companies to require routine testing when insurance policies provided for more than $100,000 in coverage. Reinsurance firms also expected testing when it was appropriate on "medical grounds."

At the core of the controversy were two matters, one superficially technical, the other a more direct confrontation with Dutch social philosophy. Could the concept of "medical grounds" be defined in a way that did not involve discriminatory judgments or the classification of all gay men as being at increased risk mainly because of their sexual orientation? Could the commercial interests of insurance firms be made compatible with the fact that life insurance is a precondition for the exercise of such basic rights as the right to purchase a home?

Conventional strategies for finding a solution—creating opportunities for those in conflict to discuss the issues at stake, attempting to find some common ground that could serve as the basis for consensus—failed in the spring of 1988, when the matter was brought before Parliament.[66]

Shortly before the parliamentary debate, the NCAB, for the first time in the AIDS crisis, called for special AIDS legislation in order to ensure access to life insurance under well-defined circumstances.[67] Parliament discussed the legislative option but ultimately urged the parties to find a solution. The Royal Dutch Medical Association, together with the society of medical advisers to insurance companies, were asked to discuss appropriate medical indications for testing for insurance policies that provide less than $100,000 in coverage. But the Medical Association informed the government that a more general discussion of the ethics of medical examinations as a condition for insurance was required before AIDS could be confronted. Faced with an apparent impasse, the government has turned to the Health Council's Standing Committee on AIDS for advice.[68]

The issues raised by the insurability of those with AIDS has implications for others with chronic conditions, and the conflict provoked by the public debate over the rights of the former has led interest groups representing the interests of those with other diseases to press their claims as well. Thus a controversy that emerged in the context of AIDS has forced the Dutch polity to confront far broader questions that go to the heart of underwriting practices.[69]

Perhaps the most bitterly contested AIDS issue in Holland has been the ethics of undertaking serological surveys of the population to determine the prevalence of HIV infection. The controversy was all the more surprising since such efforts had been approved in a number of more dissent-prone countries, including the United States and Canada, with virtually no protest. In Holland, all parties agree that epidemiological surveillance is essential for assessing the seriousness of the situation for planning programs and for assuring the adequacy of the network of social and medical services. Two major cohort studies of those at great risk—gay men and intravenous drug users—provided Dutch policymakers with a rather detailed picture of the progress of the epidemic. But as the focus of concern shifted to the spread of HIV infection in the general population, it was clear that such studies would have to be supplemented.[70]

Following methods devised by CDC, Roel Coutinho and epidemiologists from the National Institute for Public Health and Environmental Protection proposed a scheme of anonymous testing, one that would permit the unconsented-to HIV testing of blood samples drawn for other reasons, once they had been stripped of all personal identifiers. The state secretary of the Welfare and Health Ministry publicly rejected the proposed system of surveillance because of doubts about the ethics and legality of using blood samples for reasons other than those for which they were originally intended without specific informed consent.[71] While a majority of the Standing Committee on AIDS of the Health Council urged the government to permit large-scale anonymous testing, a minority asserted that evidence of a threat of substantial spread of HIV among the general population was insufficient to warrant such surveillance.[72] Although the NCAB was divided on the issue, a majority rejected anonymous surveillance.[73] Faced with this clash of experts, the government sided with those who opposed anonymous screening without consent, basing its conclusions on the grounds that such studies would not provide data useful to planning for health care or prevention.

Pressed by the repeated public challenges of Coutinho and the support he was able to elicit, the ministry turned again to the Health Council, which unanimously recommended that anonymous testing be permitted only in exceptional circumstances for particular groups that appear to be at risk for secondary HIV transmission, and only when other surveillance methods could not provide the needed data. For epidemiologists who had argued for the necessity of anonymous surveillance, this compromise represented a rigid application of ethical principles in a way that hampered efforts to protect the public health.[74]

As was true of the insurance controversy, the debate over seroprevalence studies posed for Dutch society a conflict of principles that went beyond the issue of AIDS—in this incidence involving a clash between the rights of privacy and the need for appropriate epidemiological data. Having faced this challenge, the government has sought to develop a policy that would meet the needs of public health while respecting the rights of individuals. Thus it has proposed a patients' bill of rights, which would permit the unconsented-to use of body tissue for surveillance purposes on the basis of presumed consent.[75] In the absence of an explicitly communicated refusal, anonymous screening would be permitted.

But controversy has centered not only on issues involving HIV testing. Toward the end of the first decade of the AIDS epidemic, the strategy of mass education has also been subject to challenge. By then, it had become clear in the Netherlands, as well as in other countries in the northern part of Western Europe, that the feared expansion of HIV infection had not occurred. If the level of HIV infection in the general population was at most 0.1 percent, and the risk of transmission of HIV during unprotected vaginal intercourse was also 0.1 percent, the chance of infection occurring as the result of a single act of unprotected sex would be about one in a million. That was a risk comparable to the danger associated with an airplane flight.

Based upon such assumptions, Coutinho issued a challenge. In his widely reported November 1989 inaugural lecture as professor of Epidemiology and Infectious Disease Control at the University of Amsterdam, he declared that current data could no longer justify public information campaigns that suggested that everyone was at risk for HIV infection. Acknowledging that this universal message might well have served the legitimate political interests of those concerned about stigmatization and discrimination, he warned that the public health effort risked a profound loss of credibility.[76] Those who challenged these observations noted that Coutinho himself bore considerable responsibility for such education programs, since he was vice-chair of the NCAB; in the end, he elected to resign from that post. This resignation has had profound significance, since it was Coutinho's participation, first as a member of the Coordinating Team and then as vice-chair of the NCAB, which inspired confidence in Dutch AIDS policy among members of the medical profession.[77]

One year after Coutinho issued his challenge, his position found new support from another member of the AIDS policy-making elite, the secretary of the Standing Committee on AIDS of the Health Council.[78] Nonetheless, the state secretary of the Welfare and Health Ministry recommitted the government to prevailing policies.

> Recent quotations in the press are based on statistical reasoning, leading to the conclusion that the *average* Dutchman runs a small risk [of contracting AIDS. Such a perspective does] no justice . . . to those in this country who have become infected with HIV as a consequence of heterosexual contact. Therefore, I distance myself from these comments. Further, I see no reason to assume that present AIDS campaigns provoke unneccessary fear. They are campaigns that aim at creating understanding for the position of HIV-infected persons and persons with AIDS, in addition to enhancing knowledge of the facts and stimulating responsible behavior.[79]

The Parliament endorsed the state secretary's reassertion of the merit of policies that had been forged in earlier days, when a broad consensus on the tasks posed by the AIDS epidemic had prevailed.

Viewed together, the controversy over seroprevalence studies and the dispute over educational strategies produce a picture of conflict that could have important implications for the vitality of the consensus that until recently has informed both the process and substance of Dutch AIDS policy.

Conclusion: Consensus and Rigidity

Dutch political life represents a compromise between Calvinism and humanism, between moralism and pragmatism. It has been relatively democratic, egalitarian, and tolerant of diversity for centuries. Although such an analysis helps to place the course of Dutch policy in the face of the AIDS epidemic in historical perspective, it cannot explain such policy. More recent events in the Dutch experience, as well as relatively contemporary decisions made with regard to homosexuality and drug use, provided the groundwork for what would emerge as the Dutch response to AIDS—one that from the start strove for inclusion and cooperation and rejected measures that in fact or symbolically, would have entailed an endorsement of a repressive stance. Thus one gay leader said during the discussion of whether or not the bathhouses should be closed, " It would make no more sense for the state to close the bathhouses than it would to close a church. Both are institutions rooted in their respective communities."

The policy of cooperation-and-inclusion, based on ongoing negotiation and the incorporation of community interests into the policy-making process, was endorsed by a broad political and social consensus. But that consensus was not given. It had to be worked for and sustained, and the extent of that achievement is striking. In three major AIDS debates in Parliament, unanimous support was given to the government's policies. AIDS thus never emerged as a matter of partisan dispute.

The formative period of AIDS policy-making occurred when a center–right coalition formed the government coalition. The Christian Democrats dominated the cabinet, which was generally considered conservative in its outlook, colored by traditional Christian values, yet its AIDS policies were liberal by all international standards. It is a mark of the strength of the prevailing consensus that when the Social Democrats entered the government in 1989 there was no change in AIDS policies.

But the consensus that served the Netherlands so well in the epidemic's first years has had its costs. In the 1990s, a certain rigidity has begun to emerge. Public debate about the appropriate course of policy has tended to be narrowly focused, and those with dissenting opinions have found it difficult to receive a careful hearing. When dissenting views could not be brought within the consensus, they have been virtually ignored. For some experts in epidemiology and infectious disease, some of the policies endorsed by government, whatever the dominant party, no longer seem appropriate. For them the consensus has taken on features of a troubling inflexibility. There are signs that one consequence of the policy of consensus has been an over bureaucratization of AIDS-related activities.

Dutch epidemiologists believe in 1991 that the number of individuals who will develop AIDS in the Netherlands will be considerably lower than had been anticipated by earlier forecasts. In this, the Netherlands is not so different from other Western European countries. In the second decade of AIDS, the question is how much the substance and process of policy-making will need rethinking.

Notes

1. Symposium "Fatale ziekten bij promiscue homoseksuelen" (Fatal diseases of promiscuous gay men). Erasmus University Rotterdam (May 14, 1982).

2. P.J.E. Bindels, J.T.L. Jong, M.J.J.C. Poos et al., "Het epidemiologisch beloop van AIDS in Amsterdam, 1982–1988" (The epidemiological course of AIDS in Amsterdam, 1982–1988), *Nederlands Tijdschrift voor Geneeskunde* 134 (1990), 390–394.

3. G.J.P. van Griensven, "Epidemiology and prevention of HIV infection among homosexual men," Ph.D. thesis (Amsterdam: University of Amsterdam, 1989). The thesis consists mainly of previously published articles: *American Journal of Epidemiology* 125 (1987), 1048–1057; *American Journal of Public Health* 78 (1988), 1575–1577; *American Journal of Epidemiology* 129 (1989), 596–603; *Genitourinary Medicine* 64 (1988), 344–346; *British Medical Journal* 298 (1989), 218–221; *Journal of Infectious Diseases* 159 (1989), 1157–1158.

4. H. M. Ginzburg, Fleming P. Leehan, and K. D. Miller, "Selected Pulic Health Observations Derived from the Multicenter AIDS Cohort Study," *Journal of Acquired Immune Deficiency Syndromes* 1 (1988), 2–7.

5. J.A.R. van den Hoek, "Epidemiology of HIV infection among drug users in Amsterdam," Ph.D. thesis (Amsterdam: University of Amsterdam, 1990).

6. C. Dudok de Wit, "Resultaten van het onderzoek op humaan immuno-deficientievirus bij bloeddonoren in 1985, 1986 en 1987" (Results of screening on HIV among blood donors in 1985, 1986, and 1987), *Nederlands Tijdschrift voor Geneeskunde* 132 (1988), 589.

7. R.A. Coutinho et al., "HIV-prevalentie bij zwangeren in en rond Amsterdam in 1989," *Nederlands Tijdschrift Geneeskunde* 134 (1990), 1264–1266.

8. J. C. Jager et al., "Prognose aangaande HIV-infectie en AIDS-epidemie in Nederland op basis van wiskundige analyse," *Nederlands Tijdschrift Geneeskunde* 134 (1990), 2486–2491.

9. J.K. van Wijngaarden, "Nieuwe homoziekte eist zestig doden" (New gay disease accounts for sixty dead), *Sek* (Journal of the Dutch Gay Association) (February 1982). J. van der Boon, "Drie gevallen van 'homoziekte' in Nederland geregistreerd" (Three cases of 'gay disease' registered in the Netherlands). *De Volkskrant* (June 18, 1983).

10. J.K. van Wijngaarden, "Nieuwe homo-ziekte eist zestig doden." J.K. van Wijngaarden and H. Moerkerk, "Op je hoede zijn, maar geen paniek" (Be on guard, but don't panic). *Sek* (June 1982).

11. Van Wijngaarden and Moerkerk, "Op je hoede zijn."

12. R. A. Coutinho "Een terugblik vanuit het beleid" (Looking back from a policy point of view), in *Dilemmas rondom AIDS* (Dilemmas with respect to AIDS) (Lisse, 1989).

13. Coutinho, "Een terugblik vanuit het beleid."

14. Letter of the Central Medical Blood Transfusion Committee (286/JM/ST) dated April 27, 1983, to all blood banks in the Netherlands.

15. Minutes of the meeting discussing the educational strategy and plans on Monday, May 9, 1983. Documentation Center of the NCAB, Amsterdam.

16. "Belangrijke mededeling voor bloeddonoren" (Important message for blood donors). Leaflet issued June 1983, in coproduction by Buro GVO Amsterdam (Office for Health Education), De Centrale Medische Bloedtransfusie Commissie van het Nederlandse Rode Kruis (Central Medical Blood Transfusion Committee), de Nederlandse Vereniging tot Integratie van Homoseksualiteit COC (The Dutch National Gay Organization).

17. Minutes of the meeting of the "Stuurgroep AIDS." This committee organized the campaign and functioned during the summer and fall of 1983. Documentation Center of the NCAB, Amsterdam.

18. Letter of the Ministry of WVC to the Municipal Health Service in Amsterdam on the appointment of the AIDS Coordinator (135945 DG Vgz/AGZ/BGZ) (November 1, 1983).

19. H. Bijkerk, "AIDS in Nederland 1982–1986," *Nederlands Tijdschrift voor Geneeskunde* 131 (1987), 676–678.

20. "Tweede advies inzake de problematiek van het verkregen Immunodeficiency Syndrome (AIDS) in Nederland. Klinische, psychosociale en ethische aspecten" (Second advice with respect to problems related to AIDS. Clinical, psychosocial and ethical aspects) (The Hague: Gezondheidsraad, March 1985).

21. Letter of the state secretary of the Ministry of WVC to the Parliament on September 22, 1985. *Tweede Kamer der Staten-Generaal* 19218, 1–2.

22. *AIDS Informatie* (July 1985).

23. "Tweede advies."

24. B.D.P. Eijrond, "Regionale AIDS-bestrijding" (Regional fight against AIDS) (Amsterdam: Documentation Center of the NCAB, December 1987).

25. "Notitie Voortgang Activiteiten AIDS XVIII" (Progress Report on AIDS Activities XVIII) (Amsterdam: Documentation Center of the NCAB, December 1986).

26. *Haagse Post* (November 29, 1986). See also *Hervormd Nederland* (December 6, 1986).

27. Conference held at the National Institute of Public Health and Environmental Control, Bilthoven, March 21, 1987.

28. Instellingsbesluit Nationale Commissie AIDS-Bestrijding (Proclamation of the Establishment of the NCAB), *Staatscourant* 188 (1987) (daily paper with government announcements).

29. AIDS Information and Prevention (policy paper, in English). (Amsterdam: Documentation Center of the NCAB, 1986).

30. J. H. Moerkerk, "Preventie, mogelijkheden en dilemmas" (Prevention, opportunities, and dilemmas), in *AIDS, ziekte, patient en samenleving*, ed. S.A. Danner et al. (Utrecht: Wetenschappelijke Uitgeverij Bunge, 1986).

31. L. H. Lumey, J. Kok, and R. A. Coutinho, "Screening for syphilis among homosexual men in bars and saunas in Amsterdam," *British Journal of Venereal Disease* 58 (1982), 402–404.

32. R. Shilts, *And the Band Played On: Politics, People, and the AIDS epidemic* (New York: St. Martin's Press, 1987), 443.

33. AIDS information and prevention.

34. Request for supplemental contributions of the "Federatie Nederlandse Junkiebonden" (Federation of Dutch Junkie Unions) to the Ministry of WVC (Amsterdam: Documentation Center of the NCAB, April 1987).

35. AIDS information and prevention.

36. "AIDS standaard antwoordenlijst." Later published as a book: K. van der Riet, *AIDS vragen en antwoorden* (AIDS questions and answers) (The Hague: Muusses/Staatsuitgeverij, 1988). Revised in 1990.

37. N. Loendersloot and F. Bruins, "AIDS Campagne 1987: Een Uitdaging" (AIDS Campaign 1987: a Challenge) (policy paper) (Amsterdam: Prins, Meijer, Stamenkovits, van Walbeek/Young & Rubicam/Reklamebureau B.V., March 1987).

38. The leaders of the advertisements were: "Vervolgcursus sexuele voorlichting" (Additional course on sex education); "Voorspel nieuwe stijl" (Foreplay new style?); "Wij moeten eens ernstig praten, Jan" (We should talk seriously, John); "Spelbreker?" (Spoiling the game? [depicting a condom]).

39. Communique bisschoppenconferentie (Communication of the conference of bishops), Informatiebulletin Kerkgenootschap Nederland (Information Bulletin of the Dutch Congregation (May 8, 1987), 358–359.

40. "Notitie Voortgang Acteviteiten AIDS I" (Progress Report on AIDS activities I) (Amsterdam: Coordination team, Documentation Center of the NCAB, 1983).

41. H. Scheijde, Letter to personal services, company doctors, and company nurses (Eindhoven: Philips, October 1987).

42. "Een nationaal belang" (A national interest). "Editorial," *NRC Handelsblad* (January 28, 1988).

43. As described in G. C. Geujen, I. Smeets, and G. W. Marsman, *AIDS in de media, Interimrapport* (Nijmegen: Katholieke Universiteit, 1988).

44. Addendum to a letter of the MDHG (Medical Service for Heroin Users [one of the junkie unions]) to the Municipality of Amsterdam, (Amsterdam: MDHG, June 7, 1984).

45. A.D. Verster, "Vijf jaar spuitomruil in Amsterdam" (Five years of needle exchange in Amsterdam) (policy paper) (Amsterdam: AIDS Coordination Amsterdam, Municipal Health Service, July 1990).

46. S. Biersteker, "Primaire preventie van AIDS/SOA in de prostitutie projectplan en aanzet tot meerjarenplan" (Primary prevention against AIDS/STD in prostitution: project planning and the outline for a long-term strategy) (Utrecht: SOA Stichting [STD Foundation], 1989).

47. Jaarverslag 89–90 (Annual Report 1989–1990), Stichting Huiskamer Aanloop Prostituées (Utrecht: 1991).

48. "De zorg voor AIDS-patiënten" (Care for persons with AIDS) (advice to the government) (The Hague: Gezondheidsraad, December 1987).

49. S. A. Danner, "Een ziekenhuisprotocol voor de zorg voor patiënten met AIDS" (A hospital protocol for the care of patients with AIDS) (The Hague: Gezondheidsraad, June 27, 1988).

50. "Jaarverslagen Verpleegkundig AIDS-consulenten" (Annual Reports of AIDS Nurses) (Amsterdam: AMC, May 1986 and May 1987).

51. "Advies centrumziekenhuizen" (Advice on centralizing hospital care) (The Hague: Gezondheidsraad, 1988).

52. T. van der Meer, "Vrijwilligers in de frontlinie. Het buddyproject van de Jhr Mr JA Schorerstichting" (Volunteers on the front line. The buddy project of the "Jhr Mr JA Schorerfoundation") (Amsterdam: Schorerstichting, 1987).

53. "Raamplan AIDS en de psychosociale zorg (Outline for AIDS and psychosocial care) (advice to the government) (Amsterdam: Documentation Center of the NCAB, April 1988).

54. H. Roscam Abbing, "Contribution to the session on legal and ethical aspects of AIDS," Third International Conference on AIDS, Washington, 1987. This contribution was of special importance, because Dr. Roscam Abbing is special adviser to the minister for health-related legal matters.

55. L. Gostin et al. "Legal Control Measures for AIDS, Reporting Requirements, Surveillance, Quarantine, and Regulation of Public Meeting Places," *American Journal of Public Health* 77 (1987), 214–218. See also M.D. Kirby, "AIDS Legislation, Turning up the heat?" *Journal of Medical Ethics* 12(4) (December 1986), 187–194.

56. A. M. Brandt, *No Magic Bullet: A Social History of Venereal Disease in the United States Since 1880* (New York: Oxford University Press, 1987).

57. R. Tielman (acting as chairman of the Department of Gay and Lesbian Studies at the University of Utrecht), "Heeft het zin om bepaalde homo-ontmoetingsplaatsen te sluiten?" (Does it make sense to close certain gay public meeting places?) (policy paper, AIDS Coordinating Team) (Amsterdam: Documentation Center of the NCAB, December 1985).

58. J.K. Wijngaarden, "Notitie homo-omtmoetingsgelegenheden" (Paper on gay public meeting places) (policy paper) (Amsterdam: Documentation Center of the NCAB, December 1985).

59. CDC, *MMWR* 36 (1987), 285–289.

60. H. A. Verbrugh, "Screening van patiënten op HIV-infectie ter preventie van besmetting van zorgverleners in ziekenhuizen" (Patient screening of HIV infection preventing contamination of health care workers in hospitals), *Nederlands Tijdschrift voor Geneeskunde* 131 (1987), 2207–2208.

61. R. Symons, "Chirurgen weigeren al patiënten te opereren die niet op AIDS zijn getest" (Surgeons refuse to operate on patients who have not been tested for AIDS), *Vrij Nederland* (weekly magazine) (August 22, 1987).

62. HA van Geuns, "AIDS en gezondheidszorg, testen of niet?" (AIDS and health care, to test or not to test?), *Medisch Contact* (Magazine of the Royal Dutch Society for Medicine) 42 (1987), 1191–1193.

63. M. Smalhout, "Testen, isoleren, verbannen . . . chaos rond AIDS-test neemt toe" (To test, to isolate, to ban . . . chaos on AIDS test is increasing), *De Telegraaf* (April 30, 1988).

64. F. L. Meijler, "Het testen van HIV-infectie in de cardiologie," *Nederlanderlands Tijdschrift voor Geneeskunde* 132 (31) (1988), 1445–1446. H. Roscam Abbing replied: "Arts mag niet ongevraagd aidstest doen" (AIDS test by physician without consent not permitted). *Algemeen Dagblad* (September 10, 1988).

65. As described in: J. K. van Wijngaarden and B.P.D. Eijrond, "Beleid toepassing serologische testen op antistoffen tegen HIV" (Policy on the use of serological testing on antibodies against HIV) (policy paper) (Amsterdam: Documentation Center of the NCAB, 1987).

66. Debate on AIDS, Vaste Kamercommissies voor Volksgezondheid, voor Justitie en voor Sociale Zaken en Werkgelegenheid (Standing Parliamentary Committees for Health, Justice and Social Welfare), UCV 51 (Records of Parliament) (April 25, 1988).

67. Smalhout, "Testen, isoleren, verbannen."

68. Letter of the State Secretary of the Ministry of WVC to the Health Council (DGVgz/AGZ/BGZ n. 122384) (Rijswijk: October 18, 1990).

69. Letter of the National Association for Diabetics to the State Secretary of the Ministry of WVC (Amersfoort: November 26, 1990).

70. "Onderzoek naar de verspreiding van HIV-infectie in Nederland" (Surveillance of the spread of HIV infection in the Netherlands) (advice to the government) (The Hague: *Gezondheidsraad*, February 1989).

71. D.J.D. Dees, Speech of the State Secretary at the Symposium "Stockholm 88" (Utrecht: June 1988).

72. "Onderzoek naar de verspreiding van HIV."

73. Advies over grootschalig HIV-seroprevalentie onderzoek op anonieme basis (Advice on large-scale HIV-seroprevalance surveillance on the basis of anonymity) (advice to the government) (Amsterdam: NCAB, Documentation Center of the NCAB, September 1989).

74. R. A. Coutinho, "Eerste resultaten van anonieme HIV-screening in de VS (First results of anonimous HIV-screening in the U.S.), *Nederlands Tijdschrift voor Geneeskunde* 134 (1990) 2173–2175.

75. "Wijziging van het Burgelijk Wetboek en enige andere wetten in verband met de opneming van bepalingen omtrent de overeenkomst tot het verrichten van handelingen op het gebied van de geneeskunst" (Proposal for changing laws in relation to the medical treatment contract) Tweede Kamer des Staten Generaal No. 11270/150–152 (The Hague: Ministry of Justice; Ministry of Welfare, Health and Cultural affairs; May 1990).

76. R. A. Coutinho, "Enkele grote lijnen in de AIDS-bestrijding (Some major features of the fight against AIDS), *Medisch Contact* 45 (1990), 21–22. Some daily newspapers reported: "Criticism on AIDS information: Risk for infection falsely stated," *Algemeen Dagblad* (November 22, 1989); "Professor Coutinho severely criticizes: Don't silence the truth about AIDS, *Haagsche Courant* (November 21, 1989).

77. Main daily newspapers reported: "Vice-voorzitter verlaat Nationale Commissie AIDS-bestrijding" (Vice-chairman resigns from NCAB), *Algemeen Dagblad* (December 5, 1989). The chairman and the secretary of the NCAB are quoted in the same article: "Such critism cannot be tolerated", "Coutinho weg na rel over AIDS" (Coutinho leaves after row about AIDS), *Trouw* (December 5, 1989). "Kleinzielig" (Petty-minded) (editorial), *De Telegraaf* (December 6, 1989).

78. As reported in many newspapers on December 5, 1990.

79. Debate on the budget of the ministry of WVC. Tweede Kamer der Staten Generaal TK 33 33-2022 (The Hague: December 6, 1990).

Chapter 9   Denmark: AIDS and the Political "Pink Triangle"

Erik Albæk

Imagine a young girl helping her equally young partner put a condom on his erect penis, then having intercourse with him, finally helping him to remove the condom. Now imagine the whole scene in close-up photography being shown on prime time television. That is what Danish AIDS policy is all about; this tableau formed part of an AIDS education program shown on prime time Danish television in 1988.

The public history of AIDS in Denmark started in December 1981, only six months after AIDS was first reported in the United States as an official clinical syndrome. Previously established contacts between cancer researchers in America and Denmark led to the first AIDS research projects outside the United States.[1] The central committees of the local organizations of the National Danish Organization for Gays and Lesbians (NDOGL) were promptly contacted. They agreed to inform their membership about the outbreak of this new disease and to request gay men's participation in the joint U.S.–Danish investigation. A few newspapers picked up the story and briefly reported on the new gay disease. Thus, AIDS was brought to the attention of the general public, the medical community, and the organized part of the gay community in Denmark at the same very early time in the course of the epidemic.

AIDS was never defined solely in biological terms. No disease is. It is always also defined in social, political, cultural, and existential terms. No single and necessary relationship, only a negotiated one, exists between diseases in their biological and social dimensions. This has been particularly so in the case of AIDS. At the very outset, AIDS was conceptualized as an infectious cancer—itself sufficient to invoke powerful connotations and metaphors.[2] AIDS was also defined as a disease of gay males, and while Danes have developed a markedly more tolerant attitude toward homosexuality than that of most other nations, gay men and women were still far from social parity with heterosexuals. In Denmark, as elsewhere, there was every reason to anticipate that AIDS would trigger a cultural and political backlash against gay people. The AIDS epidemic, it was feared, could be used by right-wing politicians and fundamentalists as an opportunity to reverse the increasingly liberal social and political attitudes toward homosexuality that had emerged during the 1960s and 1970s.

Elsewhere, increased homophobia has indeed had serious repercussions on how society has dealt with the AIDS epidemic.[3] But anti-gay arguments have had virtually no impact on Danish AIDS policy. The social conception of AIDS and the definition of policy choices have, from the very start, been owned almost exclusively by a political alliance consisting of medical professionals and various groups perceived as being at risk of contracting AIDS, most notably gay men. The object of this alliance has been the initiation of massive nonrestrictive AIDS policies to combat the disease. While the alliance succeeded in preventing the adoption of restrictive AIDS measures, it met substantial opposition when it sought public funding for AIDS. But this opposition only marginally reflected homophobic attitudes. Instead, the political conflict over AIDS policy in Denmark is best understood as a classic struggle over scarce public resources.

The Nordic Context

When the five Nordic countries attract the attention of the international social science community, it is most often due to their comparatively striking egalitarianism.[4] The degree to which they have been able to combine a high level of GNP per capita with a very even distribution of income and social welfare is unique, even to the extent that it has been common to speak of a distinct Scandinavian welfare state model. This egalitarianism is more often stressed by non-Nordic than by Nordic authors. Especially to many American scholars, the Nordic countries seem to have created something very close to the "good life," including equality, in contrast to the less communitarian and more competitive American society. The development of the Nordic welfare states is often explained by the historically strong position of social democracy in this region. Comparative studies measuring the good life, using both objective indicators such as education, health, and income, and subjective indicators of quality of life, always place the Nordic countries at the top of the list.[5] The same holds true for comparative studies measuring egalitarian social attitudes.[6]

The Nordic countries are considered unique in another respect: secularization is generally believed to be further advanced there then elsewhere. Yet this picture is not confirmed by comparative studies. While the role of religion in society has declined in most Western countries over the last decades, as has the role of institutions and social values traditionally associated with religion, the five Nordic countries are not distinguishable from the rest of Northern Europe.[7] However, two countries *do* differ from the rest: Sweden and Denmark. Despite the fact that some 90 percent of the Danish population are members of the Lutheran State Church, comparative surveys conducted in the beginning of the 1980s showed that fewer people believe in God or attend church in Denmark than in any other country investigated except for Sweden. Furthermore, attitudes about family and social values such as abortion, homosexuality, divorce, and prostitution turn out to be markedly more liberal in Denmark than in any other country, including Sweden.[8] Recent European Economic Community (EEC) statistics have shown that 45 percent of all children are born out of wedlock in Denmark.[9] However, even though Danes have a more relaxed attitude toward traditional family values, they prefer spending more time with their families than do any other people in Europe.[10] All this makes Denmark perhaps the most "post-materialist" country in the world.[11]

Attention to the comparatively more advanced secularization of Denmark and Sweden has been limited. Seen from a historical perspective, this modern trend has its roots in several factors related to the development of European society. The Nordic countries were located so far from Rome that they were never fully subject to its control. During the Reformation, they made a quick and complete break with the Catholic Church and adopted Protestantism, which is less resistant to secularization. In later centuries, the Nordic countries developed a marked religious homogeneity and built up their own distinctive cultural institutions. State-building in these countries never needed the strong nationalist ideology that is often coupled with strong family and sexual morals.[12] Modernization started early in the Nordic region, as did the development of a politically and culturally strong, relatively homogeneous working class. Both modernization and socialism may have been secularizing forces.

These processes started earliest in the distinctly more urbanized Denmark. Denmark was closer to the continental trade network and developed a stronger merchant capitalism than did the rest of Scandinavia. In general, it has been a more open society, economically and culturally, than the rest of the region. For more than a thousand years this small country has managed to retain its independence. Flexibility is a key: As merchants, Danes have shunned the luxury of adhering to fixed ideas and morals, opting instead for a flexible, adaptable, and pragmatic approach to morality. These qualities also characterize Danish politics.[13]

Religion and traditional family values continue to have less impact on political behavior and the formulation of policy in Denmark than in most other Western democracies. Bishops and ministers are essentially civil servants in clerical garb, which imposes important limitations on their freedom to act politically in the name of God. Since a heated debate in the Danish Folketinget, (Parliament), at the beginning of this century, religious matters have been excluded from Danish politics; it has been practically impossible to invoke God in support of political arguments. The minister of ecclesiastical affairs is a politician who need not be a church member—he may even be an atheist—who busies himself with church business but not religious issues.

As moral attitudes gradually grew more permissive after the Second World War, there was a move in most Western countries towards a separation of law and morality. Denmark was no exception. It was among the first countries to repeal legal restrictions on the publication and consumption of pornography, in 1967, and to ensure women an unrestricted choice of lawful abortion within the first twelve weeks of pregnancy, in 1973. Increased moral permissiveness, and especially the relaxation of pornography laws, triggered a Christian countermovement in Denmark; this resulted in the formation of the Christian People's party in 1970. This party, represented in the Danish Parliament since 1973, has struggled to pass the 2 percent electoral threshold. Its support peaked in 1975, at 5.3 percent, but in the 1988 election, it received only 2 percent of the popular vote. Since the beginning of the 1970s, issues such as abortion, pornography, and alcohol consumption, which from time to time have polarized the other Scandinavian countries, have been nonissues in Danish politics. This does not mean that all Danes personally approve of pornography or abortion, but reflects the fact that, over the years, religion, morality, and sexuality have been individualized and privatized.

This perspective is shared by the younger generation. Despite a marked turn to the right during the 1980s with respect to attitudes on economics, Danish youth has a liberal attitude about questions related to social mores, such as attitudes to foreigners, women's work outside their homes, and nuclear power. People in their twenties are at least as liberal as the radicalized generation of ten years ago.[14] The youth organizations of the nonsocialist parties are often outspokenly liberal on moral questions, and except for the youth organization of the Christian People's party, none of them opposes gay rights.

Private homosexual activities between consenting adults were decriminalized in 1930. Until the 1970s, homosexuality was not something that most people approved of, but it was dealt with as a fact of life. In the liberal climate of the 1960s, the topic became more acceptable in public discussion; in 1976, homosexuality was given limited legal parity with heterosexuality by making the age of consent the same for both. Paradoxically, the increased visibility of gays owing to AIDS has increased the popular and political legitimacy of homosexual political demands. In 1984, the Parliament set up a royal commission to investigate the situation of gays and lesbians in society. Two year later, two important gay rights laws were adopted: a rule that prohibits discrimination on the basis of sexual preference, and another liberalizing inheritance laws to allow two members of the same sex living together to inherit from one another. Finally, in 1989, in a vote freed from party discipline, the Parliament became the first national legislature in the world to pass a law effectively accepting "homosexual marriages," registered partnerships. Nonsocialist members of Parliament were overwhelmingly opposed, including four ministers from Det radikale Venstre, a traditionally very pro-gay center party which only a year earlier, before joining the Conservative-led government, had supported an identical bill. The government felt the proposed marriage-like registration came too close to parliamentary approval of homosexuality and regarded its implementation as technically problematic. It proposed negotiations on alternative legislative means to remove judicial discrimination against homosexuals, but the parliamentary majority prevailed.

In the general population, the law met almost no opposition, and in the media, only the small *Christian Daily* expressed hostility. The Christian People's party made its opposition to the proposed law a major plank in its platform during the 1988 general election. Its position was not supported by the clergy, and in an election survey only one of 670 respondents mentioned registered partnerships as an important issue.[15]

The changed attitudes toward homosexuality in Denmark are perhaps best illustrated by popular response to major public figures. In 1987, one of Denmark's most popular top athletes, a primary school teacher and the leading player on the national handball team, agreed to play the part of a gay soccer player in a Danish youth film. When he appeared in a full frontal nude scene and in a bedroom scene with a male high school student, his popularity did not decline. On the contrary, most felt he had shown great courage in support of a good cause, as had a well-known former member of the Danish marine corps who appeared in the same film. At about the same time, one of Denmark's leading rock stars disclosed that she was living with a twenty-two-year-old woman; they later decided to have a baby with an anonymous father. This nontraditional family is treated like other well-known people by the Danish tabloids. In 1989, the singer released an album of modern psalms with her own music and texts written by a well-known minister of the Danish State Church; the album met with tremendous success.

Paradoxically, no member of Parliament has thus far come out of the political closet. This even holds true for those gay M.P.s who have actively supported gay issues and who have been instrumental in formulating the Parliament's response to AIDS. Their reasons for not coming out to the general public vary. Some may anticipate a negative response from the electorate. Moreover, there is no tradition of community identification in Danish politics or social life. In the United States and elsewhere, the individual depends on the support and solidarity of his or her ethnic, religious, or sexual community. But the concept of community has no foundation in the homogeneous Danish culture: Denmark constitutes a community in itself. Thus, a Dane would find it utterly strange to identify strongly with just one aspect of his life—for instance, sexual orientation—and there is no community to urge him to do so. This does not imply that such matters as religion, ethnicity, or sexuality have no impact on Danish culture, but only that these are considered private matters with no significance in public affairs.[16] It would be considered odd for a politician to stress sexual orientation as significant for his or her job as a politician. Only when journalists are invited into politicians' homes would it be proper for them to discuss such private matters.

Nor are there distinct, geographically concentrated cultural communities. In Denmark, only recent immigrants or guest workers are clustered in separate sections of the major cities; gays do not live together in separate, identifiable districts.[17] Gay Danes consider their sexual orientation central to their identity to a lesser extent than do gay Americans; they also adhere less to a specifically gay or lesbian way of living. Consequently, the concept of a gay community is used in the Danish context in a somewhat different sense than is usually the case in English-language literature: it refers to Danes who declare themselves to be gay and who take an active interest in gay affairs of a social, political, or cultural nature.

Political Pluralism

The formation of the government in Denmark is controlled by the 175-seat Parliament. The Cabinet must enjoy the support of a majority of the members of the Parliament, or at least there must not be a majority opposing it. Folketinget can pass a vote of no confidence at any time, leading to new cabinet negotiations or an election. Each cabinet minister heads one or more ministries and is responsible, politically as well as legally, for his ministry. Party representatives are elected to Folketinget on the basis of proportional representation. Due to the low threshold requirement for entering the Parliament, the country has many parties, and since the beginning of this century, no single party has held a majority. A great many decisions are made by negotiating compromises among the parties, which in turn demand a high degree of party discipline from their members. The cabinet may be formed either by a single party or by a coalition.

During the 1980s, eight or nine parties have been represented in Folketinget. Since 1982, nonsocialist party coalitions under the leadership of the Conservative party have formed the government, and each of these has been a minority government. From 1982 to 1988, cabinets were formed by a coalition consisting of Det Konservative Folkeparti (the Conservatives), Venstre (the Liberals, in the classic sense of the word), Centrumdemokraterne (the Center Democrats, a party founded by politi-

cians who broke with the Social Democratic party) and Kristeligt Folke-
party (the Christian People's party, a liberal party stressing moral and
Christian values). After the 1988 election, the coalition consisted of the
Conservatives (with 35 seats in Folketinget), the Liberals (22 seats), and
Det radikale Venstre (a social liberal party with the rather misleading
name the Radical Liberals, 10 seats). The Center Democrats (9 seats) and
the Christian People's party (4 seats) provided tacit support for the ruling
minority coalition. On the right, the government's opposition came from
Fremskridtspartiet (the Progress party, a highly libertarian, antitax and
antiwelfare state party with 16 seats). To the left was a socialist bloc
consisting of Socialdemokratiet (the Social Democrats, since the beginning of this century the largest party in Danish politics, 55 seats) and
Socialistisk Folkeparti (the Socialist People's party, 24 seats). This very
fragmentation in the party system has reinforced the tendency toward
broad agreements.

Local government has considerable power. An extensive amalgamation
and administrative reform in 1970 was followed by a massive transfer of
functions from the central government to county and local authorities,
which are also elected on the basis of proportional representation. The
division of functions between the three tiers of government follows the
principles of proximity as well as economic and administrative capacity.
Local expenditures in Denmark constitute the largest percentage of the
total public expenditures in any Western European country.[18]

County authorities are responsible for managing the universal national
health insurance system. They also administer the hospital system, almost
entirely public. County government administers and finances all medical
and dental services. Practically all public social welfare functions are administered by the 275 local authorities. They are responsible for social
assistance, visiting health services, and home nursing and home help
schemes. Consequently, the fourteen counties have been understandably
alarmed by the prospect of skyrocketing costs due to AIDS.

At Risk

Between 1981 and December 1990, 718 cases of AIDS were reported in
Denmark; more than half had died. Three quarters have been among gay
and bisexual men, and about 4 percent were intravenous drug users (see
Table 9.1).

The epidemiology of the epidemic has had a profound impact on the
course of Danish AIDS policy. The two major actors in the formulation of
AIDS policies have been the medical profession and the gay community.
AIDS was first linked to urban homosexual males, and the gay community
is still numerically the most affected group in Denmark. Furthermore, the

Table 9.1. AIDS Cases by Year of Report and Category of Risk Exposure for Denmark, 1980–1990

Risk category	1980	1981	1982	1983	1984	1985	1986	1987	1988	1989	1990	Total
Homosexual/bisexual activity	1	3	3	10	17	34	55	76	96	126	124	545
Homosexual/bisexual activity and IVDU	0	0	0	0	0	0	1	3	2	0	3	9
IVDU	0	0	0	0	0	0	1	3	6	8	14	32
Blood products	0	0	0	0	0	2	6	5	6	4	7	30
Heterosexual activity	0	0	0	2	0	1	1	8	10	19	21	62
Mother to child	0	0	0	0	0	0	1	1	1	4	2	9
Other/unknown	0	0	0	0	0	1	4	4	4	10	8	31
Total cases	1	3	3	12	17	38	69	100	125	171	179	718

Source: Epidemiologisk Afdeling, Statens Seruminstitut, Denmark.

gay community is better organized than are other high-risk groups, is equipped with more resources financially and with respect to voluntary manpower, has greater experience in dealing with governmental agencies, and has developed an informal network which includes various policymakers. At the beginning of the AIDS epidemic, the NDOGL had several thousand members. By comparison, the membership basis for the Danish Hemophilia Society (DHS) roughly equals the number of Danish hemophiliacs, 325, and no other risk group is organized.

The NDOGL was further strengthened during the early 1980s, as the radical Gay Liberation Front and the Lesbian Movement gradually weakened in a climate of declining interest in grass-roots activities. Practically speaking, the Gay Liberation Front no longer exists, and the Lesbian Movement is much less visible than before. A number of former Gay Liberation Front activists joined the NDOGL. They were instrumental in moving the organization away from its traditional begging-for-tolerance-and-acceptance attitude, toward a more aggressive formulation of policy demands. During the 1980s, the NDOGL very skillfully managed to become a mainstream interest organization, with a full-time staff growing from one in 1984 to twenty-four in 1990, close contacts with public agencies, and deep involvement in formulating and implementing public policies.

The NDOGL speaks as the single political voice of the gay community. Nevertheless, the NDOGL, with approximately three thousand members in 1990, has had only limited success in organizing gays. Most of its members are motivated to join because of reduced cover charges at NDOGL-run discotheques. The organization speaks for large sections of the gay community, even though few members actively attempt to influence the formulation of the organization's policy positions.

From the outset of the AIDS epidemic, the gay community found itself confronted with a dilemma. For years, the top priority of gay politics had been "deregulating" homosexuality, by keeping public authorities at bay. This goal was finally achieved in 1976, when the age of consent was made the same for homosexuals and heterosexuals. The next step was to press for antidiscrimination ordinances and officially sanctioned gay marriages. While such moves may appear to reintroduce the state as a regulator of sexuality, in fact, they were not seen as such by the gay political leadership. As long as gays lacked the legal right to make the same choices as heterosexuals, it was argued, the state discriminated against gay people.

With AIDS, the situation suddenly changed. The strategy had been to ensure that the state was kept out of gay affairs; now the aim was to involve the state more directly and actively. Thus, the government was asked to support AIDS educational and counseling services, research, and hot lines. This fissure in strategy runs through the entire conceptualization of AIDS by the gay community. On the one hand, the political leadership of the community has demanded financial support for research, treatment, and education. On the other hand, the community has blocked any attempt at public regulation of sexual behavior in order to avoid any invasion of privacy and the prospect of stigma.

Voluntary Cooperation as Strategy

Public health intervention to combat infectious and epidemic diseases, including sexually transmitted diseases, is not new. Historically, intervention has involved drastic attacks on traditional civil liberties, both in Denmark[19] and elsewhere,[20] including compulsory testing, reporting, quarantine, detention and internment. In this century, however, public health measures to deal with sexually transmitted diseases (STD) in Denmark have become markedly liberalized.

The first Danish legislation concerning sexually transmitted diseases dates to 1496, when syphilis first spread through Europe. Denmark was the first nation to provide for public payment for the treatment of sexually transmitted diseases, in 1773, and in 1788 the first legal provisions on the obligation to seek treatment were introduced. These two principles, the right to free treatment and the obligation to seek treatment, have subsequently been maintained; they were central to the most recent act of Parliament singling out STDs as a special category of diseases, the 1973 Act on Venereal Diseases.[21]

This revision represented a considerable legal liberalization. With the 1973 law, the patient's obligation to provide information concerning the source of infection and those whom the patient may have infected was replaced by a call for voluntary cooperation. As expressed in a circular from the National Board of Health (NBH), doctors were to use "considerable care" in obtaining this information. The 1973 act specified that individuals who suspected they were STD-infected (including persons who had been informed by a doctor that they might be infected) had to submit to medical examination and treatment. But in place of fines and imprisonment, the law authorized the health inspector, after first having tried to get a patient to go voluntarily to the doctor, to compel him or her to do so. If the patient did not comply with this requirement, the health inspector could request assistance from the police, and the court could require medical examination and treatment. Earlier legislation authorized sentencing a person to up to two years of imprisonment for having infected others. The new law restricted imprisonment to instances where a person "repeatedly or under otherwise aggravating circumstances" intentionally puts others at risk, and the maximum sentence was reduced to six months' imprisonment. The 1973 liberalization meant that STD infection and treatment were to be handled by the Danish health system in essentially the same way as are other infectious diseases.

Traditionally, the medical and social construction of infectious diseases has paralleled the discourse on the designation of social outcasts. In both instances, there have been demands to restrict civil liberties. Occasionally, the higher frequency of infectious diseases among marginalized groups has nourished fears and fostered calls for repression. Ghettoized minority groups have, of course, historically been exposed to epidemic diseases to a greater extent than has the population in general. In Denmark, the syphilis rate among gay men and Eskimos in Greenland has for a number of years been dramatically higher than in the rest of the population.

With the emergence of AIDS, the leadership of the gay community did not feel it could afford to distinguish between epidemiological arguments for restrictive measures and homophobia. Restrictive public health measures could easily trigger a new stigmatization of gays and lesbians, jeopardizing the hard-won social and legal freedoms gay people had gained over the past two decades. Thus, gay leaders opposed all restrictive measures affecting gay men, including restrictions affecting gay men who had been exposed to the AIDS virus. In general, the gay community has been highly successful in blocking restrictive and potentially stigmatizing AIDS policies.

This strategy has at times been controversial. The first conflict occurred in the summer of 1983, when the NBH requested that gays refrain from donating blood. Persons with syphilis and hepatitis were already excluded from blood donation. With AIDS, however, the situation was different, since a screening method to detect the agent responsible for AIDS had yet to be discovered. In the opinion of the NBH, the situation required removing, not just AIDS patients, but an entire at-risk group—homosexuals—from the donor pool.

The president of the NDOGL denounced the recommendation as "a very dramatic step" that effectively singled out homosexuals as "second-rate citizens." There was, he claimed, no evidence that the contamination of the blood supply was caused by gay people. In his view, the NBH merely nourished the myth that homosexuals were sick.[22] To the gay community, the call represented not so much an invasion of privacy (after all, any withdrawal would have to be voluntary) as an unfair and needless stigmatization. This was the closest the NBH came to introducing public health measures that the NDOGL saw as a potential threat to gays and to those who were HIV-positive.

Calls for restrictive measures such as quarantine or internment of HIV-infected individuals found their way into the Danish news media—and sometimes even Folketinget—but never gained much support. Twice, Kresten Poulsgaard, an M.P. from the right-wing Progress party, put questions to the minister of the interior (responsible for public health until the creation of the Ministry of Health in 1987) regarding what steps the minister intended to take to prevent AIDS-infected persons from transmitting the disease. Poulsgaard referred to media stories concerning persons who reportedly had chosen not to change their sexual behavior despite being HIV-infected. On December 12, 1985, shortly after an abortive attempt by the Progress party to incorporate AIDS into the Venereal Diseases Act, Poulsgaard asked the minister to comment on a report in *Jyllands-Posten* about "the persons who despite the fact that they know they have contracted AIDS continue to infect others with the disease."[23] The article claimed that an HIV-infected sexually active immigrant had refused to curb his sexual activities. The minister answered that she had been informed by the hospital treating the patient that there was no reason to believe that he had not followed its advice regarding his sexual activities.

Three months later, on March 25, 1986, Poulsgaard put yet another question to the new minister of the interior. "Which measures does the minister intend to take to prevent people who have contracted AIDS from continuing to have sexual intercourse?" His question was motivated by a television program in which a young girl reported that she continued her normal sexual life despite the fact she was HIV-positive. The girl had been informed by the hospital that her partners should use condoms if she continued to have sexual intercourse, but she ignored the advice. Poulsgaard argued that if the proposal of the Progress party to have AIDS included in the Venereal Diseases Act were adopted—as in Sweden—it would be possible to prevent people "from infecting others with this fatal disease."[24]

It was the punitive provisions of the Venereal Diseases Act that Poulsgaard believed would have a preventive effect. In the newspaper *Aktuelt*, he argued that AIDS-infected persons should either stop their sexual activities altogether or be quarantined.[25] The minister responded that the most relevant measures to limit the spread of AIDS were information, voluntary testing, and counseling on safer sex. He did not find the penalties of the Venereal Diseases Act suitable for the struggle against AIDS.[26]

Proposals for measures as drastic as those advanced by Poulsgaard were never taken seriously by policymakers. Nevertheless, policies to promote the rights of HIV-infected persons were not secured without controversy. The most seriously debated controversies occurred in 1985, when AIDS antibody testing became available. The issues raised in the Danish debate—privacy, public health and welfare, social and economic discrimination, coercion, and liberty—were similar to those raised in other countries, and the arguments essentially followed the same pattern.[27] Concerns were raised about the responsibility of blood banks to inform donors of test results; the use of test results by insurers in making underwriting decisions; the use of tests by health care workers, the police, and prison officials to identify HIV-positive individuals as self-protective measures; the reporting of the names of people with positive test results to public health authorities; and mandatory or large-scale screening.

The Danish debate was less vehement than in most other countries, however, and the policies adopted by the government have been remarkably sensitive to the concerns voiced by gay leaders. In a famous and oft-cited resolution adopted March 31, 1987, Folketinget acknowledged "that Danish efforts to combat AIDS continue to be based on voluntary cooperation and anonymity." The resolution might as well have been written in the offices of the NDOGL, so faithfully did it reflect the concerns of the gay community. AIDS has been treated with much greater sensitivity than have other sexually transmitted diseases. Because AIDS and HIV infection were not included under the 1973 Venereal Diseases Act, none of the special obligations imposed on those with STD have been brought to bear, nor have the penalty provisions of the act ever been applied to AIDS.

Consequently, Danish AIDS policies have been remarkably nonrestrictive. In contrast, AIDS policies in Sweden are among the most restrictive in Western Europe. For historical reasons, public policies in rationalist Sweden tend to be more restrictive than those of the more pragmatic Denmark. Swedish political and administrative culture permits regulations that, from a Danish perspective, are considered violations of individual rights. The Danish nickname for Sweden is "Prohibition Sweden," the country where nothing is permitted. Such moralistic, restrictive policies are cited by critics as examples of the totalitarian tendencies they claim to be inherent in Swedish social democratic ideology. A report that Swedish authorities were establishing a camp for HIV-infected persons in the Stockholm archipelago only served to reinforce Danish prejudices about Swedes.

The principle of voluntary cooperation embodied in the resolution of the Danish Folketinget has been strictly observed. Thus, prison inmates may voluntarily submit to testing for the HIV antibody. If the test result is positive, prison management is notified and may choose to inform its personnel. Danish citizens may choose to have the test taken anonymously by using a pseudonym; however, only a small percentage choose to do so. The policy of anonymous HIV testing differs from the policy and practice on testing for venereal diseases. The 1973 Venereal Diseases Act did not allow for anonymous testing, and although anonymity became theoretically possible when the Act was repealed in 1988, venereal disease clinics do not as a matter of practice offer patients this option.

When the HIV test is not taken anonymously, test results are entered in a file available to others only in very narrowly specified circumstances. In accordance with the practice concerning sexually transmitted diseases, the general practitioner is not automatically informed of the test results by the hospital; nor is such information provided to other wards in the hospital. Sharing of such information requires the explicit consent of the person tested. In addition, the "red system," a computerized system that registers relevant medical information on all hospital admissions in Denmark, is not informed of a patient's HIV test results. Formally, the NBH has argued that information on HIV should not be shared because it is a condition, not a disease, and thus does not trigger treatment. In fact, the exceptionalism surrounding HIV is motivated by the very concerns that surround all sexually transmitted diseases, and by the sensitivity of the medical system to fears voiced by the gay community.

Full-blown AIDS is a reportable disease, subject to the standard practices that surround other medical conditions. Despite the legal distinction between HIV and AIDS, a gray zone exists, since many patients with HIV-related conditions but without full-blown AIDS are treated in hospitals. In those circumstances, almost without exception, patients have accepted the sharing of information among physicians as vital to their care.

AIDS cases were made reportable by name to the health authorities in May 1983, a step that aroused virtually no opposition, but attempts to make HIV infection reportable by name have been opposed by the NBH. Not until 1990 did HIV become reportable, and then only in an anonymous form. The examining doctor only reports the sex, age, county of residence, and, if possible, the risk behavior of the HIV-infected person. This mirrors the reporting provisions on most sexually transmitted diseases, which also exclude personal identifiers. Only with syphilis is there an exception. Blood samples that test positive have, since 1919, been entered with the individual's central personal register number into the Wassermann Reaction Register (WRR). But in a reflection of the heightened sensitivity to matters of confidentiality provoked by AIDS, access to such data requires the patient's explicit consent.

Interestingly, the Greenland Board of Health and the Commission on Scientific Research in Greenland have adopted their own AIDS policies.[28] A research project has been established to survey the spread of HIV. As in Denmark, testing is done only with the specific informed consent of the patient. There is an option of anonymity, but it is almost never exercised. The names of those with HIV infection are recorded by the chief medical officer in Greenland for surveillance purposes only. Personally identified records are never released. For the public health authorities, this move was dictated by the unique demographic characteristics that prevail in Greenland: almost half the population is less than twenty-five years of age, and the prevalence rate of STD is extraordinarily high. Thus, Greenland's population was primed for the rapid spread of HIV infection. Since there is little reported homosexuality in Greenland—the epidemic of STD there is linked to a culturally normative pattern of promiscuous behavior among heterosexuals—little opposition to this system of reporting came from the Danish gay community.

Throughout Denmark, mandatory screening is prohibited. Large-scale anonymous, blinded seroprevalence screening—in which blood samples drawn for purposes other than HIV testing are stripped permanently of all personal identifiers and then tested without consent—has been proposed by epidemiologists and public health officials for many of the same reasons that have been brought forward in other countries: the problem of selection and participation bias in volunteer studies as well as the long latency period between HIV infection and the development of AIDS.[29] Not until the spring of 1990, however, did the minister of health agree even to consider introducing such surveillance measures in Denmark, reflecting the opposition to the very concept of testing blood without the informed consent of the supplier as well as to the specific studies that have been proposed.

Among epidemiologists, the most widely supported proposals for blinded seroprevalence studies have centered on screening pregnant women. Such women were, by definition, sexually active; they were considered to be a sufficiently representative cross-section of the population, and blood specimens from pregnant women were already routinely collected and tested for syphilis at the State Serum Institute in Copenhagen.

Opponents have expressed reservations about the epidemiological value of such proposed studies,[30] and female doctors assert that sexism is involved.[31] Politicians have argued that it would be ethically unacceptable to conduct studies that would, by their very nature, preclude physicians from informing pregnant women that they were infected. However, what has most stirred opposition is the fact that this screening would be conducted without the explicit consent of the tested individual. During the past decade, Danish society has given ever greater attention to a number of ethical issues—environmental questions, gene technology, the conditions of animals in modern farm production, and medical practice—which have been vehemently debated. Concerning medical practice, a consensus has emerged that emphasizes the right to informed consent. Whether the issue is autopsy or organ donation, the rights of the individual are given priority. Presumed consent to such procedures is now widely viewed as unethical.[32]

It was against this background that the issue of blinded and unconsented-to seroprevalence studies had to be confronted. When, in the spring of 1990, the minister of health finally agreed to consider such surveillance, a working group with wide representation of medical experts was established to review the matter. The group was asked to consider blinded screening of women seeking abortions, as well as persons being tested for STD, presumably because they would be less subject to potentially disruptive stress than women planning to carry their pregnancies to term. The working group rejected the proposal, because the numbers of individuals involved would fail to provide a statistically significant picture of HIV prevalence in the population. Instead, the group urged that all pregnant women be included in the surveillance. In the proposal put before the NBH and the minister of health, all individuals would be notified of the existence of such screening, though in a general form, and would have the right to exempt their specimens from testing. The minister has once again rejected the proposal.

No law prevents insurance companies from requiring individuals applying for life insurance to take an HIV test. In late 1986, Baltica, a major insurance company, intended to introduce a questionnaire that asked applicants if they belonged to a known AIDS risk group. This scheme was immediately interpreted by members of the Folketinget as an attempt by the insurance company to establish an unacceptable, and probably illegal, register of sexual behavior. The Conservative chairman of the Parliamentary Committee on Justice, Hagen Hagensen, remarked that "of course, insurance companies have the right to exclude terminally ill persons from purchasing life insurance. But establishing a register and evaluating people's worth on the basis of sexual behavior is a violation of the freedom and integrity of the individual."[33]

The reaction of several M.P.s provoked the company management into taking the unusual step of writing a letter to all members of Parliament, explaining that the firm had no intention of recording sexual behavior but sought only to determine if the applicant belonged to one of the AIDS risk groups defined by the NBH. Other insurance companies supported the idea of such a questionnaire. The executive committee of the Danish Insurance Association indicated that it planned to begin discussions regarding the precise formulation of the questions to be asked of those seeking insurance. Those who were at risk would be required to take an HIV test. A refusal to do so would automatically mean a rejection of the application.

The chairperson of the Test Committee of the Danish Medical Association found the proposed questionnaire unacceptable and suggested that the association would order its members not to complete it.[34] The Socialist People's party prepared to take legal action to prevent insurance companies from inquiring about sexual behavior. Underwriting decisions, it asserted, could only be based on the presence of actually diagnosed illnesses. A proposed statute prohibiting insurance companies from seeking information about sexual behavior stood a good chance of passing. Then, in April 1987, the Danish Insurance Association yielded to the opposition it had provoked. The resistance to the insurance industry effort reflected the commitment of the Danish authorities to protect the social interests of those with HIV infection, a commitment that had broad-based support in Danish society.[35]

The proposed questionnaire stirred up animosity towards the insurance companies. They had sought to put profit before people, it was asserted; they had attempted to avoid the challenge of dealing with "bad lives." An attempt to punish those most in need of help was a deep offense, given the egalitarian character of Danish political culture. Its image tarnished and its actuarial foundations threatened by what it feared would be an ever-growing threat posed by AIDS-related claims, the insurance industry donated over $1 million to AIDS research and prevention programs.

The right of HIV-infected children to attend school never became a controversial issue. When the press reported a great deal of anxiety among kindergarten teachers because of AIDS, the NBH instructed the teachers to take the same precautions with children with AIDS that they took when dealing with all children. Similarly, the rights of those exposed to the AIDS virus to keep their jobs never became a major concern. The most notorious case involved the firing of a cook working in the canteen of a major Danish newspaper, but even there the facts were unclear. The paper vigorously rejected the charge of discrimination made by the NDOGL, and asserted that it had offered an alternative post to the man, who had cut himself several times at work and was too ill to continue his responsibilities.

In the controversies over testing and in the reaction to charges of discrimination, Danish officials have revealed their commitment to the protection of privacy and confidentiality. Whenever violations of these principles have been brought to the attention of central government authorities, they have made it clear that such breaches would not be tolerated. Doctors who have screened blood without the consent of patients have been reprimanded. The establishment of registers making possible the identification of HIV-infected individuals within the medical and police systems has been assailed; in 1987, for instance, the drug squad of the Copenhagen police force was asked to remove photographs of HIV-infected intravenous drug users from a bulletin board at the central police station.[36]

In the summer of 1987, three Copenhagen physicians published an article in the *Journal of the Danish Medical Association* on the case of an HIV-infected man who refused to tell his wife of his infection. Not only the wife but also their unborn child were at risk. The doctors found it "extremely difficult to accept" that they could not breach medical confidentiality to inform the wife.[37] The matter was submitted to the NBH, which ultimately ruled that the principle of confidentiality was inviolable, whatever the risk to the woman and her fetus.[38] Although the board noted that it was not informed of the case until the woman was more than five months pregnant, past the point of elective abortion, the physicians involved claimed that the woman was actually in the eighth to tenth week of gestation. It is uncertain how the board would have decided, had it viewed abortion as an option. What is clear is that the privacy rights of the infected man were deemed more important than the interest of his wife in knowing of her potential exposure.

For many observers, the article in the *Journal of the Danish Medical Association* was viewed as part of a campaign to have AIDS brought under the Venereal Diseases Act—so doing would compel the NBH to relax its confidentiality standards. The article, and the publicity that it generated, came just before the annual meeting of the Danish Medical Association, at which the issue of AIDS and confidentiality were to be discussed. Nevertheless, the Medical Association was unconvinced of the desirability of a change in the law.[39]

The demand for nonrestrictive public health measures, expressed by the gay community and endorsed by the NBH as well as by the Danish Medical Association, was echoed by other risk groups. Most of the debated restricitve measures, such as registration, affected hemophiliacs only marginally. They were already so dependent upon continued contact with the health system that registration of yet another piece of information made little difference. Only at the outset of the epidemic, when the Danish Hemophiliac Society supported the NBH call for the exclusion of gay men from the blood donor pool, did conflict emerge over the strategy of prevention. Despite the failed effort to reach an understanding in that instance, the DHS supported, albeit not very audibly, the nonrestrictive posture of the NBH. They too feared that such measures might stigmatize not only gays or intravenous drug users, but all individuals with AIDS.

Drug users themselves have publicly expressed few concerns over public health AIDS measures. Their cause has been advanced by professionals who work with them, notably social workers and doctors. Their goals have been twofold: to avoid restrictive measures, such as mandatory testing or registration, which might have the counterproductive effect of driving intravenous drug users underground; and to preserve the elements of Danish drug policy instituted before the emergence of AIDS. This has meant preserving the system of easy access to sterile syringes and needles at pharmacies, developed earlier to prevent the spread of hepatitis. With the emergence of AIDS, those who spoke on behalf of intravenous drug users could point to the wisdom of this policy. In Copenhagen, surprisingly the only urban area in Denmark where drug users are affected by HIV, seroprevalence is estimated at between 10 and 25 percent. The contrast with Sweden is striking: there, needle exchange has been fiercely resisted and the level of HIV infection among intravenous drug users is much higher.

The fact that the interests of the gay and the medical communities coincided to a large extent was critical to preventing the introduction of restrictive AIDS public health measures in Denmark. Such an alliance was rooted in the contingencies of the AIDS epidemic; it was not the result of their historic relationship, which had been an unhappy one. As late as the 1950s, Danish doctors carried out castrations on homosexual men.[40] Though the mistrust of physicians and the medical establishment is profound and widespread within the gay community, the leadership of the NDOGL recognized the necessity of overcoming past antagonisms if its own interests were to be served.

For critics of Danish AIDS policy, even the theoretical possibility of transmission provided the justification for the mandatory identification of individuals with HIV infection and for their special treatment. But for the leadership of the medical community, the putative public health benefits of introducing restrictive measures had to be balanced against the social costs. Restrictive measures might have driven the AIDS epidemic underground if infected individuals, fearful of discrimination, chose not to cooperate with public health officials. Equally important, medical leaders believed that alienating the political leadership of the gay community would subvert an alliance that was crucial to any effective campaign against AIDS. The Danish medical establishment also sought to avoid the charge of homophobia, which for the educated elite would be tantamount to an accusation of racism.

Nevertheless, there were calls for mandatory testing of high-risk groups and for registering HIV-infected individuals. As news coverage of AIDS grew, an increasing proportion of the population became concerned about its own susceptibility. Some groups, notably trade unions, voiced concerns about the safety of their members—laboratory workers, hospital porters, kindergarten teachers, social workers, and even garbage collectors— which received broad media coverage. The most visible and persistent advocacy of such an approach came from the police force, which saw in AIDS not only a threat to officers' safety but also an opportunity to press for restrictive measures to deal with drug-related problems.

Since contagious diseases have historically provoked calls for restrictions on infected individuals, it comes as no surprise that public opinion polls have shown that a large proportion of the Danish population supports such measures, despite the absence of any epidemiological justification.

An August 1987 poll found that 79 percent of the respondents believed that the treatment of AIDS should be regulated by the venereal diseases law.[41] In an important way, this finding may have been compromised by the fact that the respondents were informed neither of the restrictive aspects of the law nor of the fact that there was at that point no AIDS treatment. Another poll conducted in the same month found that 46 percent of the respondents would not preclude the possibility of using coercive measures, including quarantine, to combat AIDS, while 42 percent favored other methods.[42]

In a 1990 survey in which the respondents were asked to choose between two conflicting norms—one stressing the rights of the individual, the other collective safety—the balance shifted: 39 percent supported the required disclosure to coworkers of a colleague's HIV infection; 44 percent held that it was the individual's right to decide whether to share such information; 17 percent were undecided.[43] Respondents who were younger and better educated were less likely to favor compulsory disclosure of HIV infection and other restrictive measures. As Table 9.2 makes clear, responses varied markedly according to the political party affiliation of the respondents. Despite the fact that the Social Democratic party had joined the Radical Liberals and the Socialist People's party in supporting the policy orientation of the NBH–NDOGL alliance, a majority of its electoral base favored restrictive measures. To a large extent, this breach between the party's leadership and those who support it can be explained by the education and age of the Social Democratic electorate. As striking, those who identified with two of the nonsocialist parties—the Conservatives and the Liberals—that participated in the four-party coalition that governed in the mid-1980s, were split between advocates of restrictive and nonrestrictive approaches to AIDS. Respondents who identified with the two smaller coalition parties, the Christian People's party and the Center Democrats, clearly favored restrictive measures.

The complex balance of political forces helps to explain why so little was done to politicize the discussion of AIDS in Denmark, and why the nonrestrictive policy of the NBH was rarely subject to challenge in Parliament. Only the Christian People's party, the Center Democrats, and the Progress party might have benefited from such a move, and the Christian People's party and the Center Democrats were members of the ruling coalition. Since AIDS was not an important political concern to voters, there was little reason to upset the coalition. A few members of Parliament from the governing parties did express support for applying the measures found in the Venereal Diseases Act to AIDS, but their views were rejected by their own parties. Soon after her appointment in 1987, the first Danish minister of health, Agnete Lausten, suggested that there

Table 9.2. Political Affiliation and Policy Preference in Denmark, 1990

	Policy Preference	
Affiliation	Nonrestrictive	Restrictive
People's party	62	22
Social Democrats	40	50
Radical Liberals	57	21
Center Democrats	35	53
Liberals	39	40
Christian People's party	25	37
Conservatives	43	37
Progress party	30	56

were circumstances where she believed confidentiality should be broken to protect an unknowing partner from the risk of HIV infection. Specifically, she asserted that confidentiality should be broken in cases like those involving the infected husband who would not inform his wife. Her own advisers in the Conservative party, of which she was a member, and the press all called her to task; soon thereafter, she retracted her views.

The most persistent political voice for incorporating AIDS under the Venereal Diseases Act was the Progress party, which made several fruitless attempts to have the Parliament pass legislation to that effect. In a remarkable turn of events, it was the Venereal Diseases Act that was to become the target of challenge. Repeal of the law, first proposed by the Socialist People's party, was supported by the Social Democratic party, the Radical Liberals, and Common Course (Faelles Kurs, a populist left-wing party represented in Folketinget with four seats from 1987 to 1988). With some reservations, the Center Democrats also supported the move.

Their arguments were straightforward: the incidence of venereal diseases had been falling for a number of years, most of the effective public health measures covered by the Act were to be found in other legislative instruments, and the coercive language of the Act stood in stark contrast to the practice of STD control, which required the cooperation of the patient. Most important, and reflecting the sensitivities that had emerged out of the encounter with AIDS, it was asserted that the act served to stigmatize those with sexually transmitted diseases.

The Progress party presented a remarkable, but in its way logical, argument. If AIDS was not covered by the act, then it was superfluous. Since the party has sought to reduce red tape, it favored the repeal of the act. The minister of health opposed repeal as did her Conservative party. So, too, did the Christian People's party. When the parliamentary Health Committee finally reported on the bill, the governing parties had changed their position, accepting repeal with some reservations. Faced with the

Figure 9.1. Articles in Danish Newspapers Dealing with AIDS, 1981–1988

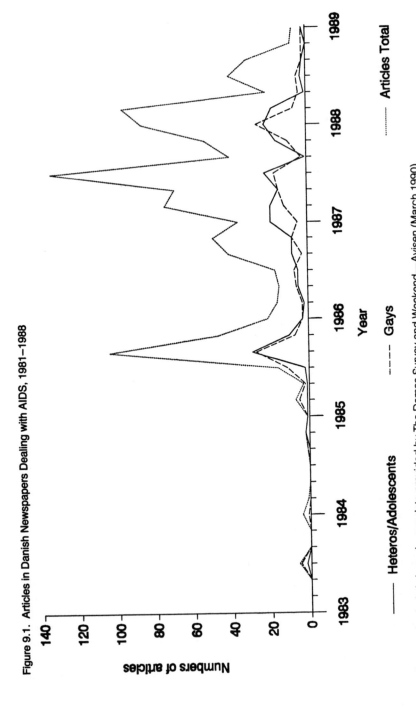

Numbers of articles

Year

——— Heteros/Adolescents   – – – Gays   ·········· Articles Total

Source: Analysis is based upon data provided by The Demos Survey and Weekend—Avisen (March 1990).

prospect of defeat, the governing parties voted for repeal. On April 7, 1988, the bill passed the Parliament unanimously.

With coercive public health measures eliminated as a potential solution to the AIDS crisis, attention shifted to education and research as the central elements of a preventive response to HIV transmission. The gay community, and gradually The medical establishment, realized the need for massive, large-scale education and counseling programs aimed at motivating people to modify their behavior in order to protect themselves and others from infection. However, it soon became obvious to both the gay and the medical communities that the necessary money would not come easily, especially in times of fiscal austerity and rule by a Conservative-led government with the explicit aim of reducing public expenditures.

Since AIDS was primarily an affliction of gay men, it was at first difficult to draw the attention of the press, much less that of the government, but without such sustained attention, it would be difficult to win support for increased funding. The medical establishment and the gay community had a common interest in de-homosexualizing AIDS: this would serve to both de-stigmatize the disease and increase general and political awareness.

One strategy was to invent what critics call "AIDSpeak."[44] "Risk behavior" replaced "risk group," thus severing the causal linkage between AIDS and homosexuality. "Promiscuous" became "sexually active," in an effort to avoid language that might imply a moral judgment of gay men who had had scores of sexual relationships. More important, however, was the effort to convince the Danish people that AIDS could spread to the population at large—in particular, to adolescents who would be at risk at the moment of their sexual debuts. If AIDS were heterosexualized, then non-stigmatized segments of the population would also begin to worry about their own susceptibility; the general public, the media, and the political leadership would then begin to consider AIDS a serious social problem meriting attention.

That this actually happened is demonstrated by an examination of media coverage of AIDS. Figure 9.1 depicts the total number of articles mentioning AIDS in ten nationwide Danish newspapers, monitored one day a week from September 1981 through December 1988. Altogether, 1,048 articles were identified, suggesting that as many as 7,500 articles mentioned AIDS in those ten newspapers during the period in question. The figure also depicts the number of articles mentioning gays and heterosexuals or adolescents in connection with the disease.

Although an initial report on AIDS appeared in December 1981, the press all but neglected AIDS for almost the next three and a half years. From 1981 until the summer of 1985, only 25 articles were recorded in the survey. By contrast, 16 articles appeared in the early summer of 1985; in August and September, coverage rose almost tenfold, to 104 articles. This dramatic increase coincided with the heterosexualization of AIDS in the press. Of the 25 articles printed prior to the summer of 1985, 17 mentioned gays, whereas only seven mentioned heterosexuals or adolescents. Of the 16 articles published during the summer of 1985, 11 mentioned gays, only two heterosexuals or adolescents. By contrast, of the 104 articles published during August and September, 27 mentioned gays whereas no less than 29 mentioned heterosexuals or adolescents. From then on, the number of articles relating AIDS to heterosexual activity or sexual contact between adolescents equaled or exceeded the number of articles dealing with AIDS and gays.

The efforts to de-homosexualize AIDS took place against an epidemiological background that did not support such a perspective. As indicated in Table 9.1, the number of Danes who acquired AIDS through heterosexual contact has been small. At the end of 1985, 68 persons with AIDS had been infected through homosexual contact. Only three had been infected through heterosexual transmission, and all three contacts belonged to a known risk group, for example, immigrants from Central Africa. In the summer of 1990, the numbers of homosexual and heterosexual cases were 480 and 47 respectively, indicating that although the number of cases traced to heterosexual contact had increased at a relatively higher rate, they still constituted a small proportion of the known cases of AIDS. In only thirteen of these cases was the source of infection not linked to sexual contact with a member of a known risk group.

Though the Danish data have never indicated a heterosexual epidemic, there were plausible medical grounds for believing that the disease might affect increasing numbers of heterosexuals at some point. After all, in Africa, the continent most seriously affected by AIDS, heterosexual contact was the most common source of transmission. It is clear, nevertheless, that the medical establishment intentionally overplayed the potential general threat of the epidemic. Even in professional public health publications, the most dramatic statistical estimates based on only weak empirical evidence were sometimes used to make extrapolations about the expected course of the epidemic. Some Danish scientists have claimed that articles questioning the official estimates were kept out of medical journals, and at medical conferences, scientists were in some instances asked to refrain from criticizing the dire projections in the presence of journalists.

Such official projections, filtered to the Danish population through the mass media, have shaped public perceptions and attitudes. More than half of all Danes responded to àn October 1985 survey that the disease would spread to all social groups, to the same degree that it was presently affecting gay men; only 24 percent disagreed. Eighty-two percent thought the disease would become more widespread; 48 percent that it would become much more so.[45] A November 1985 poll confirmed this picture.[46] AIDS, it was believed, would become the most dangerous disease in Denmark within five years.

Toward an Activist AIDS Policy

The media affects not only the general public's response to social problems but also the government's agenda.[47] Prior to the increased media attention of mid-1985, only limited political notice had been paid to AIDS. The central government's response had been limited to the following measures: in May 1983, cases of AIDS were made reportable to central health authorities, and doctors were given advice on how to deal with the disease; in September 1983, donors from high-risk groups were asked to refrain from donating blood; in mid-1984, members of high-risk groups were offered medical checkups, partially paid for by the central government; and in autumn 1984 the NBH, in collaboration with the NDOGL, produced an information package for distribution to gay men. That was all. But when media coverage of AIDS intensified, members of Folketinget began to question the government's ministers, often relying on press reports to frame the issues.

In the spring of 1985, just prior to the upsurge in media attention, the NBH submitted a report on AIDS to the minister of the interior, then responsible for public health matters. The report recommended a substantial government initiative to prevent the spread of AIDS, primarily through a massive upgrading of educational programs directed both at the population in general and at specific high-risk groups.

Minister of the Interior Britta Schall Holberg was highly displeased with the report, primarily because it proposed a substantial increase in the public health budget. Even before reading the report, she publicly declared that she did not find AIDS in Denmark deeply alarming and did not think the government should "spend public resources on more active preventive measures."[48] Furthermore, Holberg was critical of the alarmist tone being taken by some physicians, for she "saw no reason to frighten the population unnecessarily." If more resources were to be devoted to AIDS, the NBH ·would have to make cuts from other areas in its own budget.[49]

The ruling four-party coalition minority government that took over from the Social Democrats in 1982 had committed itself to reducing public expenditures. Venstre, the Liberal party, was a particularly firm advocate of budget reductions, and Britta Schall Holberg, the Liberal minister of the interior, was among the most outspoken advocates of cutbacks. Unable to reduce expenditures in 1984, she was determined to do so in the 1985 budget. Furthermore, the minister of finance insisted that she fulfill her promise to save funds.

The call for expanded AIDS expenditures was, thus, particularly unwelcome. Unable to judge whether the proposal was medically justified or just an attempt, as she put it, to "blackmail" the minister in a time of scarce resources, she found the report "naughty." The NBH, she scribbled in the margins of the report, could "go and boil its ugly head"; the episode would "only become one more death blow to the future of the NBH." When these private remarks became publicly known, the minister's position was interpreted as an arrogant refusal to do anything about a deadly epidemic.

At a moment of growing public concern about AIDS, the media were practically unanimous in their condemnation of Holberg's unwillingness to institute an active AIDS policy. She became known as "Blood Britta." Shortly after a TV interview in which she stated that "for me as a politician, there is an essential difference between a hypothesis on a piece of paper and a demonstrated fact," one tabloid headline read: "BRITTA WANTS DEAD BODIES ON HER TABLE,"[50] implying that she wanted to see the hard facts of death before she would act. She was attacked in several editorials, including one in the *Christian Daily*. The medical establishment and other interest groups joined the fray. For the first time the Socialist opposition in Folketinget—which could expect some support from the small, very pro-gay, Radical Liberal party that held the key to the parliamentary majority—paid serious attention to AIDS. The opposition leaders used these events to launch a personal campaign against the widely disliked minister.

The Danish press has almost never linked AIDS to the decline of traditional family or Christian sexual morals, and has rarely given credence to claims that AIDS embodied the punishment of God, that homosexuality was unnatural or that premarital sex was immoral. The survey of Denmark's newspapers found that only forty of almost thirteen hundred articles, half in the small *Christian Daily*, made such a linkage (some of these articles noted such a link only to reject it). It also has been unacceptable for mainstream politicians to express such viewpoints. In the heat of the political battle over AIDS funding in autumn 1985, Minister Holberg referred to Gaetan Dugas, a Canadian airline steward who was reported to have had 1,100 sexual partners. She opined that when people "have more than 1,100 sexual relationships a year, it has to go wrong"—a remark immediately denounced as indefensibly homophobic. Her observation not only misstated the facts, but more significantly represented a breach of the expectations that had come to surround public discussion of homosexuality.

With the option of discrediting those who demanded increased funding for AIDS foreclosed because of the climate of sexual tolerance, the minister of the interior had to belittle the concerns of those campaigning for more official activism. There were reasons to believe that such a strategy would work. Earlier efforts to fund campaigns geared toward the prevention of illness had largely failed. It has been hard to stimulate sufficient interest and group pressure to force such issues onto the political agenda, since calls to protect the collective good often have had a remote quality, and the benefits have been difficult to prove. Although AIDS was considered important by the general population as late as 1987, few viewed it as a major political issue.[51] In a September 1987 survey, it was ranked as the fifth most important out of twenty-three possible issues discussed by the media, surpassed by pollution, the environment, refugee problems, the upcoming general election, and the Persian Gulf; in a second survey, AIDS ranked ninth of twenty-seven issues. But less than half of one percent termed it an important political issue. With so little political salience, the governing coalition could minimize the challenge of the epidemic.

The partnership of the NBH, the NDOGL, and the socialist opposition in Folketinget were important preconditions for changing the government's response to AIDS. But the crucial role, ironically, was played by the small Danish Hemophilia Society.

For almost a year the DHS had begged for a screened or heat-treated supply of Factor VIII. The powerful Danish medical industry opposed this request, which won the support of neither the NBH nor the minister of the interior. But in September 1985, a policy window suddenly emerged.[52] The press was informed that three victims of a traffic accident, all of whom eventually died from the injuries they had sustained, might have received HIV-infected blood during emergency treatment at a Danish hospital.

One newspaper ran a front-page headline declaring "AIDS IN DONOR BLOOD: WE MAY ALL BECOME INFECTED."[53] The chairman of the DHS prepared a press release describing the plight of hemophiliacs, which he delivered by bicycle to the most important newspaper editorial staffs in the Copenhagen region. That night, he was interviewed as part of the lead story for the evening news in Denmark. Informed of the TV program by her secretary, the interior minister panicked; before the news program ended, the anchor announced that the minister had called to inform the public that the requests of the hemophiliacs would be met immediately. As is often the case in such anarchic situations, the end result was a decision that no one had called for.[54] The hemophiliacs were given suspenders as well as a belt: the minister decided to introduce screening as well as heat treatment of blood.

The hemophiliacs had skillfully managed to place the interior minister in a highly difficult political situation. At a time of increased media and political attention to AIDS, the DHS managed to stir widespread fear of the potentially dramatic consequences of failing to screen the blood supply. In contrast to the attempts of the gay community to keep sexual transmission of HIV a private matter, the DHS had defined transmission through the blood supply as a public matter and a public responsibility. It was the government's duty to provide screened or heat-treated blood products.

But more was at stake. If at some point it could be proved that a hemophiliac had become infected in the prior twelve months, when methods to inactivate HIV in Factor VIII had been available but not adopted by the Danish health authorities, it would be possible to hold the minister of the interior directly accountable.

A furious Minister Holberg tried to hold the NBH responsible for putting her in this situation, accusing the board of having failed to give her the necessary expert medical and political advice. She used the situation to launch a frontal attack on the NBH. Holberg was not the first minister to be displeased with the health board; many Social Democratic ministers before her had expressed similar sentiments. In general there was a political consensus that the NBH was a powerful, possibly too powerful, agency. As the highest medical authority in the country, the board is the most important administrative health agency; it provides expert as well as political advice to the minister and the government. The board has greater independence than do most other administrative agencies and has used this position to lobby for the medical profession. Faced with the crisis surrounding the blood supply as well as the demand for increased resources for AIDS, the minister attempted to use the dispute as an opportunity to restructure the NBH and bring it directly under her political control.

Britta Holberg was, however, the wrong minister choosing the wrong case at the wrong time. Although the Social Democrats might have agreed in principle to greater political control over the NBH, the party was unwilling to help this particular minister. Furthermore, her attempt to blame the NBH for the blood debacle was interpreted by the opposition as a form of revenge for the board's proposal to increase government resources to promote its AIDS policy. In effect, the minister laid the groundwork for her own undoing: her attack on the NBH forged a powerful alliance between the NBH, the parliamentary opposition (most notably the Social Democratic party), and, with respect to AIDS politics, the NDOGL. This alliance was nicknamed the "Pink Triangle."[55] Minister Holberg had become a political liability and ultimately was shifted from her post to the Ministry of Agriculture.

With the change in leadership in 1986, appropriations for AIDS-related central government activities were passed by Parliament and an AIDS secretariat in the NBH established. Among the first to be hired for positions in the new bureau was the then-chairman of the NDOGL, and ever since, the AIDS policy of the NBH has largely paralleled the concerns expressed by the NDOGL. This policy has been supported by all parties in Parliament except the Progress party. A 1987 parliamentary resolution states: "Folketinget acknowledges that Danish efforts to combat the AIDS illness continue to be based on voluntary cooperation; anonymity; open, direct, and honest information; the individual's assurance of confidentiality in all contacts with health authorities; as well as the desire to avoid all forms of discrimination."

The NDOGL is now involved in formulating, implementing, and administering central government AIDS activities. It has become a mainstream Danish interest group. Resources for NDOGL AIDS education and counseling in the gay community are provided for in the national budget, as are resources for the DHS. A nationwide AIDS hotline is provided for in the budget and located in the Copenhagen offices of the NDOGL. Gay concerns have also been influential in the formulation of large-scale educational programs implemented under the auspices of the NBH, providing education about the importance of condoms in preventing the transmission of HIV infection without sexual moralizing.

Most AIDS education campaigns have been open, direct, and colorful. They have been directed toward the population in general, though the main target group has been young people between the ages of thirteen and twenty-five, and have been intentionally humorous and life-affirming. Contrary to the public information campaigns in other countries, there are no symbols of death such as skulls, crosses, or a cowled man with a scythe; and there is none of the prudishness and xenophobia of the Swedish AIDS campaign. Indeed, the Swedish campaign has been particularly pointed in warning about Denmark as a source of AIDS contagion. Swedish blood donors have been warned against having sex with Danes, much as Swedish public officials tend to blame Copenhagen for all of Sweden's drug problems. One advertisement funded by the Swedish authorities, warning gay men about AIDS, carried the text: "One year ago he was in a gay club in Copenhagen." The implications were all too clear.

The NBH campaigns have been tremendously popular and have often attracted international attention. In 1987, buses in the Copenhagen region were decorated with eight-yard-long condoms. In early 1988 and again in 1989, a television campaign urged the use of condoms. Two hundred twenty-two well-known Danes—politicians, musicians, athletes, actors, authors, and entertainers—volunteered their time. The campaign also consisted of longer educational programs, among these the program showing a girl helping her boyfriend put on a condom mentioned at the outset of this chapter. An attempt by a parish minister to halt the presentation of this particular program before it was shown gave it such publicity

Table 9.3. Danish Expenditures in the National Budget Specifically Earmarked for AIDS-related Activities, 1984–1990 (in 1990 U.S. dollars)

	1984	1985	1986	1987	1988	1989	1990
AIDS testing at local government hospitals	7,609	99,129					
National AIDS hot line			88,420	260,196	327,839	297,297	339,262
Compensation to HIV-infected hemophiliacs				1,344,685	200,802	107,976	
Compensation to HIV-infected transfusion recipients					532,739	71,984	
AIDS project-pool					467,563	1,219,518	941,048
The AIDS organization of the NDOGL					127,857	112,296	128,435
NDOGL					245,879		
DHS					665,567	57,587	65,429
The HIV-positive support group					32,783	28,793[a]	33,118

SOURCES: Stabsregnskab for finansarene 1984–1989; finanslov for foraret 1990.

[a]Because of the fluctuation in the international exchange rates, it appears that the expenditures in 1989 were lower than they actually were. There was in fact no decline in expenditures for the HIV-positive support group when measured in Danish kroner.

that it was among the most widely viewed television programs in Danish history, seen by 69 percent of all Danes over the age of 18.[56] Eighty-seven percent of these viewers found the program in no way offensive; 83 percent thought it was informative.

The NBH campaigns have been paralleled by official efforts at the county and local levels, as well as by private initiatives. The Association of County Governments launched its own campaign, followed by individual county campaigns. In a collaborative effort between the Association of County Governments, the NBH and the Local Government College, fifteen key professionals from each county were trained in initiating AIDS-related activities. Most educational programs in schools, youth clubs, and sports clubs, and most programs for drug addicts, have been sponsored locally. Within the Danish system of government, these are also the agencies that would be most directly affected if HIV infection were to continue spreading.

AIDS educational programs in the schools have not stirred up noteworthy opposition, a reflection of the fact that mandatory sex education has not been controversial in Denmark for decades. (In the mid-1970s, one student's parents brought the mandatory sex education law to the European Commission of Human Rights but lost their case.) And without controversy, the Danish Railways handed out free condoms to teenagers buying Interrail tickets in the summer of 1990.

Whether enough resources have been granted for AIDS research and prevention remains a matter of debate. As Table 9.3 shows, appropriations in the national budget specifically earmarked for AIDS-related activities took off in late 1986, with a grant to the national AIDS hot line run by the NDOGL. In 1987, Parliament began to support a number of other activities, but they were not started until 1988, when AIDS-related activities in the NDOGL, the DHS, and the HIV-positive group were subsidized. In addition, an AIDS pool was established to support AIDS prevention and care projects, especially those run by voluntary organizations. Most remarkably, 44 percent of the national AIDS appropriations from 1984 to 1990 have involved compensation to HIV-infected recipients of blood transfusions and hemophiliacs. Since local authorities spend considerable sums on AIDS (precise data are thus far unavailable), Table 9.3 shows only a small fraction of the total public expenditures on AIDS during the period in question.

When appropriations for AIDS began to rise, the NDOGL became a mainstream organization involved in ordinary interest group politics, where voices pressuring for more resources have a greater chance of being heard. It has close contacts with the political parties and key bureaus. For decades, Denmark, like the Netherlands, has had a tradition of interest organization involvement in the formulation and implementation of public policy. Government officials operate together with, rather than separate from, interest groups. The role of the NDOGL has followed this familiar Danish pattern.

While the political leaders of the homosexual community have tried to de-homosexualize AIDS, they have also sought to monopolize the disease. It was important to them that as many resources as possible go to the gay community—any effective interest organization would have similar ambitions. Because of the gay monopolization of AIDS, it often has been hard for the concerns of other risk groups to be heard.

Relatively little attention was paid to the hemophiliacs until a policy window opened in the autumn of 1985. But when this occurred, because hemophiliacs were able to define their risk of infection as a public matter, they were able to pressure Parliament to accept public fiscal responsibility for their having been infected with HIV. In what was a clear political victory for the DHS in 1987, Parliament granted economic compensation to HIV-infected hemophiliacs and recipients of blood transfusions who had been infected before the serological test for exposure to HIV had been developed. No other risk group was able to define its risk of infection as a public responsibility. By privatizing sexual conduct, the gay community removed the possibility of claiming public responsibility for their infection, and even made it possible to distinguish "blameless" victims from those "responsible" for HIV infection through their own private acts. The leadership of the gay and the medical communities opposed giving economic compensation to hemophiliacs. Once again, the DHS was exceptionally skillful: Parliament had recently given economic compensation to persons who, some thirty years earlier, had participated in medical experiments with LSD without their knowledge or consent and who still suffered from the after effects. Though HIV infection and the LSD experiments were dissimilar, the DHS was able to press its concerns, in a political climate in which the hegemony of the medical profession over health policy was increasingly being questioned.

Among those at risk, intravenous drug users fared worse. Until 1986, they were not even mentioned in the NBH's policy proposals, and central government has done little on their behalf. There have been no special AIDS budget appropriations to meet their needs. Modest initiatives have been undertaken in Aarhus and Copenhagen, where the Danish drug problem is concentrated.

While sterile needles and syringes have been available, often without charge, and while there have been information campaigns directed at intravenous drug users, little has been done to expand the options for treatment. Although individual physicians increasingly prescribe methadone, there has been no national commitment: thus, there remains a shortage of detoxification programs, ambulatory services, long-term meth-

adone maintenance, residential care, and social supports for patients being treated by family doctors.[57] Unorganized and marginalized, drug users
have not been able to plead their own case, and their advocates have
failed to secure the level of resources made available to gay men and
hemophiliacs.

Conclusion: AIDS in the Mainstream

There have been noisy political battles over AIDS in Denmark. Yet,
homophobia has had little impact either on the recognition of AIDS as a
problem or on the specifics of policy adopted by the government. On the
contrary, the political-administrative system has been more sensitive to
the concerns voiced by the gay community than to the concerns of any
other risk group. The gay and medical communities concurred in their
definition of AIDS, and on the policy alternatives that followed from this
definition. Moreover, the gay community had greater resources, was better organized and had more experience in dealing with government than
other groups. In the end, the NBH and the NDOGL became the two
central actors in the formulation of central government AIDS policies.
They formed a powerful alliance, later to be bolstered by the support of
the socialist parties in Parliament. When the much weaker Danish Hemophilia Society was able to launch its successful assault on a reluctant
conservative governing coalition, winning compensation for its members,
the NDOGL became a mainstream interest group.

From an organization of outsiders, which opposed government intervention in matters affecting gay people, the advent of AIDS turned the
NDOGL into an interest group with close ties to the major political parties
and bureaus. As a result, it became deeply involved with the formulation
and implementation of government policies. As NDOGL became mainstream, AIDS became ordinary interest group politics in Denmark.

Notes

1. R. Shilts, *And the Band Played On* (New York: St. Martin's Press, 1987),
111; P. Ebbesen, M. Melbye, and R. J. Biggar, "Sex habits, recent disease, and
drug use in two groups of Danish male homosexuals," *Archives of Sexual Behavior*
13 (1984), 4.

2. S. Sontag, *Illness and Metaphor* (New York: Farrar, Straus, 1978); *AIDS
and its Metaphors* (New York: Farrar, Straus, 1988).

3. B. A. Misztal and D. Moss, eds., *Action on AIDS: National Policies in
Comparative Perspective* (New York: Greenwood Press, 1990); S. Watney, *Policing
Desire* (Minneapolis: University of Minnesota Press, 1987); D. Altman, "Legitima-
tion through disaster: AIDS and the gay movement," in *AIDS—The Burdens of*

History, ed. E. Fee and D. M. Fox (Berkeley: University of California Press, 1988); M. Gronfors and O. Stalstrom, "Power, prestige, profits: AIDS and the oppression of homosexual people." *Acta Sociologica* 30 (1987).

4. O. Listhaug, *Nordiske Vaerdier* (working paper). (Universitetet i Trondheim, 1987).

5. R. Estes, *The Social Progress of Nations* (New York: Praeger, 1984); S. Abizadeh and A. Basilevsky, "Socioeconomic classification of countries: A maximum likelihood factor analysis technique," *Social Science Research* 15 (1986).

6. R. Veenhoven, *Conditions of Happiness* (Dordrect: Reidel, 1984); J. Stoetzel, *Les valeurs du temps present: une enquête européenne* (Paris: PUF, 1983); R. Inglehart and J.-R. Rabier, "If you're unhappy, this must be Belgium," *Public Opinion* (1985).

7. Listhaug, *Nordiske Vaerdier.*

8. Stoetzel, *Valeurs.*

9. *Politiken* (July 7, 1990). However, the fertility rate of Danish women is above the EEC average.

10. Stoetzel, *Valeurs.*

11. Inglehart, *Culture Shift* (Princeton: Princeton University Press, 1990).

12. G. Mosse, *Nationalism and Sexuality* (Madison: University of Wisconsin Press, 1985).

13. Sometimes the adaptability may be carried too far, as was the Allied opinion of the Danish politics of collaboration during the German occupation from 1940 to 1945.

14. P. Svensson and L. Togeby, *Hojrebolge?* (Aarhus: Politica, 1991).

15. J. Elklit and O. Tonsgaard, eds., *To Folketingsvalg* (Aarhus: Politica, 1989). I am grateful to my colleagues in the election studies group at the Institute of Political Science, Aarhus University, for agreeing to include this issue in their survey.

16. Thus, for instance, Jews are fully assimilated in Danish society. When participating in public life, they are never identified, and they seldom present themselves as Jewish, with the exception of the Chief Rabbi of the Copenhagen temple. Most Danes would be surprised to learn that well-known public figures with last names like Meyerheim, Rubenstein, Metz, Salomonsen, Israel, Koppel, and Nathan may be Jewish or of Jewish descent.

17. While there is a gay night life scene in Denmark, even in the greater Copenhagen area with a population of close to 1.8 million people, there are only some five bars and a single discotheque catering primarily to gay people. In Aarhus, the second largest city, with a population of 260,000, there is only one gay bar/disco open three days a week.

18. OECD, *National Accounts Vol II, 1976–1988* (Paris: OECD, 1990).

19. H. Zachariae, *Konssygdomme efter antibiotika og piller* (Copenhagen: Belingske Leksikon Bibliotek, 1974).

20. A. Brandt, *No Magic Bullet* (New York: Oxford University Press, 1985).

21. Zachariae, *Konssygdomme.*

22. H. Jorgensen, "AIDS—myter, skraemmemiddel og homopolitik," *Pan* 30 (1983).

23. *Folketingets Forhandlinger* (1985–86), columns 4920–4921.

24. *Folketingets Forhandlinger* (1985–86), columns 9796–9797.

25. K. Poulsgaard, "AIDS og asbest." *Aktuelt* (April 7, 1986).

26. *Folketingets Forhandlinger* (1985–86), columns 9797–9798.

27. R. Bayer, *Private Acts, Social Consequences* (New York: Free Press, 1989).

28. M. Melbye, ed., "AIDS and Other Sexually Transmitted Diseases in the Arctic Regions," *Arctic Medical Research* 49, Suppl. 3 (1990).

29. R. Bayer, L. H. Lumey, and L. Wan, "The American, British and Dutch Responses to Unlinked Seroprevalence Studies: An International Comparison," *AIDS* 4 (1990).

30. T. Wisborg and G. Brattebo, "HIV-screening af gravide," *Ugeskrift for laeger* 150 (1988), 15; S. Kroon, B. Kvinesdal, and A. G. Poulsen, "Rutine-maessing HIV-testing af gravide er ingen garanti mod AIDS-smittede born." *Ugeskrift for laeger* 9 (1988), 150.

31. Kroon et al., "Rutinemaessig HIV-testing."

32. According to a recent survey, this policy coincides with the opinion of the overwhelming majority of the population. The respondents were confronted with two claims: one that stressed an individualistic norm of requiring consent of individuals to use organs for transplantation after their deaths; the alternative stressed a more collectivist norm: the rights of living sick persons to obtain lifesaving organs. Less than one-quarter of the respondents (24 percent) supported the latter claim, while 67 percent supported the former. Remarkably few were in doubt (3.8 percent responded "Don't know" and 5.1 percent chose "Don't agree with any of the two claims"). The survey was even more remarkable in that the distribution of the answers did not correspond with the distribution of the respondents on four other questions concerning individual rights versus collective responsibility. And there was no variation with respect to education, party preference, occupation, and public/private sector employment. J. Poulsen, "Hjertets ejer," *Weekend Avisen* (August 31–September 1, 1990).

33. *Jyllands-Posten* (December 1, 1986).

34. *Jyllands-Posten* (April 6, 1987).

35. This dynamic was repeated in 1990 when the press focused on a proposal by Falck, the largest private ambulance corps in Denmark, to exclude persons above the age of sixty from taking out ambulance insurance if they had not taken out insurance before they turned sixty. The proposal was met by a storm of protest, most of it misunderstood. The company was thought to be unwilling to insure old people as such, which was not the case. With the population growing older, the company wanted people to be act on the principle of social solidarity, to take out insurance before they would benefit from it most, in old age. Less than twenty-four hours after it had first been covered in the press, the director withdrew the proposal after a corporate crisis meeting on a Saturday morning.

36. *Folketingets Forhandlinger* (1986–87), columns 13442–13443.

37. A.-M. Worm, C. S. Peterson, and J. Sondergaard, "AIDS-dilemma," *Ugeskrift for laeger* 35 (1987).

38. L. de Neergaard, "Svar," *Ugeskrift for laeger* 35 (1987).

39. Not only had the doctors strategically waited ten months to publish their

story, one newspaper later discovered that the husband's adviser at the hospital had a different version of the story than the doctors'. He claims that the man was depressed about the situation and deeply concerned about his family. Furthermore, the patient belonged to a religious community which forbids the use of contraception. The man felt unable to break the news to his wife and the adviser suggested that the hospital could be helpful in this situation. According to the adviser, the doctors were unwilling to accept this arrangement. Cf. A. Brockenhuus-Schack and P. Birch Eriksen, *AIDS—mellem linierne* (Copenhagen: Sommer og Sorensen, 1989).

40. E. Albaek and K. Hansen, *Velkommen pa prutten* (Aarhus: GRUS, 1981).

41. *Observa—Jyllands-Posten* (August 13, 1987).

42. *Gallup—Berlingske Tidende* (August 22, 1987).

43. J. Poulsen, "AIDS er politisk dynamit," *Weenend Avisen* (May 4–9, 1990). I am grateful to Jorgen Poulsen for including the AIDS issue in his survey.

44. Shilts, *Band*, 315.

45. *Gallup—Berlingske Tidende* (August 22, 1987).

46. *Observa—Jyllands-Posten* (November 28, 1985).

47. J. Kingdon, *Agendas, Alternatives, and Public Policies* (Boston: Little, Brown, 1984).

48. *Politiken* (June 6, 1985).

49. *Ekstra Bladet* (June 26, 1985).

50. *Ekstra Bladet* (September 14, 1985).

51. Elklit and Tonsgaard, *Folketingsvalg*.

52. Kingdon, *Agendas*.

53. "AIDS i donorblod: Vi kan alle blive smittet" (Aids in Donor Blood: We May All Become Infected), *BT* (September 3, 1985).

54. M. D. Cohen, J. G. March, and J. P. Olsen, "A Garbage Can Model of Organizational Choice," *Administrative Science Ouarterly* 17 (1972) 1–25; Kingdon, *Agendas*.

55. A. Brockenhuus-Schack and P. Birch Eriksen, *AIDS—Mellem Linierne* (Copenhagen: Sommer og Sørensen, 1988).

56. *Observa—Jyllands-Posten* (February 25, 1988).

57. Peter Ege, "Stofmisbrug og HIV infektion." *Ugeskrift for laeger* 151 (1989), 616–618.

Chapter 10 # Sweden: The Power of the Moral(istic) Left

Benny Henriksson and Hasse Ytterberg

Sweden has a reputation for being liberal, tolerant, open-minded, caring, egalitarian, and concerned about violations of human rights. Why, then, is Swedish AIDS policy marked by open isolation of some who are HIV-positive, compulsory testing, the reluctance to initiate needle exchange programs, and prejudiced mass information campaigns—initiatives one would anticipate in such bastions of authoritarianism as Cuba or Bavaria? Why has AIDS provoked a contain-and-control response from a government famous for its defense of a welfare policy that protects marginalized groups against conservative ideologies?

"The HIV Man"

In February 1990, a single HIV-infected man became a national scourge. Social workers, infectious disease officers (IDO) and police officers, aided by the tabloid press, presented Sweden with a picture of an extremely dangerous terrorist, against whom innocent citizens had to be protected. Actually, the central figure in this story is a rather confused drug user. Many years earlier, the authorities had given up on efforts to wean him from drug use. In 1990, they became interested in him again for one reason only: he was HIV-positive, a fact that by itself would not have created a situation of moral panic. But this man had another secret, which would become critical in the process of creating the picture of a desperado: seven years earlier, he had been convicted of sexually abusing teenage boys.

"Contagious Rapist Released," read the indignant headline of an article in *Svenska Dagbladet.*[1] The story told the tale of a forty-five-year-old HIV-positive man who had been sentenced to isolation in a hospital because he had been assaulting young boys. What the story did *not* note was the fact that the sentence had been imposed years before, long before the man knew about his HIV infection.

The infectious disease officer of Stockholm who requested his isolation did so because he believed that the man's history demonstrated a potential public hazard. The County Administrative Court[2] of Stockholm, and

317

later the Administrative Court of Appeal, agreed and imposed isolation. After serving part of his sentence at a major psychiatric hospital in Stockholm, he was transferred to Gothenburg, where he resided. There, the local infectious disease officer decided to release him, since apart from his HIV infection, he did not have any contagious diseases and seemed to pose no other threat. His release provoked Stockholm's IDO, who informed the media that this dangerous individual might once again seek out a healthy adolescent who would become HIV-infected.

One week after its initial story, *Svenska Dagbladet* reported that day-care centers in Stockholm had begun to lock their doors because of the information "that a released HIV-infected man was in the neighborhood." Rumor about the "HIV Man's" presence reached the Office of Social Workers in Stockholm, which in turn called every day-care center in its district. A teacher at one center told the press: "We informed the parents about the situation and saw to it that no children went home on their own."[3] The tabloid *Aftonbladet* wrote about "parents in fright," and about social workers and policemen who complained that Swedish laws protecting confidentiality prevented them from discovering the potential predator's identity. An ambiguous statement by Minister of Health and Social Affairs Ingela Thalén addressed the importance of providing parents with "accurate information." To the readers of *Aftonbladet* there could be but one meaning to the minister's remark: parents had a right to know more about the man who could put their children at risk.[4]

On February 20, 1990, the tabloid *Expressen* cited a police officer who declared: "I seriously want to warn against this man. He is extremely dangerous. I know him well."[5] The next day, the newspaper continued its alarmist coverage. Under the headline "Are Children to be Sacrificed for the Sake of the HIV Man?" the same officer stated: "There is no reason for hysteria, but rather for increased vigilance, particularly around schools. The main ambition of the forty-five-year-old man is to get himself into relationships with small boys; he makes no secret of that."[6]

That same day, the *Aftonbladet* headline blared "He will Strike Again—Anytime," while reporting that the "HIV Man" had locked himself in a public toilet with a man ten years his junior—the implication being that they were engaged in unsafe sexual acts.[7] Despite this, the story complained, the IDO could not intervene. Another tabloid, *Expressen*, reinforced the sense of imminent danger by telling its readers that the "HIV Man" had held a sixteen-year-old boy as his "prisoner," neglecting to state that it was recounting an event that had occurred in the past.[8]

Days later, the forty-five-year-old man was apprehended by the police while trying to buy drugs. The infectious disease officer of Stockholm once again isolated him, after a ruling by the National Board of Health and Welfare that reversed the Gothenberg IDO's decision to release him. But for those who had been provoked by the threat of this hounded individual, that was not enough. "The fact that the runaway is caught does not mean that order has been restored. Everything that has happened to him during the past two months reveals how helpless our society is against the HIV-infected man."[9] In the face of such panic, Minister of Health and Social Affairs Thalén called for the creation of clinics to isolate presumably dangerous HIV-infected people.[10] There was serious talk of turning an island in the Swedish archipelago into a kind of AIDS prison.

When, months later, the "HIV Man" eluded his captors, his identity was revealed by the *Aftonbladet*, thus breaking a longstanding principle of Swedish journalism that protects the confidentiality of the accused.[11] (Not even during the trial of the man charged with murdering Prime Minister Olof Palme was the name of the accused published.) The press ombudsman did not challenge this departure from convention, nor was there significant challenge to the efforts to isolate the "HIV Man." The justice ombudsman reviewed the episode and found no basis for criticism. No objections were raised by the media, political parties, or human rights advocates. Only a physician who works with AIDS patients and the lawyer who defended the rights of the "HIV Man" complained.

The tale of the "HIV Man" reveals a great deal about Swedish thinking on AIDS and about the breadth of consensus regarding policies that in other nations would have provoked real controversy. The history of Sweden's AIDS policy suggests the profound contradictions within the conception of the humane welfare state.

At Risk

The first confirmed case of AIDS was reported in Sweden in 1983, although one patient who died in 1982 as the result of an unidentified immune deficiency disease has been retrospectively diagnosed. By the end of 1990, 487 cases had been confirmed among adults, and only four children had been diagnosed.[12] The vast majority of the cases (72 percent) have been among gay and bisexual men. HIV infection came late to intravenous drug users, and by mid-1990 only twelve cases had been recorded among them (see Table 10.1). Measured in terms of the rate of AIDS cases per million inhabitants, Swenden ranks low in Europe. Its forty-eight cases per million stand in striking contrast to France (173), Spain (135), and its Nordic neighbor Denmark (112).

Swedish AIDS Policy: The Beginnings

Since the mid-1980s, Swedish government has taken seriously the challenge of AIDS. The expenditure of public resources, especially for AIDS

Table 10.1. AIDS Cases by Year of Report and Category of Risk Exposure for Sweden, 1982–1990

Risk category	1982	1983	1984	1985	1986	1987	1988	1989	1990	Total
Homosexual/bisexual activity	1	5	11	34	24	60	54	90	90	369
Homosexual/bisexual activity and IVDU					n/a					
IVDU	0	0	0	0	10	0	1	0	6	17
Blood products	0	1	0	4	2	14	14	13	9	56
Heterosexual activity	0	0	0	2	0	9	12	13	23	59
Mother to child	0	0	0	0	0	0	3	0	1	4
Other/unknown	0	0	0	0	0	0	1	1	2	4
Total cases	1	6	11	40	36	83	85	117	131	509

SOURCE: National Bacteriological Laboratory (SBL).

prevention, has been especially striking, given the number of reported cases. For fiscal year 1990–1991, the budget explicitly designated for AIDS programs was 230 million Swedish crowns, approximately $38 million,[13] and total expenditure on national and local AIDS programs was more than double that amount. Discrimination against HIV-infected persons has not been a widespread problem. HIV-positive schoolchildren have not been barred from school. HIV-infected persons and those with AIDS get generally good hospital care, reflecting the virtual absence of discrimination in the health care system and universal coverage of the cost of health care by the welfare state.

It was not the government, however, that undertook the first efforts to prevent the spread of AIDS. Rather, it was the Swedish Federation for Gay and Lesbian Rights (RFSL) that spearheaded the campaign and pressed the authorities to act. In Sweden, gay men and lesbians are relatively well organized. The RFSL, founded in 1950, today has twenty-five local chapters throughout the country. Since the end of the 1970s, the RFSL has been recognized by the government as the group representing gay interests and as the organization with which it must negotiate on matters affecting gay concerns. In 1978, the age of consent for homosexual and heterosexual relations was made the same: fifteen years of age. In the same year, a parliamentary commission was appointed to investigate the living conditions of gays and lesbians, and one year later homosexuality was removed from the official classification of diseases. In 1987, anti-discrimination legislation was enacted, and in 1988, gay men and lesbians were included in the cohabitation act that provides social rights for unmarried couples.

The well-established role of the RFSL and the existence of a gay and lesbian subculture in Sweden's larger cities has had a profound impact on AIDS prevention. Even before the AIDS epidemic began, the RFSL had organized health examinations for gay men in Stockholm and Gothenberg, primarily because of the epidemic of hepatitis B. Since gay men had complained of their treatment in public clinics, it was decided that only gay physicians and gay male nurses would provide the needed services. These clinics, subsequently incorporated in the public health system, regarded educating gay men about venereal diseases as a critical part of their work.

As early as January 1983, well before government authorities paid attention to AIDS, the RFSL and a few physicians recommended that gay men not donate blood. The RFSL saw its recommendation as dictated by the need to protect the blood supply, at a time when the cause of AIDS was still unknown. Interestingly, this statement, made two months before the Centers for Disease Control in the United States delivered a similar recommendation, provoked the National Board of Health and Welfare

(Socialstyrelsen) to charge that the RFSL was creating hysteria. Even suggesting that tainted blood could be a source of disease might prevent people from donating, the board claimed, and might frighten those in need of transfusions.

The first public discussion of AIDS in Sweden was organized by the RFSL during Gay Pride Week in the summer of 1983. A year later, it produced the first Swedish pamphlet on the use of condoms and the avoidance of penetrative sex as strategies of AIDS prevention. Although the pamphlet's principal message was "Sex is Great; Don't Let AIDS Stop You," some within the gay community saw it as hostile to sexual pleasure, as "sex negative." But such opposition paled in significance when compared to the antagonism of the government, which refused to provide even modest financial help.

As concern about AIDS intensified, a number of organizations emerged to provide counseling and support to members of high-risk groups and to persons with HIV infection and confirmed AIDS. Gay and bisexual men as well as drug users organized support groups for those who were infected. Local chapters of the RFSL, and later Body Positive, actively promoted prevention by organizing safe-sex workshops.

In 1986, a group of gay physicians created the Noah's Ark Foundation, loosely patterned after New York City's Gay Men's Health Crisis, which mobilized volunteers to assist those with AIDS and HIV infection. Noah's Ark also operates the national AIDS Hot Line. It has been chosen by the Swedish Red Cross to distribute the resources it contributes to the struggle aginst AIDS, over $2 million a year, and also receives funds from the government. For some in the gay community, the funding of Noah's Ark represents an effort on the part of the Red Cross and the government to create an alternative to the RFSL, which has been more aggressive in its sexual politics and which has invested in educational efforts openly directed at gay men.

Government Policy: AIDS as an Infectious Disease

Not until 1985, almost two years after the epidemic began in Sweden—and the moment when it became clear to Swedish officials that heterosexual transmission of HIV was possible—did the government react by appointing an AIDS Delegation, headed by the minister of health and social affairs. Although the delegation's official role was to coordinate public efforts to stop the spread of HIV, it effectively established political dominance over AIDS. Politicians, joined by medical and epidemiological experts, became the architects of national AIDS policy. By bringing representatives of all political parties into the delegation, the government was able to neutralize whatever conflict might have been voiced in Parliament. Across the political spectrum, from the conservatives to the Communists, there has been a policy of consensus on AIDS.

The government's decision to act when concern was mounting about heterosexual transmission, and when Swedish tabloids had begun to publish articles calling for decisive action to prevent the spread of the "gay plague," provoked anxiety among the most politically active segments of the gay community. The first decision of the AIDS Delegation only confirmed those fears. It called for defining HIV infection as a venereal disease covered by the Infectious Diseases Act (IDA), a recommendation approved by Parliament. This decision—rare among the industrialized democracies—brought into play a number of legal restrictions. The act states that infected people must be registered, that contact tracing must be carried out, and that a person can be isolated in a hospital when his physician believes he is not following instructions deemed important to prevent the spread of disease. Although in recent decades the act had become almost a dead letter, it was now being revived for AIDS.

Under the stipulations of the act, individuals who believe that they have been exposed to an infectious condition must report to a physician for examination. In the case of possible exposure to HIV, the law could thus be read to require any individual who has had sexual relations with a partner who might be infected to get a medical examination and an HIV test. During the examination, the physician is obliged to determine the potential source of infection and the identities of those who may have been subsequently exposed by the patient. All those named in this process of contact tracing can be subject to mandatory testing if they refuse to take the HIV test voluntarily.[14]

Despite the statutory provisions of the IDA, individuals have not been tested solely on the basis of risk group membership. Even in the case of contact tracing, there are few reported cases of mandatory testing. Most individuals identified through contact tracing agree to be tested, reflecting the success of the health authorities' efforts to portray the HIV antibody test as beneficial. In addition, many physicians choose not to enforce the letter of the law, relying instead on their patients' reports that they always practice safe sex.

Mandatory testing is also permitted by a special 1988 act on HIV infection in criminal cases. Under the law, those guilty of sexual assault may be tested against their will in order to inform their victims about the possibility of their having contracted HIV infection as the result of an assault. When the HIV status of an accused may be relevant to a determination of whether an assault should be classified as aggravated, the penal code also permits a compulsory HIV test.[15]

If a physician determines that an individual is infected with HIV, the doctor must report this finding to the National Bacteriological Laboratory as well as to the local IDO. In lieu of the patient's name, a unique numerical identifier is used, which includes the date and county of birth and the sex of the individual; this serves as the prefix for each citizen's personal identity number. In the case of those with HIV infection, the county of residence and risk group to which the individual belongs are added. It is not normally possible to use this code to identify a particular person; indeed, that is the argument used by the government in rejecting the accusation that it has created a register of HIV-infected individuals. However, in rural areas only one or two persons might have the same code, thus making identification possible. Furthermore, those with access to other registries such as social security files or drug abuse records who are especially determined may compare them to determine the identity of the infected person.[16] As a result, the Swedish agency responsible for data control has classified the HIV file as listing "identified individuals."

This system of reporting is fully consonant with the Swedish tradition of keeping extensive records about the population. Church records dating back hundreds of years note births, deaths, and changes in residence; the Swedish state itself maintains detailed files on all citizens, each with a common civic registration number. City authorities also maintain extensive records, including social security and school records. Such record-keeping, which in other nations might be the source of deep concern over intrusions into one's privacy, is made possible by a high level of trust in government, a widely held conviction that the state serves the interest of the people. Hence, the creation of a special file on HIV-infected cases has provoked virtually no protest.

Nevertheless, many physicians, especially those who work at sexually transmitted disease clinics, believe the reporting requirements discourage individuals in need of care. At one clinic, doctors note that the waiting room is crowded with gay and bisexual men when it is known that the clinic will protect the anonymity of its patients and almost empty when it is believed that the law on reporting will be enforced.[17]

The treating physician must also inform the infected patient of behavioral regulations promulgated by the National Board of Health and Welfare for persons with HIV infection. Such individuals must seek regular medical examinations, inform all potential sexual partners not known to be infected about their HIV status regardless of the nature of the sexual acts involved, and tell physicians and dentists who are treating them of their infection as well as of any condition for which they are being treated. There has even been discussion of creating a formal contract indicating agreement with these behavioral expectations that all infected persons would have to sign, a copy of which would be included in the patient's medical file.

The treating physician is obligated by the IDA to determine whether the patient can be expected to adhere to these norms of behavior. When it is suspected that someone has failed or is unlikely to comply, the physician must inform the local infectious disease officer, who is empowered to examine all medical and social records relevant to the investigation of the case. When the IDO determines that the infected person has, in fact, failed to follow the rules of the National Board of Health and Welfare, police and social work authorities must be notified. In turn, they must report back to the IDO if they observe noncompliant behavior.[18]

This extraordinary system which turns the physician into a confessor linked to the state agencies of control has only been brought to bear in a few instances. Some gay men who have not told their sexual partners of their HIV infection have been warned by their physicians that they were courting legal problems, regardless of whether they practice safer sex; in other instances, physicians have only warned their patients who engage in unprotected sex. Warnings have been more common with intravenous drug users, a smaller and essentially voiceless group in Sweden. Such flexibility has softened the harsher aspects of the law, but to those concerned about the rights of individuals with HIV infection it suggests the possibility of arbitrary enforcement. It is the specter of a rigid enforcement of the law, demanded by police, social workers, and right-wing groups, that is most troubling.

The prospect of isolation, the ultimate sanction available under the Infectious Diseases Act, is what makes the Swedish approach to AIDS so striking. The IDO may ask a county administrative court to impose such restrictions simply on the basis of suspicion; there need be no evidence that an individual has deliberately spread disease. If an infected drug user informs his physician that he does not plan to use condoms, this is sufficient basis for a court to issue an isolation order of three months, which may be extended for an additional six months and then, indefinitely, for further six-month terms.[19]

The case of the "HIV Man" shows a willingness to use this power of control. So too does the case of Ylva, a prostitute sentenced to isolation on the basis of testimony by social workers and the police who saw her on the streets frequented by sex workers in Stockholm after it was known that she was infected with HIV. Ylva claimed that she only engaged in safer sex, but that was deemed irrelevant. As of 1990, seven individuals had been isolated, all either drug addicts or female prostitutes, and one had been incarcerated for four years.

The regulation under which these individuals were isolated is currently being challenged as an unconstitutional limitation on the right to privacy and freedom of movement beyond what is required to prevent the spread of HIV infection.[20] It has also been criticized by some of Sweden's leading AIDS experts, among them Sven Britton, the chief physician at the Roslagstull's Hospital in Stockholm.[21]

> Prostitutes are isolated for the sake of convenience. Applied to HIV infection, the isolation paragraph of the Infectious Disease Act becomes arbitrarily cruel, astronomically dear, and epidemiologically inefficient. One of the prostitutes has now been isolated for four years at the cost of 13 million Swedish crowns, money that could have been used better for the care of sick people. . . . I appeal above all to the Minister of Health and Social Affairs to reconsider this situation.[22]

Rather than recognize the compelling nature of such criticism, the government has proposed authorizing other, presumably more compliant, health professionals to supervise those who are isolated.[23]

Sweden's willingness to rely upon repressive measures to control AIDS is further demonstrated by the 1987 parliamentary decision—unique in Europe—to close gay bathhouses (saunas). Beginning in 1986, a number of journalists began to target these settings. "Shut the AIDS brothels" became a rallying cry. These reports mobilized police and social workers, who were appalled at the existence of such institutions. Under pressure to show that it could do something to stem the AIDS epidemic, the government quickly moved to close the bathhouses. This move, which permitted the authorities to distinguish between responsible or "good" homosexuality and promiscuous or "bad" homosexuality, was supported by some voices on the left, who saw the bathhouses as oppressive milieus. In the end, few opposed the government's decision. The gay media, the RSFL, and some social researchers who saw closure as repressive and counterproductive were lonely dissenters.

Those in the gay community who opposed shutting the bathhouses were not unmindful of the potential for the spread of HIV infection. They recognized that a too-casual attitude toward sexually transmitted diseases in the 1970s, inspired by the availability of antibiotics, had permitted the hepatitis B epidemic to take hold among gay men; they had targeted the bathhouses and porno video clubs for safer-sex education. These efforts, which reflected the capacity for self-organized counseling programs, were ignored in the government's decision to close an institution that could have served as an important locus for AIDS prevention.

Swedish policy toward drug users also demonstrates the appeal of harsh measures and official reluctance to consider policies that could effectively reduce the spread of HIV infection through unorthodox means.

In Sweden, there are an estimated 12,000 intravenous drug users. Most are addicted to amphetamines: in Stockholm, for example, it is estimated that there are 3,000 amphetamine users, 400 heroin users, and 600 who use a mixture of drugs. Over 60 percent of the heroin users are thought to be infected with HIV, in sharp contrast to the 4 percent among amphetamine users and 12 percent among mixed drug users. There were twelve known cases of AIDS among drug users as of mid-1990. Two years earlier, there had been none.

Sweden is internationally known for its restrictive drug policy, with severe sentences for selling drugs. But Sweden has also has one of the best voluntary drug prevention and treatment programs in the world. Two decades ago, there was much discussion about the failures of compulsory alcohol and drug treatment programs. Drug users' organizations, trade unions, and youth organizations spearheaded the move for radical reform. As a result of such pressure, many new ventures based on voluntary treatment received considerable support from the government.

The AIDS epidemic spawned a new alliance on drugs. The opposition in Parliament, conservatives, and leading social workers called upon the government to take stronger measures to control the drug problem. In 1987, a government committee published a report that proposed broader reliance on compulsory treatment programs for adult Swedes. Despite some evidence that such efforts would be counterproductive, the government agreed with the committee's finding, and also proposed that the duration of legally required treatment be extended from two to six months.

For the government, the fight against drug use is among the highest priorities in the struggle against AIDS, and compulsory treatment of drug users is a principal tool. In the 1988–89 budget of the minister of health and social affairs, almost $6 million was allocated to aid local authorities in establishing new facilities for compulsory treatment of HIV-positive drug users. Despite recognizing the severity of the drug problem and the importance of preventing the spread of HIV infection among drug users, the government has been unwilling to endorse the distribution of sterile injection equipment to intravenous drug users, fearing that such an effort would legitimize drug use.

Only reluctantly did the government approve a pilot needle exchange project in the city of Lund, in which drug users are given clean needles upon request.[24] The Lund experiment was praised by Alec Carlberg, secretary general of the Swedish Association for Aid to Drug Users (RFHL), who stated in a 1990 article in *Dagens Nyheter:*

> Giving access to clean needles would be a health care measure with a positive approach to drug users that could lead to continued treatment. Most important, however, is preventing the spread of [HIV] infection. In Lund, no drug user has been infected since November 1986, when the

[needle exchange project] began. In Stockholm 155 drug users have been infected during the same period.[25]

The chief physician in the Drug Users' Treatment Department in Lund, Kerstin Tunving, who had won the right to establish the pilot program in Lund and another in Malmö only after a bitter struggle, has repeatedly criticized the government's reluctance to develop similar programs elsewhere.[26] Writing in the *Svenska Dagbladet,* she declared in 1990:

> The current Swedish health care policy will undoubtedly lead to an increased spread of HIV infection among injecting drug users and through them to the population at large. There is a shortage of clean needles in Stockholm, no matter what official, orthodox drug policy says. . . .[27]

But needle exchange proposals have met with opposition from the government and those responsible for its drug use prevention efforts. Anna Lindh, president of the Social Democratic Youth Organization, a member of Parliament, and president of the government's Committee for Drug Use Prevention, has stressed the benefits of compulsory treatment, while proudly defending Sweden's refusal to follow the path of other European countries.[28] Gertrud Sigurdsen, president of the AIDS Delegation, and a former minister of health and social affairs, has sought to undermine the legitimacy of physicians who have argued for needle exchange:

> The struggle against drugs is first of all a question for the National Board of Health and Welfare, the National Police Authority, the National Board of State Penitentiaries, the National Customs Authority, etc., with the support from organizations like Parents Against Drugs, FMN, etc. The struggle against drugs is [only] to a very small extent a medical problem.[29]

The reluctance to support needle exchange, coupled with the imposition of the controls mandated under the Infectious Disease Act, has produced a set of contain-and-control policies that distinguish Sweden from most European nations. In October 1989, Sweden was the only member of the Council of Europe not to endorse the recommendation of the Committee of Ministers concerning ethical rules for the treatment of HIV infection. This is the first time that Sweden has been unwilling to support a Council of Europe document dealing with human rights and discrimination.[30]

The unique posture of the Swedish government has provoked some physicians to protest. The organization Doctors Against AIDS has demanded that HIV infection be removed from the list of diseases regulated by the Infectious Diseases Act. In place of the provisions that afford IDOs extraordinary discretion in incarcerating individuals with HIV, the group has proposed that cases involving the intentional spread of HIV infection be handled within the framework of the penal code.[31] The Association of Infectious Disease Physicians has also sought to limit the scope of the government's power to isolate by restricting such interventions to the most extreme circumstances.[32]

Whatever the role of containing AIDS through the Infectious Diseases Act, Swedish authorities have also recognized that the changes in sexual practices required by efforts to control the spread of HIV infection necessitate strategies that reach deep into Swedish society. The government's policy centers on the strong encouragement of voluntary HIV testing.

The gay community in Sweden has been deeply suspicious of this strategy. As early as 1985, the RFSL declared its opposition to testing without the promise of absolute anonymity; at that time, there were already intimations that the government might elect to include the AIDS under the Infectious Disease Act. Additionally, when testing first became available on a large-scale basis, virtually no counseling services were provided to those who tested positive. Indeed, many people learned their HIV status by mail.

Although there have been periodic calls for mandatory testing of the entire population, an approach supported by the National Organization for a Drug Free Society,[33] the government has rejected such an extreme measure. Instead, it has relied on a campaign of persuasion. Each year since 1985, when testing began, approximately 350,000 tests have been done: by 1990, there had been more than 1,500,000 HIV tests,[34] in addition to more than two million tests performed on blood donors during this period.[35] No one knows exactly how many individuals have been tested, since some people have been tested more than once, but it is clear that a substantial proportion of the 8.4 million Swedes has followed the government's advice.

Among those most at risk for HIV infection, heroin users and gay and bisexual men, the rates of testing have been very different. Approximately 80 percent of heroin users have been tested; much of this testing can be attributed to a large prison-based study of HIV infection. In addition, some drug treatment programs require HIV testing as a condition of admission.

Awareness of the risks, both psychological and social, associated with being identified as HIV-infected has inhibited gay and bisexual men from seeking testing. Between 1985 and 1987, approximately ten thousand tests were administered to those who had engaged in homosexual behavior. Since 1987, the numbers of gay men seeking the test have declined each year. Thus, a small fraction of those most at risk have elected to take the test. Concern evoked by the legal regime surrounding HIV infection has functioned as a significant disincentive.

Those being tested are mostly the worried well, the population toward whom the government's information campaign is directed. "AIDS is spreading," the campaign declares; "everybody can get it. If you for a moment think that you may have been exposed to the virus you should take the test."

The issue of testing within the health care setting has surfaced for reasons having little to do with the modification of behavior linked to the spread of HIV infection. Many physicians and nurses have demanded that patients be tested prior to surgery so that they can take additional protective precautions. Such efforts, which reflect an unwillingness to accept recommendations regarding the adoption of general precautionary strategies, have been rejected by the National Board of Health and Welfare. Nonetheless, there have been reports of testing in hospitals without patient consent. In 1989, the RFSL learned that all patients coming to the country's largest gynecology clinic were being routinely tested. Although the hospital within which the clinic is located has promised to change its policies, it is unclear how widespread this practice of involuntary testing is.

Paralleling the discussion of testing patients has been the question of whether health care workers should be tested. There has been little support for such screening, although in some hospital wards the personnel have collectively decided to undergo testing, in the belief that a negative test result would enhance their chances of receiving insurance compensation in case of an accidental transmission of HIV from an infected patient.

In other employment settings, things have been very different. Testing has typically been offered on a voluntary basis by physicians working for private firms. The Swedish International Development Authority recommends testing to those of its employees who serve in areas of the world with high levels of HIV infection.

Some private employers have sought to make an HIV test a condition of employment, a practice that is legal in Sweden. The most noted case of HIV testing involved SAS, the national airline. On the basis of a preliminary study that suggested the possibility of early neurological problems in individuals with asymptomatic HIV infection, SAS decided to screen and exclude all new pilots who were infected.[36] This was done despite the recommendations of an expert panel convened by the World Health Organization, which found no justification for such exclusionary policies.[37] Critics argue that the policy of SAS, as well as some other firms, is best explained by a desire to avoid investing in new employees who might eventually become too sick to work because of their HIV infection.

Insurance companies also have had an economic interest in identifying individuals with HIV infection. Application forms for life insurance now routinely request information about HIV status.[38] If an applicant is believed to belong to a group at increased risk, an HIV test is required. Those who are infected may still be insured, although the premium charged may be as much as five hundred times the normal rate and HIV-positive individuals must have their health status reevaluated every five years. As with private employers, the government has not regulated such screening practices.

In a country so committed to the identification of those with HIV infection, it is not surprising that there would be calls for the compulsory screening of immigrants. The government has rejected such a course, although in 1990 the AIDS Delegation recommended that all refugees seeking to establish residence in Sweden be offered an HIV test. When asked about the government's response to those who refused to be tested, the first secretary of the AIDS Delegation responded that experience indicated that such refusals "hardly occur"—in seeking asylum, who would dare to appear uncooperative?[39] Ironically, and reflecting the tensions within Swedish ideology provoked by AIDS, there have been instances where a positive HIV test proved to be the decisive element in the decision to offer asylum.

Screening to track the epidemiology of HIV infection has also been undertaken through anonymous or blinded seroprevalence studies. As in the case of United States, but unlike in many European countries, such studies, which cannot be used to identify particular individuals, because the samples are stripped of personal identifiers, have provoked no controversy.

Prevention, Education, and the De-homosexualization of AIDS

The AIDS epidemic has reinforced anti-gay sentiments in almost every society, even those that have sought to counteract the legacy of discrimination and prejudice. In Sweden, where the ideology of the welfare state makes the overt expression of homophobia unacceptable and where charges of neglect of the needs of those infected with HIV would have been a profound embarrassment, the influence of homophobia has taken a unique form—one that in other societies might be viewed as an expression of both concern and tolerance. Every effort has been made by the state to sever the link between homosexuality and AIDS—thus the striking absence on the AIDS Delegation of any expert on homosexuality or gay culture. This policy is reflected as well in the effort to de-homosexualize AIDS through a process of "normalization." The carefully created picture is one of AIDS spreading from those initially affected to the broader society. AIDS thus concerns everyone; hence, the centrally coordinated AIDS prevention campaign has been directed at the "general population." A strategy that many would consider enlightened has excluded from its central focus men who have engaged in homosexual activity: gay and bisexual men all but disappeared from the official campaign to control the spread of HIV.

The government has relegated primary responsibility for educating gay men to the RFSL, providing a modest sum—only $350,000 of the $27 million AIDS prevention budget—to support its efforts. Despite the authorities' early refusal of support to the RFSL, because its initiatives were too explicit, since the initiation of the government's major AIDS campaign in 1986 there has been no attempt by the AIDS Delegation to censor such material.

The RFSL has not concerned itself with the issue of multiple sexual partners—a matter it has viewed as irrelevant if not pernicious—but instead with encouraging the adoption of safer sex, the use of condoms, and alternatives to penetrative sex. Celebrating the pleasure of homosexual relations, the RFSL has popularized the slogan: "On me but not in me."

While in other countries, such as Germany and France, a similar demarcation of responsibilities has been lauded, to the RFSL the creation of separate realms—the government addressing itself to the heterosexual world, the RFSL speaking to the community of gay men—has been problematic. This approach ignored the fact that many men who have had sex with other men do not consider themselves gay, and so are beyond the reach of the RFSL. It represents an abdication of the responsibility of government to address the needs of all Swedes. And it conveys the message that the mention of homosexuality and gay relationships, especially in messages directed to adolescents, is to be officially avoided.

While the government has undertaken a number of steps to meet the needs of gay men confronted by the AIDS crisis, its efforts distinguish sharply between "good" and "bad" homosexuals. Both the government and the local authorities have provided grants to establish gay centers in Sweden's larger cities. The newest, which opened in Stockholm in 1988—shortly after the bathhouses were shut—includes a restaurant, disco, pubs, and meeting rooms. As part of its effort to support "good" gays, the government also introduced legislation in 1988 that recognizes a marriage-like status for gay and lesbian couples and bars discrimination on the basis of sexual orientation. [40]

To fully appreciate the extent of the government's efforts to create an AIDS prevention program that offends no one, that would win the support of the average Swede—that would be "lagom," extremely middle-of-the-road—it is necessary to look more closely at the media campaign launched in 1986.

From its initial plans, made public in 1985, it appeared that the AIDS Delegation would follow the tradition of the relatively successful drug prevention campaigns implemented in the early 1970s. But a year later, the development of an AIDS policy changed dramatically. A large multinational advertising firm, the Ted Bates Agency, with no prior experience in health, social program, or prevention campaigns, received a multimillion-dollar contract to carry out the information campaign.

From the outset, the firm's strategy was clear: keep the campaign clean; make AIDS a "decent" disease. As a consequence, it elected to develop messages that appealed only to heterosexuals, justifying this approach on the unpersuasive grounds that messages that also spoke to gay and bisexual men would be screened out by the general population.

Four broad themes emerged from the campaign. Foremost was the message of fear, which was meant to motivate behavioral change, and to encourage a recognition that taking the HIV test was crucial to self-protection, the protection of others, and the conquest of AIDS-related anxiety. "Love can make you crazy. Chlamydia can make you sterile. HIV can make you dead. Use Condoms." stated one advertisement. A poster warning about potential infections as the result of a sexual encounter during a visit to New York stated: "Could I have been HIV-infected? The answer is yes even if the risk is small. You should have a test. An HIV test is just a blood sample and you can have it done anonymously and free of charge. But will you dare? Or rather, how long can you take not knowing? Precisely because the risk of your being infected is so small, you will surely find the courage sooner or later. For your own sake and for your dear ones."

This AIDS campaign also sought to create a sense of guilt in those whose histories might expose them to HIV, a sense that becoming infected was one's own fault. "You decide yourself whether or not you will become HIV-infected. . . . We know how this infection is spread. . . . Now it is up to you to decide whether you will become HIV-infected or not."

In addition, the campaign stressed the dangers of promiscuity. "Between the two of you there will be 23 altogether," says one poster. "She has slept with Bjorn, Staffan, Lasse, Joakim, Per, and a few others. He has had even more. If they go to bed with each other, they are (in a sense) going to bed with all their previous sex partners. And if only one of them was an HIV carrier, HIV could also be accompanying them now." Another poster warned: "What did you say your name was, again? HIV never introduces itself. . . . You can never see if a person is infected with HIV. Someone who has been recently infected would not know himself. . . . We cannot protect you but you can." One of the few advertisements addressed to gay men reiterates this theme. "He will get all his experiences. Perhaps you have only had a few sexual encounters with other men before. The one you go to bed with, on the other hand, may have had many partners before you."

Finally, there was the repeated theme of the risk posed by encountering foreigners or by having sex in foreign places. "What happened in New York in 1983, Peter?" read a poster addressed to heterosexual men. Another, targeted to women, depicted a Swedish blonde next to a darker-skinned male and stated: "What you bring back is not love. Several Swedish girls have been infected with HIV while vacationing abroad. No one could have imagined that the beautiful young man she fell in love with was an HIV-infected drug user." Here was xenophobia tinged with racial prejudice. In an advertisement that warned women about bisexual men, the theme of contamination from abroad—Denmark, in this instance—was also present. "A year ago he was at a gay club in Copenhagen. Now you love each other, but how were things before you met?"

Only in 1989—after protests by the RFSL and others angered by the emphasis upon anxiety, testing, and "sex-negative themes," and after a critical review by the National Audit Bureau—did the content and style of the educational messages change.[41] From the bureau's perspective, the entire campaign had been too moralistic, had mistakenly focused on matters of life-style (the number of sexual partners) rather than upon the adoption of safer-sex practices, and had wrongly failed to concentrate on those most at risk of HIV infection.

The shift is evident in a 1989 poster which, using the backdrop of an erotic oriental print, declares: "Eroticism is dead. Long live eroticism! . . . Sex and eroticism are, and always have been, lovely games. But they are also games of love. HIV and AIDS will never change that. As long as we are for eroticism at home, and as long as we use condoms when we are hunting for it with others." In 1990, a playful campaign focused on the importance of condom use, another shift away from the dour warnings of the past.

AIDS and the Moral Left

What accounts for the fearful tone of the AIDS campaign in Sweden, at least until 1989? How is that tone connected to the emphasis on contain-and-control reflected in the extension of the Infectious Disease Act to AIDS and the resistance to needle exchange programs for intravenous drug users?

Analyses of the politics of AIDS have focused on the significance of the Moral Right. Concepts such as moral panic and homophobia have been analyzed in the context of the influence of Christian as well as politically conservative ideologies, to explain negative attitudes toward safer-sex education.[42] For Sweden, however, it is necessary to focus on the influence of what can best be termed the Moral (or Moralistic) Left—the influence of the ideologies that have shaped the Swedish welfare state. Two critical factors emerge: the early labor movement's wish to raise a

new human being, "the down-to-earth, reliable worker,"[43] and the socialists' urge to put life in order for all people.[44]

It was vital for the early labor movement to dissociate itself from what it
viewed as the hedonistic, depraved upper classes. Hard work, economiz-
ing, a sober life, and an absence of dissipation were critical. This agenda
left scant room for individualism, pleasure, or eroticism. Instead, labor's
ideology entailed an obsession with purity. Many of the early socialists
dreamed of building a new egalitarian society, where children would have
a fine upbringing, with good schools and good housing. A social security
net would provide protection in case of mishaps. Beginning in the 1940s,
the metaphor of a People's Home most influenced the social democratic
architects of the good society, foremost among them Gunnar and Alva
Myrdal. They sought to combine science, reason, and political reform in
building the new welfare state.

Driving this worldview was the belief that social problems would disappear in the new society. In the "blue-and-yellow socialism" of Sweden
there would be no poverty, no problems associated with alcohol or drugs,
no oppression of women, no prostitution, and no sexual deviation. In
putting this vision to work, the labor movement emphasized the role of
the state as the Good Parent who would put its children's lives in order.
An idealized conception of social engineering, guided by the vision of the
problem-free welfare state, took hold.

These same ideals informed the Swedish government's response to
AIDS. The government, acting as a Good Parent, was driven to look after
its children, to assure that they behaved, that they didn't drink too much,
that they didn't visit "bad" places, that they were not involved with dangerous sexuality. Neither hatred of homosexuals nor erotophobia, but
instead a profound commitment to the well-ordered life, inspired Swedish
socialists. If gay men sought anonymous sex in the back rooms of bars,
bathhouses or parks, it could only be because they were oppressed and so
had not developed the political consciousness necessary to live normal
lives. Their self-affirming sexual exuberance was interpreted as a kind of
false consciousness.

The AIDS epidemic provided the Swedish government with evidence of
society's failure to raise its children properly; corrective education and
formal social control were needed. The lecture came in the form of closing
the gay bathhouses, a campaign to encourage HIV testing and promote
stable relationships, and to discourage prostitution, drug use, and the promiscuity of gay men. An elaborate set of regulations reinforced the lesson
that was to closely govern the life of those who were HIV-positive. They
authorize quarantine for those who fail—or even those, like the "HIV Man"
who are suspected of failing—to obey the established rules of behavior.

Notes

1. "Smittad våldtäktsman släpps fri" (Contagious rapist released), *Svenska Dagbladet* (February 10, 1990).
2. Länsrätten.
3. "Fritidshem låstes mot smittad man" (Day-care center locked against infected man), *Svenska Dagbladet* (February 1990).
4. *Aftonbladet* (February 20, 1990). "Ministern: Läkaren kan tvångsisolera mannen innan han gör nya brott" (The minister of health and social affairs: "The physician can isolate the man before he commits new crimes").
5. "Hivmannen ar extremt farlig: Polisen varnar skolor pa Östermalm" (The HIV Man is extremely dangerous: The police warn the schools in the eastern parts of Stockholm), *Expressen* (February 20, 1990).
6. "Ska barn offras för hivmannens skull?" (Are children to be sacrificed for the sake of the HIV Man?), *Expressen* (February 21, 1990).
7. "Hivmannen: 'Lås in mig': Han slår till igen, när som helst" (The HIV Man: "Lock me up": He will strike again, any time), *Aftonbladet* (February 21, 1990).
8. "Sextonårig pojke hans fånge" (Sixteen-year-old-boy his prisoner), *Expressen* (February 22, 1990).
9. Editorial in *Expressen* (February 27, 1990).
10. "Specialklinik för hivmannen?" (Special clinic for the HIV Man?), *Dagens Nyheter* (March 9, 1990).
11. "Läkaren lät hivmannen fly" (The doctor let the HIV Man escape), *Aftonbladet* (May 10, 1990).
12. EPID-aktuellt 6 (1990). (Statistics from the National Bacteriological Laboratory, the SBL).
13. Regeringens proposition 1987/88:79 om atgarder mot aids (Government's bill on measures against AIDS.), 48.
14. Infectious Diseases Act Section 25. (25 § Smittskyddslagen.)
15. Penal Code of Procedure Chapter 28 Section 26. (26 kap 12 § rättegångsbalken.)
16. Infectious Diseases Act Section 26. (26 § smittskyddslagen.)
17. Statement from Dr. Anders Karlsson, physician at the hospital of Sodersjukhuset, during a public hearing with the Minister of Health and Social Affairs on May 25, 1987.
18. Infectious Diseases Act Section 30. (30 § smittskyddslagen.)
19. Infectious Diseases Act Section 40–41. (40–41 §§ smittskyddslagen.)
20. Hasse Ytterberg, "Lynchjustis vid HIV" (Lynch justice for HIV positives), *Svenska Dagbladet*, (August 21, 1990).
21. "AIDS ut ur smittskyddslagen" (AIDS out of the Infectious Diseases Act), *Dagen Nyheter*, (March 22, 1988).
22. "Socialministern måste stoppa HIV-isoleringen" (The minister of health and social affairs must stop HIV isolation), *Aftonbladet*, (April 25, 1990).
23. Skrivelse fran socialstyrelsen till socialdepartementet, 28 March 1990 (Dnr

s90/1752/S). (Letter from the National Board of Health and Welfare to the Ministry of Health and Social Affairs.) Skrivelse fram smittskyddslakarmyndigheten i Stockholm till socialdepartementet (August 28, 1990) (Dnr s90/3901/S). Letter from the IDO of Stockholm to the Ministry of Health and Social Affairs.

24. Kerstin Tunving, et al.: "Fria sprutor till narkomaner—akutåtgärd för att begransa hivsmitta," Läkartidningen 10, *Swedish Medical Journal* (1987).

25. "Cyniskt inte ge fria sprutor" (It is cynical not to give out free needles), *Dagens Nyheter* (October 10, 1990).

26. "Rena sprutor räddar liv medan tid är, det ar cyniskt att inte vilja använda alla till buds stående medel att bekampa aids, menar Kerstin Tunving." (Clean needles save lives while there is still time, it is cynical not to use all possible ways of fighting AIDS," says Kerstin Tunving), *Svenska Dagbladet* (July 23, 1990). Bengt Ljungberg, Kerstin Tunving, and Bengt Andersson, "Rena sprutor till narkomaner, hivforebyggande atgarder enligt Lunda-modellen" (Clean needles to drug users, HIV preventative measures according to the Lund model.) (Studentlitteratur, 1989).

27. "Viktigast stoppa HIV/aidsepidemin" (Most important is stopping the HIV/AIDS epidemic), *Svenska Dagbladet* (June 22, 1990).

28. " 'Vansinne liberalisera drogpolitiken,' säger Anna Lindh." ("To liberalize drug policy would be insane," says Anna Lindh) *Svenska Dagbladet* (June 12, 1990).

29. "Kampen mot narkotika inte läkarnas bord." (The struggle against drugs is not the task of physicians.) *Dagens Nyheter* (November 11, 1989).

30. "Tjurskallig strutspolitik," *Dagens Nyheter* (August 17, 1990). (Article on Swedish AIDS policy by Benny Henriksson.)

31. Skrivelse från Läkare mot aids till socialdepartementet (June 7, 1990) (Dnr 590/2833/S). (Letter from "Doctors Against AIDS" to the Minstry of Health and Social Affairs.)

32. Skrivelse till socialdepartementet fran Svenska Infektionsläkarföreningen den 15 juni 1990 till socialdepartementet (Dnr S90/3056/S). (Letter from the Association of the Infectious Diseases Physicians to the Ministry of Health and Social Affairs.)

33. "Aidstest för ålla RNS-krav" ("AIDS test for everybody demands the RNS"), *Dagens Nyheter* (December 1, 1989).

34. Figures from Birgitta Eriksson at the National Bacteriological Laboratory.

35. Socialstyrelsen informerar om AIDS 2 (1988). (Information from the National Board of Health and Welfare.)

36. "SAS testar alla nya piloter" ("The SAS tests all new pilots"), *Svenska Dagbladet* (April 14, 1988).

37. Global Program on AIDS, World Health Organization.

38. Ylva Brune, Bengt-Erik Ginsburg, Luis Abascal, *Rädd för det okända. Hiv/aids i ett mångkulturellt samhälle.* (Stockholm: Brevskolan, 1990).

39. "AIDS tvingar fram ny praxis" ("AIDS brings out new policies"), *Svenska Dagbladet* (April 14, 1988).

40. Regeringens proposition om homosexuellas situation i samhället (1987). (Government's bill on the situation for homosexuals in Swedish society.)

41. Riksrevisionsverket (National Audit Bureau): Informationskampanjen om hiv/aids. Samhällsinformation som styrmedel. Regeringsuppdrag. (Stockholm: Riksrevisionsverket, 1989).

42. Jeffrey Weeks, "Love in a Cold Climate," and Simon Watney, "AIDS, 'Moral Panic,' Theory and Homophobia," in *Social Aspects of AIDS* ed. Peter Aggleton and Hilary Homans, (East Sussex, Eng.: The Palmer Press, 1988).

43. Ronny Ambjörnsson, *Den Skötsamme Arbetaren (The Well-Behaved Worker.)* (Stockholm: Carlsson, 1988).

44. Yvonne Hirdman, *Att lägga livet till rätta. Studier i svensk folkhemspolitik (To Put Life in Order for People. Studies of Swedish Welfare Policy)* Stockholm: Carlsson, 1989).

Chapter 11 Japan: AIDS as a "Non-issue"

Eric A. Feldman and Shohei Yonemoto

On July 28, 1985, as the story of Rock Hudson's battle with AIDS dominated morning newspapers throughout the United States, another hot and humid summer day had just passed in Tokyo. Hudson's illness, while described as "the single most important event in the history of the epidemic" by American AIDS experts, only reinforced the perception of most Japanese that AIDS was foreign, distant, and unthreatening.[1]

Yet, at that time, HIV had already entered Japan, and was slowly spreading through certain parts of the population. As the result of the widespread use of contaminated blood products, HIV had become a serious threat to hemophiliacs. Among homosexuals, safe-sex education was rare, and the response of gay bathhouse operators was to exclude all non-Japanese clientele while continuing to provide a venue for anonymous, unprotected sex. Even though Japan's first AIDS case was confirmed months prior to the news about Rock Hudson, it was to be another year and a half before Japan was rocked by its own AIDS scare.

Nonetheless, despite the failure to learn from the AIDS epidemic in the United States and Europe, the impact of AIDS in Japan has been modest (see Table 11.1). At the end of 1990, only 371 cases had been diagnosed. Of these, 280 were hemophiliacs, 44 were homosexuals, and 23 were foreigners (including 13 foreign homosexual men).[2] Twenty-two of the remaining patients were heterosexuals; 19 were listed as "other," because the etiology of their infection had not been determined. Two homosexual patients were also intravenous drug users.

The number of people who had tested HIV-positive was correspondingly low. As of the end of 1990, there were 1,412 indentified HIV carriers in Japan, including 1,204 hemophiliacs, 58 women, and 799 who were below the age of thirty.[3] Official figures concerning HIV-positive people represent only the number of tests that yielded positive results. More important are estimates of the number of infected individuals.

A Yokohama City University study predicts that in 1992 there will be 2,000 HIV-positive hemophiliacs and 150 to 195 AIDS patients, 1,350 to 2,350 HIV-positive homosexuals and 132 to 151 AIDS patients, 150 HIV-positive heterosexuals and 50 AIDS patients, and an unpredictable number of patients and carriers of unknown etiology.[4] The Ministry of Health

Table 11.1. AIDS Cases by Year of Report and Category of Risk Exposure for Japan, 1985–1990

Risk category	1985	1986	1987	1988	1989	1990	Total
Homosexual/bisexual activity	6	4	8	10	6	10	44
Homosexual/bisexual activity and IVDU	0	0	0	0	0	0	0
IVDU	0	0	0	0	0	0	0
Blood products	0	0	0	0	0	0	280[a]
Heterosexual activity	0	0	5	7	3	8	23
Mother to child0	0	0	0	0	0	1	
Other/unknown	0	1	1	2	7	13	24
Total cases	6	5	14	19	16	31	371

SOURCE: Ministry of Health and Welfare.

[a]No year by year statistics for hemophiliacs are included; hemophiliacs were made an exception to reporting requirements by the AIDS Prevention Law.

and Welfare (MHW) estimates that in 1992 there will be about 260 to 300 AIDS patients and about 3,000 carriers.[5] Other estimates place the current number of HIV-positive people at between 2,000 and 4,000.[6]

At Risk

The epidemiological profile of Japan's HIV population, like the number of actual AIDS cases and HIV-positive individuals, provides a sharp contrast to the West. AIDS in Japan is not characterized by a high incidence of infection among homosexuals, it is not a disease of the urban poor, and it has not been rapidly spreading among those who use intravenous drugs. Instead, the majority of those who are HIV-positive or have died from AIDS are hemophiliacs.

Among those who are HIV-positive or have AIDS, there is a clear popular delineation between "innocent" and "guilty" victims. Hemophiliacs are perceived as the passive recipients of tainted blood; homosexuals are seen as putting themselves at risk by their own behavior. This distinction has made it easier for hemophilia groups to speak out effectively against AIDS policy, while it has inhibited an already muted gay voice.

The use of controlled substances is severely limited by various factors, among them two laws, the Narcotics Control Law (Mayaku Torishimari Ho) and the Stimulant ("Awakening Drug") Law (Kakuseizai Torishimari Ho). The legislation imposes a jail sentence of three years to life and a fine of up to $33,000 (in 1990 U.S. dollars) for anyone caught buying or selling a controlled narcotic. In 1988, 20,716 people were arrested for violating the Stimulant Law, but only a small percentage of these violators administered the drugs intravenously.[7] Other socioeconomic factors, such as a low unemployment rate and a high overall standard of living, also contribute to the infrequency of narcotics abuse.

The culture of intravenous drug use in Japan is quite different from that in the United States. Drug users tend to be private, shooting up alone rather than in urban shooting galleries, which accounts for the limited sharing of needles. The only available figures regarding AIDS and drug abuse, based on data collected before February 1989, indicate that out of 2,753 drug users given an HIV test, only one tested positive.[8] Thus, drug abuse is currently an insignificant factor in the spread of AIDS in Japan.

Gay relationships have long been a part of Japanese social life, whether through samurai connoisseurship of homosexuality, relations between priests and acolytes, male prostitution in urban centers, or the involvement of actors with the patrons of Kabuki theater. In contemporary Japan, however, acceptance of homosexuality has been largely replaced by discrimination and exclusion.

Although neither homosexuality nor sodomy are illegal, few legal protections are afforded to gays. Fear that gossip could harm their professional and personal lives keeps gays from being open about their personal choices. When jobs or housing are denied on the basis of sexual preference, gays will rarely go to court.

In fact, "homosexuality" is an ambiguous term in Japan, since many gays have conformed to social pressures. These men would be labeled "bisexual" in the West, living with wives and children but frequenting gay bars and bathhouses. As it becomes more socially acceptable to marry later or not at all, there is speculation that this behavior may slowly be changing.

Information about gays and bisexuals in Japan is sparse. The editors of *Barazoku*, a gay magazine with a circulation of 70,000, believe that one out of every four or five gay men buys each issue; other guesses range from 30,000 to 500,000. Yet considering that in addition to *Barazoku*, there are four other popular gay magazines (*Adon, Zaigei, Sabu,* and *Samson,* each popular among a particular readership), that nationwide there are approximately 2,000 gay venues and 50 bathhouses, and that Japan's population is over 120 million, an even higher number is possible.

Anecdotal evidence suggests that anal intercourse, a particularly risky behavior in terms of AIDS transmission, is far less common in Japan than in many Western nations. While a gay phone counseling service reports a trend toward more frequent anal sex, it has been estimated that less than 25 percent of the patrons of gay bathhouses engage in anal intercourse. One explanation for this may be widespread intestinal problems in Japan and the correspondingly high frequency of hemorrhoids, which could make anal sex painful.

Cultural differences in the way affection and sexual desire are expressed may also be important. Homosexuals in Japan have fewer sexual partners than their Western counterparts and are less drawn to aggressive forms of sex. Like heterosexuals, Japanese homosexuals read a great deal of pornography and have vividly erotic sexual imaginations, which they partly substitute for actual physical contact.

Among those who do engage in anal sex, condom use has not become the norm. For many, safe sex has come to mean relations among Japanese only, and avoiding "unsafe" Westerners has substituted for a change in life-style.[9]

One explanation for the absence of safe-sex practices is the lack of a gay community in Japan. Membership in gay organizations is minuscule; most operate out of personal apartments, without lounges or social areas. Leaders of these groups talk enviously of organizations in the West, their multimillion-dollar budgets and their well-appointed offices. During the past several years, the number of groups concerned with gay issues has increased. The largest is AIDS Action, part of the International Lesbian and Gay Association. International Friends is a gay support group, and the HIV–Human Rights Information Center unites hemophiliacs and homosexuals critical of government AIDS policy. Not alarmed by the statistics on AIDS and HIV infection among gay men, and anxious to avoid publicity, these groups have played a limited role in the development of a national AIDS policy and the creation of safe-sex education programs.

The central role of hemophiliacs in Japan's AIDS policy was cemented in 1983, when reports from the United States indicated that AIDS could be contracted from contaminated blood products. The hemophilia associations demanded that the Ministry of Health and Welfare stop importing U.S. blood products, which accounted for 90 percent of Japan's supply. They feared that this blood might carry the as yet undiscovered agent responsible for AIDS and wanted blood products produced exclusively from domestic supplies. But the MHW, falsely encouraged by the fact that no AIDS cases had yet been reported in Japan, did little.[10]

A year later, several laboratories in the United States had announced procedures that allowed blood plasma to be heat treated, and thereby purified, without destroying its effectiveness. The Japanese MHW adopted these procedures for hemophilia patients in 1985. But for Japanese hemophiliacs, it was already too late.

Of a hemophiliac population estimated to number about 5,000, between 30 and 60 percent are now thought to be HIV carriers. A 1984 study testing 1,747 hemophiliacs found 678 to be HIV-positive, a rate of 38.8 percent.[11] In contrast to the 1 percent of AIDS cases traced to hemophiliacs in the United States, about half of Japan's AIDS cases are hemophilia-related.[12] Besides being the only Japanese group significantly touched by AIDS, hemophiliacs also consider themselves victims of Japanese prejudice against those with genetic disorders. Prior to AIDS, they were sometimes excluded from schools, had difficulty finding jobs, and were treated as unable to function in other aspects of daily life. These difficulties have been a unifying factor for hemophiliacs, who have successfully organized around such issues as insurance coverage for medical expenses and self-administration of medication. Consequently, despite the stigma of hemophilia and the personal tragedies many hemophiliacs have had to endure as a result of HIV, hemophilia associations have been remarkably successful in organizing their members to oppose aspects of the Japanese government's AIDS policy.

The Two Prostitutes

While the first AIDS case was officially reported in Japan in March 1985, AIDS attracted little attention until almost two years later, when two female AIDS patients were diagnosed.

The first case involved a Filipina working as a bar hostess and prostitute in Nagano Prefecture. She apparently went to a clinic for a blood test, was discovered to have HIV, and was quickly sent back to the Philippines in November 1986, on the pretext that her visa had expired. Few details were reported in the press, and there was no protest over why and how her test results reached the immigration authorities. The government conducted follow-up tests in the bar where she worked, in an attempt to discover whether she had infected any of her customers. Although there is no public information concerning how many of her possible clients were identified or tested, no other AIDS patients or carriers have been publicly linked to this case.

Then, on January 18, 1987, a Japanese woman was discovered to be dying of AIDS. "Japan's First Female AIDS Victim Is Kobe Prostitute," announced an English-language daily, and other papers ran similar stories. The victim was said to be a twenty-nine-year-old prostitute particularly drawn to Caucasian men, and was supposedly exposed to AIDS by a Greek sailor. The MHW's AIDS Surveillance Committee added that she had practiced prostitution for several years after she was infected. The patient died two days later, making it impossible to learn about all of the places where she had worked and rendering the local health authority unable to trace accurately the course of her infection. Although neither the national nor local government released the name or address of the patient, two widely circulated weekly tabloids discovered the location of her funeral. They ran a photograph of her displayed on her coffin (a custom at Japanese funerals), and published it, along with a story on where she had worked and her struggle with AIDS. The woman's outraged parents sued for invasion of privacy.

Attorneys for the magazines argued that government reports saying an unnamed woman had died of AIDS delivered an inadequate warning to those who may have had sexual contact with her. They asserted that publishing a photograph was a way of telling men the identity of the victim so that they would know if they had had sex with her and so should be tested for HIV. Divulging the identity of the woman, they argued, was therefore critical to curbing an AIDS epidemic, and was thus more important than the privacy of one individual.

The Osaka Regional Court issued a judgment in favor of the family in 1989.[13] The court pointed out that the local government had acted to help those who believed that they might have had sexual contact with the woman by publicizing how and where to get tested. The judges further asserted that the magazines interested in curbing the spread of AIDS could have accomplished this by publishing only the age, sex, and residence of the deceased; publishing a photograph was an ineffective and unnecessary way of educating the public. This decision was immediately appealed in the Osaka High Court, which as of late 1991 had not yet ruled in the case.

The Kobe woman's death triggered widespread fears that all Japanese, not only members of "high-risk groups," were threatened. Suddenly, every worry about AIDS generated by grim reports from the West found expression in Japan. *The Japan Times* editorialized: "Rarely has the death of a single human, unknown and indeed anonymous, aroused so much concern among people throughout our society."[14]

Between the announcement of her illness and her death, a period of only three days, 2,487 people contacted the AIDS headquarters of Hyogo Prefecture where Kobe is located. In public meetings people expressed concern about getting AIDS on trains and public places. By mid-February of 1987, 200,000 handbills, pamphlets and posters had been printed by the Kobe city government, an AIDS hot line had received over 100,000 calls, and almost 20,000 people had visited health clinics.[15]

Barely had the dust begun to settle from the Kobe case when the Japanese press was again agitated—this time because a woman in Kochi Prefecture who had tested HIV-positive was pregnant. The MHW reported that she was infected by a hemophiliac AIDS patient she had dated prior to her marriage, and that she had been advised to avoid pregnancy because it would pose a risk to her child. As late as the eighth month of her pregnancy, both the national and local health authorities continued to advise her to terminate the pregnancy. She did not do so, and thereby sparked a debate about her behavior, the first time the ethical issues related to a woman's responsibility for the health of her fetus, or attitudes toward in utero genetic defects, had surfaced in Japan. The child in Kochi was born and as of late 1991 apparently was not HIV-positive.

The Impulse to Containment

The Nagano, Kobe, and Kochi cases prodded the government to consider a national AIDS policy. Beginning in mid-January 1987, when the Kobe case was reported, there had been discussion about AIDS legislation. The Ministry of Justice pressed the MHW to implement a policy that would prevent foreigners with AIDS from entering Japan.[16] Prime Minister Nakasone, feeling public pressure as the result of the news reports of women with AIDS, ordered the Infectious Disease Department of the MHW to draft an AIDS bill immediately.

On February 19, 1987, legislation under consideration by the MHW was leaked to the press.[17] It included penalties of up to $2,000 or as much as a year in prison for AIDS patients and carriers who engaged in unsafe sex acts or donated blood.[18] Such persons could be imprisoned for six months or fined as much as $1,300 for giving false replies when examined by medical authorities, and physicians could be fined up $700 for failing to report an AIDS diagnosis to the prefectural government. The bill also included the mandatory reporting of the existence and names of all AIDS patients and individuals with HIV infection to the prefectural government,[19] the reporting of their names and addresses if they were suspected of disregarding their physician's advice and spreading the disease, and an amendment to the Immigration Act aimed at the exclusion of foreigners.[20]

Cabinet members disagreed about how stringent the AIDS bill should be. MHW officials, led by Chief of Infectious Diseases Dr. Masaharu Ito, advocated a slightly more moderate approach to legislation, to avoid alienating groups whose cooperation would be necessary for the control of AIDS. Other influential government officers, particularly conservative senior Liberal Democratic Party (LDP) politicians, insisted that the law impose stiff penalties on both physicians and patients. It was to gauge public reaction that a strong version of the legislation was leaked to the press by the MHW.

Criticism came quickly, especially from the liberal wing of the legal and medical establishments, hemophilia groups, and others concerned about human rights and public health. One general concern was that the privacy of individuals with AIDS required far more protection than the draft offered. The only law directly governing medical confidentiality, the Doctors' Law (Ishi Ho), was enacted in 1948 to prohibit physicians from allowing others to gain access to information obtained in the course of medical consultation. Physicians who violate its provisions are subject to up to seven months in jail and a $70 fine. The law prevents only lay persons from examining medical records, but allows doctors free access to the records of other physicians.

Opponents of the AIDS bill believed that this law was inappropriate when applied to testing and treating persons with HIV infection. Critics also argued that severe punishments for patients would only serve to drive away those possibly in need of medical care.[21] Groups representing hemophiliacs claimed the bill would accelerate prejudice against those with genetic defects. "The Hemophiliac Association encourages patients to openly acknowledge their illness, not to conceal it," stated Yoshiaki Ishida, chairman of the Kyoto Branch of the Hemophiliacs' Association of Japan. "We have made enormous strides in improving public understanding, but now the government's AIDS bill will turn the clock back."[22]

Pressure to reform the draft legislation may also have been exerted by certain Diet members sympathetic to physicians and the Japan Medical Association (JMA). Many physician–Diet members maintained strong ties to the JMA and served as internal lobbyists for the Association. Since physicians have traditionally enjoyed autonomy, those sympathetic to the doctors' role would have found the proposed penalties against doctors objectionable.

But tough measures were supported by the chairman of the AIDS Problem Countermeasure Subcommittee of the LDP (AIDS Mondai Taisaku), a physician and former director of the Okinawa branch of the JMA. He advocated better education regarding AIDS, stricter immigration controls to prevent infected foreigners from entering Japan, and tight government regulation of high-risk groups. Under pressure from Nakasone to act quickly, the MHW had not had the time to draft original legislation. Instead it turned to its archives of infectious disease laws in search of something that could quickly be adapted.

The first law for the control of infectious diseases in Japan, enacted in 1895, was the Infectious Disease Prevention Law. Aimed at eleven different diseases, including cholera and dysentery, the law granted broad authority to public health officials. It permitted prefectural governors to isolate particular geographic areas, stop trains, and close roads. Physicians who diagnosed one of the controlled diseases were required to make a report to the prefectural government's health bureau. The official report indicated that a patient was diagnosed, described the symptoms, and discussed the results of the physician's attempt to trace the source of the infection. Unofficially there was a close relationship between physicians and government health officials, who could obtain detailed information about patients if they so desired. When those who believed that they had come into contact with an infectious disease failed to request a medical examination, physicians or officials would sometimes require them to submit to testing. Once diagnosed, people with one of the infectious diseases would be sent to an isolation hospital until they were cured or died.

In fact, these powers were rarely exercised, since there had been few outbreaks of controlled diseases since 1895.[23] Moreover, many of the documented cases were traced either to foreign travelers in Japan or to Japanese who contracted a disease while traveling overseas.

The 1948 Venereal Disease Prevention Law represents another attempt to protect public health in Japan. The law, intended to prevent the spread of venereal disease through prostitution, gave physicians who encountered victims of venereal disease the authority to "guide them through" the medical system. Physicians could require patients to submit to medical treatment, and were either to pursue noncompliant patients themselves or else to report them to the police. Each physician was required to file a report with the district health office about the existence and address of every venereal disease patient and had to report the name and address of patients who could infect others to the prefectural governor. Most reported patients were prostitutes, who were usually ordered to abandon their trade. If the patient was not a prostitute, physicians would often provide treatment without making a report to government officials. [24]

The Prostitution Prohibition Act, passed in 1957, made prostitution a criminal offense. At that point, physicians stopped complying with the requirements of the Venereal Disease Prevention Law because they believed that the 1948 law had become antiquated in light of the 1957 act. In addition, some physicians were concerned about patient privacy, and feared that the reporting requirements would dissuade patients from making medically necessary visits. [25] To this day, the government cannot maintain accurate records on the prevalence of venereal disease; official figures are many times lower than its actual extent.

Public health officials have rarely attempted to enforce the Venereal Disease Prevention Law, since prostitution is officially outlawed. Yet prostitution continued to thrive with little official interference after it was banned. Today, many prostitutes operate from what are known as "soaplands," establishments where male customers are invited to be bathed and massaged but where a great deal more actually occurs. It was in the "soaplands" that the government feared an AIDS epidemic could begin. Not surprisingly, the MHW used the 1948 Venereal Disease Prevention Law as a model for its AIDS legislation.

Within three weeks of the draft legislation, the MHW submitted a final draft of the bill. [26] It required physicians to report, without names, the age, sex, and route of infection of all patients infected with HIV to the prefectural governor within seven days. A physician who deemed that a patient was not following medical advice and might be infecting others was to report the name and address of the patient to the prefectural governor. A physician who believed a patient had transmitted AIDS to a non-patient could give the name and address of the non-patient to the prefectural governor. Prefectural governors could recommend that people suspected of being HIV-infected and infecting other people be tested for the virus. They could also require a test for individuals who did not voluntarily comply. Punishments included fines of up to $2,000 or one year in jail for physicians or public officials who unjustifiably breached an AIDS patient's confidentiality, and a fine of up to $700 for persons who defied the prefectural governor's order to be tested, or who gave false answers to questions about AIDS asked by the prefectural authorities. [27] An amendment to the 1951 Immigration Act granted immigration authorities the power to deny entry to foreigners "who it is feared could infect a number of other people with this virus." [28] Absent from the bill were the penalties to be leveled on physicians for failure to report AIDS patients to the government, as well as penalties for spreading the disease or withholding AIDS-related information from physicians.

Like the earlier draft, this legislation was widely criticized. Foreigners complained about the potentially unfair immigration controls. Physicians questioned the ambiguity of provisions aimed at monitoring patient care by public health authorities. Hemophiliacs, again the most vocal critics, echoed earlier fears of discrimination. Yukuo Yasuda, vice chairman of the National Association of Friends of Hemophiliacs, stated: "The law would fuel people's prejudice and discrimination against AIDS victims. It treats carriers as if they were socially dangerous."[29] Citing the possibility of children with hemophilia being denied entrance to schools and being ostracized by other children, hemophiliac groups insisted that society should react to AIDS with compassion and let hemophiliacs monitor themselves.[30] The proposed AIDS law, formally introduced in the Diet on March 31, 1987, was not discussed for almost two years. This long hiatus was possible because the intitial AIDS panic sparked by the first reports of female AIDS cases had all but vanished. The political costs associated with pressing for the enactment of legislation that had provoked such controversy seemed to outweigh the benefits of such an effort. Meanwhile, the government attempted to mollify the group most vociferously protesting against the law by creating a financial relief scheme for hemophiliacs.

Hemophiliac Exceptionalism

Persistent lobbying by the hemophilia associations led to a close working relationship with Dr. Ito of the MHW and others closely involved with AIDS legislation. The hemophilia groups continued to be outspoken, hoping to gain concessions from the government; in turn, the government was searching for a way to satisfy the group most critical of the proposed law. What resulted was a system of providing financial relief to hemophiliacs affected by AIDS, lessening the sting of the AIDS bill—a method of compromise called *ame to muchi* (candy and a whip) by the Japanese.

In April 1988, the Ministry of Health and Welfare announced the establishment of a relief scheme for hemophiliacs. Funds were collected from companies selling imported blood products in Japan, which were eager to avoid costly litigation. Under the scheme, beneficiaries are separated into two groups. HIV-positive people infected by blood-clotting drugs who have AIDS-related symptoms and have stayed in the hospital for more than eight days receive $200 a month for an indefinite period. Those who have been diagnosed with AIDS receive varying amounts: those under eighteen years old receive $600 a month, while those over eighteen get $1,400 monthly. Families who have lost a hemophiliac family member to AIDS receive a flat sum of $38,000 if the victim was not the primary breadwinner, and $1,100 a month for up to ten years (minus the time the person received money as a patient) if the person was the primary breadwinner. By October 1990,

207 hemophiliacs were receiving relief; no rejected applicants had filed formal complaints.[31]

Although this scheme would appear to represent a significant concession to the hemophilia groups, they did not treat it as a major victory, because financial relief was viewed as small consolation for having been infected with HIV. At the same time, some hemophiliacs argued that the level of payment should be significantly higher. Moreover, hemophilia groups rejected the government's attempt to sidestep moral responsibility for mishandling the blood policy by calling the payment scheme relief (*kyusai*) rather than compensation (*isharyo, hosho*)—the latter implying an acknowledgment of guilt and an apology. Hemophiliacs differed about whether an apology alone or an apology coupled with a large payment would be an acceptable government response, but since neither was forthcoming, some hemophiliacs have refused to accept the proffered relief and instead have taken their grievance to the courts. Two lawsuits, filed in 1989 and still in court in late 1991, argue that the MHW and the companies that imported blood plasma into Japan in the mid-1980s ignored evidence that it could be contaminated, and so should be required adequately to compensate affected hemophiliacs.

Despite being treated as different from and more "innocent" than others who were affected by AIDS, hemophilia groups were not easily silenced. Their protest continued, but the AIDS bill was not to be defeated.

Discussion of the proposed legislation was resumed in late 1988. After deliberating for several days, the Social and Labor Committee of the Lower House of the Diet incorporated four changes into the text. In the revised measure, the national and local government were required to educate the public correctly about AIDS. The MHW and local governments must coordinate their education efforts. Cases of HIV-positive persons infected through blood products do not have to be reported to the government. And the prefectural administration cannot rely on suspicion to question or control those thought to be HIV-positive, but can only contact those with HIV whose behavior endangers others.

These revisions, like so many other aspects of the creation of an AIDS policy in Japan, resulted from the lobbying of hemophilia groups. Yet despite their exemption from most provisions of the bill, hemophiliacs did not feel victorious. Before the bill was passed, most HIV-positive hemophiliacs had already received medical care; when their identities were known to the hospitals in which they were treated, they had been reported to prefectural health authorities. For them, exemption represented little more than a hollow gesture.

The Social and Labor Committee of the Diet's Upper House appended six additional provisions. These included a government-sponsored counseling system; a call for research on drugs that could prevent and cure

AIDS; maintaining the secrecy of medical records mandated by the AIDS law; confidential AIDS testing; a prevention program for infectious and sexually transmitted diseases; and a system of blood donation within Japan, especially for hemophiliacs. While the relief fund for hemophiliac patients had already been engineered, the lawmakers also indicated their support for this scheme. In contrast to the controversy surrounding earlier drafts of the legislation, final passage caused scarcely a ripple. Most Japanese were no longer obsessed with the possible dangers of contagious foreigners; they had returned to the concerns of daily life.

The Substance of AIDS Policy Prevention Efforts

The Japanese Red Cross began to test all donated blood in 1986. Out of 13,709,401 tests conducted over the next two years, twenty-six were HIV-positive, a rate of 0.000189 percent.[32] While domestic donations account for almost all whole blood used for transfusions in Japan, more than 90 percent of blood products are imported. In response to the spread of HIV among hemophiliacs because of contaminated blood, the MHW has pushed to make Japan totally self-sufficient in its blood supply.[33]

Sex has long been a taboo subject in Japanese schools. Adolescents learn about sex on their own, and they usually do so by reading magazines and talking to friends. The magazines they read may include such standard Western fare as *Playboy*, but far more common are Japanese *manga*, book-length comic books that highlight violent, misogynistic, and sado-masochistic aspects of sexual relations.

Mainstream magazines have occasionally included safe-sex tips, but such advice is sometimes tarnished by racist comments. In *Shukan Playboy*, a weekly magazine for young men, a 1987 article stated:

> Casually ask your date if she's ever had sex with whites, blacks, Central Americans, East Africans, merchant marines, American military personnel, people with weak bodies [hemophiliacs], and homosexuals. Also inquire if she's had sex with [Japanese] men who have been abroad on business. Be wary of women who like reggae, Prince, Michael Jackson, African music, and black contemporary. Special caution is needed with women who like soul and frequent discos where blacks hang out.[34]

Along with the public interest in AIDS in 1987 came a great deal of talk about AIDS education. The Japanese Foundation for AIDS Prevention, started that year by the MHW, has commissioned a variety of AIDS education posters, but their messages are not always clear. One shows a rear view of a naked couple holding hands. "Protect your loved one from exposure to HIV," it reads. The couple pictured is Caucasian, suggesting that it is Westerners from whom one actually requires protection. Other posters are too vague to convey any useful information: one shows synchronized swimming as a metaphor for shared responsibility in sexual relations. Yet even this bland poster was rejected by high school administrators because it was considered too explicit.[35]

Within the homosexual community there has been some self-education. In 1985, *Barazoku* magazine published a special issue on safe sex; and at least four phone services with sporadic hours provide gay men advice and counseling on sexual and other matters. But those who could make the most important contribution to educating the gay community have refused to do so. Gay bar owners have rejected attempts by concerned groups to place wallet-sized cards with safe-sex information on their premises, either refusing outright or saying that this would promote sexual activity and be bad for business. Operators of gay bathhouses have also resisted attempts to distribute information about AIDS at their establishments for fear that this would drive away potential customers. Instead, most have posted notices asking foreigners not to enter the premises.

There is also concern on the part of government officials about educating businessmen who travel abroad.[36] For many years, group tours have shuttled men to Bangkok and Manila, where they deposit their golf clubs in airport luggage compartments and partake of the entertainment for which those cities are famous. As reports about the prevalence of HIV-positive prostitutes have reached Japan, it has become clear that these tours pose a serious health threat.

As with education, interest in AIDS testing peaked in 1987, when hospitals and the Prefectural Health Bureaus implemented testing programs that guaranteed anonymity and cost just $7. Many people were voluntarily tested because of their worry about being infected. The Tokyo Metropolitan Government has since publicized a $10 anonymous test through advertisements in gay magazines, and *Barazoku* magazine also runs a testing center.

Despite claims of anonymity, there is a suspicion of testing centers. The HIV–Human Rights Information Center has been conducting research about test sites to determine what type of information must be provided by a client and whether places that claim to be anonymous really are. Stories of individuals who have traveled to the United States to be tested suggest deeply felt skepticism about claims to anonymity. One other aspect of HIV testing bears mention: As a way of reassuring regular customers about the quality of services offered, some managers of "soaplands" have produced pamphlets saying that all employees have been tested and are "safe."

AIDS has had no real impact upon the delivery or financing of health care, since insurance schemes organized either around the workplace or around the place of residence provide adequate coverage for about 90 percent of the population. But the health insurance system provides no coverage for home care, and this allows hospitals to realize large profits from extended stays.

One aspect of medical ethics in Japan has had a particularly unfortunate impact on the spread of HIV. In the case of terminal illness, particularly cancer, physicians have considered it improper to disclose the diagnosis to a patient. They claim that patients who know they are terminally ill will lose hope, become depressed, and live their final days with an unnecessary burden.

In the case of HIV, some doctors have decided not to disclose information about test results to hemophiliac patients. Out of 454 hemophiliacs who responded to a 1988 survey, 106 had taken an HIV test but were not informed of the results.[37] Takeshi Abe, a physician in Tokyo who has almost 100 hemophiliac patients, says: "Until we can have a procedure to conquer AIDS, we prefer to hide the real data from the HIV test. . . . We injected the contaminated blood preparation, and they got the infection. . . . I am a criminal."[38] Physicians who treat hemophiliacs fear that if hemophiliacs are told they are HIV-positive, they might commit suicide or become irresponsible and intentionally infect others. Physicians also claim that many hemophiliacs do not want to know their test results, despite a survey that showed that 87 percent of them would prefer to know the truth.[39] Consequently, many hemophiliacs do not know that they are infected with HIV and continue to have unprotected sexual relations. At least two spouses have become infected in this manner, and have joined the suits by hemophiliacs against both the MHW and pharmaceutical companies.

There has been little if any public criticism of government spending on AIDS-related areas, partly because it is so difficult to get an accurate picture of how much is actually being spent. The only comprehensive breakdown of the AIDS budget in Japan was done by the MHW just prior to the passage of government AIDS legislation and issued to members of the press (see Table 11.2).

Being a hemophiliac in Japan has always been difficult. One prominent hemophiliac, for example, was educated at home after the high school he was planning to enter refused to admit him, despite entrance test scores far higher than those required. Since AIDS has become identified with hemophilia, such incidents of discrimination have become more common.[40]

One family reports that the teacher of their hemophiliac child demanded that the student bring evidence to school that he was not HIV-positive. When the child did so, the teacher posted the report at the entrance to the school. Other hemophiliac children have had "AIDS" written on their belongings, or are greeted with chants of "You are an AIDS patient."[41] Many adult hemophiliacs have been required by employers to show copies

Table 11.2. Total AIDS Expenditures in Japan, April 1988 and March 1989 (in 1990 U.S. dollars)

	April 1988	March 1989
AIDS basic research and development		
Research for AIDS prevention	3,923,000	6,283,000
Research to prevent HIV-positive individuals from progressing to disease[a]	1,810,000	2,900,000
Related research for AIDS vaccine	517,000	458,000
Management, etc. of blood donation	172,000	458,000
Medical drugs related to AIDS	2,586,000	3,267,000
Special research for coordination with U.S. researchers	103,000	92,000
Total	7,300,000	10,558,000
AIDS prevention policy		
Research into AIDS statistics in Japan	345,000	305,000
Government counseling for AIDS:	888,000	1,611,000
Health and Welfare counseling re: housing, etc.[a]	440,000	664,000
Educational courses for AIDS counselors[a]	0	123,000
Special courses for medical practitioners[a]	61,000	54,000
Special course for school teachers[a]	0	435,000
Total	1,233,000	1,916,000
National AIDS center—planning	733,000	1,359,000
Payment to WHO	1,457,000	2,428,000
Total	10,723,000	16,261,000

SOURCE: Ministry of Health and Welfare, unpublished press packet (October 1988).
[a]Related to the hemophiliac compensation scheme.

of HIV test results, have had to change jobs, and have been shunned by neighbors.[42] A 1988 survey found that hemophiliacs are routinely turned away by dentists, internal medicine specialists, surgeons, and pediatricians.[43] Coupled with all of the other problems HIV has brought to the hemophiliac population, this additional discrimination—not addressed by legislation—has created unnecessary additional suffering.

As early as 1985, the international press reported that Japan planned to deny entry to foreigners suspected of being HIV-positive.[44] But while the amended Immigration Act gives broad powers to exclude foreigners, it has become increasingly clear that the government has no intention of screening all foreigners entering the country. International pressure may have played a critical role here.

At the 1988 World Health Ministers' AIDS conference in London, there was a general discussion of immigration controls; the Japanese press reported that the idea was strongly criticized by Japan's allies. The government, aware of this criticism, realized that international opinion would be hostile if a restrictive immigration policy was implemented. While more extreme measures would have been seriously considered if the prevalence of AIDS in Japan had been greater, the authorities now use the powers granted by the Immigration Act to deny entry only to women who plan to work as prostitutes and who are suspected of being infected with HIV. There have been no reports about any other individuals denied entry to Japan on the basis of the AIDS law.

Westerners living in Japan have experienced various types of discrimination since the onset of fear about AIDS. Soon after the Kobe case, a black woman from the United States, living in Tokyo, was denied entry to her local public bath. Traditionally, the bathhouse is a spot where locals go to bathe (even now, many homes do not have bathing facilities) and socialize. The owner of the bathhouse was worried that the presence of a foreigner—someone who might have AIDS—would cause regular patrons to go elsewhere. The woman found a sympathetic reporter at a city newspaper, complained that her exclusion was based on race rather than nationality, and finally convinced the owner of the bathhouse to allow her access to the facilities.

Almost every foreigner living in Tokyo has experienced similar problems, or knows someone who has. Some find themselves suspiciously comfortable on a crowded rush-hour train, or else are required to show proof of a negative HIV test before obtaining employment or before swimming in a company pool. Still others hear children whispering "*gaijin* (foreigner)—AIDS" as they walk through their own neighborhoods.

Discrimination against foreign homosexuals by Japanese gay men is also widespread. Rather than identifying themselves as sharing concerns with homosexuals from other nations, many Japanese gay men and the bathhouses catering to them have adopted a policy of exclusion. Before the era of AIDS, Western men were treated as particularly desirable partners, and welcomed at entertainment establishments; now they are seen as infectious and dangerous. Almost all gay bathhouses post "Japanese Only" signs at their entranceways and in their advertisements in gay magazines. In bars and other social settings, Westerners are also avoided. Like much of the rest of Japanese society, many gay men in Japan have found it easier to view AIDS as an exclusively foreign phenomenon, thus obscuring the failure of the Japanese gay community to educate itself effectively about AIDS.

Not only have some members of the gay community in Japan engaged in discrimination against foreign gays, but Japanese homosexuals themselves have also had to confront issues of discrimination. A researcher studying sexual practices among Japanese gay men, for the purpose of learning about high-risk behavior related to AIDS, discussed his methodology and goals with members of gay groups, was given their backing, and placed a notice soliciting respondents in a widely read gay magazine. After extensive data collection a controversy arose among the groups that had initially given their support as to whether data about gay sexual practices would lead to discrimination and persecution of homosexuals. Enthusiastic support turned to opposition, and the researcher, who felt that the cooperation of gay groups was essential, indefinitely delayed reporting his findings.

The first legal case regarding discrimination against gays was filed in February 1990 and involved the refusal of the Tokyo Metropolitan Government to rent a meeting space to a gay group because of complaints from other organizations. Ironically, the group turned away was OCCUR, whose 250 members fight for gay rights in relation to AIDS and other issues. The group brought a still-pending claim in Tokyo District Court against the Tokyo Metropolitan Government for the cost of its more expensive rental and for damages associated with emotional distress. A government spokesman responded to the lawsuit by declaring, "our thinking may be old-fashioned, but in Japan, homosexual groups are not yet recognized."

Whether one is a hemophiliac or homosexual, man or woman, Japanese or foreign, persons with AIDS face common problems. Companies have fired workers with AIDS, and landlords have turned people with AIDS out of their homes. The most acute problem is finding a physician willing to provide care. Many AIDS patients report that some private hospitals have turned them away. Hospital administrators claim that they do not have the facilities or expertise to care for AIDS patients. Such explanations are pretexts. In fact, they believe that the presence of AIDS patients is bad for business. AIDS patients must therefore rely on public hospitals. The most desirable is Tokyo's Komagome Hospital, which has the country's only AIDS ward of only five beds. When AIDS patients are hospitalized, they find themselves treated differently from other patients. They are normally not permitted to share rooms with other patients, but are instead required to stay in private accommodations, which can be extremely expensive and are not covered by insurance.

Conclusion: A Success Story?

From 1987 through 1991 there was increasingly less attention given to AIDS by government and the media. Officials took credit for having effectively dealt with the epidemic. Then, in early 1991, there was an upsurge in concern, driven by fears of infection through Japanese businessmen with foreign prostitutes. It was fear of AIDS that was the official explanation for maintaining a ban on birth control pills, viewed as less effective than condoms for protecting against HIV. But there was little else to indicate that the MHW had decided to take AIDS prevention seriously.

The number of those suffering from HIV-related diseases continues to rise, if slowly. And affected individuals have begun to speak with a unified voice. On October 17, 1990, five people visited the offices of various Diet members and MHW officials influential in the creation of AIDS policy. Men and women, HIV positive and physically untouched by HIV, homosexual and hemophiliac: all shared an interest in persuading the government to institute a more humane and effective AIDS policy. They carried with them an appeal signed by about twenty thousand Japanese citizens. It read:

> In Japan, only a few medical institutions are positively engaged in treatment of HIV patients. It is not an overstatement to say that even the few medical facilities we have, that are positively helping HIV patients, receive meager support and depend on the dedication of a limited number of physicians.

> Denial of treatment for HIV patients and carriers is prominent in Japan, and, in addition, since the enactment of the "AIDS Prevention Bill," there has been a decrease in the number of people receiving the HIV Antibody Test. In the midst of such unreasonable prejudice and spread of discriminatory acts, HIV victims are being deprived of their basic human right of health, which is tantamount to denying them the right to live.

> Japan is said to be a major economic power. We must not continue to ignore the pitiable condition of HIV patients and carriers. Victims are increasing throughout the world. It is time for Japan to take an international stance with regard to a policy on HIV.

The document went on to demand accessible medical facilities for HIV-positive people, a more generous compensation system for hemophiliacs, free anonymous HIV testing, HIV education, the elimination of discrimination against HIV patients and carriers, and a bigger budget for HIV research. As copies of the petition were distributed, letters of support from AIDS experts in the West were also displayed, to indicate international support for a changed AIDS policy in Japan.

Many of the Diet members targeted to receive the petition were at least superficially sympathetic. By contrast, the MHW bureaucrats appeared distant and defensive. Several weeks after the meeting, newspapers reported that a group of government officials had been assembled in order to review national AIDS policy in light of criticisms that had been so strikingly made public. But as of the end of 1991, no changes had occurred.

The extent to which the ruling Liberal Democratic party and the MHW decide to revamp the current strategy for confronting HIV is likely to depend as much on the spread of AIDS in Japan in the future as on the pressure exerted by particular groups and individuals. Nevertheless, citizen action continues. Most significant is the increasing presence of gay groups, such as OCCUR with its small membership committed to vocal opposition to discrimination and government indifference toward homosexuals. A split in the gay community between those who are willing to remain marginalized and others who insist that gays must be more outspoken has begun to surface. Criticizing the heterosexual publisher of the gay publication *Barazoku,* the leader of OCCUR stated, "He doesn't talk about AIDS, discrimination, safe sex, and other matters. He still views homosexuality as a form of recreation and not a life-style."[45]

As part of the effort to better educate the public about AIDS, a group of activists and concerned citizens brought a section of the NAMES Project's quilt to Japan's major cities. Seeing the response to the quilt, a journalist who frequently covers AIDS-related stories commented that "the Japanese have begun to gain in only six months (up to 15 May 1991) a more immediate awareness of the worldwide AIDS disaster than they had acquired in all of the last six years."[46] While hyperbolic, the observation contains some truth. In each city where the quilt was displayed, people of all ages and backgrounds came to learn about HIV. Japanese panels were also included; the earliest ones contained no names, but later ones bore initials. Most poignant was the panel of a recently deceased hemophiliac AIDS patient who signed his name in his own blood.

Other small but significant incidents have also occurred. For example, a toymaker marketing a game called Bacteria Panic, in which the player left holding a card marked "AIDS" is the loser, recently decided to recall all unsold units. This action was taken after the Japan Patients' Council and the Tokyo Friends of Hemophiliacs complained that the game was "insensitive" to people with AIDS.[47]

Taken together, these events—the petition, the lobbying, the quilt, the protests—demonstrate that those most affected by HIV have begun to cooperate, publicly speaking out on the needs of people with HIV, the shortcomings of government policy and the failure of the medical system in a manner inconceivable when the AIDS controversy first reached Japan.

Notes

1. Randy Shilts, *And the Band Played On* (New York: St. Martin's Press, 1987), 579.

2. *Nihon Ishi Shimpo* #3470 (October 27, 1990).

3. *Ibid.*

4. Kenji Soda, "Present Situations of AIDS and HIV Infection in Japan," *HIV Ekigaku Kenkyu-han Kenkyu Hokoku-sho (Report of HIV Epidemic Study Group)* (March 1989), 291.

5. *Yomiuri Shinbun* (January 9, 1988), 3.

6. Interview with Dr. Yoshiki Sakurai, chief of Education and Medical Information Unit, Department of Medical Information on AIDS, National Medical Center (October 9, 1990).

7. Ministry of Justice, *White Paper on Crime* (1989), 24.

8. Soda, "present Situations," 19.

9. *Ibid;* personal communication with Jim Fredrick, International Friends (October 6, 1990).

10. Yoshiaki Ishida, "Objection to the Legalization of AIDS Countermeasures," *Asahi Shinbun* (February 9, 1987).

11. Soda, "Present Situations," 287.

12. Institute of Medicine, National Academy of Sciences, *Mobilizing Against AIDS* (Cambridge, Mass.: Harvard University Press, 1986), 26.

13. *Asahi Evening News* (December 29, 1989).

14. *Japan Times* (January 23, 1987), 22.

15. William Weatherall, "Japan Curses Gaijin and AIDS Still Spreads," *Far Eastern Economic Review* (April 9, 1987), 111.

16. "Health Ministry Mulls AIDS Prevention Law," *Mainichi Daily News* (January 20, 1987), 1; "Law Considered to Bar Entry of AIDS Carriers," *Japan Times* (February 4, 1987), 12.

17. "AIDS Reporting Plan Proposed in Drafts of Prevention Bill," *Japan Times* (February 19, 1987), 2; "LDP Has Draft AIDS Bill," *Mainichi Daily News* (February 21, 1987), 12.

18. While the draft did not explicitly limit penalties to those who engaged in *unsafe* sexual acts, this limitation can be implied from the language of the bill.

19. While the draft did not explicitly say that names had to be reported, this requirement can be implied from the language of the bill.

20. "AIDS Bill Draft Watered Down," *Daily Yomiuri* (March 7, 1987), 1.

21. See, for example, Jocelyn Ford, "Innocent Victims of AIDS Worry that Government Ignores Their Rights," *Daily Yomiuri* (March 1, 1987), 2.

22. Yoshiaki Ishida, "Objection to the Legalization of AIDS Countermeasures," *Asahi Shinbun* (February 9, 1987).

23. *Kosei no Shihyo* (Tokyo: Kosei Kei Kyokai, 1989), 426.

24. Personal communication with Dr. Masayoshi Negishi, Department of Infectious Diseases, Tokyo Metropolitan Komagome Hospital.

25. Masayoshi Negishi, "AIDS Kansensha no Jinken Mamori" (Protect the Rights of HIV-Positive People), *Asahi Shinbun* (March 11, 1987), 5.

26. "LDP Panel Approves Ministry's AIDS Bill," *Japan Times* (March 7, 1987), 2.

27. *Law Concerning the Prevention of Acquired Immunodeficiency Syndrome,* Ministry of Health and Welfare (March 6, 1987).

28. *Ibid.*

29. Yayoi Uchiyama, "Draconian AIDS Legislation," *Mainichi Daily News* (May 15, 1987), 6.

30. *Ibid.*

31. Interview with Dr. Yoshiki Sakurai (October 9, 1990).

32. Soda, "Present Situations," 290.

33. "Foundation To Spur Domestic Blood Supply," *Daily Yomiuri* (August 2, 1990), 2.

34. Weatherall, "Japan Curses Gaijin," 112.

35. Robert Holloway, "Lack of Awareness Hurts AIDS Prevention in Japan," *The Daily Yomiuri* (August 11, 1990), 3.

36. Interview with Dr. Yoshiki Sakurai (October 9, 1990).

37. "Hemophiliacs Targets of Abuse, Poll Shows," *Daily Yomiuri*, (April 12, 1988), 2.

38. "Doctors Keep Hemophiliacs in the Dark," *Mainichi Daily News* (March 24, 1987), 12.

39. *Ibid.*

40. Kyoto Chapter of Friends of Hemophilia Society, "Yunyu Ketsueki Seizai Higai Jitai Chosa Anketo" (Survey of the Actual Damage from Importation of Blood Products) (February 1989).

41. "Hemophiliacs Targets of Abuse," 2.

42. *Ibid.*

43. *Ibid.*

44. "AIDS Becomes a Notifiable Disease in Japan Despite Protests," *Nature* 326 (March 19, 1987), 232.

45. Marcia Stepanek, "Japan's New Gay Activists Battle Bias, Indifference," *San Francisco Examiner* (May 26, 1991), 1.

46. Dan Furst, "On Seeing the Memorial Quilt," *Asahi Evening News* (May 15, 1991), 5.

47. "Toymaker Recalling AIDS Card Game After Protests, "*Asahi Evening News* (May 4, 1991), 4.

Conclusion # The Second Decade of AIDS: The End of Exceptionalism?

David L. Kirp and Ronald Bayer

In the Beginning, There Was America

"The American is a new man . . . whose labors and posterity will one day cause great changes in the world," J. Hector St. Jean de Crèvecoeur predicted more than two centuries ago in *Letters from an American Farmer.* In America's responses to AIDS are imbedded as many different and contradictory meanings as Crèvecoeur's prophesy contains.

During the first decade of the AIDS epidemic, the United States produced the very best policy—and the very worst. To the other industrialized democracies, AIDS initially was dismissed as "the American disease," and the xenophobic reactions in nations as different from one another as Japan and Sweden revealed that national borders could be regarded as separating innocence from guilt. Yet, as epidemiological patterns first reported in the United States surfaced in other nations, the American experience became a kind of Rorschach inkblot. Onto the record could be projected all the hopes for a quick cure and humane treatment of those with AIDS—also all the fears of a pandemic of death and intolerance that the epidemic evoked.

The best was represented by what came to be called the San Francisco model. This model—more accurately, a series of ad hoc accommodations to crisis—included private care-giving, with everything from emotional counseling and cooked meals to pet care provided for people with AIDS by organizations largley staffed with volunteers and partly subsidized by government. It featured privately produced education campaigns, noteworthy for their sophistication and their candid talk about taboo sexual topics. The model provided for expert medical attention, by doctors with large AIDS practices and in Ward 5A of San Francisco General Hospital, the world's first AIDS unit. It incorporated research on new treatments, often carried out by the care-givers themselves, for the opportunistic infections that flourished in those with HIV-weakened immune systems.

From every one of the ten other industrialized democracies whose policy history is told in this volume, government officals, medical experts, gay leaders, and journalists flocked to San Francisco. There were times when Ward 5A seemed to have more international visitors than patients, more reporters and TV crew members than nurses. It was no surprise that the Australians came to San Francisco, or the Germans or the Dutch, since their governments were predisposed to embrace the kind of inclusionary approach that San Francisco represented. More interestingly, the British health minister, who earlier had downplayed the significance of AIDS for his country, returned from his 1986 visit to San Francisco a chastened, changed man—and an advocate for an aggressive government policy. So did an emissary from the British Columbia health department, where AIDS had previously been an almost unspeakable word. Even the Japanese, while publicly minimizing the relevance of AIDS for their island nation, secretly sent a high-level mission to the United States.

Many of the elements of an AIDS policy that were in place in most industrialized democracies by the late 1980s originated in the United States: blood screening, HIV testing and counseling, and community-based prevention programs. The epidemiological model for tracking AIDS developed by the Centers for Disease Control was adopted world-wide. To be sure, the French did compete with America for research preeminence during the epidemic's early years. A dispute over whether the Pasteur Institute's Luc Montagnier or Robert Gallo, at the National Institutes of Health, first isolated the AIDS virus wound up in the courts; and in the mid-1980s, many Americans with AIDS, most famously Rock Hudson, went to France for treatments unavailable in the United States. But eventually the French research stalled.

Elsewhere, scientists piggybacked on American AIDS research, either participating in American-developed protocols, as in Australia, or simply awaiting American research findings, as with the demonstration of AZT's efficacy as a treatment for the progression of HIV infection. Many influential scientific assessments on AIDS were lifted straight from American journals, then translated into a dozen languages.

It wasn't just governments but care-givers and pressure groups as well that took their cues from America. Buddy systems to deliver emotional support, pioneered by the Gay Men's Health Crisis in New York City and San Francisco's Shanti Foundation, sprung up in Germany and France, Australia and Canada, the Netherlands and Denmark and Britain. Later, confrontational strategies to "zap" officials tarred for their inaction on AIDS, and chiefs of pharmaceutical firms accused of profiteering on death, proliferated world-wide. "Silence = Death," the movement's motto, became an international slogan.

America also showed other countries what *not* to do.

Uniquely among the industrialized democracies, the United States does not guarantee universal access to health care. During the 1980s and early 1990s, there has been wide-ranging American criticism of the patchwork of private insurance and public health care, private practitioners and health maintenance organizations and public clinics: the system is at once too expensive, it is said, and too inequitable. America probably did more for those with AIDS than for people dying of less attention-grabbing causes; certainly the San Francisco model of care-giving represents a great advance over earlier practice. Still, AIDS horror stories—about patients forced to bankrupt themselves to get medical care, about noisy struggles to make promising new treatments available to people without money— confirmed officials elsewhere in the wisdom of having a national health policy capable of incorporating AIDS care more or less naturally into a system already in place.

Similarly, AIDS revealed—or rather reminded—that the welfare system in the United States leaves many unhelped. One anecdote speaks volumes about the differences in how nations help the poor. When a German AIDS expert visiting the Centers for Disease Control in Atlanta walked into a gay bar in that city, he saw a large cardboard box, into which patrons put canned goods for poor people with AIDS. To Americans, this was a familiar example of the sense of communal responsibility that AIDS had fostered among gays. But the German visitor was shocked that, in the world's richest country, dying people had to depend on handouts to survive.

AIDS panic and discrimination, dubbed AFRAIDS early on, were also widely attributed to America. Notoriously, the United States spawned politicians and preachers, even leaders of regional medical associations, who described AIDS as God's will, as a punishment on evil homosexuals and depraved drug users. There were headline stories given international circulation about Americans with AIDS turned out of their houses or booted out of public swimming pools, about rapidly rising levels of gay bashing sparked by fear of AIDS, about hundreds of workers in the telephone company walking off the job because a man with AIDS was allowed to work—and about the torching of the Ray family's house in Arcadia, Florida, when the family's three sons, hemophiliacs carrying the AIDS virus, were admitted to public school.

It is unfair to attribute AIDS panic exclusively to America, for everywhere the epidemic struck, AIDS provoked home-grown panic. It prompted local moralists, in no need of instruction from the Reverend Jerry Falwells and Lyndon LaRouches, to launch their own crusades. In every democratic country—even in nations as proud of their enlightened attitudes as Sweden, Denmark, and the Netherlands—there were calls to quarantine those with the HIV virus, to create an Elba for people with AIDS.

Many of the industrialized democracies had their own identifiable villains upon whom could be projected all the horrors of this disease: the Japanese prostitute, the English prison chaplain, Sweden's "HIV Man," the flight steward from Montreal who (according to *And The Band Played On,* by American journalist Randy Shilts) had almost single-handedly introduced the disease to the United States. Everywhere, too, there were those described as innocent victims: the Australian infants exposed to AIDS because of a tainted blood supply; above all, hemophiliacs, who in Britain, Japan, Canada, Denmark, and Australia have received financial benefits not offered to others who are similarly afflicted—others presumably less innocent or at least less well organized.

By the end of the first decade, even as AIDS-infected children in Spain were being banished from school, Berliners were panicking at the sight of an HIV-infected man in a public swimming pool, and the "HIV Man" scare was being played out in the Swedish media, the United States had largely contained AIDS panic. Following the lead of many states, the national government adopted legislation that outlawed discrimination based on HIV infection. Popular concern had also diminished: the news that a dentist with AIDS had apparently infected five patients did not stir calls for a witch-hunt. But in a realm where perception matters at least as much as reality, bigotry toward those with AIDS is elsewhere in the world widely regarded as another invention of that "new man," the American.

Containment-and-Control versus Cooperation-and-Inclusion

As democratic nations were forced to confront the public health challenge posed by the AIDS epidemic, it was necessary to face a set of fundamental questions: Did the history of responses to lethal infectious disease provide lessons about how best to contain the spread of HIV infection? Should the policies developed to control sexually transmitted or other communicable diseases be applied to AIDS? If AIDS were not to be treated this way, what would justify differential policies?

To understand the importance of these questions, it is necessary to recall that conventional approaches to public health threats were typically codified in the latter part of the nineteenth or the early part of the twentieth century. Even as public health laws have been revised in subsequent decades, they reflect the imprint of their genesis. They typically provide a warrant for mandatory compulsory examination and screening, breaching the confidentiality of the clinical relationship by reporting to public health registries the names of those with diagnoses of "dangerous diseases"; imposing treatment; and, in the most extreme cases, confining infected persons through the power of quarantine.

As the century progressed, the most coercive elements of this tradition were rarely brought to bear because of changing patterns of morbidity and

mortality, the development of effective clinical alternatives, and limitations on the conception of the appropriate scope of compulsory government power in liberal democracies. Nevertheless, the specter of past
coercion troubled proponents of the rights of privacy and gay rights, as
well as those who spoke on behalf of hemophiliacs, as they considered the
potential direction of public health policy in the dawning era of AIDS.
Would there be widespread compulsory testing? Would the names of the
infected be recorded in central registries? Would such registries be used
to restrict those with HIV infection? Would the power of quarantine be
used, if not against all infected persons, then at least against those whose
behavior could result in the further transmission of infection?

Although in every nation there were public health traditionalists who
pressed to have AIDS and HIV infection brought under the broad statutory provisions established to control the spread of sexually transmitted
and other communicable diseases, they were in the distinct minority.
Typically, it was those identified with conservative political parties or
movements, such as the Christian Social Union in Bavaria, who endorsed
such efforts, although not all conservatives pursued such a course. Liberals and those identified with the democratic left tended to oppose such
efforts, although there have been striking exceptions, such as the Sweden's Social Democrats. In the end it was those who called for "HIV
exceptionalism" who typically came to dominate public discourse. Even in
Japan, where the governing conservative party used the extant venereal
disease law as a model for proposed AIDS legislation, the harsher aspects
of the proposal were substantially modified before passage.

A new approach to prevention was required because AIDS was incur-
able, afflicted marginalized or threatened populations with historically
rooted fears about the state and antagonism to its institutions, carried with
it great stigma, required modifications in the most intimate behaviors that
were difficult to undertake and sustain, and was primarily transmitted in
contexts that involved well-defined sexual acts or the sharing of drug
injection paraphernalia by consenting adults. The new strategy had to
eschew all the trappings of coercion and threats to privacy if the epidemic
was not to be driven underground.

Thus, in the first decade of the epidemic, an alliance of gay leaders,
proponents of privacy, physicians, and public health officials began to
shape a policy for dealing with AIDS that reflected the exceptionalist
perspective—a perspective that sought to foster the inclusion of those
with HIV or at risk of HIV infection rather than advocating their control.

Among the most striking reflections of the shift in perspective was the
regulation—or the lack of it—of settings where gay men met to engage in
sexual relations. In America, the move by some public health officials to
close gay bathhouses came reluctantly and only after enormous public

debate. In the Netherlands, where the debate was short-lived and re-stricted to a small circle, closure was rejected, as it was in Denmark and Germany. Even in Japan and Spain, the baths remained open despite the weaker position of the gay community and the relatively late embrace of the norms of democratic political life. Only in Britain, where gay bath-houses were essentially unknown, and in Sweden, which came closer than any of the democratic nations we have studied to imposing the restrictive measures of the traditional public health perspective, were the baths closed with hardly a sign of protest.

Just as public health officials came to recognize the bathhouses as a potential site for preventive education, the confrontation with the AIDS epidemic fostered a rethinking of the strategy for dealing with intravenous drug use. Instead of a single-minded—even intensified—application of a repressive abstinence-oriented approach, there emerged efforts to work with drug users to modify their most dangerous AIDS-related behaviors. The Netherlands, with its commitment to "harm reduction," has served as a model. In Australia, Denmark, and Spain, needle exchange efforts were also launched in an effort to engage drug users rather than to control them. Even in the United States, the United Kingdom, Germany, and Sweden, where needle exchange met with fierce resistance on the part of conservative politicians and some elements of the drug treatment estab-lishment, there was grudging willingness to support local experiments.

The commitment to engaging those most at risk for HIV infection on a voluntary basis was also reflected in the rejection of calls for compulsory screening, so much a part of the conventional approach to epidemic con-trol. Concerns about privacy, recognition of the logistical problems that would attend efforts at mass population screening, and the absence of therapeutic interventions that could benefit either the infected individual or the public health by reducing infectivity all played a role. With the exception of blood donor screening, which was universally recognized as an appropriate public health strategy, democratic nations rejected unconsented-to HIV testing, except in narrow and limited circumstances. The United States went furthest by screening all military recruits and prisoners in some states, but the official emphasis remained on voluntary testing. Even in Sweden, where the law permitted the mandatory testing of some individuals suspected of being infected, that authority was rarely exercised.

To encourage voluntary testing, governments often made provision for anonymity, thus precluding the reporting by name to public health regis-tries of those who were infected which is otherwise common with regard to sexually transmitted diseases. There were examples of efforts to require named reporting—in some states in the United States, for instance, and in Canada's largest province—but in the epidemic's first decade these were the exception rather than the rule. Even in Sweden, HIV infection was only reportable by code.

The centrality of informed consent to testing was made clear in the fate of proposals to undertake unconsented-to screening for epidemiological purposes in blinded seroprevalence studies, in which samples that are stripped of all identifiers are tested for HIV. In the United States such surveillance provoked little objection, since it was recognized that by the very design of such studies no individual could be identified and hence placed at risk. But in the United Kingdom, such studies provoked opposition from ethicists and were viewed skeptically by the public health establishment. Only after two years of controversy did the government decide to permit them to go forward. In Denmark, too, blinded studies were a source of concern; in the Netherlands they have remained largely unacceptable. Here is very striking evidence of how differences among national cultures may lead to very different conclusions about how to proceed—even when a commitment to very high standards for the ethics of research is present and when a recognition of the importance of privacy prevails.

If the importance of protecting the confidentiality of AIDS-related medical records has been accorded recognition is every democratic country, there are notable variations regarding the limits of that principle. Among the most complex and troubling questions to confront clinicians is how to respond when an infected patient reveals that he or she will not inform a partner of that fact. Should the duty to protect confidentiality yield to an ethical obligation to warn an unsuspecting individual whose life may be placed at risk? And if such breaches are to occur, what impact will they have on the willingness of patients to speak candidly to their caregivers?

Physicians have had to deal with these questions in the past as they treated communicable diseases. But they took on particularly difficult dimensions in the AIDS epidemic, where confidentiality was so crucial to the interests of the individual as well as to the public health strategy of encouraging the cooperation of those most at risk for HIV infection. By decade's end, the importance of notifying unsuspecting partners was to receive greater attention because of the prospects of early clinical intervention. Nevertheless, in Denmark and Holland, the principle of protecting confidentiality was viewed as trumping all other concerns. By contrast, in the United States, after some reluctance, many states adopted laws that permitted breaches of confidentiality to warn unsuspecting sexual and needle-sharing partners. Australia, too, recognized exceptional circumstances where confidentiality could be breached. In Sweden, the law was much more explicit in stipulating the circumstances that would obligate physicians to act to protect individuals from the threat of HIV infection.

The question of how to respond to individuals whose continued behavior might place sexual and needle-sharing partners at risk inevitably provoked consideration of the extent to which the coercive powers of the state could legitimately be brought to bear to protect the public health. While all democratic states rejected the calls for mass quarantine on the Cuban model, they have differed markedly in their willingness to consider legislative provisions that would extend to AIDS the tradition of public health controls. In the United States, many states did so, although the powers provided by such legislation have almost never been used to isolate. More typically, but still comparatively rarely, American states have used their authority to warn or counsel those whose behaviors posed a threat of transmission. In that way the United States did not differ markedly from Britain, or from Australia, which had developed a system of staged interventions designed to encourage behavioral modification and which provided for restrictions only as a last resort. Sweden has demonstrated a unique willingness to incarcerate "irresponsibles" for extended periods—but even there this power has been used in only a handful of cases involving prostitutes and drug users. By contrast, the Netherlands and Denmark have rejected as a matter of principle the exercise of such restrictive authority.

More common than the use of the public health power to isolate has been the use of the criminal law to sanction individuals whose behaviors have resulted in the infection of unsuspecting or nonconsenting partners. This trend has been most evident in the United States and Germany.

Even where a willingness to employ the traditional interventions of public health has been most pronounced, every country has recognized that a strategy of mass persuasion represents the most certain approach to controlling the spread of HIV. This has been true in the Netherlands and Denmark, which most clearly exemplified a model of inclusion and cooperation in response to AIDS; true also in the United States and Germany, which, while adopting some elements of the contain-and-control strategy, were largely committed to policies that fostered cooperation; and true in Sweden, which came closest to adopting the standard of traditional epidemic control. Thus, despite the important differences among democratic nations in terms of how they have responded to AIDS, all adopted a program that could broadly be defined as based on cooperation and inclusion rather than on containment and control.

The democratic ethos demanded as much.

While the content and style of national campaigns have differed markedly—from Australia's Grim Reaper to Denmark's yards-long condoms on the sides of public buses—all national efforts have recognized that community-based organizations have the capacity to reach deeper and more effectively into constituencies most at risk. Thus, public funds have been used to support gay organizations involved in AIDS prevention education everyplace except Japan. By funding such groups, government has made possible the large-scale distribution of literature characterized by candor and language that government itself is unwilling to use. Although politically and culturally conservative groups have at times succeeded in limiting the boldness of the messages presented, what is more striking is how much latitude has been accorded such efforts.

If the first decade of the epidemic was characterized by HIV exceptionalism, there is evidence from many of the democracies that the second decade will be very different. Fissures have begun to emerge in the alliances that supported the exceptionalist perspective. The prospects for enhanced therapeutic intervention have weakened the claims of those who have sought to argue that AIDS is so fundamentally different from other sexually transmitted and communicable diseases that it requires unique public policy responses. Treatment means early identification; this, in turn, means access to drugs that prolong life expectancy and allow people with AIDS to lead more normal lives. Drug development has also cut the ground, at least in some countries, from rights-rooted objections to partner notification programs, another familiar public health strategy that had been largely rejected in the epidemic's early years. Now the knowledge that someone has been exposed to AIDS is not just epidemiologically interesting or relevant to delivering counsel to those infected but also medically significant.

The speed and the precise nature of the changes that will occur depend on the political configurations in each nation. In some instances there will be a transformation of traditional approaches to sexually transmitted disease in light of what has been learned as a result of a decade of AIDS. That is what has occurred in Denmark and to some extent in Canada. But the effort to preserve a set of policies that treats HIV infection as fundamentally different from all other public health threats will be almost impossible to sustain.

AIDS will be absorbed into the nations' routines, even as convulsions of very different types—the labor movement in Australia, populism in America—have historically been assimilated. HIV exceptionalism will almost certainly be viewed as a relic of the epidemic's first decade. But historical experiences do not vanish without a trace. What will remain from the era of HIV exceptionalism? Will the principle of requiring informed consent to HIV testing be extended to other clinical tests? Will the importance of using community-based groups in mobilizing an effective campaign for health promotion and disease prevention be recognized? Will the importance of involving those most at risk for disease in the shaping of public policy be acknowledged? Will the potentially counterproductive consequences of reliance on coercion to effect the radical modification of behavior be understood? It is in the answers to these questions that the legacy for the future of public health of the terrible epidemic that struck in the 1980s will be found.

The AIDS Policy Pentacle

For AIDS as for all domains of public policy, every strategy of policy design can be grouped under one of five frameworks: create a regime of legal rights; rely on professional expertise; utilize bureaucratic norms of consistency and internal accountability; let the political system settle matters, producing either ideological clashes or the give-and-take of interested parties; or leave matters to the market, subject to varying degrees of regulation.[1]

Each of these frameworks tends to fall in and out of favor over time. Markets replace bureaus in education with talk of vouchers; rights are substituted for markets in safeguarding the environment. Each framework has its distinctive and predictable potentialities as well as its distinctive pathologies. Few real-world problems are defined exclusively in terms of any single framework. Instead, as with AIDS, policymakers draw on elements of several frameworks to fashion a complex policy.

Conflict and strain among the frameworks is the norm, since they represent alternative values and also come with built-in constituencies. Professionals regard expertise as a superior form of problem-solving because it avoids petty partisanship, while the politician disparages claims of expertise as masking political judgments. Bureaucratic norms are said by administrators to produce the fairness that results from checking discretion, while lawyers say that rights provide firmer protection because they can trump other kinds of claims.

The balance struck among these frameworks matters greatly. It determines what services will be provided, by whom, and on what terms; it also determines how varied these services will be and who will benefit most. Defining a policy problem primarily in terms of rights, for instance, creates a different client class with a different stake than does treating the issue as one fit for professional discretion or the ministerial responsibility of a bureau or the price-setting mechanisms of the marketplace. In short, choices among policy frameworks are choices about how power gets allocated.

For any issue, maintaining this tension among frameworks—paying attention to both the rights-minded and the professionals, for instance—means inviting competing conceptions of the good into the house of policy. That is often wise. Because any single framework can offer only a partial response to a problem, trouble usually arises when one approach dominates: when, for example, professionals deny clients a say in decisions concerning their lives, or when bureaucratic rules undermine the wise exercise of professional discretion, or when the triumph of market values puts the necessities of life beyond the reach of those who cannot purchase them.

Initially, the mix of AIDS strategies adopted by the industrialized democracies varied greatly. Some countries treated AIDS largely in political terms, others left matters to the experts or the bureaucrats, one (the United States) relied heavily on rights. Yet by the end of the epidemic's first decade, some convergence was apparent: The professionals and the bureaucrats had reclaimed much of the authority that had earlier been assumed by political actors inside and outside government.

Rights

"Scarcely any political question arises in America," observed Alexis de Tocqueville in *Democracy in America,* "that is not sooner or later converted into a legal question." And so it has been, a century and a half later, with AIDS. The right to attend school, hold a job, rent an apartment—even the rights of prisoners with AIDS not to be quarantined—have been vindicated by American courts. There are enough AIDS cases on the books to fill a thousand-page law school casebook with leading examples. While there are instances of harsh criminal penalties meted out to those found to have deliberately spread the disease, in the most noteworthy rulings judges have upheld individual claims based on liberty or nondiscrimination against more utilitarian arguments premised on appeals to the general welfare.

At least as important as these legal rulings is the fact that the language of rights deeply informs American policy-making on AIDS. It is the basis for the 1990 Americans with Disabilities Act, which parallels numerous state laws in outlawing discrimination against people with AIDS and HIV infection. Concern for rights also explains why privacy and confidentiality are taken so seriously in debates over closing gay bathhouses, requiring AIDS tests for marriage licenses, regulating the blood supply, and named reporting of AIDS cases and HIV infection. Rights-based concern has limited what American governments may do under the banner of promoting public health.

Confidentiality and privacy are not uniquely American concerns, of course, yet the framework of legal rights is far less salient in other countries, including those that did not incorporate AIDS into the laws governing sexually transmitted diseases or contagious diseases. This reliance on officials to do the right thing in matters concerning privacy and liberty has mostly gone unquestioned.

Nowhere has discrimination and the need for special protection been acknowledged so openly as in the United States. Almost never have there been new civil rights laws, despite reports of people with AIDS losing jobs, being evicted from their homes, turned away by hospitals, and kept out of schools. In Britain, gays, the group most seriously touched by AIDS, lost civil rights when the Thatcher government pushed through legislation preventing local authorities from "promoting" homosexuality. In much of the industrialized world, the civil rights issue has scarcely surfaced and courts have done little to protect the liberty of people with AIDS. Even in Germany, with its strong tradition of judicial safeguards of individual liberty, no special AIDS civil rights legislation has been introduced. The rulings of the German courts, so deferential to official judgment, are reminiscent of early-twentieth-century American opinions upholding quarantine orders. Elsewhere, only when the blood supply has been tainted have courts been inclined to intervene. Typically, they award money damages to those who contracted AIDS from contaminated blood; in one country, Spain, hospital administrators were jailed for criminal negligence in ignoring hazards to the blood supply. But beyond the matter of blood, reliance on the idea of civil rights has been an American exceptionalism.

Politics

AIDS has surfaced on the political agenda of all the industrialized democracies. While the political question has sometimes been framed in ideological terms, as a battle for the moral high ground, to a surprising extent the politics of AIDS has more often been driven by an ambition to avoid conflict and locate consensus.

Such consensualism could be anticipated in countries like the Netherlands, Sweden, and Denmark, with their entrenched if quite differently styled commitments to social welfare and social tolerance. Political leaders in those nations have downplayed controversy, deploying nonpartisan committees of politicians and experts to settle potential disputes, but ideological disagreements have emerged nonetheless. In Sweden, with its vigorous campaign to eradicate drug use, there have been debates over needle exchange; in Denmark in 1985, a health minister who demanded proof that AIDS was a menace before committing new public resources was dubbed "Blood Britta" in the press. Consensualism has been most evident in the Netherlands, where government literally speaks with a single voice. Consensus-building of a different kind has prevailed in Japan, where conflict avoidance is a norm and except for a brief flurry of fear AIDS has generated almost no political debate.

What's more interesting is the fact that consensualism has held sway whatever the political complexion of the government, even where ideological passion is usually a more visible presence on the political landscape. The delicate political maneuverings to limit dissent that have been performed everywhere reveal parallels in countries otherwise very different from one another in their political cultures.

In France, which has seen three different governments assume power since the onset of AIDS, Jean-Marie Le Pen's reactionary National Front demanded that every Frenchman be tested for AIDS, with quarantine in "Sidatoriums" for all who tested positive, but the idea went nowhere. The moralist right-wing government that ruled Britain from the time of the onset of AIDS might have used the issue to manufacture convenient scapegoats. Instead, it contented itself with the occasional diatribe from Conservative back-benchers and the occasional rumbling from former prime minister Thatcher that AIDS was a matter best left to individuals or to the Church. Subsequently, British AIDS policy has taken a less ideological and more interventionist tack, as the Parliamentary Select Committee on AIDS has tended to substitute expertise for passion in political debates.

In Germany, a conservative Christian Democratic federal government effectively resisted pressure from a single state, Bavaria, to adopt rigid contain-and-control measures, preferring instead a less confrontational approach. AIDS surfaced as a noisy issue during the 1984 Australian national elections, when conservative candidates tried blaming the contamination of the blood supply on the permissiveness of the ruling Labour government. But party leaders agreed in a preelection summit conference that AIDS would not be a topic for partisan squabbling, and at the national level this consensus has been maintained. AIDS produced its share of political drama in Canada, when the health minister was burned in effigy by AIDS activists; there, the Conservative government's response was not to exacerbate conflict but rather to contain it by crafting a national AIDS strategy. In Spain, criticism has come from the Catholic Church, which—to no evident effect—has berated a social democratic government for its efforts to promote the use of condoms.

The American AIDS story is most often recounted as a pitched ideological battle for the nation's soul. There is some truth to that description, since at all levels of government there have been prominent politicians inclined to use AIDS as a weapon for bashing "deviants." Sometimes this point of view shaped policy, as when Senator Jesse Helms convinced Congress not to pay for "offensive" AIDS advertising, thus preferring moralizing disguised as supposed aesthetics to saving lives. What is more remarkable, though, is not how much of the Moral Majority's agenda was adopted, but how little. Beginning in the mid-1980s, Congress as well as two national AIDS panels appointed by conservative Republican presidents forced exponential increases in federal AIDS funding. Nondiscrimination became the law of the land, with overwhelming bipartisan support.

Centralized governments, predictably enough, responded more uniformly than federalized systems, but federalism turns out to mean a host of different things in the context of AIDS. In Canada, there was little national AIDS policy to speak of; there, the provinces ran the show, with Ottawa unwilling to use even its funding and coordinating authority to exercise any leverage until the end of the 1980s. In Australia and Germany, by contrast, inclusion-and-cooperation-oriented national governments warred from the outset against powerful states bent on a contain-and-control strategy; in both countries, most of the states with a sizable AIDS caseload followed the national lead. In the United States, California and to a lesser extent New York, the two states with the most AIDS cases, took the early lead. Both states spent far more per capita on AIDS than did the federal government. Both have established their own AIDS research programs, a rarity in a realm where Washington usually holds sway. In another major departure from precedent, California adopted its own fast-track drug approval regime. A $20 million foundation grant encouraged cities across the United States to emulate the San Francisco model of AIDS care. By the end of the 1980s, however, policy leadership had largely shifted to Washington, which set new nondiscrimination rules as well as providing new funding for research and, in cities with the heaviest AIDS caseloads, money to pay for health care as well.

To its admirers, multilayered government offers opportunities to test and experiment with policy ideas; in the well-worn phrase, states are laboratories for democracy. To its detractors, though, federalism brings redundancy and prompts turf wars—or else invites dances of avoidance, as each level of government insists that someone else should be taking the initiative. The experience with AIDS provides ammunition for both sides of this endless debate.

Anticipated policy initiatives were taken in politically progressive states all around the globe, among them South Australia, California, Ontario, Catalonia, and Hessen, even as little was done about AIDS in other states, such as Florida. Elsewhere, most famously in Queensland and Bavaria, the devolution of authority permitted states to inflict repressive measures. A federal structure also enabled some locales to launch policies that the national government was unwilling to adopt: needle exchange programs in several U.S. cities as well as the Basque region of Spain, a mobile van delivering condoms and needles to Sydney's hustlers, explicit educational materials in Montreal and Toronto. Even Britain and Sweden, two nations where political power is highly concentrated in the center, effectively federalized needle exchange by leaving touchy policy decisions to local officials.

In the United States, the Reagan administration was widely criticized for its inaction, as if this demonstrated a failing of federalism. But while the charge of inaction is well-founded, the critique takes no account of the policies that an interventionist and moralist White House, where quarantine was a topic of conversations, might have proffered. In this instance, political neglect at the center may have been *truly* benign.

The advent of AIDS substantially increased the influence of interest groups in most of the democracies, especially organizations representing gays and people with HIV infection, including hemophilia associations. In America, where homosexuality remains a crime in twenty-four states, and where a conservative national administration was hostile to the interests of gay people, public health officials repeatedly met with gay organizations in developing AIDS policies. Even in Britain and France, with their pattern of elite-run government, gays were consulted on policy, and terms like "empowerment" found their way into official texts.

The influence of outsiders on AIDS policy-making is part of a broader expansion of interest group participation during the past two decades. Discussions of policy about the environment, energy, the treatment of women, racial and ethnic minorities, and the handicapped—all once the exclusive province of political insiders, bureaucrats, and experts—have been forced into the open. AIDS fits this pattern of broadened participation, especially since organizing among gays had begun in earnest during the previous decade. While initially some gay groups tended to minimize the significance of AIDS, fearing that the disease would be used as an excuse to deny them their newfound liberation, the evidence soon persuaded them to push for more government help: more money, more research, quicker access to new therapies, and better care.

Familiar concerns about the danger of being coopted by officialdom surfaced in conflicts among different groups of outsiders over what strategy to follow: whether to rely on traditional forms of influence, including participating on blue-ribbon commissions and proposing legislation; or instead to turn to direct action, with government treated not as a partner to negotiate with but an enemy to be attacked. Direct action was almost unheard of in Sweden, the Netherlands, and Denmark, where little dissent was registered; or in genteel Britain; or in Spain and Japan, with weak gay or AIDS-focused groups. Elsewhere, internecine interest-group battles were sometimes fierce. This was particularly so in the United States. "The only good use for the AIDS quilt [which memorializes tens of thousands of those who have died from AIDS]," said one American ACT UP activist, "would be to set it on fire and toss it onto the White House lawn." But since these groups were usually pressing for the same policy outcomes, squabbles over tactics translated into the political equivalent of a "good cop, bad cop" strategy.

Professionalism

It would never have occurred to Dr. Rieux, the narrator and hero of Albert Camus's *The Plague,* to decide how to respond to the calamity that befell his city by counting votes or by worrying overmuch about popular reaction. As Rieux saw matters at the outset of the plague, there was only one right course of action: to slow the spread of the epidemic by isolating those affected by it, to contain and control its spread; meanwhile, to depend upon conventional scientific research to determine its cause and develop a cure.

But even Rieux faltered in his resolve when the plague struck close to home, personally caring for a friend and so violating the quarantine strictures he himself had set. So, too, during the AIDS epidemic, the professionals—physicians and epidemiologists and laboratory researchers—have found themselves subject to conflicting tugs and pulls.

The penchant of medical experts is to define problems in terms that can be solved only by them. This means constructing AIDS as a scientific problem, subject to the familiar norms of treatment and research. But those norms have been under siege.[2] During the 1970s, it was the intellectuals of the left (Ivan Illich and Michel Foucault, among others) who advanced a critique of the entire institution of medicine as a profit-driven "medical-industrial complex" run by experts who monopolized control over our bodies. In the age of AIDS, distrust of the medical expert cuts across the political spectrum. The very fact that an entirely new and devastating epidemic could emerge cast doubt on the prevailing expectation of steady, rational medical progress. As William McNeill writes in *Plagues and Peoples:* "A world where sudden and unexpected death remains a real and dreaded possibility in everyone's life experience makes the idea that the universe is a great machine whose motions are regular, understandable and even predictable, seem grossly inadequate to account for observed reality."

Concerning AIDS, scientists have been caught in a classic double bind. They cannot readily offer guarantees, since guarantees are not a language in which science traffics. And if they venture definite-sounding claims, the false assurances of the not-so-distant past make them appear less than credible. With Bhopal, Chernobyl, and Love Canal etched in contemporary memory—with the closer-to-hand, newly discerned dangers posed by that toxic dump down the street or, more intimately still, by silicone breast implants—there exists a deep-seated suspicion about what the experts say about AIDS, a hard-to-erase worry about another possible Big Lie of modern science.

To the right, the concern has been apocalypse now—or very soon, at least—if strict controls are not put into place. The dire predictions of scientists like Sweden's Michael Koch, a prophet not just in his own country but also in much of Western Europe, and pseudoscientists like Lyndon LaRouche, fueled these anxieties. For its part, the left, which numbered among its membership the groups hardest hit by AIDS, was hostile to a scientific establishment that had long returned the favor. At least until the 1970s, the prevailing expert view was that homosexuality was an illness to be cured, not a legitimate sexual orientation. During the AIDS epidemic, some leading medical spokesmen argued that gay concerns were getting too much attention: that San Francisco's bathhouses would have been closed much earlier had the disease been concentrated in heterosexuals, that in Australia sound national policy was being sacrificed to satisfy gay political interests. To those directly affected by AIDS, these assertions compounded questionable claims of scientific expertise with homophobia. But even in the Netherlands, the most inclusion-and-cooperation-minded of the democracies, some leading scientists have begun to challenge policies promoted by gay groups.

It took three years for HIV, the retrovirus that causes AIDS, to be identified. If that is speedy in scientific terms, it seems agonizingly slow when the metric is the toll on lives. Had the 1984 promise of U.S. Health and Human Services Secretary Margaret Heckler come true—had the discovery of the virus led to a vaccine and a cure by the end of the decade—the preeminence of the professionals would have been less subject to attack, since everyone hoped for that magic bullet. But Heckler's promise proved to be delivered not as a scientific judgment, but rather for partisan gain and national advantage (the United States asserting its research preeminence over France). Even as scientists learned a great deal about this exotic new retrovirus, the body count kept growing. With no end to scientific uncertainty in sight, with even the paradigm of AIDS as caused by a retrovirus under highly publicized assault from within the establishment, the professionals had to give ground.

The best defense against AIDS became, by default, education to encourage widespread change of the most intimate behavior, sex and drug use. Even HIV testing, available in all these countries by the mid-1980s, was widely resisted on the grounds that, in the absence of a treatment let alone a cure, a positive test result did more psychological harm than medical good. Traditionally, the very fact that education was so "unscientific" made it the stepchild of medical science. This meant that the real experts in AIDS education were not the epidemiologists, clinicians, and lab researchers but those who spoke the street language of people most at risk of contracting AIDS, those who thought up Condom Man and Bleach Man. In country after country, gay spokesmen were called on to develop educational strategies, even as mainstream ad agencies and renowned directors produced spots like the scarifying Grim Reaper commercials in Australia and the xenophobic Swedish campaign.

Beginning in the late 1980s, however, the experts began to reassert their authority. Even as a host of drugs like Compound Q, promoted by the antiestablishment underground, proved to offer false hope, the scientific establishement started coming up with treatments for specific HIV-caused maladies: first AZT, then Pentamadine and DDI. These were not panaceas; many were highly toxic, and there was substantial skepticism, especially in Europe, about the wisdom of using them prophylactically. Questions about the cost of the new drugs sparked controversy in British Columbia and Australia, among other places. But the efficacy of AZT and its progeny undermined much of the politically based opposition to HIV testing. By the 1990s, there were signs everywhere that responses to AIDS were more and more driven by expertise—that AIDS was neither a metaphor nor a rallying cry but an illness, and so properly the province of doctors and scientists.

Bureaucracy

This reclaiming of professional hegemony over AIDS is largely repeated in the story of the role of the public health bureaucracy. That is not surprising, for health bureaucrats are usually professionals wearing a second hat. They are subject to the autonomy-driven norms of their calling as well as to the demand for regularity and standard operating procedures that drives bureaucracies.

While historically public health has been powered by a contain-and-control model, the more recent emphasis placed on changing behavioral patterns—altering diet, discouraging drinking and smoking—has spawned a new generation of bureaucrats, more cooperation-, education- and prevention-minded. The tussle between these two types of professional bureaucrats—and the related conflict between administrators primarily concerned with health, on the one side, those more interested in stopping drug use, on the other—has been evident in AIDS policy-making. In the early years of the epidemic, as politicians dithered and traditional medical professionals balked, prevention-minded public health officials came to the fore. Typically, they were careful not to call too much attention to themselves, not to upset their political masters. But reformist bureaucrats led the way in France, the Netherlands, Britain, in parts of Canada and in Australian, Spanish, and American states, as well as in the U.S. Centers for Disease Control.

Across the globe, AIDS prompted the creation of new bureaucratic entities focused on a single medical syndrome, unimpeded by the traditions of the health departments in which they nested, more prestigious than the old sexually transmitted disease units. Some of these new bureaus engaged AIDS activists to run the official show. While bureaus can take on a life of their own, the characters of those who lead them are often crucial.

So it has been with AIDS. Some officials, most notably former U.S. Surgeon General C. Everett Koop and health ministers in Australia, Germany, and a few Spanish and Canadian states, pushed for an education-driven strategy with varying levels of intensity. In nations including Denmark and the Netherlands, gay leaders assumed official authority. Elsewhere, as in Sweden, Germany, Canada, France, and the United States, the bureaus funneled public support to gay groups that could be less euphemistic in their AIDS prevention efforts than their government.

Yet bureaucratic innovation has generally slowed as the demographics of AIDS has changed. Attention was powerfully concentrated when AIDS looked to be decimating the gay population, with its considerable political influence—and especially in 1986, after the international meetings in Paris, when it was widely forecast that AIDS would spread rapidly into the heterosexual population. But there has been a push to reincorporate AIDS into old bureaucratic structures as the incidence of HIV infection has dropped dramatically among gay men, as the perceived threat to the general heterosexual community has subsided, and as the incidence of HIV infection is increasingly in concentrated intravenous drug users, their sexual partners and offspring—groups with no political voice. Within the research-minded agencies, this change coincides with the renewed claim that too much money is being spent on AIDS at the expense of other illnesses, that in financially strapped times the payoff, in terms of lives saved, does not warrant so large a public investment. While that argument is empirically questionable, and while it ignores the general failure of the researchers to pay special attention to the distinctive needs of children and women with AIDS, it is receiving more attention as AIDS becomes the disease of the most marginalized.

The Market

In all the industrialized democracies except the United States, the private sector has not been a major player in shaping AIDS policies. The delivery of health care and the financing of medical research are either handled directly or else are tightly regulated by the government. This is not coincidental. The fact that the market sets prices for goods, and so makes access depend on personal wealth, means it is widely regarded as an inappropriate way to deliver a necessity of life or to decide which illnesses deserve researchers' attention.

Internationally, market values do predominate in one domain: life insurance. The insurance companies' explicit need to develop underwriting standards that discriminate in picking policyholders has only buttressed the determination of AIDS policymakers to keep the market in its limited place.

America's response to AIDS reinforces this antagonism to marketplace values. Insurance companies have denied not only life insurance but also health insurance to those suspected of being infected as well as to people suspected of merely being gay. Pharmaceutical houses have reaped windfall profits from AZT and other drugs; only under sustained political pressure have prices been rolled back.

With respect to AIDS research, though, there may be some reason to rely on market competition, supplemented with generous government funding and the relaxation of inhibiting regulations. While France, Spain, and other nations have concentrated almost all their research in a single institute, the United States has encouraged a proliferation of inquiries in for-profit as well as nonprofit and government institutions. Despite its unwieldiness, this system has yielded almost all the advances in pure science, where the competition is for a Nobel Prize, as well as in the development of drugs, where making money is the driving force.

AIDS in 2001

Imagining the future is a useful exercise, not so much for its predictive powers, its summoning of utopias or dystopias, as for the light it sheds on present tendencies. Speculate for a moment about conditions in the year 2001, the beginning of the third decade of the AIDS epidemic. For all the early hopes of a vaccine or a cure, the virus is lingering and mutating, and, world-wide, new cases are being reported daily by the thousands. Historians of science express no surprise, since no sexually transmitted disease has ever been eradicated.

Some notable Cassandras predicted in the early 1980s that AIDS would be the epidemic of the millenium, dwarfing the Black Plague in its toll.[3] In 2001, the Third World—particularly sub-Saharan Africa, as well as swatches of Southeast Asia and Latin America—is indeed being devastated by AIDS. Millions have died from the disease, as many millions of children have been left orphaned. With the World Health Organization reporting 40 million people with HIV infection and 10 million cases of AIDS since the epidemic began, tens of millions more deaths are anticipated before the virus spends itself.[4] Attempts to change the heterosexual practices responsible for much of the transmission of this disease in Africa have largely failed in the face of powerful traditions.

From time to time, Africa's AIDS miseries are recounted in the world press. But these grim tales now hold little interest to the public—or to policymakers and politicians, who have grown largely innured to Africa's suffering. In Africa in 2001, an estimated 30 million people are at risk of starving to death and 10 million more may perish from preventable conditions like measles and diarrhea.[5] Still, there are no funds even to pay for widespread HIV testing in this devastated corner of the planet, let alone for the costly life-prolonging drug treatments commonplace in the developed world. AIDS in the Third World has become just another in the litany of calamities, even as Malthusian academicians in Chicago and Oxford commons rooms talk about AIDS as a form of population control.

In the industrialized democracies, the AIDS epidemic has evolved very differently. Since the late 1980s, the epidemiologists have been lowering their projections of the likely numbers of AIDS cases. And while even the remotest county in the United States (still the hardest-hit Western nation) has now reported at least one AIDS case, and while the 1991 revelation that renowned basketball star Magic Johnson was infected with HIV had a momentarily sobering effect, there is no longer much concern that AIDS will spread beyond its primary targets to touch the heterosexual, non-drug-using population in sizable numbers.

It was this fear of an "AIDS breakout" that mobilized democracies around the world to act with unaccustomed speed during the epidemic's first decade. While the policy particulars differed, almost every country exponentially increased the level of AIDS spending. Once despised groups, particularly gays, were brought into the policy process, even empowered. The conduct of medical research changed, as new models of disease prevention which departed from the traditional medical paradigm took shape, stressing cooperation with rather than control over those most at risk.

But during the 1990s, things changed once again. In all the industrialized democracies, AIDS struck mostly at the most marginal members of the society: intravenous drug users, their sexual partners, and their children. Around the world, racial and ethnic minorities were disproportionately affected: Hispanics and blacks in the United States, Australian Aborigines, Greenland natives governed by Denmark, Surinamese who had settled in the Netherlands, and *pieds noirs* in France. A demographic pattern that had initially surfaced in Spain, Italy, and the inner cities of America had become the norm. Social commentators described AIDS as another intractable urban problem, like homelessness and drug abuse.

This demographic shift changed the politics of AIDS. Far from being empowered, drug users and their intimates must depend on health and social work professionals, who often behave less like advocates than like handlers. Even for children, the classic "innocent victims," the official response has generally been more generous in rhetoric than substance. Everywhere the health and social services systems, strained by mounting caseloads and increasing costs, are struggling to provide children with rudimentary treatment and to find adults willing to be foster parents to those who will die young. In several countries, the orphanage has been revived to care for these doomed children.

Looking back, the late 1980s and early 1990s turned out to have marked the high-water mark of AIDS policy-making around the globe.

Governments of widely varied ideological coloration had taken aggressive action. The World Health Organization had promoted enlightened international standards on such matters as job discrimination and travel restrictions. Angry activists were everywhere pushing officials to do much more. In Japan, a petition with ten thousand signatures calling for a less head-in-the-sand policy, a rarity in that conflict-abhorring country, had been presented to government leaders.

But in 2001 the generation that launched groups like ACT UP has long since moved on to other causes; and its slogan, "Silence = Death," is now graffiti barely visible on cosmopolitan sidewalks. A few private organizations continue to provide care and counseling for those with AIDS, but these groups have found the going hard, with volunteers suffering from burnout and money hard to raise. Now that AIDS is no longer regarded as a fashionable cause, the more enterprising private groups have found new missions—even as, in the 1950s, the March of Dimes looked for new diseases after a polio vaccine was developed. But other groups of patients—including women with breast cancer, long subject to the absolute rule of doctors—have been learning new tactics, such as zaps and street theater, from old ACT UP members.[6]

Governments have disbanded their separate AIDS units, and public funding for private organizations, a mainstay of the earlier years, has essentially ceased. Every industrialized country, even the United States, now has some form of universal health care. But everywhere the health and social services systems are straining under mounting caseloads and increasing costs for a host of diseases, and this has meant proportionately less money is being spent to treat patients with AIDS. As the pace of scientific discovery has slowed, many of the laboratories' brightest stars have gone back to cancer research or on to gene-splicing. AIDS research budgets have been trimmed, first in the United States and then in all the countries that once looked to America for leadership in research.

As early as the mid-1990s, AIDS education had become a routine part of health promotion campaigns: the daring advertisements of a few years earlier, with their nubile couples of all sexual persuasions, had mostly given way to talking heads. Across the globe, the health education books used in secondary schools now include a chapter on AIDS, often sandwiched between the discussions of the perils of smoking and drinking.

In many of the democratic nations, AIDS activists and people with AIDS are now ignored in policy circles. Doctors and researchers, who in earlier years were obliged to pay attention to nonscientist activists, are firmly in the saddle once again. With continued advances in life-prolonging drugs, concerns about infringing privacy and liberty, once regarded as primary everywhere from Australia to the Netherlands, have given way to an emphasis on testing, contact tracing, and treatment. The isolation of people with

AIDS regarded as "irresponsible," which in the epidemic's first decade had been seriously attempted only in Sweden among the industrialized democracies, is now more common even in countries with longstanding liberal traditions. The criminal law is more regularly used to incarcerate those who deliberately spread the disease.

In short, by 2001 the era of AIDS exceptionalism is history. The epidemic has been brought into the mainstream of health policy and practice—it has been "normalized," as the current crop of AIDS specialists say, intending all the meanings of that word. Yet the impact of AIDS exceptionalism lingers. Nondiscrimination laws have become the rule, not the exception. Gays, initially empowered by AIDS, continue to enjoy some access to the political mainstream, with openly gay politicians in the national assemblies of most democracies. In place of the hyper-caution (driven by memories of the Thalidomide debacle) that used to characterize drug approval, speed has now joined safety as an official priority. Reliance on international testing, rather than redundant country-by-country reviews, is becoming commonplace.

For the citizens of the industrialized democracies, AIDS has been a mirror in which aspects of individual character could be glimpsed. In this sense, it resembles the London Blitz—or those moments in Nazi-occupied Europe when ordinary Gentile Poles and Danes and Frenchmen had to respond to Jews who sought sanctuary, whether by identifying with their plight or turning their backs or joining the persecution. Analogously, official responses to AIDS have revealed something about what used to be called national character—or, more accurately, national characters, for everywhere there has been a tension between containment-and-control and cooperation-and-inclusion strategies. Many countries had their Bavaria or their Queensland, where antipathy toward those with AIDS translated directly into policy. And in almost every country there were also voices like those that predominated in Denmark and the Netherlands, where the afflicted received the public equivalent of love.

These same questions of individual and national character have been posed in the wake of other epidemics. They contribute to the continuing universal appeal of Camus's *The Plague*, which focuses on an epidemic that decimated just a single city for just a matter of months. By 1981, the industrialized democracies had come to believe that these plague stories were only history lessons, that epidemics belonged to an earlier time or were the fate of more primitive peoples. The advent of AIDS, of course, consigned that belief to the dustbin of hubris.

In 2001, in some corner of the globe, other deadly viruses, other potential AIDSs, are being launched into the populace. Almost all will vanish unnoticed, nature's false starts. But some day soon, one such virus will begin spreading world-wide.[7] When this happens—in the year 2002, perhaps—what lessons will these two decades of experience with AIDS have taught?

Notes

1. This model is elaborated in David L. Kirp, "Professionalization as a Policy Choice: British Special Education in Comparative Perspective," *World Politics* 34, no. 20 (1982), 137–181.

2. This section is adapted from David L. Kirp, *Learning by Heart: AIDS and Schoolchildren in America's Communities* (New Brunswick, N.J.: Rutgers University Press, 1989).

3. Among the eminently respectable Cassandras: Sweden's Michael Koch and the U.S.'s Steven Jay Gould.

4. The World Health Organization, in 1991, predicted 20 million cases of AIDS by the end of the century. See generally Peter Piot et al., "The Global Epidemiology of HIV Infection: Continuity, Heterogeneity, and Change," *Journal of Acquired Immune Deficiency Syndromes* 3 (1990), 403–412.

5. These guesses assume that things will not improve in the coming decade; in 1991, thirty million people were at risk of starvation in Africa; six million children were severely malnourished.

6. In the United States, the beginnings of this change in tactics, especially among women with breast cancer, were reported in spring 1991.

7. This prediction has been made by many scientists, including Harvard University Professor Jonathan M. Mann, who headed the AIDS program of the World Health Organization until 1990 and who has written the Foreword to this book.

List of Contributors

Erik Albæk is an associate professor of public policy and administration at the Institute of Political Science, Aarhus University. His recent research interests have focused on political agenda-setting and the utilization of policy and evaluation research.

John Ballard is a senior lecturer in political science at the Australian National University. He has served as a member of the National AIDS Forum and the Commonwealth AIDS Research Grants Committee, and is currently completing a book-length study of the Australian response to HIV.

Ronald Bayer is a professor at the Columbia University School of Public Health. His recent work has focused on the ethical and political dimensions of the AIDS epidemic. He is the author of *Private Acts, Social Consequences: AIDS and the Politics of Public Health.*

Eric A. Feldman is a Fulbright Graduate Research Fellow at the University of Tokyo's Institute of Social Science. His research is currently centered on the legal, political, and sociological dimensions of Japanese health care.

Guenter Frankenberg is a professor of constitutional and administrative law at the Fachhochschule and senior research fellow at the Institute for Social Research in Frankfurt am Main. He is the author of *AIDS— Bekämpfung im Rechtsstaat: Aufklärung ewang Prävention,* an analysis of the legal problems of HIV/AIDS prevention strategies.

Benny Henriksson is the director of the Swedish Institute for Social Policy in Stockholm and a researcher at the department of social work at the University of Lund. His research involves the study of issues involving youth, sexuality, policy evaluation, and HIV/AIDS prevention.

David L. Kirp is a professor at the University of California (Berkeley) Graduate School of Public Policy. His research interests have focused on the public policy dimensions of education, housing, gender, and race. He is a journalist as well as an academic, and is the author of *Learning by Heart: AIDS and Schoolchildren in America's Communities.*

Evert A. Lindquist is an assistant professor in the Department of Political Science at the University of Toronto. His research interests center on how governments mobilize expertise to deal with complex challenges and the ways in which policy communities function as learning systems.

Jonathan M. Mann is a professor of epidemiology and public health at the Harvard School of Public Health and Director of the International AIDS Center, Harvard AIDS Institute.

Jesús M. de Miguel is a professor and chairman of the Department of Sociology at the University of Barcelona, where he is also on the faculty of the School of Public Health. His research has focused on the relationship between social inequality and health, and he is the author of *Salud y Poder.*

David M. Rayside is an associate professor of political science at the University of Toronto. His research has centered on language, class and gender divisions in society, and he is the author of *A Small Town in Modern Times,* an ethnographic study of an eastern Ontario community. As both an activist and researcher, he has most recently been concerned with gay rights, lesbian and gay movements, and gay-related policy issues such as AIDS.

Monika Steffen is a researcher in political science at the National Center of Scientific Research (CNRS) in Grenoble. The author of numerous articles on public health policies in France, as well as on the comparative analysis of health policy, she is presently conducting a study of AIDS policy in four European countries.

John Street is a lecturer in politics and director of the Center for Public Choice Studies at the University of East Anglia. He is the author of several articles and chapters on British AIDS policy and its politics.

Albert Weale is a professor of politics at the University of East Anglia. He is the author of a number of publications on health care politics, including *Cost and Choice in Health Care.*

Jan K. van Wijngaarden is Medical Officer of Health for Infectious Diseases, Department of the Chief Medical Officer of Health, Ministry of Welfare, Health, and Cultural Affairs of the Netherlands. He served as National AIDS Policy Coordinator and director of the Office of the National Committee Against AIDS between 1983 and 1988.

Shohei Yonemoto is head of the Life Science and Society Program at the Mitsubishi Kasei Institute of Life Science. His research has focused on the history and sociology of science and he is the author of *Biomedical Revolution: Its Philosophy and Institution.*

Hasse Ytterberg is currently a junior judge in the district court of Borås. Over the last decade, he has been actively involved in issues regarding civil rights for gay men and lesbians and has served as president and secretary general of the National Swedish Federation for Lesbian and Gay Rights.

Index

ACT UP, 375; Australia, 157–158, 164–165; Britain, 189; Canada, 84; United States, 39

activism 362; and bureaucrats, 378–379; of gay organizations, 368–369; role of interest groups in, 375

—Australia: of community groups, 153, 158, 159; of gay organizations, 135, 137, 139–140, 145, 157

—Britain: of gay organizations, 185, 193, 198–200; and loss of influence, 188–189, 201, 215

—Canada: of community groups, 68, 70, 71, 73, 74, 76, 78, 82, 85, 86; of gay organizations, 50–51, 52, 55, 57–66, 68–69, 71, 73–76, 77, 78, 81, 83–85, 91; as response to government inaction, 49–50, 62–66, 68, 78

—Denmark: of gay organizations, 281, 287–290, 293, 311–312, 313; of hemophiliacs, 312; of intravenous drug users, 312–313

—France, 236–237; and broad-based representation, 244–247; of gay organizations, 232

—Germany: and broad-based representation, 100, 121; of gay organizations, 104, 120–122, 129

—Japan, 356–357; and criminal law, 346, 349; of gay organizations, 342–343, 357–358; of hemophiliacs, 343, 349–350

—Netherlands, of intravenous drug users, 261

—Spain, of gay community, 169, 173–175, 177

—Sweden: of gay community, 321–322, 326, 329, 331, 332, 333; of gay and intravenous drug users' support groups, 322; of physicians, 328

—United States, of gay community, 11–14, 22, 23–25, 27, 29, 39–40, 42

advertising campaigns, see education

AZT, 362, 377–378; Australia, 141, 164; Britain, 211–212; Canada, 63, 69, 70, 80, 87, 92; France, 248; Spain, 172; United States, 41

bathhouses (saunas), 365–366, 371; Australia, 143; Britain, 189; Canada, 84; France, 236; Germany, 116; Japan, 339; Netherlands, 260–261, 269–270; Sweden, 326; United States, 19–21

behavior modification, 365, 368, 377, 378; and lifestyle, 5

—Australia, 141, 144, 150, 159

—Britain, 205–206; and lifestyle, 196; survey of, 186

—Canada, 59

—Denmark: recording of, for insurance purposes, 296; refusal to undertake, 292

—France, 248

—Germany, 100–101

—Japan, physician monitoring of, 348

—Netherlands, and rejection of Christian dogma, 259

—Sweden, and testing rationale, 330

—United States, 9, 14, 24, 33

blood: safety of, 373; screening of, 362, 366, 371

—Australia: exclusion of high-risk groups from donating, 138–139, 143; safety of, 134–135, 138; screening of, 135

—Britain, exclusion of high-risk groups from donating, and screening of, 206

—Canada: regulation of, 53; safety of, 79; screening of, 74

—Denmark: banks, 292–293; exclusion of high-risk groups from donating, 291, 298, 305; screening of, 307–308

—France, safety of, 232–236

—Germany, and donation, 99

—Japan: for hemophiliacs, 351; safety of, 343

—Netherlands: banks, 256; education of donors, 260–261; exclusion of high-risk groups from donating, 256; safety of, 255–256

—Spain: banks, 176; safety and screening of, 176

—Sweden, and high-risk donors, 321–322

—United States: banks, 22–24; safety and screening of, 21–23